KU-255-474

Opening the Gates

A Century of Arab Feminist Writing

EDITED BY

Margot Badran and Miriam Cooke

VIRAGO

Published by VIRAGO PRESS Limited 1990
20-23 Mandela Street, Camden Town, London NW1 0HQ

This collection and introduction copyright © Margot Badran and Miriam Cooke 1990

Copyright © in each contribution held by the author 1990

All rights reserved

A CIP record for this title is
available from the British Library

Printed in Great Britain

Arab women today live in more than twenty sovereign states, as well as in occupation or exile; they come from an area that stretches from Morocco to the Arabian Peninsula. Here, for the first time, a collection of Arab women's writing is organised within a feminist framework. It brings together many women's voices; some are familiar – Etel Adnan, May Ziyada, Nawal al-Saadawi, and Huda Shaarawi – many have never been read in English before. In these wonderfully diverse documents – personal letters, memoirs, speeches, fiction and poetry, spanning over a century – women eschew their role as silent helpmates. These documents in all their diversity and sophistication not only challenge Arab patriarchy, but also eloquently refute the myth of a monolithic western feminism.

Margot Badran took degrees in Middle East Studies at Harvard and Oxford. She was Visiting Associate Professor in History and Women's Studies at Hamilton College in 1984/85. She edited and translated *Harem Years: Memoirs of an Egyptian Feminist* by Huda Shaarawi (Virago, 1986) and is currently researching on contemporary feminist and Islamist currents in Egypt; several of her articles have appeared both in English and Arabic. She now divides her time between Cairo and the United States.

Miriam Cooke earned her Ph.D from Oxford in 1980. After publishing a collection of translations and a major study of the life and works of the Egyptian male writer Yahya Haggi, she turned her attention to Arab women writers. Her book *War's Other Voices: Women Writers on the Lebanese Civil War* (1988) explores the liberating and radicalising effect of the civil war (1975–82) on the lives and writings of women. Miriam Cooke teaches modern Arabic literature at Duke University. She lives in North Carolina.

Contents

✿

Preface

❧

We first met each other at Oxford in the seventies when we were pursuing graduate studies on the Middle East, specialising in history and literature. Since then we have met over the years in the Middle East, the United States and England exchanging ideas. We each came to feminism in the Middle East in different ways. Margot Badran, an historian, did research in Egypt on the pioneering Egyptian feminist, Huda Sharaawi, and the feminist movement she headed earlier this century. This led her into feminism in other Arab countries and the rise of pan-Arab feminism. Miriam Cooke, a literary critic and a specialist in Arabic literature, conducted research on women writers in Lebanon during the war discovering a feminist school that had emerged during this cataclysm. Our everyday experience in the Arab world, our contacts and debates with Arab women, and with men, as well as our studies have informed our feminist thinking in ways that transcend more purely academic interests.

In 1984, we decided to collaborate on an anthology of Arab women's feminist voices. These were voices that had shaped our own thinking and had often given us pause in debates on feminist theory going on in the west. Some of these voices are known in the West, such as those of Nawal al-Saadawi and Fatima Mernissi, but we became excited about what might happen if more Arab women's feminist voices spoke directly to western audiences. It was then that we decided to pool some of the writings with which we were familiar. Over the past five years we amassed so many texts that selection for the anthology became difficult. Finally, we had to limit our choice to less than sixty pieces. We were also forced, in a few cases where the texts were particularly long, to trim a little. Most of these texts appear here for the first time in English translation, though a few have never been published before. We have seen our work as a conscious effort to retrieve texts that have been buried in public archives and libraries, or in private houses. We hope to assist in the global recovery of women's feminist voices, either previously unknown, lost or forgotten. We were guided by the importance of individual voices rather than by an attempt to be proportionally representative of the entire Arab world, and hence

we did not attempt to correct the preponderance of Egyptian or
Lebanese writers. This preponderance is due to the early centrality
of writers from these countries in the cultural renaissance of the
Arab world.

A book like this owes its existence to the co-operation and help of
many people. First we would like to thank all the authors whose
writings appear in this book for their permission to include their
work. We also thank the translators for their generous help. These
include: Nayra Atiya, Ali Badran, Beth Baron, Marilyn Booth,
Patricia Francis Cholakian, Donna Robinson Divine, Simone Fattal,
Elise Goldwasser, May Ibrahim, Elizabeth Oram, Charlotte Petrey,
Michelle Raccagni, Noha Radwan and Mona Yacoubian. We would
like to thank Wadida Wassef for her autobiographical sketch;
Elisabeth Oram for her introduction to the lecture she transcribed
and translated; and Beth Baron, Marilyn Booth and Simone Fattal
for also providing biographies and introductions to the pieces they
translated.

There are others we also wish to thank. We thank Marilyn Booth,
a specialist in modern Arabic literature who has been researching
and translating Egyptian women writers, for retrieving works of
Warda al-Yaziji, Aisha al-Taimuriya, Zainab Fawwaz, and May
Ziyada, and for making selections; Simone Fattal for providing the
short stories of Ulfa Idelbi and May Muzzaffar; Nimet Riyad for
assisting our retrieval of articles in *Hawa* by Amina Said; and
Ahmad al-Dimardash for providing information on his mother,
Qut al-Qulub. We are grateful to those who read and reacted to all
or parts of the manuscript at various stages. In particular we would
like to thank Ali Badran, Marilyn Booth, Claudia Koonz, Bruce
Lawrence, Carol Meyers, Jean O'Barr, Karen Offen, Midge
Quandt, Sandra Robinson, Josefina Tiryakian, Jing Wang, Rahel
Wasserfall and William Zeisel. We are especially grateful to Albert
Hourani, who has trained and influenced generations of students
of the Middle East, including the two editors, for his close reading
and detailed comments that have helped us in the difficult task of
introducing and presenting the rich materials before us.

To those who have provided friendship, support and hospitality
during the years we spent on this project we thank: Edit and
Hedley Cooke, Joseph Farranto, John and Evgenia Farranto,
Andrée Fahmy, Nelly Hanna, Frank Woods, Mary Coon, and Liz
and Tex Wueste.

At Virago Press we thank Ursula Owen for her early enthusiasm
for the project and Melanie Silgardo for careful and sensitive
editing. At Indiana University Press we thank Janet Rabinowitch
for her eager response to the almost final version. Special thanks go

to Gail Woods for her good-natured typing, re-typing, and re-re-typing of an evergrowing manuscript.

Finally, a word on transliteration from Arabic. We have followed a standard system for transliteration into English but have elimin-ated long vowel marks not to distract the general reader. The specialist will recognise where they belong. The hamza or glottal stop is not indicated nor is the Arabic letter, ain. In the North African pieces the reader will find transliteration into French. We have mainly, but not always, used a standard transliteration for personal names. We have tried to be as consistent as possible but realised there were a few instances where leeway seemed best.

We would like to end with thanks to our mothers, Edit Cooke and Margaret Woods Farranto, who have supported our intellec-tual journeys from the start and whose influences have found resonances in our work. In honour of their memory we would like to include a personal dedication.

Margot Badran
Miriam Cooke
1990

But I was incapable of learning, and I had no desire or readiness to become refined in the occupations of women. I used to flee from her [mother] as the prey escapes the net, rushing headlong into the assemblies of writers with no sense of embarrassment. I was certain that to become one of this group of people would be the most perfect and complete of blessings.

Aisha al-Taimuriya, *The Results of Circumstances*, Cairo, 1888

I was unable to compose poetry; my inner voice was weak in protest against everything that had caused my silence. I was expected to create political poetry while the corrupt laws and customs insisted that I remain secluded behind a wall, not able to attend assemblies of men, not hearing the recurrent debates, not participating in public life.

Fadwa Tuqan, *Difficult Journey – Mountainous Journey*, Nablus, 1984

I am female . . . so I'm nothing. I hold my pen and write . . . in the darkness of the night I write . . . so that I don't see what I'm writing . . . and get scared. I take the first train . . . ask for a one-way ticket . . . and sit in it hoping it travels into no place and no truth . . . Don't ask me about my name . . . my stop . . . when I'm coming back or where I'm going . . . because I don't know.

Noura al-Saad, Doha, Qatar, 1982

Introduction

⊱⊰

This anthology of poems, tales, novels, short stories, memoirs, essays, journalistic articles and speeches is the first collection of Arab women's feminist writings.[1] Revealing the range of feminist expression over a century and a quarter, *Opening the Gates* is the recovery of a debate presumed not to have existed.

What do we mean by the terms, feminist discourse and feminist vision? Are the connotations the same for the Arab world as for Europe and America? Or, are there discrete feminisms that emerge in response to indigenous circumstances? In our research and through our contacts with Arab women, we have explored expressions of feminist consciousness beyond the horizons of western expectations.

Historically, a term connoting feminism first appeared in the Arab world in 1909 when Malak Hifni Nasif under the pen-name, Bahithat al-Badiya, a name meaning 'Seeker in the Desert', published a collection of articles and speeches in a book entitled *Al-Nisaiyat*.[2] We say 'a term connoting feminism' because *nisaiyat*, conventionally signifies something by or about women. However, the content of *Al-Nisaiyat* revealed its feminism: it advocated improvement of women's lives, including new education and work opportunities, and the recuperation of lost freedoms understood to be granted by Islam. The publication of *Al-Nisaiyat* by the press of *Al-Jarida* paper, the liberal nationalist organ of the Umma Party, helped the feminist voice reach a broader public of both women and men. Two years later, Bahithat al-Badiya sent demands adumbrated in *Al-Nisaiyat* to a nationalist congress. By 1923, Egyptian women belonging to the Egyptian Feminist Union began to use the term, *nisai*, unambiguously as feminist. While in French – the dominant language of the Egyptian Feminist Union women – the distinction between *féminine* and *féministe* is clear, in Arabic *nisai* remains ambiguous and is clarified only by content. To this day there is no unambiguous term for feminist in Arabic.[3]

However, Arab women produced a discourse that can be identified as feminist before there was an explicit term for feminism. The first written evidence occurs in the poetry of an Arab woman published in the 1860s. This means that for about half the time span covered in this book, a period during which the seclusion of middle and upper class women and the segregation of the sexes predominated in cities and towns, there were no Arab women who called themselves feminists and there was no women's discourse labelled feminist.

The first explicit identification of middle and upper class Arab women as feminists coincided with the founding of The Egyptian Feminist Union and the public political unveiling by two upper class women in Egypt in 1923. This represented a symbolic and pragmatic announcement of the rejection of a whole way of life built on hiding and silencing women. This anthology reveals how early feminist consciousness and voices were for the most part hidden from the 'larger world' or confined to the world of women while female seclusion and the segregation of the sexes prevailed. Much of Arab women's feminist expression has eluded people because of its invisibility.

In her work on the history of feminism in Egypt, Margot Badran has made the distinction between invisible and visible feminisms. This distinction, she argues, rescues feminism from being understood as an exclusively public and explicit phenomenon, and thus provides an analytic framework within which to locate and explain the more comprehensive feminist historical experience. There are historical moments when patriarchal authorities suppress public feminist movements, as was the case in Egypt from the middle 1950s until the early 1970s.[4] There are private moments when authorities within the family, usually husbands, enforce silence. Feminism may be removed from sight, but it is not necessarily extinguished.

Opening the Gates accordingly includes voices of Arab women who both did and did not call themselves feminists. Even after the term came into use and feminism was explicitly understood, there were women writing who did not call themselves feminists and who would not see their work as embodying an outlook which others could and did recognise as feminist. Miriam Cooke's analysis of the war writings of the Beirut Decentrists in the late 1970s and early 1980s illustrates how literature which is not promoted as feminist, nonetheless portrays and even accelerates feminist transformations.[5]

In this book we employ a broad working definition of feminism deriving from the expression of Arab women's voices and activism over nearly a century and a quarter. It involves one or more of the following: an awareness by women that as women they are systematically placed in a disadvantaged position; some form of rejection of enforced behaviours and thought; and attempts to interpret their own experiences and then to improve their position or lives as women.

Texts in this book indicate, contrary to popular thinking, that feminist debates did not begin in the Arab world in 1899 with the publication of the Egyptian male lawyer Qasim Amin's book, *The Liberation of the Woman*. It is important to distinguish between the feminism of women and the feminism of men. Margot Badran has noted fundamental differences between early female and male generated feminist discourses in Egypt.[6] The starting points of the two discourses were different. Men's pro-feminist stands arose out of contact with European society in which women were generally visible. Women's feminism was initially an upper class phenomenon and it grew out of expanded learning and observation of their own lives during times of great change. Muslim women, argued that Islam guaranteed women rights of which they had been deprived because of 'customs and traditions' imposed in the name of religion. Through the correct understanding and practice of Islam women could regain basic rights, and their families and societies would also benefit.

The more visible male-generated feminist debates were known through books including Qasim Amin's *The Liberation of the Woman*, and also the Egyptian Murqus Fahmi's *Woman in the East* (Al-Mara fi al-Sharq, 1894) and the Tunisian Tahir al-Haddad's *Our Women in Islamic Law and Society* (Imraatuna fi al-Sharia wa al-Mujtama, 1929). These men argued that Arab society was backward because women were backward, and women were backward because of lack of education and because of social constraints, such as veiling and seclusion practised in the middle and upper classes. They affirmed that these practices were not sanctioned by religion. These pro-feminist men – who also included the Egyptian intellectual Ahmad Lutfi al-Sayyid, founder of *Al-Jarida*, and the Iraqi poet, Jamil al-Zahawi, imprisoned in 1911 for advocating unveiling – demanded that women be liberated from bondage to constraining social practices so that their countries might advance. The two disparate starting points of women's and men's feminism help to explain subsequent developments and challenge the notion of a monolithic discourse.

Arab feminism has been greatly misunderstood and misrepresented both in the Arab world and in the West. Distortions date back to the end of the nineteenth century when Amin's *The Liberation of the Woman* triggered acrimonious public debate in Egypt and became particularly shrill again, for example, with the publication of Nazira Zain al-Din's book, *Unveiling and Veiling* (Al-Sufur wa al-Hijab) in Beirut in 1928 and Tahir al-Haddad's

Our Women in Islamic Law and Society in Tunis in 1929 and Nawal
al-Saadawi's *Women and Sex* (Al-Mara wa al-Jins, 1971). Some Arabs
have attacked feminism as being: western – the cultural arm of
imperialism or neo-imperialism out to destabilise local society and
to destroy indigenous cultural identity; anti-Islamic – undermining
the religious foundations of the family and society, and elitist, and
therefore irrelevant to the majority.

Some Arab women have claimed that Arab feminism is at once
indigenous to the Arab world and part of a universal phenomenon;
others, that it is a western import into the Arab world that
nonetheless assumes an adversarial relationship with western feminism; others, that it is *sui generis*.[7] Westerners have variously
contended that an indigenous Arab feminism is impossible because
of an Islam that is interpreted as being oppressive of women; or
that it was exported from the West to the Arab world; or that it
exists as a unique Arab phenomenon, or is a local manifestation of
a universal feminism.[8]

While affirming the universality as well as the diversity of
feminism, scholars have begun to use the term 'feminisms' to
acknowledge the plurality within the unity. Within the context of
the third world, Badran's work on the history of the feminist
movement in Egypt from the 1920s through the 1940s and Eliz
Sansarian's study of feminism in Iran during this century demonstrate that feminist agendas in these two Middle Eastern countries
are grounded in nationalism and Islam. At the same time, they
illustrate divergent roles of the state: the Egyptian government
tolerated the existence of an independent feminist movement,
whereas the Iranian government from the mid-1930s until the end
of the 1970s orchestrated women's advance. Both studies also
illuminate universal dimensions of women's experience. Kumari
Jayawardena observes common threads in the early feminist
experience of Asian women. She asserts that this commonality
arises out of similar colonial and socioeconomic pasts, and situates
Asian experience in the context of global feminism.[9]

While eastern feminisms are being uncovered and studied,
understanding of western feminisms is being refined. For example,
Karen Offen's work on European feminism notes essential differences between Anglo-Saxon and French feminisms. She distinguishes the former as primarily individual, and the latter as
basically relational, or family based. Elaine Marks and Isabelle de
Courtivron discuss multiple feminist traditions in a single country.[10] Black feminist theorists like Barbara Christian and Barbara
Smith demonstrate differences between black and white feminisms
in America.[11] Nancy Cott's recent history of early twentieth cen-

tury American feminisms provides data and a vocabulary for dealing with this plurality.[12] This new scholarship undermines the myth of a monolithic western feminism and refines our understanding of feminisms as products of particular times, places, classes and races. It also sensitises the reader to the danger of essentialising Arab feminism.

In the Arab world, the period from the 1860s to the early 1920s witnessed the evolution of 'invisible feminism'. We find expression of this in books produced by middle and upper class women which were circulated in the harems and in women's journals such as *Al-Fatah* (1892), *Anis al-Jalis* (1893), and *Fatat al-Sharq* (1906) and in some men's journals such as Bahithat al-Badiyya's articles in *Al-Jarida*. The feminism of this period was mainly centred in Egypt.

The second period from the 1920s to the end of the 1960s witnessed the rise of women's public organised movements. There were active movements in Egypt between the 1920s and mid-1950s, in Lebanon, Syria and Iraq in the 1930s and 1940s and Sudan in the 1950s. In the 1950s and 1960s, states started to co-opt independent feminist movements, repressing but not totally eliminating women's independent, public feminist voices. States for their own purposes articulated their own agendas for women's advance.[13]

The third period from the 1970s to the present witnessed a resurgence of feminist expression in some countries such as Egypt, Lebanon, Syria and Iraq. However, during this same period many other Arab countries experienced their first wave of feminism. This period was fuelled to some extent by the United Nations Decade of Women (1975–1985). Outside stimulus encouraged Arab states to support limited public debate on the woman question. However, the rise of Islamic fundamentalist forces has increasingly inhibited these same states from promoting, and even sustaining, women's advance. We shall explore this historical experience more fully below.[14]

Methodology
The selections in this anthology question embedded patterns of dominant ideology and prescribed behaviour. As Rachel Blau Du Plessis writes: 'One of the major powers of the muted is to think against the current.'[15] Questioning the inherited 'wisdom' passed down by patriarchal authorities and surrogates, the women anthologised here shape a new ideology reflecting their changing everyday lives. Through their words they reject imposed patterns of thought, and they breach walls of silencing. By affixing their

signatures to their words, they eradicate namelessness. This is a radical act for women in societies where women's voices were not supposed to be heard nor their names pronounced. Women's voices were even considered by some to be *awra* (something shameful to be hidden; usually refers to private parts of the body). The feminist discourse of Arab women writers destroys patriarchally produced female archetypes and replaces them with their own prototypes: women who have their own aspirations, desires, needs.

We have organised our selections within a deliberately fluid classificatory framework that opens up a new way of thinking about women's writings. The rubrics we have chosen are: Awareness, Rejection, and Activism.[16] These are not firm categories. They are loose arenas that do not pin down the discourse but rather open it up for debate and allow its complexity to emerge. It is interesting to note that there are more selections under Awareness and Activism than there are under Rejection. This suggests a predominantly positive mode: the importance of awareness and its catalysing of activism. How far this would hold for the entire corpus of feminist discourse we cannot say, but it is provocative to ponder.

Some texts fall more neatly into one category than another. Others, as the readers will see, express two or even three dimensions. In these instances we have placed the piece in the section where we believe its most striking dimension is highlighted. For example, the essay by Marie-Aimée Helie-Lucas involves both awareness and activism. Her articulation of a feminist consciousness finally freed from imprisonment within a nationalist agenda a quarter of a century after the Algerian War of Independence was so myth-shattering that despite its patently important activist aspects it seemed more appropriate to include it in the section of awareness. Amalatrauf al-Sharki's memoir, which narrates her emerging awareness in the Yemen of the seventies and eighties, her rejection of certain institutions and her activist stands, spans all three modes and indeed connects them. We chose to place this piece in the section on Activism, as the most remarkable element in her life story is her self-construction resulting from her daring initiatives. Readers will find, and we hope debate, many more examples of overlapping modes.

The first section includes texts that illustrate a range of forms of awareness. In her memoirs, the Palestinian Fadwa Tuqan reveals her grasp of the paradox between her father's demands for political poetry and the life of domestic seclusion that the patriarchal system imposed upon her. She also shows how women function as male surrogates upholding at once patriarchal and class orders. The short story by the Palestinian Samira Azzam signals the understanding that men also are oppressed by patriarchal rules.

The section on rejection displays modes ranging from overcoming some of the isolation of strict domestic confinement through fantasy to violent annihilation or mental derangement. Aisha al-Taimuriya 'rejected' her extreme isolation in a nineteenth century elite harem in Egypt through writing tales and poems for other secluded women. In their more contemporary short stories, the Egyptian Andrée Chedid and the Iraqi May Muzaffar fuse women's rejection and physical violence in two quite different contexts. The Syrian Samar Attar demonstrates how rejection through partial rebellion against prevailing norms can catapult women into limbo and can also lead to psychological disorder. Nawal al-Saadawi connects rejection of the extreme control of females with loss of mind. These writings link women's rejection of intolerable conditions or roles with drastic, life-eradicating ends. The texts in this section illuminate the depths of women's pain and despair.

The final section demonstrates a wide range of activist modes of expression. While some writers criticise aspects of prevailing patriarchal systems, others work toward building and validating a new order. Within the first category are texts that claim rights for women. Examples include the Lebanese Zainab Fawwaz's essay insisting upon political rights for women in 1891 which is echoed in the first half of the twentieth century by Egyptians like Huda Shaarawi, Duriya Shafiq and Inji Aflatun. The essays of Nabawiya Musa ground appeals for educational and work rights for women within the nationalist struggle. In their journalistic articles, Duriya Shafiq and Amina Said expose the defective logic of certain Islamic religious figures and criticise their use of religion to oppress women. In fiction, women take activist stands, for example, Qut al-Qulub's Ramza who, through a marriage of her own choice, challenged both patriarchal control and class barriers. The Palestinian writer Nuha Samara sketches a woman's new emotional and sexual behaviours unleashed during wartime. Some memoirs such as that of the Yemeni Amatalrauf al-Sharki, in which she describes how she transcended practices of strict invisibility and sex segregation, reveal how women go about constructing new lives beyond prevailing social norms.

The texts that speak more directly to women and demonstrate the construction of new institutions or a new order by women include the Lebanese Hind Nawfal's 1892 editorial announcing her journal, the first by and for Arab women. Bahithat al-Badiya's

speech to women in Egypt early this century describes the process
of individual liberation. Several essays trace the development of
women's feminist literary criticism that helps to articulate a tradition of women's writings. Recognising a feminist discourse and
further shaping and validating it, these essays answer the need to
go beyond the confines of patriarchal linguistic structures and
literary conventions.

Issues of nation, class, sexuality, morality, and gender are
reflected in these activist texts. The texts show that feminist
activism comes not only from conscious, organised, collective
actions but may occur as everyday acts of life carved out with little
or no clear feminist consciousness.

Historical Context
Who are the women whose discourse this anthology presents?
They are women of the nineteenth and twentieth centuries who
share a broad Arab-Islamic culture. They share a common language, Arabic, though because of a colonial past and for reasons of
class not all write in this language. Arab women today live in more
than twenty sovereign Arab states as well as in occupation, in exile
or emigration.

They come from an area that stretches from Morocco in the
West to Iraq and the Arabian Peninsula in the East. The majority
of Arab lands in the nineteenth and early twentieth centuries were
under Ottoman rule. However, as Ottoman sovereignty declined,
European colonialism spread. Egypt was the first country to
establish *de facto* independence from Ottoman control early in the
nineteenth century, only to be occupied by the British in 1882. The
Arab East, or the Mashriq excluding Egypt, remained under direct
Ottoman rule until after the First World War. In the 1920s, the
territory was broken up into the states of Lebanon, Syria, Palestine
and Transjordan under French and British mandates. In the late
nineteenth century, Sudan fell under Anglo-Egyptian control. In
the Maghrib or Arab West, Algeria in 1830 and Tunisia in 1881 fell
under French colonial rule, while Morocco and Libya were occupied early in the twentieth century by the French and Italians
respectively. In the Arabian Peninsula, the Ottoman pressures and
controls on the cities and caravan routes in the nineteenth century
were eliminated in the early twentieth century. Although the
Arabian Peninsula was never colonised, much of the western
littoral of the Indian Ocean became Trucial States under British
control, and South Yemen (Aden) became a strategic outpost. By
the 1960s, most Arab lands had thrown off colonial rule and the

final vestiges of foreign occupation. Palestine was the exception. In 1948, it was taken over by the new state of Israel.

Different degrees of colonial control influenced secularisation as well as educational and linguistic patterns. Whereas British colonial policy left indigenous cultures and religions more or less intact, French and Italian colonial policies promoted aggressive cultural and religious assimilation. The British imposed administrative and financial superstructures, while the French and Italians, in addition, created extensive infrastructures and implanted vast settler communities.

In the Mashriq (including Egypt and Arab lands in western Asia excluding the Arabian Peninsula), there was a move towards secularisation directed by new Arab elites and state authorities. They wrested control of the national educational systems from the Islamic authorities and restricted the scope of Islamic legal jurisdiction mainly to laws governing the family. In the early and middle decades of the nineteenth century, Christian missionaries opened up French, English and American schools in Egypt, Palestine and Lebanon, and later in other Arab countries. By the end of the nineteenth century, new state educational systems, derived from European models but using Arabic as the language of instruction, had been introduced. Arabic remained the language of the majority in the urban and rural areas. In turn-of-the-century Egypt, French supplanted Turkish among the aristocracy. Elsewhere in the Mashriq, Turkish remained the language of the elite until the 1920s when English and French took its place. Although English and French became the spoken languages of the elites throughout the Mashriq, Arabic remained the official language and it continued to be widely spoken among the educated who commonly knew two or more languages. Following independence in the middle of the twentieth century and the spread of free education through university level, Arabic gained ascendancy as both the written and spoken language.

The situation was very different in the Maghrib. Education was absorbed into the metropolitan colonial system with destructive intrusion into indigenous culture. French and Italian replaced Arabic (or Turkish) as the language of government and schools. They also became the everyday languages across the classes. The law of the coloniser in some cases superseded Islamic law, including family law. So pervasive were some forms of enculturation that even after independence in the fifties and sixties, French and Italian still remain widespread today as written languages. The Arab women from the Maghrib anthologised in this book all write in French. In the Arabian Peninsula, which was neither under colonial rule nor absorbed into the European dominated market system until the discovery of oil in the 1930s, Islamic authorities retained fuller control over everyday life. The Arabic language and Islamic/Arab education remain in force.

Modern education was introduced differently to women and men. While foreign missionary schools in Egypt and Lebanon before the mid-nineteenth century began to admit girls and boys more or less simultaneously, state schools opening later in the century were quicker to provide education for boys than for girls. Male tutors brought into the household instructed upper class Egyptian girls in Arabic, Turkish and Persian. In the final decades, European governesses taught French and even English, but there were no state secondary schools for girls until the twentieth century. Whereas in Egypt the first state institution offering secondary school education for girls on an equal level with boys opened in 1925, similar institutions were not opened in Saudi Arabia until the mid-1950s. University education leading to degrees was made available to women in Egypt in 1929, and in the Arabian peninsula only in the 1960s.

These new educational opportunities disturbed patriarchal patterns of control over women. In the nineteenth century Arab world, urban upper and middle class Arab women lived within the harem system which ordained the segregation of the sexes and women's seclusion in the home. Face veils maintained distancing of the sexes if or when women left their homes.[17] Many lower class urban women veiled, but the peasant women whose work would not allow for it did not veil. Bedouin women living in the desert, however, could veil while grazing their flocks.[18]

During the final decades of the nineteenth century, while modernisation brought Egyptian women some change in everyday life, basic attitudes remained the same. Egyptian society was more open to change because British colonialism had not undermined the culture of indigenous daily life; they had even tolerated the upper classes' 'use' of the French language and fashions as a counterpoise to their cultural influence. In countries under severe forms of colonisation threatening the culture itself, as in the Maghrib, women's adherence to received norms such as veiling and seclusion became forms of nationalist/cultural defence.[19] Thus, Egyptian women could fight for nationalist as well as feminist goals without incurring the criticism that their feminist demands were dividing the nation against itself. In Algeria, however, as the essay by Marie-Aimée Helie-Lucas shows, it took women twenty-five years after Independence to release themselves from the hold of patriarchal nationalism articulated in the discourse of cultural authenticity.

The ending of the harem system and the disappearance of the face veil started to become widespread among upper and middle class Egyptian women in the 1920s, in the rest of the Mashriq from the end of the 1930s, and in Sudan and the Maghrib from the 1950s and 1960s following national liberation. In the Arabian Peninsula, with the exception of Saudi Arabia, changes began in the 1970s and especially the 1980s.

In the Arab world, women's feminism first arose in a pre-colonial context following the rise of capitalism and the modern state. In Egypt, the rise of women's feminist consciousness preceded the emergence of a nationalist consciousness. From the start women grounded their feminism first in Islam and later in nationalism. Islamic modernism, initiated in nineteenth century Egypt by Shaikh Muhammad Abduh, reconciled Islam and modernism. Using *ijtihad*, or independent inquiry holding that Islam is directly accessible to every thoughtful, well-educated and concerned individual, Muslims reinterpreted the Quran.[20] Women discovered that certain so-called Islamic practices, such as veiling, segregation and seclusion imposed upon urban women, were not ordained by Islam as they had been led to believe. To the contrary, women found that Islam guaranteed Muslims basic rights irrespective of gender. Huda Shaarawi's memoirs reveal the existence of women's debates on Islam and veiling in a Cairo harem salon of the 1890s. Nazira Zain al-Din extends this argument in *Unveiling and Veiling* (1928).

From the late nineteenth century, with the rise of nationalism, the first feminists grounded their growing feminist consciousness in nationalism, as can be read in the new Arab women's journals in Cairo and Alexandria. These women added new dimensions to nationalist debates and activism. Badran has investigated Egyptian women's militancy in the national revolution from 1919 to 1922 in which feminist nationalists advocated a society restructured on feminist principles.[21]

Following independence, Egyptian women organised a public movement under the aegis of the Egyptian Feminist Union. In the late 1930s, during the Arab Revolt in Palestine, women from the Mashriq, who had earlier channelled their energy mainly into philanthropic and literary societies, became active as nationalist and feminist militants. In 1938 and 1944, at pan-Arab conferences in Cairo, they joined forces in cementing Arab feminist consciousness. In 1944, they formed the Arab Feminist Union.[22] Among Palestinian women during the mandate period and after the creation of the state of Israel, women's nationalism took priority with the impending and actual loss of their country.[23] In Sudan, women participated in the national independence struggle in the mid-1950s and continued as an organised feminist movement. During the Algerian Revolution, 1954–62, most of the women who participated were young and only much later did some become feminists. In the late seventies and eighties, Palestinian women increasingly asserted themselves as feminists and nationalists simultaneously. Meanwhile women in the Arabian Peninsula took advantage of new educational opportunities, and state policies to reduce large foreign work forces opened new possibilities for work. In Kuwait, where women have more opportunities to organise and are freer to express controversial views, feminism has the most visible face, while in Saudi Arabia, where greater constraints are imposed upon women and candid expression, it is the least visible.

In the mid-1980s pan-Arab feminism re-emerged within the framework of the Arab Women's Solidarity Association (AWSA) under the presidency of Nawal al-Saadawi in Cairo. Arab feminists met in large numbers at the non-governmental forum in Nairobi in 1985 marking the end of the United Nations Decade of Women. There are now AWSA offices in various Arab countries and also in Europe. In some Arab countries, AWSA has invisible nuclei. The new pan-Arab feminism is aiming to combat reactionary or conservative moves throughout the Arab world to drive women out of the public workforce back into the home and to challenge the rescinding of even minimal gains in family laws. The new patriarchal conservative thrust, which most progressive men do not challenge, is led by Islamic conservatives and is symbolised by the veil. While some Arab feminists like the Moroccan, Fatima Mernissi and the Egyptians Nawal al-Saadawi and Amina Said, remain outspoken, most are guarded or publicly silent. However, as Mernissi writes in the introduction to the 1987 edition of her classic, *Beyond the Veil*: 'Are we all going back to the veil, back to the secluded house, back to the walled city, back to the national, proudly sealed, imaginary boundaries? . . . It is very unlikely.'[24]

Literary Context
Before the middle of the nineteenth century there were no known published writings by women. However, there was a lively oral tradition. Arab women were sometimes the custodians of knowledge: in the Western Sahara, nomads entrusted their wives with the key to the howdah bearing the Quran and other sacred texts.

Grandmothers passed on tribal wisdom in stories they told their grandchildren. However, until comparatively recently oral traditions were little known beyond the community that generated them. In recent decades, with a growing awareness of the importance of this oral tradition, scholars are now collecting folktales in danger of extinction.[25]

Despite a tradition of women's discourse, both the oral and the literate sources have until recently been difficult to locate. The majority of women in pre-modern Arab lands, as virtually everywhere, have been illiterate. Their individual voices have not come down to us, although as storytellers and poets they have been part of folk traditions. Among the elites there have always been the exceptional literate, and sometimes highly gifted women. The genealogical line of known Arab women writers and poets goes back to pre-Islamic Arabia when women competed with men in public debates. The elegies of al-Khansa of the Mudar tribe are counted among the masterpieces of Arabic poetry. In early Islamic Arabia, Aisha, a wife of the Prophet Muhammad, issued religious interpretations. In the eighth century, the mystic Rabia al-Adawiya composed esoteric verse. Among the medieval Abbasid court poets in Baghdad were Ubaida al-Tamburiya, Sakina and Queen Zubaida whose lyrical correspondence with the Caliph Harun al-Rashid has been much praised. In the late eighteenth century, the Egyptian historian, al-Jabarti, spoke of Cairene women distinguished by their learning. By the late nineteenth century Arab women intellectuals, like Zainab Fawwaz and Maryam al-Nahhas, the mother of Hind Nawfal, the founder of the first women's journal, had catalogued their foremothers along with more contemporary sisters in the new biographical dictionaries and compendia of women. These compendia served a hortatory function: they pinpointed desirable qualities in great Arab and non-Arab women of the past to reclaim their experience for contemporary women.

Arab women in the nineteenth century began to benefit from the spread of education. Although their contributions remained largely invisible in the public realm, these women were part of what in the Mashriq was called the *nahda* or cultural renaissance. In Egypt, where Arab feminist discourse first appeared, women's feminism preceded that of the men. Yet, it is Qasim Amin's books – rather than women's writings and their debates in the harems – which were *seen*. Therefore, his has been considered the pioneering discourse even though he was not the first. Already in the 1860s and 1870s women were writing to each other, transcending the highly segregated and secluded world of the nineteenth century that even cut women off from each other. Discursively they were

breaking through conventional patriarchal barriers of circum-
scribed kin-centred female social relations. Such communication
includes for example an 1860s poem by Warda al-Yaziji, to Warda
al-Turk, two women of Greater Syria. From the 1870s, al-Yaziji
and Aisha al-Taimuriya, an upper class Turco-Circassian woman
living in Cairo, exchanged poems and essays. Early in the twentieth
century, Bahithat al-Badiya sent letters and verses to May Ziyada
from the Fayyum, an oasis east of Cairo. She subsequently published these letters in the press.

By the 1890s in Egypt, Eugenie Le Brun Rushdi, a Frenchwoman
who had married an upper class Egyptian and converted to Islam,
held a salon which served as a forum for upper class women to meet,
compare, debate and analyse their condition as women. The women's
salon of the 1890s paved the way for other collective intellectual
activities such as women's lectures. In 1914, Huda Shaarawi, supported by princesses of the Egyptian royal family, spearheaded the
founding of the Intellectual Association of Egyptian Women. May
Ziyada was a member and Labiba Hashim, the founder of the
women's paper *Fatat al-Sharq* (1906), was its Arabic secretary.[26]

Already at this early stage, women writers knew of each other
and appreciated the revolutionary potential of writing; when
women write they enter the field of power and knowledge. When
Warda al-Yaziji died in 1924 a group of Lebanese women wrote
her obituary, and, as Ziyada writes in her biography of al-Yaziji,
they 'contributed to a portrait and donated it to the public library
in Beirut so that the poet's picture should hang next to those of the
great men'[27]. It was the first time that women had publicly
acknowledged another woman in this way. In 1918, Shaarawi's first
feminist speech was the eulogy she delivered at the commemoration for Bahithat al-Badiya when she died. By this period, communications between female and male littérateurs were becoming
widespread. One of the best known correspondences is that
between Ziyada and Gibran Khalil Gibran, the Lebanese writer
who had emigrated to America in the late nineteenth century.

Arab journalism began in the nineteenth century in Egypt.
Unlike most other Arab lands, independence from Ottoman
controls allowed a free press to emerge. Its earliest foundations
were laid mainly by women and men who had emigrated from the
Arab province of Greater Syria. In the 1880s, women were already
contributing to male-founded journals: Aisha al-Taimuriya published in *Al-Adab* and various Syrian women contributed to journals
such as *Al-Lataif* and *Al-Muqtataf*.[28] Early in the twentieth century,
Bahithat al-Badiya published feminist essays in *Al-Jarida*. These
women pioneered in finding space in male-run journals.

In Saudi Arabia, the continued segregation of the sexes has not kept women as journalists and editors out of the pages of the male-run major dailies, such as *Al-Riyad*, although they have been housed in separate editorial offices and are subordinate to male administrative and editorial authorities. Women's ability to publish a feminist discourse within the framework of a male-run paper depends on the policy of the paper, few of which have been as liberal and pro-feminist as newspapers like *Al-Jarida*.

Towards the end of the nineteenth century, women began to create their own journals to publish what they wanted to say to mainly remote audiences. These journals gave women a new sense of identity, community and changing roles, helping many for the first time to conceive of themselves functioning outside the home. In 1892, Hind Nawfal, a Syrian woman living in Cairo, founded *Al-Fatah*, the first women's journal in the Arab world. Many others followed it. The first militantly feminist journal in the Arab world appeared in Egypt in 1925 when the Egyptian Feminist Union founded *l'Egyptienne*. It lasted fifteen years. In 1925, Fatma Yusif, a Lebanese immigrant to Egypt, was the first woman to found what would become a major mainstream journal called by her stage name, *Ruz al-Yusif*. Until today, it is an important Cairo magazine. In 1937, *Al-Misriya*, a sister journal to *l'Egyptienne* in Arabic, was initiated. In 1945, the Arab Feminist Union published the first pan-Arab women's journal called *Al-Arabiya*. Nine years later, its editor Amina Said started *Hawa*. This journal has brought important gender issues to a broad readership, although recently under new direction it has become conservative and many of its articles are trivial. The seventies and eighties saw the founding of other journals such as the Moroccan *Thamanya Mayu* (Eighth of May), the tunisian *Al-Nisa*, the Sudanese *Ahfad*, the Libyan, *Al-Bait* (The Home), and the Saudi *Sayyidati*, which is published in London, and most recently *Al-Mara al-Arabiya* and *Bint al-Ard* in Egypt. In 1989, nearly half a century after the first pan-Arab women's journal was founded, the Arab Women's Solidarity Association (AWSA) began to publish a magazine called *Nun*. With the continued proliferation of women's newspapers and magazines in response to a growing readership, writing to publish became more or less acceptable for middle class women.

From the end of the nineteenth century women also gained limited access to male publishing houses, as entries in this volume attest. Notwithstanding a small number of liberal men who favoured women's emancipation and opened their journals to women and whose presses published their books, the very issue of literacy for women was inflammatory and remained anathema to

entrenched male patriarchy which has linked female immorality
with literacy. It was alleged that literate women would fall prey to
immorality: they could absorb subversive ideas and engage in
dangerous communication which would lead to unseemly behaviour. Nabawiya Musa confronted such male fears in her 1920
essay, 'The Effects of Books and Novels on Morals'. Patriarchal
elites showed a class as well as a gender bias, construing literacy as
inappropriate and *politically* dangerous in men of the lower classes,
yet not *morally* threatening to men as it was for women of any class.

While progressive male reformers read works by women, most
men did not. The most effective means of keeping the silence was
contemptuous neglect.[29] In the view of most men, women were not
writing important texts. How could they when they did not have
important roles in society? At best, they were deemed harmless and
therefore irrelevant. At worst, as when writers like Nawal al-
Saadawi later in the twentieth century began to link women's
oppression with class oppression, women's writing was seen as
threatening to patriarchal interests. Socialist men did not welcome
new allies.

However, despite persistent male contempt and neglect as well as
domestic constraints or tyrannies, women continued to write. The
Egyptian Alifa Rifaat spoke of a husband who could not tolerate
seeing his wife's words in print. In order to write, she locked
herself in her bathroom. Nawal al-Saadawi divorced two husbands
hostile to her literary pursuits but would not give up her writing.
The Algerian Fadhma Amrouche did not dare show her husband
the memoirs which she wrote in 1946 and only published them
after his death.[30]

Women have also attempted to subvert patriarchal control of the
distribution of their writing. The Egyptian Feminist Union issued
its own publications from the 1920s, but only in the 1980s have
women founded and run their own publishing houses, such as the
press run by the Arab Women's Solidarity Association in Cairo, the
Ghada Samman Publishing House in Beirut, and the Post-Apollo
Press founded by the Lebanese Simone Fattal in California.

Novels, poetry and short stories were the preferred genres after
article writing. Fiction and poetry retain the screen of apparent
non-accountability. Intimate and critical reflections can be safely
expressed in a form that appears to draw attention to itself rather
than to the author and her message. These can be powerful
vehicles for feminist thought, especially when invisibility is needed
or sought.

Aisha al-Taimuriya and Warda al-Yaziji wrote and distributed poetry and tales in the late nineteenth century. They were brought up in liberal families, and they had fathers who supported their learning. These men, disregarding gender 'rules', foiled their wives' efforts to produce ladies of the needle rather than women of the pen. The fathers brought in special tutors and encouraged their daughter's literary inclinations. In this environment, the girls were allowed to develop and express alternative perspectives on their society until they were ready to be married and then they were expected to conform. Al-Taimuriya's poetry has been commonly considered traditional and 'genderless', yet a careful reading of *Hilyat al-tiraz* (Embroidered Ornaments, 1909) displays anger:

> I challenge my destiny, my time
> I challenge the human eye
>
> I will sneer at ridiculous rules and people
> That is the end of it; I will fill my eyes with pure
> light, and swim in a sea of unbound feeling
>
> I have challenged tradition and my absurd position,
> and I have gone beyond what age and place allow.[31]

Al-Yaziji's poetry anthology *The Rose Garden* (Hadiqat al-Ward) was the first book by an Arab woman to appear in print. Published in 1867, it enjoyed considerable success and was republished in increasingly expanded form in 1887, 1894 and 1914. May Ziyada lauded it as the first anthology by an Arab poet to be reprinted more than twice in the nineteenth century.

The first half of the twentieth century was a time of experimentation and innovation in Arabic literature. The short story and the novel were new genres from the West that writers tried to appropriate. Most were concerned with the plight of the individual, and particularly of women in a society in rapid transition. The short stories of the Egyptian, Suhair Qalamawi,[32] and the Syrian Ulfa Idelbi and the novels of the Egyptians Amina Said and Latifa Zayyat fall in this period.

While organised public feminist movements made headway during the first half of the twentieth century, it was not until the sixties and seventies that women's feminist voices found wider published literary expression. During this period a Lebanese woman's novel caused the first wave of excitement: Laila Baalbaki's *I Live* (Ana Ahya) came out in 1958. Like many other Arab women's novels, it has been described as an autobiographical narration of a middle class woman's revolt against social conventions. This label of autobiography has until recently been a common tool for diminishing women's literary voices – they have only one story, their own. However, whether it was called autobiography or novel mattered little.[33] The message of refusal was so strong that it unleashed a wave of feminist literature.

Women wrote mainly short stories and poems that questioned social norms that systematically oppressed women. In the 1960s, many women throughout the Arab world were publishing. These include Andrée Chedid and Ihsan Assal in Egypt; Ghada Samman and Huda Naamani in Syria; Emily Nasrallah and Nadia Tueni in Lebanon; Nazik al-Malaika and May Muzaffar in Iraq; Samira Azzam and Fadwa Tuqan in Palestine; Khannata Bannuna in Morocco. The Algerian Revolution provoked women like Assia Djebar and Zoubeida Bittari to write not only about oppression but also liberation.[34] These writers usually described women's lives as a constant struggle to find a space of their own. The more outspoken, like Samman, attracted disapproval. Yet these voices were beginning to resonate.

Although women's feminist literary expression does not follow a strictly chronological progression, the seventies and eighties generally witnessed a bolder literary attack on patriarchal institutions and traditions. While rooted in indigenous experience, these writers acknowledge the universal dimension of the feminist struggle. Nawal al-Saadawi has used fiction in a campaign to raise consciousness throughout the Arab world.

In Lebanon, the civil war (1975–82) opened opportunities for women to express themselves and to publish in a situation where norms had given way. As the war progressed and the men left, women like the Lebanese Emily Nasrallah, the Palestinian Nuha Samara and the Iraqi Daisy al-Amir wrote of a society reconstructed in terms of a feminist consciousness. They went beyond criticism to subversion of patriarchal structures. Not simply the authors of a number of compelling individual books, they have through their collective discourse gained recognition as a radical feminist school. Indeed, it is important to note that what has been seen as the first Arab women's literary school is feminist.[35]

The emergence – however unplanned and unconscious – of a feminist school of women writers has implications for the further development of women's literature. The volume of Arab women's writings published in places like Lebanon and Egypt inspired women elsewhere. It is striking how, in Saudi Arabia, women have begun to write in full awareness of other women writers. Titles of some Saudi women's stories and novels self-consciously intertext with other women's works, especially those of the Syrian Ghada

Samman. The Saudi Fawziya al-Bikr's 'Swimming in the Lake of Nothingness' (Al-Sibaha fi Buhairat al-Adam, 1979), recalls Samman's *Swimming in the Lake of the Devil* (Al-Sibaha fi Buhairat al-Shaitan, 1974), while her compatriot Raja Muhammad Auda's *He is my Destiny* (Innahu Qadari, 1982) refers to Samman's *Your Eyes are my Destiny* (Aynak Qadari, 1962).

The writing and publication by Arab women of their own memoirs and journals is mainly a twentieth century phenomenon. Personal and family lives have been deemed private, and not to be talked about in public. The first feminist memoir was dictated by Huda Shaarawi in the mid-1940s; in it she candidly recounted her life as a girl and as a woman and analysed gender experience.[36] Other Egyptian feminists have written memoirs such as Munira Thabit, who has recalled her life in journalism[37] and politics; Nawal al-Saadawi and Farida al-Naqqash – who does not call herself a feminist – have written prison memoirs. The Palestinian Raimonda Tawil has published a journal of life under occupation, *My Home My Prison* (1978).[38] We have included part of the 1984 memoir of the Palestinian poet Fadwa Tuqan, an autobiographical essay by the Lebanese poet and artist Etel Adnan and extracts from the Algerian Zoubeida Bittari's *O Mes Soeurs Musulmanes, Pleurez!* (1964).

Warda al-Yaziji's poem to Warda al-Turk written in 1867 was a first step towards recognition of sisterhood in writing. One of the first women to evoke a self-conscious sense of literary sisterhood was May Ziyada (1886–1941). In 1913, five years after her arrival in Cairo, she began a weekly salon frequented by men and women – the literary luminaries of the day. In her biographies as well as in her Press Club Speech in Cairo in 1928 she praised Warda al-Yaziji, Aisha al-Taimuriya as well as Bahithat al-Badiya. By invoking these names she was giving public recognition to foremothers, women with whom she could link herself in a line that gave weight and substance to what they and other later women might say. When Ziyada died in 1941, the recognition that she had bestowed on women writers was reciprocated by the Egyptian Feminist Union which published a commemorative volume remembering and honouring their literary sister.

The cultivation of such a tradition, while begun earlier, achieved a new level of activity in the 1970s and 1980s, when Arab women increasingly wrote introductions to each other's writings as well as critical reviews on essays. Works like these reveal a growing tradition of Arab feminist literary criticism. Mary Eagleton has written: ' . . . the search for women writers has constituted an important challenge. To ask the questions – where are the women writers? What has aided or inhibited their writing? How has criticism responded to their work? – introduces into literary criticism the determinant of gender and exposes literary tradition as a construct'. [39] In the 1980s, the number of women writers has increased so dramatically that mutual awareness and acknowledgement or competitive rejection has become the norm.

Arab women's feminist discourse has addressed universal issues such as education and work, rights concerning marriage, and suffrage, and at the same time has confronted less universal issues such as breaking out of gender segregation. Like women in many other third world countries, and unlike western women, Arab women have typically had to pioneer their feminist expression in agrarian societies, more recently experiencing modern urbanisation, and in societies where religion has remained an important regulator of everyday life and a source of identity. These Arab and other third world societies have typically experienced European colonial rule and/or western imperialist hegemony while Arab women's feminisms were beginning to be articulated. Arab women's feminist voices have always run the risk of being discredited as anti-nationalist or anti-religious. Women in the Arab world have had more complex battles to fight than have feminists in the West with their strikingly different histories and circumstances.

Today, conservative Islamic forces in Arab countries threaten women's expression in ways that outsiders can scarcely perceive. We can begin to appreciate the price of feminist expression when we see that not only Nawal al-Saadawi but also a moderate feminist like Amina Said have had round-the-clock protection by state guards.

What are Arab feminisms? Meanings are not the same everywhere, that we know, but exactly in what way they differ we are still only discovering. When one woman writes to another praising her poetic expression, as al-Yaziji wrote to Warda al-Turk, one might ask, 'How can this be feminist?' It seems to be no more than an exchange of poems between women. However, when we recall the circumstances in which these women lived, when visiting was at best confined to female family members, when most women did not write because the act of writing was considered inflammatory and a moral threat, such a communication takes on special meaning. An analysis of Arab women's discourse allows us to see feminism where we had not previously thought to look.

NOTES
1 While this is the first anthology of Arab women's feminist writings there have
been some more general collections. There are four Arabic anthologies of
Arab women's literature. In 1975, Yusuf al-Sharuni published *The 1002nd
Night* (Al-Laila al-Thaniya bada al-Alf), a selection of Arab women's fiction
from the 1920s to the early 1970s. Laila Salih edited two volumes on women's
literature that include brief studies and very brief excerpts: *Women's Literature
in Kuwait* (Adab al-Mara fi al-Kuwait, 1978) and *Women's Literature in the
Arabian Peninsula and the Gulf* (Adab al-Mara fi al-Jazira al-Arabiya wa
al-Khalij, 1983). Salih writes that all eighteen studies of literature from the
Arabian Peninsula that had been compiled by 1980 uniformly excluded
women writers. Hence, all of her research had to be done *in situ*. Rose
Ghuraiyib, *Breezes and Storms in Contemporary Arab Feminist Poetry* (Nasamat wa
Aasir fi al-Shir al-Nisai al-Arabi al-Muasir, 1980).
  In English there are five anthologies. In 1978, Elizabeth W. Fernea and
Basima Bezirgan published *Middle Eastern Women Speak* which also includes
some scholarly articles by western area specialists. In 1978, Kamal Boullata
published *Women of the Fertile Crescent. An Anthology of Modern Poetry by Arab
Women* (Washington D.C.), a collection of women's poems from Egypt, Iraq,
Jordan, Lebanon, Palestine, Saudi Arabia and Syria. Fernea's *Women and the
Family in the Middle East: New Voices of Change* (1985) brings together the voices
of women and some men most of whom speak of women's socio-economic
condition. Nayra Atiya's *Khul Khaal: Five Egyptian Women Tell Their Stories*
(1984) crafts interviews with five working class, mostly illiterate, women into
biographies. Fatima Mernissi's *Le Maroc Raconte par ses Femmes* (1984) was
translated into English as *Doing Daily Battle: Interviews with Moroccan Women*
(1988). It is a collection of eleven interviews that the sociologist conducted with
women from various sectors of Moroccan society.
2 Meaning women's pieces or feminist pieces.
3 On feminist terminology, see Margot Badran, 'Dual Liberation: Feminism and
Nationalism in Egypt, 1870–1925', *Feminist Issues*, Spring 1988, pp. 27–28 and
Irene Fenoglio Abd al-Aal, *Défense et Illustration de l'Egyptienne Aux Débuts d'une
Expression Féminine*, Cairo, 1988. Karen Offen writes that the term 'feminism'
first became current in France in the 1890s (see Offen, 'Defining Feminism. A
Comparative Historical Approach', *Signs*, 14/1, Fall 1988).
4 Margot Badran, 'Independent Women: More Than a Century of Feminism in
Egypt', paper presented at Georgetown University Symposium 'Old Bound-
aries. New Frontiers', ed. Judith Tucker, forthcoming.
5 Miriam Cooke, *War's Other Voices. Women Writers on the Lebanese Civil War*,
Cambridge, Cambridge University Press, 1988.
6 Margot Badran, 'The Origins of Feminism in Egypt', *Current Issues in Women's
History*, London, Routledge & Kegan Paul, 1989.
7 See Marnia Lazreg, 'Feminism and Difference: The Perils of Writing as a
Woman on Women in Algeria', *Feminist Studies*, 14, no. 1, Spring, 1988. See
Leila Ahmed, 'Feminism and Feminist Movements in the Middle East' in Aziz
al-Hibri (ed.), *Women and Islam*, New York, Pergamon, 1982, 153–168; May
Ghoussoub, 'Feminism – or the Eternal Masculine – in the Arab World', *The
New Left Review*, 161, Jan/Feb 1987, 3–18.
8 For a critique of western women's writing on Arab women's experience and
feminism, see Lazreg, ibid.
9 Margot Badran, 'Huda Sharawi and the Liberation of the Egyptian Woman',
Oxford D. Phil Thesis, 1977; Eliz Sanasarian, *The Women's Rights Movement in*

Iran, New York, Praeger, 1982; and Kumari Jayawardena, *Feminism and Nationalism*, London, Zed, 1987.

10 Elaine Marks and Isabelle de Courtivron, *New French Feminism*, New York, 1981.

11 Gloria T. Hull, Patricia B. Scott and Barbara Smith (eds.) *All the Women are White, All the Blacks are Men, bu Some of Us are Brave*, New York, Feminist, 1982; Barbara Christian, *Black Feminist Criticism. Perspectives on Black Women Writers*, New York, Pergamon, 1985.

12 Nancy Cott, *The Grounding of Feminism*, New Haven, Yale University Press 1987.

13 Badran, 1977. See note 9.

14 For a broad historical overview see Margot Badran, 'Feminism as a force in the Arab World' (Al-Nisaiya ka Quwa fi al-Alam al-Arabi) in *Contemporary Arab Thought and the Women* (Al-Fikr al-Arabi al-Muasir wa al-Mara) Cairo, 1989. This is the second volume in a series from the Arab Women's Solidarity Association Press. Also Margot Badran, 'Feminists, Islam and the State in 19th and 20th Century Egypt', in Deniz Kandiyoti, ed. *Women, Islam and the State*, Macmillan, London and University of California Press, 1990.

15 Rachel Blau Du Plessis, *Writing Beyond the Ending; Narrative Strategies of 20th Century Women Writers*, Bloomington: Indiana University Press, 1984, p.196.

16 Before arriving at this typology, we considered other options: 1) a chronological line that would highlight the unexpected appearance and reappearance of multiple themes over time, it would also allow the writings to be more easily situated in an international context; 2) a geographical clustering that would demonstrate the variety of national discursive productions; 3) organisation under categories of experience; 4) organisation by life-cycle stages.

17 On nineteenth century harem life in Egypt, Badran, 1977. See note 9.

18 Judith Tucker, *Women in Nineteenth Century Egypt*, Cambridge, Cambridge University Press, 1985.

19 Frantz Fanon, *A Dying Colonialism*, Paris, 1962.

20 On Muhammad Abduh and Islamic modernism see Albert Hourani, *Arabic Thought in the Liberal Age*, Oxford, 1962; Muhammad Imara (ed.), *Al-Islam wa al-Mara fi Ray al-Imam Muhammad Abduh* (Islam and Woman in the Opinion of Imam Muhammad Abduh), Cairo, n.d.

21 Badran, 'Dual Liberation: Feminism and Nationalism in Egypt, 1870–1925'. See note 3.

22 See Badran, 1977.

23 On Palestinian women's feminism and nationalism in the 1920s through the mid-1930s see Matiel Moghannam, *The Arab Woman and the Palestine Question*, London, 1937.

24 Fatima Mernissi, *Beyond the Veil*, Cambridge, 1975; new ed. Bloomington, Indiana University Press, 1987, p.3.

25 Malika al-Assimi's work on women's folktales in Morocco is a case in point. She explains that under the French protectorate, the art of oral narration flourished. Arab and Berber traditions and stories were sources of pride and opposition to the French. However, in 1956 when the French left, there was no more need for the preservation of an oral indigenous culture. Moreover, modernity had so encroached upon every facet of life that there was less inclination to sit around for evenings on end listening to a crone's fabulations. Television had taken over, and as the old people died, so did the stories. In *Al-Hikayat al-Shabiya: Hikayat al-Nisa* (Popular Tales: Tales of Women, thesis for 3rd Cycle doctorate, Muhammad V University, 1987), al-Assimi brings

together 240 stories out of the Marrakesh area, the Moroccan capital for six centuries. She divides the stories between those that can be told at any time (*tarfih*) and those that can only be told at night. The latter can last for over an hour and they are usually connected with sexuality.

26 On the women's salon, see Huda Shaarawi, *Harem Years: The Memoirs of an Egyptian Feminist*, London, Virago, 1986 and Feminist Press, New York, 1987, pp.76–82, 94–99. Eugenie Le Brun wrote two books under the pseudonym, Niya Salima: *Harem et Les Musulmanes*, Paris, 1902, and *Les Répudiées*, Paris, 1908.

27 May Ziyada *Warda al-Yaziji*, Cairo, 1924, p.25.

28 Byron Cannon, 'Nineteenth Century Writings on Women and Society: The Interim Role of the Masonic Press in Cairo – *Al-Lataif*, 1885–1895', *International Journal of Middle East Studies*, Vol. 17, no. 4, 1985, pp.463–84.

29 Joanna Russ, *How to Suppress Women's Writing*, Austin: University of Texas Press, 1983.

30 Amrouche wrote, 'This is the epilogue to the story of my life which I wrote in Muxula-Rades in the month of August 1946 in memory of the fiftieth anniversary of leaving the school of Tadder-on-Fella in Kabylie . . . I tried to open it (the notebook containing the memoirs) at Ighil-Ali in 1953 but I realised it would displease his [her son's] father, and as I did not want to pain him I returned the notebook to its drawer to which he alone had the key hanging from his watchchain.' Fadhma Amrouche, *Histoire de ma vie*, Paris, Maspero, 1976, p.199.

31 Translations from Mahmoud Bikheet al-Rabie, 'Women Writers and Critics in Modern Egypt 1888–1963' unpublished Ph.D. thesis, School of Oriental and African Languages, London University, 1965, pp.45, 59, 93.

32 Suhair Qalamawi was a member of the youth group of the Egyptian Feminist Union called the Shaqiqat, see Badran 1977, pp.174–175.

33 Estelle Jelinek, *Women's Autobiography: Essays in Criticism*, 1980; and Carolyn Heilbrun, *Writing a Woman's Life*, New York, Norton 1988.

34 On women's writings on the Algerian Revolution see Miriam Cooke, 'Deconstructing War Discourse: Women in the Algerian Revolution', Working Paper, *Women in International Development*, East Lansing, June 1989.

35 Cooke, *War's Other Voices*. See note 5.

36 Her memoirs have been published in Arabic as *Al-Raida al-Arabiya al-Haditha*, with an introduction by Amina Said, Cairo, Dar al-Hilal, 1981, and in English as *Harem Years: The Memoirs of an Egyptian Feminist*, previously cited.

37 Munira Thabit's memoir is entitled *Revolution in the Ivory Tower* (Thawra fi al-Burj al-Aji) Cairo, 1945.

38 On prison memoirs see Marilyn Booth, 'Prison, Gender, Praxis: Women's Prison Memoirs in Egypt and Elsewhere', MERIP, 149, Nov.–Dec. 1987, pp.35–41.

39 Mary Eagleton, ed., *Feminist Literary Theory*, Oxford, Basil Blackwell, 1986.

AWARENESS

❧

My life is lack,
misery, pain,
hell, boredom
So why live?

My life is tears
and flames of a burning heart
The light of all candles has hid
Why a life of grief?

My life is anxiety,
ice and a winter night
and a slow death . . . extinction
Is there no mercy, O Time?

My life is a desert,
a fence . . . oppression
Where is the light, the day?

Dalila al-Zaituni, 'My Life' (Tunisia, 1982)

Translated from the French
by Miriam Cooke

Etel Adnan

(1925–)

Etel Adnan was born in Beirut, Lebanon. Her father was a Muslim Syrian and her mother a Christian Greek. Beirut and Damascus, she said in an interview with Margot Badran, 'the landscape of my childhood, represented two poles, two cultures, two different worlds and I liked both.'

She attended a convent school until the age of sixteen. The war interrupted her education and she went to work for the French Information Bureau. Three years later, she attended the newly opened École Supérieure des Lettres. She taught for three years at the Ahliya School for Girls. In 1950, she went to Paris to study philosophy at the Sorbonne. Five years later she moved to America where she studied at Berkeley and Harvard. Between 1959 and 1972, she taught philosophy at Dominican College in San Rafael, California.

Adnan is a poet, a writer and a painter. She has said that it is only while painting that she can express herself in Arabic, and much of her writing is illustrated not only with plates but also with flourishes and bursts within the text itself. In *Apocalypse Arabe* (1980), each segment of the poem is pockmarked with signs that weave above the often dense text a system of meaning: STOP, she writes, but the arrow points on, and on . . . In 1972, she worked as literary editor of the Beirut daily, *L'Orient-Le Jour*. In 1976, she left Lebanon. She now divides her time between Paris and Sausalito, California.

In the twenty years following the publication of her first volume of poetry, *Moonshots* (1966), Adnan has published eight books in English and French of which two are written in prose: *Sitt Marie Rose* (1978, translated into English in 1982) and her 1986 'essay in the tradition of Siddharta' *Journey to Mount Tamalpais*. Her poetry collections include *Five Senses for One Death* (1971), *Jebu et l'Express Beyrouth-Enfer* (1973), *L'Apocalypse Arabe* (1980), *Pablo Neruda is a Banana Tree* (1982), *From A to Z* (1982), *The Indian Never Had a Horse* (1985).

'Growing Up to be a Woman Writer in Lebanon' is the text of the keynote address she gave to the first meeting of the Association of Middle Eastern Women's Studies during the 1986 annual convention of the American Middle Eastern Studies Association at Boston. In it she explores her evolution into a woman artist.

Growing Up to be a Woman Writer in Lebanon

1986

❦

The thing that I remember as the oldest my memory has retained – the first object in my private archaeology – is a circular stone fountain, low and made of what I think now was soft limestone. And that fountain was empty.

I don't know if I lived in the house which had that garden and the fountain, or if I visited it with my mother. But it is there with a singular and haunting clarity.

The house I remember very well, the one in which I see the little girl I was, was an old big house, with huge windows, lace curtains, a flower stand painted in green with ferns or other permanently green plants in pots, and a garden with a tall wall delineating its territory from the street. It was in Beirut. I remember light all over the place, I remember it to be cool, with my bed in my parents' bedroom, and a kitchen which had a door to another side of the same garden. I remember flowers as clearly as I remember my mother and her cat. Bijou was our cat and she had kittens regularly.

I was an only child and it seemed like I lived in a magic place. I liked it. I had space to run, I had places to inhabit. There were four rooms each one with a different personality, I could be a different person in each one of them. One of them was sunny and my father used to shave in it. It had sunshine. The sun was like something real coming through the windows. It had existence. It jumped off the mirrors of the tall cupboards. The bedroom was cooler. Its light was more evenly distributed along the year. The third one was well furnished but I did not often go into it. My mother used to close its door. The fourth one was useless. It had a window bearing on the living room inside. It was dark, almost black, and reserved for the cat when she had her kittens. Nobody needed that room.

I was much aware that I was a little girl. There was something nice about being a little girl, something warm and comfortable. Something electric also. I was aware that I was more like my mother than my father. But as I did not have other children around me to compare the way they were treated, I felt more like something alive, a 'being', a person, than specifically a little girl. And I did not go to school until I was five.

There is related one event which stays clear in front of my eyes: we had a little boy visiting us. He was half French by his mother and his name was Pierrot. His father was a French citizen from Indo-China. The little boy was an orphan. His French mother had died in Beirut. He came to us to spend his vacations from his boarding school. I remember that one day, very likely before noon, we were playing in the space between a couch and the wall with its windows. Pierrot offered to uncover himself if I would do the same so that we see 'how we are made'. So we did take some of our clothes off and I think that we heard my mother moving around in the house and pulled back our clothes. That was all. I don't know if my memory is faithful. But it seems that I took the experience as something I learned, something I saw, with a kind of numbness, the feel of the pure looking at something. But I did not forget. The moment remains singular and clear. And close to age sixty, I found that it had made its way into a poem I wrote recently: 'An alley of linden trees, and lightning . . .' It reads:

> This is why I kept company with
> archangels and ants
> as well as with a seven-year-old
> child who since has died
> leaving no trace
> one day over the radio it was said
> that he received two bullets
> in the head
> it was in Saigon the day the war ended

I lost track of Pierrot far back in my own childhood; the war in Vietnam happened and I put my energies into the anti-war movement, writing my first poetry in the language and the land of America, and then, sometime in 1985, writing a long poem about my earlier years, Pierrot and his Indo-Chinese origins and the Vietcong . . . all came together through the mystery as well as into the mystery of poetry.

As I said, my parents sent me to school at the age of five. My mother was a Greek from Smyrna, and my father was a Syrian from Damascus who belonged to a family where the men served in the Army of the Ottoman Empire. He was the commander of Smyrna during the First World War and although he was already married and the father of a boy and of two girls, he married my

mother who was about twenty years younger than he was. His first
family had remained in Damascus. At the end of the war he came
to settle in Beirut and I was born in the city of Beirut in 1925.

Lebanon was newly created as a state by the French. The French
turned Syria and Lebanon into mandates under their rule. They
expanded the already existing French schools in the country and
favoured the establishment of new ones. They created in Lebanon,
and imposed on it, a system of education totally conforming to
their schools in France, an education which had nothing to do with
the history and the geography of the children involved.

So at age five I started speaking French and then, only French, as
Arabic was a forbidden language in these French schools. They
were in their entirety run by members of the French Catholic
Church. And Arabic was forbidden. The Lebanese children spoke
it at home. My mother not knowing Arabic, French took over as the
language at home: we spoke less and less Turkish or Greek and
more and more French.

These schools were for boys or girls only. The co-educational
system was instituted in Lebanon in the fifties.

The French nuns were stern. They behaved like colonialists and
like missionaries: they had the dual purpose of extolling the virtues
of French civilisation, and the infallibility of the Church in matters
of religion. They created for children an authoritarian and dogma-
tic environment. They were so thorough in their system that very
few students of their schools ever questioned the education they
received. Dogmatism has the effect of occupying the totality of
one's mental space to such a degree that the things it purports to be
true become as 'natural' as the sky or earth: they become the only
things the mind can distinguish, they become the very tools of one's
thinking. They become taken for granted.

So I grew up thinking that the world was French. And that
everything that mattered, that was 'in books', or had authority (the
nuns), did not concern our environment. This is what is called
alienation.

I loved school because there I found other children to play with,
and recreation time was my favourite time. We had fifteen minutes
at ten in the morning and fifteen minutes at two in the afternoon.
A square courtyard with a kiosk and an empty fountain in its
middle was our playground, and was for me an enchanted garden
that still recurs in my dreams.

I was very much aware that I was a little girl because of my
mother's careful attention to my dresses: little pieces of silk cloth
were going to the dressmaker to make me elaborate little dresses
which were worn for special occasions and given to the 'poor' in

perfect condition one or two years later. I still miss them and am left with the feeling that I never wore them to the full.

One day I was caught by the nuns while climbing the fence of the courtyard: it was a low fence made of slim painted iron poles, and it was easy to press oneself on the railing and slide to the other side. But the nuns caught me and with a stern voice accused me of being a 'tomboy' which in French is called 'garçon manqué' ('something that failed to be boy')! It made being a boy both appealing as a fact and shameful as a desire. One should say that with their obsession with sins – French Catholicism having a Calvinistic streak in it – the nuns did their best to spoil our natural innocence. I could say that my earlier creative works were the invented confessions of non-existent sins at the confessional. The priests were always asking for more, implying that we had sins that were hidden from them; so I invented (and other children did too, I learned later) stealing candy, telling lies to my mother, hurting Jesus' feelings during mass by chatting, and having bad thoughts . . . not knowing that the priests meant sexual daydreaming by bad thoughts. So I consider now these early fabrications as a sort of story-telling, little moments of imaginative thinking.

I was made aware early in my life that little girls were in 'danger'. My mother never let me go alone anywhere, and allowed me to go playing with friends of only two families, one in our street, the other about two American blocks from our house. She used to give me counselling. It was very simple: do not go behind the counter at the grocery store, do not accept candy from strangers, stay always outside and visible. Once she said: do not go behind the counter because the storekeeper can pull out a knife and kill you in the belly. I still shudder at the image, but I was only puzzled then, wondering why the old man with his cap down over his ears, sitting endlessly behind huge sacks of lentils and rice in his tiny store would have ever done such a thing. He barely talked to me.

The admonitions grew more serious when I was an adolescent. And when at college age I expressed the desire to go to Paris to study, my mother just said: 'There the men will devour you.' She managed with a few sentences here and there to create an image of the world that I discovered later in movies like *Jack the Knife*, where men are like the Chaos of Greek mythology, the original void, the unending vertigo.

Looking back at those years, I also wonder if my mother didn't suffer from the fact that I was her only child and that she didn't have a son.

It must have been the month of June, when school was out and summer was officially ushered in; was I ten or nine when she bought a piece of black satin and made a costume for me on her sewing machine: billowing and extremely short pantaloons of shining and black satin, and a white satin blouse with long sleeves? She also made a flowing black tie. She took me to the hairdresser, the neighbourhood coiffeur, whose store smelled of soap and *eau de cologne*. She asked him to cut my hair very short, 'à la garçon', a hair-do I discovered later was very chic and popular in French fashion magazines of the time. My hair was cut the way Rimbaud had his hair in one of his famous pictures that one sees on the cover of editions of his poems. There was a picture of me taken that summer, in the family album, a precious book of photographs ranging from the First World War to the forties. That album was entrusted to an Armenian family who were friends of mine – the three sisters who had stayed in Beirut fled during the Civil War in Lebanon and they destroyed or dispersed the things I had left with them for a few decades. They thought they would never locate me, but it happened that I met one of them, after many years of absence, on a Beirut sidewalk the day after the destruction of the most important documents I had inherited from my parents.

Being dressed as a boy made me feel very happy. I felt special: no other girls that I knew ever dressed like that. (In fact, no boys, either). It was a dress suitable for the movies or the theatre. I thought I looked beautiful in it, if not beautiful, certainly touched by some magic. In fact it must have reinforced my identity of being neither just a girl, nor a boy, but a special being with the magical attributes of both.

In fact, my singularities accumulated. I was the only 'only' child at school, the only one among the children considered 'natives' by the ever-present nuns. I had met one or two girls who like me had neither brothers nor sisters, but they were French, and French people were expected to have few children as opposed to the large Lebanese families. It was regarded as a sign of aristocracy to be among few at home. There were also French families with ten or eleven children, but they were very 'Catholic', they went to church in a row, and somehow they looked poorer, more 'common'. They did not fit the image of the superior and aloof French.

I was also the only child of mixed background: my father was a Muslim and my mother a Christian. Such a mixed marriage was an anomaly. It attracted attention and often mysterious remarks: there was a hushed antagonism. My mother was scorned by some for having married a Muslim. She was pitied by others: 'Such a beautiful woman like you married to a Turk', some women neighbours would say. For most people my father, although an Arab, was a Turk, because of his service in the Ottoman Empire.

To marry a Muslim Turk was somehow worse than having married an Arab, at least in the eyes of the Maronite Christians who were more and more in positions of power in the new Lebanon. My mother took it in her stride, but once in a while she would feel guilty, and turning to a lit olive oil lamp in the corner of our bedroom and the icon, she would ask the Greek Virgin Mary, in Greek, sometimes with tears, 'Oh Panaya, have I done something wrong in marrying him? Will you forgive me?!'

I absorbed that sense of guilt, or at least the sense that there was something in our family which was unique, this uniqueness being sensed by me as a privilege mixed with some shame: I felt both rebellious and apprehensive any time an allusion was made to the religious make-up of my family.

This question of religion or religions haunted my life. By the end of the kindergarten year the French nuns called in my mother and said something along these lines: 'This child is six years old already and is not baptised. Do you realise that if anything happens to her she will go to limbo.'

My mother must have been made to feel ashamed that she had not resolved that question with my Muslim father. She was a Greek, a woman in a new country and a new culture, respecting authority. The sisters told her that I was asking to be baptised because I loved the little Jesus so much. My father, who was twenty years older than his wife, and also a rather defeated man, let her decide. She decided that as I was going to a French school and that the sisters were so nice as to insist and worry, they could arrange a baptismal ceremony. As children were usually baptised at birth I felt proud and very special in having in a way witnessed my own ceremony. It was in the French church of Beirut, the rite was Latin. For the sisters I was becoming practically a French child, and they were particularly fond of me for years to come. I was something they had worked for and conquered.

I was very conscious of my new privilege, but a division remained and settled in my heart. My father and I used to go very regularly to Damascus, where my aunt Fahima lived with her husband and her two sons. My father loved Damascus, the city of his own childhood, with tenderness. He was different when he was there: relaxed, mysterious, romantic. And I was happy there, in a house where Arabic and Turkish were spoken, and never French. It was another world, with Muslim feasts involving dinners on huge copper trays put on the rugs, and trays of sweets brought in from the market by boys carrying them on their heads.

Damascus was the East, with its splendour, its specific qualities, its hushed conversations, its sense of history and grandeur. There I was a child of city Arabs mixed with Turkish blood and culture, of Arabs who were wondering if the Ottoman Empire was really any worse than the new colonisation. In Beirut it was puzzlement and everyday life, in Damascus it was magic and recreation. In Beirut I was a little Christian. In Damascus I was at the door of the Islamic world.

Thus I got used to standing between situations, to being a bit marginal and still a native, to getting acquainted with notions of truth which were relative and changed like the hours of the days and the passing of seasons.

I ended up not being religious, seeing in the discourse held by the nuns some vague trap, some temptation I was refusing, some challenge to the world of my father, a father who always appeared weaker than my mother but always dignified. In my adolescence I viewed him as a tragic figure.

The world of a writer, even at its most fictional, and particularly the world of a poet, are not pure constructs of the mind. The energy that carries creative work to its expression, and the very content of creative work, comes from life experiences, and maybe even from some memories carried in our genes. I cannot separate the events that shape my day-to-day existence from whatever I write and paint.

There is a dialectical relation between one's life and one's work. The former obviously influences the latter, but one's work also becomes an influence on one's life. It is a two-way affair, a mysterious process where what we call life and what we call creation, merge and do not merge, cross feed each other.

I loved the fact, the act, of writing, as far as I can remember. In elementary school we were given words around which to build a sentence. I used to write long paragraphs, enjoying the pen, the ink, the page, and the words coming one after another with a feel of roundness, a comfort for the body and the mind. Later, we had composition classes. We had to write a few pages on a given topic. My writings were often singled out by the teacher and read out loud in the class as a model. Once I was accused of having cheated, copied what I wrote, because the teacher could not believe that I had written the text I turned in to her. I also used to write the homework of my class mates. The pleasure of inventing little stories, of achieving a sort of triumph, of winning a sort of victory, of having kids come around me for sentences and words, while I was not best at running or at volleyball, made me feel early in life that writing was my little domain, a world where I had no fear, no tension, no problem.

I speak of writing and not of reading books because the homes in Beirut in the twenties and thirties did not have shelves of French books, of children's or adult's books in French. Some had no book shelves at all. Books were rare, considered expensive, and in the libraries of scholars. What was called an average home had just a few, usually some religious or poetic works in Arabic. My parents, each having been uprooted many times, we had at home my father's Quran, my mother's book of the Gospels in Greek, a Turkish-German dictionary from my father's War College days in Istanbul, and a few novels in Greek about Cleopatra, Egyptian Saints of the Desert, and love stories . . . books my mother at some time in her life read aloud to her niece who came to live with us for a while.

So I was more interested in writing than in reading, a pattern which fitted the other patterns of my existence: as an only child I had to invent my games, imaginary game companions, and my stories. This must have been true to such a point that I remember in pre-kindergarten times the mirrors of the cupboards, in which I was looking, and imagining that the little child I was seeing, which was myself, was a little friend of mine who came to visit.

The years that qualify most as being a writer's or poet's formative years are the years of our adolescence. These are years when our reason and our senses grow conspicuously but in separate ways, and develop as if independently from one another. This is why they are years of violent emotions and mental confusion. We are then like some young trees whose branches grow in separate directions giving the impression that the stem will break apart under opposite pulls.

A young girl in Beirut in the late thirties was seen as an endangered species to be protected from future predators. Mothers were sentimental about them, looking into the not-so-far future where a young man would appear on the horizon and marry their daughters. A little girl was a daughter, a school girl, and a future wife. She was never considered as an autonomous being whose life could turn out to be something other than what was considered to be the social norm.

Rape was never discussed socially and never mentioned in the newspapers or in classrooms, but mothers thought about it all the time and made sure that their daughters were not playing in courtyards, gardens, or the streets, with boys who were friends of their sons. The division of the world between a masculine universe and a feminine universe was established by the time children were seven years old, what the Catholic church called the age of reason, a division which also exists in the Islamic world.

Not having a brother at home, I did not see little boys of my age until I went to college. I was in girls' schools, visited with my mother families where only little girls sat with us. But I went to the movies at an early age, early enough so that the sisters called in my mother and told her that my imagination was running wild because I was going to the movies. There was indeed a fire in the house! Movies were then mostly for adults and the kids I went to school with were marvelling at the fact that my parents took me to the movies. Maybe because I was an only child and it was normal for my parents to take me with them wherever they went – my father to Damascus, my mother on visits and to the movies.

My image of men, of love, of interaction with the outside world, the world at large, was formed uniquely by the cinema of the thirties and the early forties. And that cinema was not local, it was the cinema of Hollywood and France. I used to go to the movies and come out of them with a fever. My head was turning and my heart beating. I developed a secret life inhabited by men and women who looked infinitely more attractive than the saints whose lives were tediously explained to us during religious studies. At age ten I was already in love with Marlene Dietrich, Garbo, and Gary Cooper while I was falling in love with the little girl sitting next to me in school. My first passion. A love which manifested itself by running and playing catch in recreation time, by holding my breath when that little being looked at me, and by exchanging stamps. My father had a collection of stamps going back to the end of the nineteenth century. I gave it all to that little girl. It was only two or three years later that my father discovered the disappearance of his collection. He asked me if I had taken it and I think I said, yes, and that I had given them all away. He shook his head taking it, I am sure, as one more defeat in his life, and never said another word about the matter.

The movies provided me with the occasion for having a parallel life outside the gaze of my mother: the thing I remember as the hardest about my childhood, and I am sure about the whole culture, the hardest to live with, was the fact that we had no life of our own, no privacy, neither physical nor moral. People in the Arab world, and certainly elsewhere in the third world, are never really left alone, they live under the scrutiny of everybody around. This is also true of Greece, Italy and Spain, at least in the popular strata of their societies.

Developing private thoughts was my first rebellion, my first emancipation. Private life came much much later. So I am accustomed to equate freedom with thinking, and I was made ready to understand political rebellion as an affirmation of the self.

By the time I reached fourteen, a new problem faced me at home: studying in a language basically foreign to my parents created a distance between us: I was engaging myself in territories alien to them and I was being estranged. I felt more and more different, with frames of reference they could not share. I was becoming a foreigner in my own house.

My father respected learning to such a point that he didn't interfere with matters of education. He must have known that there was no use fighting an unavoidable national situation. He was too much of a military man not to understand that military defeats carry with them a multitude of consequences which affect every aspect of life. My mother viewed the world in rather simplistic ways. All she saw was that I was growing to be different from her and it must have increased her loneliness and her sense of exile. At that time I could not understand what was going on. I only knew that I was subjected to tensions which gradually evolved into hostility: I started hating her because her views, her authority, and what must have been her desperation, were becoming unbearable to me.

She began hating the very education she was striving to give me at school. She was hating the books, and my friends, and was starting to harass me by putting out the lights when I was reading or obliging me to go to bed early to make sure I would not sink into some book or magazine that she viewed as enemies and intruders.

By the time I was fifteen the Second World War was in full operation and I was taken out of school. My mother declared that prices had gone up enormously and that we were too broke for the family to afford a private school, public schools being practically non-existent in Beirut.

But things were not as simple as I was made to believe they were. I must say here that a few years before I interrupted school my mother had taken charge of a little boy, the son of her niece who used to come to visit us. That young woman had fallen in love and was expecting a child. She was not married and she panicked. My mother convinced her to keep the child and promised to take care of him. She assumed his upbringing.

By the time I was sixteen, the war was on, the presence of the French army in Lebanon increased, and the French, in their war effort with their English allies, needed local help. Beirut became a boom town. Offices multiplied. Young girls were finding jobs as secretaries both in the military and in the civilian sectors of the war economy. The first generation of Arab girls going to work in offices

with men was being born. Inflation and job opportunities made
families accept that their girls should work. This new way of life
shook society and a little revolution took place, a social revolution,
that went unnoticed. Girls were still required to come home just
after work but you could see them steal away for a few hours that
they spent with boy friends in the coffee shops and the tea houses
that mushroomed in Beirut overnight and as if by enchantment.

In that city, exploding socially, but in subtle ways, in ways nobody
talked about, everybody behaved as if life hadn't changed. My
mother decided that I should take a job she found in the French
Information Bureau, a job consisting at first of filing papers and
receiving the mail that the postmen, or the British soldiers called
dispatch carriers, were regularly bringing in large leather pouches
hung over their motorcycles. It was the beginning of adventure.
And it happened inadvertently. I was in the midst of exciting
hours, history was being made practically before my eyes. I was
following, on maps, with French and British officers and officials,
the advance and the retreat of armies. Black pins for the Germans,
red pins for the Russians, blue pins for the Allied Forces were
moving day to day like the soldiers they represented.

I gained the confidence of the administrator of the Bureau I was
working for, and although my pay was the lowest, maybe just ahead
of the office boys', I started to type and sometimes answer letters on
my own. The news was formulated in the office and distributed to
the daily papers. I witnessed how political influence was wielded
and how much propaganda was part of warfare. I had no theories,
I had not the means to draw large-scale conclusions, I had no
political upbringing, no college training, but I was watching events
in their rawness, I was participating in my own limited ways in a
cosmic adventure. The magic of these years still haunts me. It is of
such stuff that literature is made, even in the most indirect of ways.

Something though was eating me: the sense of having left school
too early, of something left unfinished, of a world which held its
own fascination for me and of which I was kept out. One October
morning (classes in Lebanon start in the early days of October) I
was crying in the office, and the 'boss', a writer and former teacher,
saw me cry and called me to his office to find out the reason was for
my sorrow. I told him that it was the first day of school, that I had
left my studies for three years, and that I was desperate. He asked
me not to worry and told me he would see what he could do about
it. I had nothing in mind, not knowing that it was even possible that
something could be done.

Jean Gaulmier, who later pursued his academic career at the
Sorbonne, in Paris, then arranged my office hours in such a way

that I was free in the morning till eleven. In exchange I had to work an evening schedule, leaving the office at eight or nine, the chauffeur of the office being charged to drive me home. These were war years, there was sometimes a curfew, and it was out of the question that young ladies walk alone at night in the streets of the city.

My life changed again. I enrolled for the French baccalaureate, a degree which is given in two terms, and is roughly the equivalent of a junior college degree. I skipped a whole year of studies, by special permission, and I went to the morning classes considered the most important for the baccalaureate. The other studies I managed with a series of tutorial courses, some on Sundays, some during school vacations.

I passed the first year exam with high honours as well as the second year one. I was the only person who had ever passed these two exams without going regularly to classes and, also, while working full time at an exciting and demanding job. The baccalaureate is a state examination and after the completion of its second part, a student is automatically entitled to enter the university of his or her choice.

I certainly was happy, aware that I was leading a double or triple life: I was living in three unconnected worlds, the one at home losing its grip on me. But I was losing contact with my parents: I was home only to sleep at night and years later I realised how their hearts were being broken. My father was ageing rapidly, my mother too, and home was not a happy and exciting place any more. With the cruelty of adolescents I had only one dream: to get away from it the best I could. My parents sensed it and they must have felt betrayed and abandoned.

I have said earlier that as a child I used to love to write. The act of writing, the alignment of sentences, the warm impact of words, the excitement of learning new ones through the subjects we studied, geography words, history words, chemistry words, all that was the discovery of an invisible world made sometimes more real than my bedroom or the street of Beirut.

By the time I was nineteen and eligible for the university, I thought that I liked mathematics above all, and architecture. There was no school of architecture, then, in Lebanon and it was the engineering school that was licensing the builders. I declared one day at home that I wanted to become an engineer: it created one more scandal. My mother was horrified as if confirmed in her belief that I was veering from the norm. She said that that was a profession for men, and she said it in a way that carried the intention to shame. There was something immoral in my demands and she said that even if I asked for a scholarship to pay for my studies she would not let me leave the office. 'We need the money,' she said. And when I remarked that her little nephew was costing her a lot of money for his schooling, she replied that he was a boy and that men deserved any sacrifice made for their education. So I could not go any further on that matter. I knew that I had no recourse.

It happened then that the French University was opening a branch in literature: an autonomous institute for literature and linguistics named Ecole Supérieure des Lettres de Beyrouth. The enrolment fees were minimal, and, most importantly in my case, the classes were scheduled for the afternoon or early evenings. By then the war was over, the war bureaus were closed, and I found a day-time job that allowed me both to bring money home and to be free to go to classes again.

The Ecole des Lettres was founded by an exceptional Frenchman who was for years the chief administrator of all the French schools in Lebanon and Syria. He was an appointee of the French Ministry for Foreign Affairs and had the prestige and the power of a top diplomat. It happened, we learned, that he disliked the control of the French University in Beirut by the Jesuits and wanted to create a separate institute for literature, linguistics, and philosophy, a place for learning where ideas would not be directed toward a religious ideology. Gabriel Bounoure was his name. He was an essayist and a major critic of French literature, sending papers on literature and poetry to the prestigious literary magazine called the *NRF*. He became, in addition to his official government functions, the director of the Ecole des Lettres and gathered in Beirut a small but exceptional staff of professors. He gave a few classes, scheduled at odd times, during vacations, or at the hours he was free from his office. I was one of the ten or twelve first students of the Ecole. Gabriel Bounoure's classes were the equivalent of these mystic encounters one reads about either in the great sufis' writings of the Islamic past, or in the works of German Romantic writers such as Novalis or Herman Hesse. These were not ordinary academic teachings, but rather initiations into the life of the spirit as exemplified by the works of Pascal and Déscartes or the poems of Baudelaire, Gérard de Nerval and Rimbaud. I entered literature by the grand door, I discovered the golden rule of the mind. I participated for three or four years in an experiment that Plato himself would have envied.

This is where and when I convinced myself that poetry was the purpose of life, poetry as a counter-profession, as an expression of personal and mental freedom, as perpetual rebellion. Poetry became a revolution, and a permanent voyage. With a few friends I felt I was living a parallel life, a life which cut all ties with home and country. I can say that I experienced the feeling of knowing what angels could be. The city itself changed in my imagination. It became an enchanted small town, orange trees perfuming some of its streets, movies and music becoming one with my thoughts. I was living at home but not seeing my parents any more, or seeing them as through a fog. I think that is what is meant by being enraptured.

Gabriel Bounoure treated us as privileged children of enlightenment. There was an equality in fervour, a fullness. Body and soul were one. Rimbaud and Baudelaire became more familiar to us than anybody we knew or could know. They took residence in Beirut. Along with Rilke. And Gérard de Nerval, who had written in the late nineteenth century a 'Voyage to the Orient', came back resuscitated among us. Gabriel Bounoure called him Gérard, and Gérard was one of us. The ten or twelve students of the Ecole des Lettres became thirty or forty, in a few years, but they did not dilute the intensity of the first years, rather they caught the fever, joined the paradise.

Of course the world view I had during the Ecole des Lettres years had nothing to do with the problems of day to day living that people have to face. It was a view suited for pure spirits. My mother was getting scared about my future. She was eager to have me married, to see me settling into situations which were familiar to her. The tensions at home were becoming unbearable. My father was totally out of the picture: he was too old and too ill.

When I said that I wasn't interested in getting married I was accused of preferring to be adventurous and irresponsible. Sometimes I was made to understand that I was in danger of losing my mind.

One thing was true, that I realised much later. I had no idea how to run my life materially. My jobs were getting menial and badly paid.

I cannot say that I then contemplated a literary career. I did not see myself as a writer, not even a poet, but rather a person for whom poetry and the poetic life were the only concern. There were no literary magazines in French in the city, so I never thought of publishing. I did not know how one achieved success in the literary world. I do not regret it; all my life I kept the notion of poetry and literature being fragile, personal, needing distance and silence around them.

One day I wrote a paper for class. I thought it was a good paper. Somehow I was late in turning it in and I think Gabriel Bounoure represented such a figure that I was hesitant to give him my first piece of writing, the one assigned by him for his class. A friend of mine, a young man who was also a student at the Ecole des Lettres, asked to read it. He read it and liked it and decided that he would give it to his best friend who was the editor of the newspaper *Le Jour*, a daily paper in French which had a regular literary page. His friend loved the piece and published it. It was my first publication. A piece of writing on the nineteenth century French writer, traveller, and painter, Eugène Fromentin.

So Gabriel Bounoure did not find my paper among the other papers of the class, but read it one morning in the newspaper laid on his desk. He called me in through his secretary and congratulated me. He said I had an exceptional literary sense and asked me why I had not asked for a French government scholarship to study at the Sorbonne in Paris. I said I was an only child and that my mother was difficult and that I couldn't face her with such a decision. He said: why don't you ask her to come and see me. He thought he could convince her to let me go.

When I told my mother than Monsieur Bounoure wanted to talk to her about sending me to Paris she got pale and nervous and started to shake. She said he was an immoral man stirring us up and separating us from our homes. Then she added that she had a doctor friend who kept hand grenades in his apartment against potential burglars and assassins. She threatened to go and ask for one of these weapons and come and blow up the school. The next day I warned the private secretary of Monsieur Bounoure of the dangers of my mother's visit. He laughed it off. But I was dead serious and vaguely scared for a while.

The idea of going to Paris stuck in my mind. I knew that it was going to be a matter of time before I went to the prestigious city. After all, since childhood, we were brought up to consider France the centre of the world, if not the world itself. My best friend, Lydia, a Russian girl whose parents emigrated because of the Revolution, a girl who was also the only child of her family, a few years older than me, and a being I equated with angels and spirits because she lived in an air even more rarefied than mine, had already left for Paris. Lydia had introduced me to Rilke and Gauguin (through reproductions). And to classical music. Now she had preceded me to the source of our dreams.

It seemed to me, then, that Paris was a mythical place where Rimbaud and Verlaine still quarrelled in cafés. I thought that every Parisian was a poet. My mother's image of Paris was no less absolute: for her Paris was hell itself, the capital of white female slavery, the chaos in which children who have left home disappear forever. We obviously lived in irreconcilable worlds.

In 1947, my father died. The house looked empty. Something was gone forever. Then Lydia also was gone. The war with its excitement (Beirut did not see the disasters of war, then, but only its romantic side) was a thing of the past. At a tea party, in the home of some family friends, I met an old gentleman who was a biology teacher who said that he taught in a school that was looking for a French teacher. I took the job a few weeks later. I taught French literature in a high school which was unique of its kind. Al-Ahliya School for girls was run by a headmistress who was a Lebanese Protestant, a woman I knew closely for the two years I stayed in her school. She was an admirable person, had gone to the American University of Beirut and had a Ph.D. in Education from a university in the United States. It was my first contact with teaching and with the Anglo-Saxon oriented milieu of Lebanon.

I had no idea what I was going to do in my life. I lived from day to day. My greatest passion was for the sea. I had swum from the age of five, and very few girls of my generation were allowed to swim. There were mainly European children who were lying on the beaches. I loved the sea not only for the pleasure of swimming, but for herself. Her colours and her movements used to hypnotise me. I started one day writing a poem about her which became a long poem that I called 'Le Livre de la Mer', 'The Book of the Sea'. It is a poem about the sea and about the sun and about their cosmic marriage. The only marriage I could care about.

At the end of 1949, I accepted the scholarship for studies in France that I was offered two years earlier. The Ecole des Lettres was not yet staffed enough to provide all the courses needed for a University degree. I had to finish the Licence ès Lettres in France. My mother was shattered. I could not ask her for much. I was disinherited, and I felt cruel and alone. But in October I was on the plane with a few clothes and the poem on the sea still unfinished in my valise. I had a very long way to go.

Written in English

Warda al-Yaziji

(1838–1924)

Warda al-Yaziji was born in the village of Kafr Shima in Lebanon.
She was the daughter of the poet and scholar Shaikh Nasif al-Yaziji
(1800–1871) and sister of the scholar and litterateur Ibrahim
al-Yaziji and the poet Khalil al-Yaziji. The family moved to Beirut
in 1840, where Warda began her schooling in French. Her father
took great care to train her early in Arabic grammar and the
structures of Arabic poetry; she is said to have begun writing
poetry at the age of thirteen. She taught at a local school and
helped to educate her many siblings. It is said that her wise advice
within the family earned her the nickname 'Shaikh Mahmud.' She
was married in 1866 to Francis Shamun and continued to write
poetry and teach at school while bringing up five children. Her
diwan (collected poetry), *Hadiqat al-Ward* (The Rose Garden), was
first published in 1867 in Beirut, republished in expanded form in
1887, and again – with new additions – in 1914, this time in Cairo.
She was in Egypt at the time; she had moved to Alexandria
following the death of her husband in 1899. She also wrote articles
on the issue of women's status for the magazine *Al-Diya* (founded
by Ibrahim al-Yaziji in Cairo, 1898). She died in 1924.

This poem was chosen from *Hadiqat al-Ward*. Warda al-Turk, to
whom her poem is addressed, was born in 1797 in Dayr al-Qamar
in Lebanon. Her father was Niqula, born Yusuf Nasif al-Turk,
court poet of the Amir Bashir al-Shihabi II ('the Great'). Her father
educated her in the Arabic language and literature; she was a
prolific poet, writing mostly panegyrics and elegies. She is one of
very few nineteenth century women poets for whom we have
surviving texts of poems in colloquial, as well as in classical, Arabic.

Warda al-Yaziji plays on the first name which poet and addressee
share – 'Warda' meaning rose or flower.

Epistolary Poem to Warda al-Turk

1867

❧

O Rose of the Turks, I am Rose of the Arabs
      Between us we have found the nearest of kinships.
      Your father gave you an art become famous
Among the learned and literary for its graces.
      Among women of the age you have ascended
To the highest position in worth and rank.
      O polisher of literary pearls that came to tell us
Of a fine nature received by people in wonder
      It is you who have impassioned the lover's heart
To listen and never withdraw
      A precious friend whose news delights my hearing
Yet she has disappeared from sight, secluded by veils.
      She has ennobled the standing of this art conspicuously
With great fineness and utter clarity of view
      Adorning the sheet of paper with a script of great
      elegance
That shines like a string of pearls.

Translated from the Arabic
by Marilyn Booth

Nadia Tueni

(1935–1983)

Nadia Tueni was born in Baakline, Lebanon, and died in 1983 in Beirut. Her father was a Druze diplomat and writer. Her mother was French. She attended a convent school in Beirut, the Institut Français in Athens where her father was ambassador, and then studied law at St. Joseph University in Beirut.

In 1967 she became literary editor of *Le Jour* and was awarded the Ordre de la Pléiade, the Order of Francophonie and Cultural Dialogue. She died in 1983, and at her funeral, she was awarded the gold medal of honour for public instruction.

She has nine collections of poetry that include: *Les Textes Blonds*, Beirut, 1963 (illustrated by the author and later considered juvenilia); *L'Age d'Écume*, 1965 (this collection won the Said Akl prize); *Juin et les Mecréants*, 1968; *Poèmes pour une Histoire*, 1972 (won the Academie Francaise prize); *Le Rêveur de Terre*, 1975; *Liban. 20 Poèmes pour un Amour*, 1979; Tueni wrote *Archives Sentimentales d'une Guerre au Liban*, 1982, her 'poetic geography', when she knew that she was dying. The last two collections have been put on records and Etel Adnan has illustrated the cover of *Archives Sentimentales d'une Guerre au Liban*.

Her unpublished materials have been organised and published posthumously. The last collection of poems is *La Terre Arrêtée*, 1984. Her numerous articles, conference papers and short stories were first published in 1986 in *La Prose Oeuvres Complètes*.

'Qui Est-Tu Claire Gebeyli?' was written to her close friend, the poet Claire Gebeyli, when she published her first collection of poetry *Poesies Latentes*. It was published in *La Revue du Liban*, 18 December 1968.

Claire Gebeyli collaborated with Nadia Tueni on the cultural supplement for *Le Jour* from its inception in 1966. She has also written some articles about Tueni.

Who are you, Claire Gebeyli?

1968

❦

Who are you, Claire Gebeyli?
What do your words mean?
Are they cries? Are they prayers?
Are they a wound out of which your blood, your truth, your
substance flow?
Are they a way of saying who you are?
You are woman, and rarely has poetry shouted this fact so loud.
It certainly was not you who declared one day: 'There are writers,
gender is of little import.'
Your poetry, for that is what it is, is the profound expression of a
crisis at the level of skin and of reason.
On the one hand, you refuse the world as it is, this civilisation cut as
it is according to a male pattern, for men's convenience, at their
will, this human comedy where woman is an accessory, glorious
perhaps but, nonetheless, subaltern.
On the other hand, how like you that is, you dive into language as
others dive into life, that is with fervour. You look for the
confrontation whether it be violent or nostalgic and you aim your
anguish as though it were a weapon.

Who are you, Claire Gebeyli?
Your poems are full.
What vertigo pushes you to viciously explore the most subtle
meanderings of the female soul? Careful. It is about games that do
not exist. Nights from which one cannot return. Things that burn
more than sun tears. It is about dialogues that should not be
started.

Who are you, Claire Gebeyli?
Do you know how to exorcise the demons that you release?
The hermetism of your verses proves once again that the poetic
phenomenon is intimately linked to the sexual process. By a reflex
of modesty, O you very feminine, you embellish and symbolise and
you sublimate also. One must dive slowly, without impatience, into
the red water of your forbidden sleep to seize the reality of the
drama that is being played.

Who are you, Claire Gebeyli?
Rigorous but docile, caressing but tense, you bend, bend again to
the rhythm of the Orient to which you belong, and from time to
time you jump in revolt, this geometric lucidity of the Greece of
your origins.

Who are you, Claire Gebeyli?
Discreet, determined as a bee, despising passion as degrading, but
extolling the intelligence of the heart. Whoever can read your
Latent Poetries will see that you wish you were less stable, less
modest, more savage and strong. Do you not say elsewhere: 'The
indomitable current will be reborn in me . . .'?

Who are you, Claire Gebeyli?
When people speak of your poetry, do they not too often use the
word 'erotic'?
You would reply (I find you once again), that all artistic creation is
by definition erotic, because it is first of all an act of love.
Every woman is 'flute and amphora'.
Every mouth is 'hungry for the sky'.
And I like you 'bleed from memories'.

Translated from the French
by Miriam Cooke

Fadwa Tuqan

(1917–)

Fadwa Tuqan was born in Nablus, Palestine. Her poetry collections
include: *Wajadtuha* (I Found it) 1958; *Atina Hubb* (Give Us Love)
1960; *Al-Fidai wa al-Ard* (The Guerrilla and the Land) 1968; *Al-Lail
wa al-Fursan* (Night and the Knights) 1969; *Ala Qimmat al-Dunya
Wahidan* (Alone on Top of the World) 1973; *Kabus al-Lail wa
al-Nahar* (The Nightmare of Night and Day) 1974.

Although most of her early poems deal with love, she has also
written more directly about Palestine in poems like 'Call of the
Earth' and 'Dream of Remembrance'. The latter deals with the
death of brothers killed in action. After 1967, she focused more on
the plight of refugees, as well as on the Israeli occupation of the
West Bank and Gaza. In *Amam al-Bab al-Mughlaq* (In Front of the
Closed Door), 1967 she has dedicated a poem to Salma Khadra
Jayusi, another Palestinian woman poet who has written about the
Palestinian cause. Abd al-Muhsin Taha Badr has written of her
post-1967 poems that 'some of them remind us of the old Fadwa,
while others come close to having an entirely new sound'.

The following piece is taken from her autobiography *Difficult
Journey – Mountainous Journey*, 1984. In it she describes her childhood and growing awareness of what it means to be a woman in an
Arab society. This is her first prose publication and it represents an
attempt to break with the male poetic tradition into which her
famous brother Ibrahim Tuqan had initiated her.

Difficult Journey – Mountainous Journey
1984

❦

When I was young I was incapable of describing life as forcefully as a poet does. My world – the world of writing – was frightening and emotionally empty. I lived amidst thoughts sown in writing, but I was isolated from the world itself. As I matured into a woman, I was like a wounded animal, sterile in its cage. Although confined and deprived of a homeland, I was asked by my father to write political poetry. He wanted me to follow in the footsteps of my brother, Ibrahim,[1] and publish for the good of the nation and its politics. Through writing, my father wanted me to respond to our national despair, but his demand made me miserable. I was unable to compose poetry; my inner voice was weak in protest against everything that had caused my silence. I was expected to create political poetry while the corrupt laws and customs insisted that I remain secluded behind a wall, not able to attend assemblies of men, not hearing the recurrent debates, not participating in public life. Oh, my nation, I want you to know the face behind the veil when I was forbidden to travel freely. I only knew Jerusalem because Ibrahim invited me there when he worked for the Palestine Broadcasting System. He wanted me to know a city other than Nablus,[2] my birthplace.

The home environment in which I was raised did not nourish an interest in the outside world, but encouraged me, rather, to turn away from the struggle.[3] Nevertheless, my father demanded that I realise the lofty aspirations he had for me. And yet, he never allowed me to establish a connection between his aspirations for me and my own inner emotions. For that reason, I was unable to compose poetry and instead sought refuge under a cover of tearful submission.

When we come of age, we are expected to concentrate our energies no matter what the personal cost, the obstacles and difficulties which preoccupy us. My father believed it was possible to solve any problem. My past had been deeply rooted in poetry, but my emotions had taken a very different direction from the course my father was urging me to follow. The poet must know the world before it can be healed through poetry. How else can the political issues be weighed? Where was I to find an intellectual atmosphere in which I could write political poetry? From the newspaper my father brought home at lunch every day? The newspaper is important, but it doesn't have the power to inspire poetry in the depths of one's soul. I was enslaved, isolated in my seclusion from the outside world, and my seclusion was imposed as a duty – I had no choice in the matter. The outside world was taboo for women of good families, and society didn't protest against that seclusion; it was not part of the political agenda.

My mother, as I recall, was one of the first members of the Society for the Welfare of Women. And yet, nothing changed for her. She did not participate in social gatherings, and unlike other members of the Society, she was not allowed to travel to meetings. In fact, she was not allowed to travel at all unless accompanied by a member of the family. This women's organisation was founded in Nablus in 1921 by Miriam Hashem, a teacher who died in 1947. Many outstanding people were members. In 1929, it became affiliated with the Arab Feminist Union, founded in Egypt by Huda Shaarawi. This affiliation stirred Palestinian women into being involved in their own political struggle.

The women in my family left the house only on rare occasions, such as family celebrations in the houses of relatives and close friends. Although my father permitted my mother to join Miriam Hashem's organisation, he restricted her activities to those associated with fundraising. If conferences were held in Egypt or in other cities in Palestine, my mother was not allowed to attend. Seclusion from the outside world deprived the home atmosphere, which women breathed, of any political or social consciousness.

Given the many prohibitions imposed on women, their movements in the home strongly resembled those of domesticated poultry who can come and go freely until they find fodder and then suffer constant temptation. But this particular domesticated poultry confined its energies to hatching the young. Women exhausted their lives with the big, copper cooking pots and gathering firewood for the stove in all seasons. As in other societies where the lives of women make no sense, the lives of Palestinian women, in every epoch and in every house, seemed devoid of significance. Such an environment had a stifling grip on me, which intensified as I approached sexual maturity.[4]

My journey through life was filled with the misery of acute emotional and intellectual struggles. During the early years, I hated politics. I tried to realise my father's wishes in order to gain his love. I was not socially liberated but in my heart I justified rebellion and rejection. How could I possibly struggle for the sake of political liberation and for my own national convictions? Just as our society needed strong political action, so too did I need political activity. And while our cultural needs were not as pressing, we were deprived in this area as well.

I was conscious of my talent but I knew it could not mature except in society. This society created barriers to restrict me. The world of the harem stood between me and society. A spirit of impotence prevailed, and I could not write poetry. I was idle. I stopped exercising my poetic talents. In my difficult journey, I concealed the gift of my poetry. The strong awareness of what I had repressed and what I could potentially express left its traces on my spiritual and bodily existence. I became very thin and my brain felt fragmented. The weariness of my soul burdened all my limbs and during the night my body felt as if it had drowned.

Let me talk about the meaning of my life, its purpose and the particular poet's anxiety which I bear. My afflictions tore me apart, but if my wretchedness increased my tears, it also expanded the sensitivity of my soul. I found relief when I thought of the wisdom of the ancient saying, 'If I am not for myself, who will be for me? And if I am only for myself, who am I?'

My commitment to life weakened as I remained secluded from the outside world. My soul was tormented because of this seclusion. My father's demands may have initiated my turmoil, but the pain always stayed with me, taking different forms throughout the journey of my life. Ultimately, at the source of my struggle was a tradition whose laws and customs constantly tested me. The process of maturing was a most painful experience in body and soul. I was oppressed, crushed; I felt bent out of shape. I could not participate in any aspect of life unless I pretended to be another person. I became more and more distant.

When I recovered, the words which intensified my feelings of subjugation and suppression also enriched the individuality and quality of my poetry. My work is existential, but it also penetrates the life of the harem which is narrow and constricted like a long-necked bottle. The talent, which I seemed initially to lack, had been blocked from view by this narrow long-necked bottle. My only bridge to society was the political poetry which I occasionally published in newspapers. I felt increasingly alienated and sensed that my poetic gifts were being plundered. I was aware of my ambition, but in those circumstances of seclusion, it appeared pathological. In the midst of my journey, my misery deepened, and one of my protectors, Nadim Salah, our family doctor, saved me from death and delivered me from my torture.

In 1948, during the Palestine War, my father died. With the loss of Palestine, my writing problems also ended. I began to write the

nationalist poetry my father had always wished me to write. I began
to devote myself to the nationalist cause, as had Ibrahim during his
lifetime. I wrote poetry spontaneously and now with no complaints
from the outside world.[5] I was convulsed by the Palestine problem,
the tragic situation of the refugees and the difficulties of the Arab
world whose armies fought the war. I did not expect miracles from
a politics which was then in its earliest stages, but I did not despair
or abandon political activity. Politics gave me the will to persist in a
struggle against the fragmentation and poverty of our war-torn
nation. My immobility ended.

*The Enclosed Environment of Women in Nablus During the 1930s and
1940s*
Because of my family's status and position, my feelings about
myself were strongly affected by the opinions of others. Even when
I was angry at the outside world, my emotions were strongly
affected by its views of me. My emotions were so volatile that I
never questioned the need to disguise them. This disguise was my
defence against criticism.

Men and women in Nablus have particular social customs which
they impose by designating certain people as the city's 'watchdogs.'
The authority these people enjoy does not stem from their special
knowledge, but rather from their hateful pretentiousness. It has
often been said that people from Nablus disapprove of everything.
Unlike other citizens of Nablus, I do not impose on other people
customs alien to their own, nor would I deprive anyone of free
discussion. For the most part, however, people in Nablus are civil to
one another without being especially warm or close.

During the 1930s and 1940s, I could not leave the house unless
accompanied by another family member, such as my mother or
aunt or sister or cousin. It was impossible to breathe freely during
these visits. I was occasionally forced to join members of my family
on their visits, although the atmosphere was hostile. I yearned for
any situation in which my mother or the other women in my family
would be allowed to go out more than once or twice a month. At
the time, women were usually illiterate or had the most rudi-
mentary skills of literacy. Their meagre education could be fur-
thered only at the government high school (*Dar al-Muallimat*)[6] in
Jerusalem where they received a secondary school education.

However, there was a group of schoolteachers in Nablus and in
other Palestinian cities who had a distinct social status. These
women teachers distinguished themselves by their education and
material possessions. They demanded and received deference
from the common people. The women teachers had established a

network of philanthropic societies which distributed pittances to people who were overwhelmed by what they considered extraordinary generosity. From these teachers, I learned the meaning of economic independence. In fact, my sisters and I began to support a woman enslaved by family and custom. This woman could not count on support from her family. Not that she was liberated from social customs and constraints. In fact, because her education was very limited, she could not change her personality and gain confidence in her own abilities and talents. In blind imitation of custom, she continued to consider male sponsorship and female subordination the rule. She believed that the power of men to make all the decisions in society was nothing more than brotherly compassion. But when the men in her family were unemployed, this woman was forced to turn to society for sustenance.

The situation for women teachers was not much better than the situation for other women in society, for they too had to abide by society's rules, which constrained their behaviour. The rules were shaped by arrogance, conceit, and pomposity. Despite their knowledge, these teachers did not have any special regard or appreciation for the books or articles published at the time. They were not cultured, nor did they engage in serious reading. Rather, the importance of this group stemmed from their fastidious dress. The money they earned as teachers enabled them to satisfy their desires for fashionable clothes. They never altered the rules and practices that existed among common people.

This educated class read in a destructive, hostile spirit. Only one woman was different. She alone possessed a craving for knowledge and culture. Sitt Fakhriya Hajawi was my former teacher in a school attended by the daughters of prosperous families in Nablus. She was very concerned with my life in and out of school. Sitt Fakhriya loved to read the newspaper to me or to read from the Egyptian journal *Al-Risala*. She was full of knowledge and would urge me to pursue my poetic journey. When I met her, I spoke to her about writing, reading, and about the structure of *qasida*.[7] She paid me attention and I was happy.

With the exception of Sitt Fakhriya, I could not respect the privileged position of educated women. In turn, they made their negative feelings clear in unpleasant and haughty encounters with me. They would say sharply: 'Her brother, Ibrahim, composed the poetry and appended her name to it.' They directed their negative comments at me until Ibrahim's death. Their hostility was painful, and I was aware of the pain even though I was very young. Once I reached the age of puberty, I began to realise that every success achieved by a woman has its price both for her and her family. It is not even possible to laugh at the antics of clowns without being criticised. But I realised this only later; at the time, I merely suffered in silence.

During the 1930s and 1940s, I was secluded in female society. Because urban society strove for outward appearances which would distinguish it from village society, it maintained an isolated and inhospitable existence for women. But the breach between me and female society grew wider. While I kept my disdain secret, I could neither contribute to society nor accept anything from it. Female society was consumed by idle chatter. The chatter manifested the illiteracy of women who had no access to the beautiful and fertile writing appearing in the larger world around them. Unable to join in their illiteracy, I was forced into a breach with the society in which I was born.

I See, I Hear, I Suffer
I didn't show my father my emotions. My feelings toward him were almost neutral: I neither loathed nor loved him since I didn't matter to him. I felt for him only when he was sick, imprisoned, or banished for political reasons. His temper cast a shadow over us; in the morning we scarcely noticed it until it would explode like a storm. I was afraid he would die and abandon us. This outweighed any other feelings I had about him, feelings of alienation or indifference. I was not aware of the significance of this until I reached adolescence when I feverishly began to scrutinise my youth.

My burdens made me suffer. Seeing this, Ibrahim compensated for my father and always showed me great tenderness, affection, and goodness. When Ibrahim died, my father still imposed shackles on my life. But when my father passed on to the next world, I was freed from the frightening duty which had stifled my emotions and which I had endured for so many years. Even though I was sharply critical of his legacy I tried not to betray it. I considered his death an attack against the family itself. From that day on I was empowered. I no longer kept my distance from controversies: I saw, I heard, and I suffered. Earlier, I had written a *qasida* called 'Life', but my true feelings had been distant, absent.

The Narrow Long-Necked Bottle
I was much more attached to my aunt than to my mother, and my attachment to my paternal uncle, Hajj Hafiz, was stronger and deeper than my attachment to my father. Because of the warmth of his heart, his joking and laughing, I felt he truly loved me. My memories of my uncle continue to be clear and vivid, although my

thoughts are fragmented and muddled. My uncle was involved in many enjoyable quarrels and controversies. One dispute between him and my father concerned my uncle's participation in family councils. The men of the city, considering my father too rigid in his views, would approach my uncle instead and meet constantly with him. I would often run to him during his meetings and he would take me in his arms and set me on his lap. My father would never do this.

During the first quarter of the year, the men of Nablus would celebrate the birthday of the Prophet Moses – Nabi Musa. The idea for this holiday began during the Ayyubid period[8] in an effort to attract large numbers of Muslims to Jerusalem when many Christians were there celebrating Easter. This presumably would put Muslims on their guard against a surprise attack by the Crusaders. Muslim youth would arrive in the holy city in huge numbers from cities and villages all over Palestine. They would meet at the tomb of Nabi Musa, which is located between Jerusalem and Jericho. During the holiday, the young men of Nablus would go out with the religious dignitaries who were in charge of the rituals. The procession began with the religious men beating on drums and cymbals and singing popular songs. The parade continued to the city's limits, then turned to Jerusalem to join a procession of religious dignitaries of Hebron and Jerusalem. The singing continued throughout the Easter celebration.

In the Nabi Musa procession, just as in the procession of a bride and groom where the Quran is recited, the parade would stop in front of our house and look for the family 'jester.' The shouting and calls for my uncle would rise higher. My uncle would leave his office chamber to join the holiday procession near the government offices. The young men would mount him on their shoulders. They would all draw weapons. My uncle would wave his sword imploring the enthusiastic crowd to reply to his words: 'We are men of the mountain of light.' In the parade, orange-blossom water would drip from the pitchers or from long-necked bottles.

I was very proud of my uncle. Eventually, I recognised the reasons for his popularity. In 1925 the National Party was founded in Nablus to support the candidacy of Hajj Amin al-Husaini[9] to the Supreme Muslim Council.[10] Other parties, like the National Democratic Party, opposed the National Party in the elections. My uncle was one of the founders of the National Party. After his own success in the municipal elections, he distanced himself from party rivalries and from the factions in both the local council and the country. Of the two parties, the National was connected to Hajj Amin al-Husaini and the National Democratic was led by Raghib al-Nashashibi, mayor of Jerusalem. These two parties created damaging divisions in the country. Unlike my uncle, my father did not avoid this political battlefield. He belonged to various political organisations and was imprisoned several times by the British mandatory authorities. Still, my uncle continued to be more popular and prominent.

When my uncle died of diphtheria in 1927, at the age of fifty-two, I began my encounter with death. As if struck by lightning, I fell into confusion and a whirlpool of inconsolable sadness. For the first time, I experienced loss, and I grieved. Man's life is a chain of distinct losses, starting as a separation from the mother's breast and ending with his own death. My uncle's death deprived me of a loving guardian. After his death, he lay still, shrouded on a bed. I was confused by the lack of worry on his pale face, his unawareness of a crying family and friends. I concealed my sadness, trying not to think of the loss of the family member I felt closest to. We deceive ourselves in thinking that we can preserve the memory of the deceased by placing little stones on his grave. That ritual doesn't compensate for the loss. To tell children that it does is only to deceive them as they are forced to confront death. I hid my own grief and drew near to it only at night, crying myself to sleep.

I am not a philosopher. As a child, I reasoned simply as children do. But I was preoccupied by the dread which death inspires. I wondered about the external appearance of death since the dead seem absolutely isolated and indifferent. Even Julia, my childhood friend, who was distantly related to me, could not share my feelings of death for she, herself, died before my eyes in the seventeenth year of her life. She struggled alone and had to struggle alone, for no beholder can partake of another's death. When I think about Julia's death, I do not remember how she looked, but rather how I felt about her. I became angry when people said that death carries our loved ones to paradise in reward. The death of my uncle marked the end of my childhood. Julia's death appeared so unjustifiable that I thought only about death for a time. I was obsessed with the questions of why people died and why they left me. I was a child. I asked these questions simply and clearly.

Shaikha
Among my earliest memories are those of an aunt we called 'Shaikha.' I knew her as a mistress of intimidation, the person who controlled all the women in the family. She also reported on the activities and behaviour of the boys in the family, serving as a sort of police, surreptitiously transmitting accounts to my uncle.

Societies in which supervision is arbitrary and repressive engender dual reactions: submission and revolt. But these reactions, in turn, intensify the repressive power and create a hegemony in family and society. In my family, it was Shaikha who not only laid the foundation for this sort of power, but who also encompassed the qualities of submission and revolt.

When she was only sixteen, Shaikha returned to her father's house divorced from a marriage which had lasted a few months. She became a follower of the Sufi Order of Shaikh Abd al-Qadir al-Qilani.[11] For Shaikha the religious order served as an escape from the frustrations of a failed marriage. In the religious community of this blind Egyptian shaikh, there was a polarisation between female members who were divorced and those who were widows. The group assembled in the house of the treasurer who, with his wife, had the authority to dispense *baraka* and facilitate ritual purity. The shaikh proclaimed his *baraka* in a way that aggrandised his own importance. So doing, he deprived his followers of their own capacity to reason. By sharpening sensations with the fragrance of musk, the shaikh could convince his followers to see what was not visible, to hear what did not exist.

The account of the shaikh's *baraka* brings to mind a story about my old Turkish grandmother, Mother Aziza. One day she was present at one of the shaikh's demonstrations. In tears, she renounced what she saw and launched a devastating attack against the shaikh. From that day, an enmity was firmly established between Shaikha and my mother, whose modern outlook, especially on the subject of death, was at odds with Shaikh's religious piety. Shaikha attacked my mother, my brother Ahmad, and me for opposing her views.

As she aged and grew weaker, Shaikha was constantly engaged in praying, fasting, or proclaiming revelations. She would fast for three months – Rajab, Shaban and Ramadan – and pray and perform sacrifices at night.[12] Her prayer beads were huge and always by her side. They consisted of a thousand individual beads, and as she touched each one she would pronounce one of the names of God. Her personality was like that string of prayer beads, displayed for public and private devotions; the beads were a concrete manifestation of her piety.

As a child, I used to love to watch people engaged in prayer especially because of the theatrics involved. I would often stop at the gate of the Al Bek Mosque facing our house in the old market area to watch the different ways in which the worshippers prayed. While their facial expressions were quite different, they all began at a speedy pace, then humbled themselves without paying attention to anything but God. My heart and spirit were moved as I watched the worshippers pray firmly and slowly.

I noticed the hand movements. They were raised behind the ears, then brought above the head and finally to the right side as prayers were whispered in undertones. Body movements began: bowing the torso to the front; raising the body and lifting the head to the sky, kneeling down, prostrating themselves while placing their hands on their legs. Raising two index fingers, the assembled group would testify to the existence of God. They would pronounce praises to God aloud and turn their heads from right to left.

Only much later did I discover why it was important to express religious submission through prayer. I learned of a continuity in religious rituals from the period of peasant paganism. All modern religions try to evoke a mysterious environment through their theatrics and expressions, which are similar to the devotions and activities of the early natural religions.

Shaikha's call to religious prayer was exaggerated and artificial. Occasionally, she seemed to imitate the rituals of dervishes. She would begin vehement, trembling motions, moving her head fiercely right and left while repeating Allah . . . Allah . . . Allah . . . Allah . . ., and so on. She pronounced the name rapidly, without pause, foaming at the mouth.

Because of Shaikha, my faith changed. Occasionally, it was said that her religious rigidity dissolved in gatherings of women visitors. I did not find that to be true. She loved to issue decrees to the women in the family and to censure them for religious impiety. Shaikha would insult people simply because they were poor or unsuccessful. Thus did Shaikha believe.

In most circumstances, she took the particular behaviour of individuals as a general commentary on all humanity. She would permit one of the girls in the family to become friendly with a relative, a school friend or a neighbourhood girl. Then seeing the two together in the courtyard she would fume with rage. This used to drive every school friend or neighbourhood companion away from the house. When I did Shaikha a favour or bought her a gift from the *suq*, she would insinuate that I was trying to buy her love. Even when she smiled or showed some gentleness her affection always stopped like a cold wall which cannot nourish green plants. In a way, I combined traits of my mother and those of Shaikha, and yet the two were very different. On the one hand, there was my mother's warmth, gentleness and softness, and on the other, Shaikha was like a desert without trees or water. She was a harsh goddess who aimed her breath at an invisible throne.

Proud and haughty, Shaikha was in control of an entire stratum of women who blindly obeyed her. This 'pious' Shaikha would lead the simple women by her example. She would sit with them during their children's illnesses. The women would hold pitchers of water while Shaikha stood near the sick babies reading passages from the Quran. The women believed Shaikha could purify and bless water as she exhaled into the pitchers. Given her devotion to God, this 'pious' Shaikha held an astonishing view of the upper class, which she expressed arrogantly: 'We are above and you are below. This is God's Wish.' During the 1930s and 1940s this view was commonly held by the classes which benefited from the established order. They legitimised their positions of authority through the name of God. One could always hear the words: 'Sayyids, ladies; at your service, Sayyids; at your service, ladies; at your service, sons of Sayyids.'

Ideas are effective as long as people accept them and do not revolt against them. We must reject Aristotle's saying 'that the slave resembles the beast' even though this idea was consistent with the venerated thought of Athenian society and not questioned at that time.

I remember what a woman once said to Shaikha: 'Honour us, O lady, with a visit during the holidays, for we visit you often and you do not visit us.' But Shaikha stared at her and said in her haughty way: 'Listen, you will visit us always and forever and we will not visit you in order to emphasise the significance of the day of our departure.' What has happened to the world! How inverted things are! The woman was ashamed and my heart was filled with sympathy for her. I left the room, rushed to my mother to tell her how Shaikha had shamed this poor woman. I was young. I did not understand the meaning of cruelty, but I distanced myself instinctively from Shaikha's views. My feelings overwhelmed me, and I fell ill.

Although it may have been unconscious, I considered pride improper. In my home, criticism of Shaikha's haughtiness was tolerated until it affected the family as a whole. Shaikha would say to us in utter simplicity: 'We are all Creations of the Lord and our fate is in God's hands,' but this harsh woman turned away from all else. It is not right to turn away from suffering in order to honour important men who hold esteemed social positions. Because she believed it was, God punished her and afflicted her with hostility to the poor. My mother told us about democracy, simply, and she could explain spontaneously how the demise of democracy affected all people at all social levels. My mother could teach us in a practical way the true meaning of the phrase, brotherly unity is no burden.

I saw Shaikha as a symbol of the hardness of society, and I did not find my efforts to destroy the symbol absurd. Ultimately, I was unable to put an end to Shaikha's religiosity and to convince her that her feelings were inhuman. She never could accept my beliefs that the true meaning of religion had been distorted and that God's attributes of love, mercy, and goodness had produced illiteracy and ignorance for most men and women. What Shaikha considered permissible and forbidden, proper and improper was a strange, soggy mixture. She would cry to me for help but considered me an apostate. 'Come on up, weak one. Buckle down. Submit more or you will enter Hell and so will your mother who sewed those disgraceful clothes for you.' Shaikha's views undermined any serenity I had in my childhood. Her simplicity confused my young mind. Peace returned only when I began to imagine that it was the god of Hell who visited with my mother. I imagined God himself as a harsh and fearful ruler without compassion.

Once, when I had raised my voice in song – 'How secure is the breath of fresh air for the beautiful beloved everywhere . . .' – Shaikha entered the room like a storm and said: 'Silence, close your mouth or you will perish and awaken in Hell. Hinkiyan . . . Hind . . . Surena . . .' My voice was suddenly broken; the song, broken and incomplete, stuck in my throat. Hind and Surena were professional singers in Nablus whom Shaikha called Hinkiyan or harpies, a term she derived from the Persian word for god.

Shaikha hurt me deeply during those days by condemning the desires I satisfied daily through music and dance. I regarded music and dance as desirable and liberating activities. I, alone, possessed the power to control music and dance; the world in which I lived did not. Shaikha could not impose her power over song, and I did not believe her when she said that song and dance were ugly.

My mother used to hum softly with her sad, tender voice. I would hum and sit on her lap listening attentively. Resting from time to time and comforting me – at family gatherings and with my friends – in warm soft light – she would make me content, which she loved to do as she would remind me of the words and music of a song. Singing delighted me and made me happy. To fulfil an ambition, my mother had learned to play the violin. But she was so devoted to that ambition that the instrument was forbidden in our house. Playing an instrument and singing represented outlets and then, at a later phase of my youthful journey, symbols of the sentimental yearnings I had suppressed. In harmony and song – both in listening and in practising – I found a release of tension. Like poetry, this release served as a means to realise my talents and liberate my imprisoned capacities.

One of the strongest of my depressing memories of Shaikha began in the girls' room. This room, in the front of the house, did not belong to her, for each of the upstairs rooms had a different name. She entered unexpectedly and came upon my older brother, Ahmad, who was answering some of my questions on poetic metre and form. Shaikha stopped silently and looked over our heads. Then she said to Ahmad reproachfully, 'Even you, then what more? For girls, words are opponents who collapse in battle.' Ahmad joked with her, using some meaningless words. Then he turned his attention once again to me and my questions about poetry.

'Even you . . .' A terrifying expression for me which Ahmad understood with indulgence and which made a loving impression on him. In contrast, Ibrahim, whom I always loved, was emancipated from family traditions and from Shaikha's harsh shackles. From that day on my attitude to Shaikha was completely hostile. I no longer hoped for anything different in the future. Shaikha was the nightmare of my childhood and adolescence, and she left her harsh traces on many years of my life.

Those who think little of their role in my life are often the ones who, in retrospect, penetrate it most deeply.

Translated from the Arabic
by Donna Robinson Divine

NOTES

1 During the period of the British mandate, Ibrahim Tuqan (1905–1941), Fadwa's brother, was considered the most prominent poet of the Palestine-Arab community.

2 Nablus, a Palestinian city of modest size, is located in what is now called the West Bank. During the last decades of the Ottoman Empire (1517–1918) many men from Nablus held high administrative positions. In the course of British rule, Nablus served as the centre of a local Palestinian-Arab cultural revival. Known as 'Jabal al-Nar' (the mountain of fire), Nablus has a reputation as the site of rebellion and resistance to government.

3 Fadwa Tuqan is referring to 'the struggle' against the Zionists in their efforts to establish a Jewish state in Palestine.

4 In a later chapter of her memoirs, Fadwa Tuqan says that at the age of puberty, she was not even permitted to attend school.

5 According to Fadwa Tuqan, people often said that Ibrahim had written the poetry and had signed her name to it.

6 Dar al-muallimat literally means 'the house of female teachers' and refers to a teacher-training school in Jerusalem.

7 *Qasida*, sometimes translated as 'ode,' is a poem of praise consisting of twenty-five to one hundred verses with rhymes arranged in a particular pattern.

8 Aiubid refers to the dynasty founded by Salah al-Din ibn Aiub, known in Europe as Saladin.
9 Hajj Amin al-Husaini, Grand Mufti and president of the Supreme Muslim Council, was the single most prominent leader of the Palestinian Arabs during the period of the British mandate.
10 The Supreme Muslim Council was newly constituted by the British in 1922 and given wide discretionary powers over the disbursement of sums of money collected for the development and maintenance of Muslim educational and charitable institutions. It became a significant vehicle for exercising political and economic power in the Palestine-Arab community.
11 Abd al-Qadir al-Jilani, founded one of the four major Sufi orders. The blind Egyptian shaikh mentioned later was probably the leader during Shaihka's time.
12 Shaikha fasted two months longer than necessary according to Muslim law and performed rituals required only during the month of Ramadan.
13 To emphasise the piety of Arab women and their deep commitment to tradition, it is commonly said that they leave their houses only on the day of their death when they are taken out to be buried.

Huda Shaarawi

(1879–1947)

Huda Shaarawi was born in Minya in Upper Egypt. The daughter
of Sultan Pasha, a landowner from Upper Egypt who had risen to
the heights of provincial administration and had become President
of the Chamber of Deputies, and Iqbal, a Circassian woman, she
was raised in a wealthy household in Cairo, and belonged to the last
generation of women to reach maturity while the harem system still
prevailed. She was a leader in the first Egyptian women's nationalist demonstration in 1919 and became president of the women's
nationalist organisation, the Wafdist Women's Central Committee.
She was a founder and the president of the Egyptian Feminist
Union from 1923 until 1947, and the President of the Arab
Feminist Union from 1945 to 1947. She founded *l'Egyptienne* in
1925 and *al-Misriyya* in 1937. She supported the founding of
al-Mara al-Arabiyya, the newsletter of the Arab Feminist Union in
1946. A member of the International Alliance of Women for
Suffrage and Equal Citizenship she became a vice-president in
1935. She gave numerous speeches in Egypt, the Arab East, and at
Alliance conferences in Turkey and Europe. Huda Shaarawi was a
self-declared Egyptian, Arab and international feminist and a
lifelong activist. She died in Cairo in 1947.

Personal memoirs can offer special insights into the workings of
patriarchal institutions and ideology because they can show how
their imperatives are internalised and suppressed or how they
cause conflict and inspire attempts to escape from their control. In
her final years, after nearly a quarter of a century of public feminist
activism, Huda Shaarawi reflected on her life. The selections below
reveal her reactions to reaching puberty, to betrothal, and to
marriage. They were extracted from the English translation of her
memoirs in Arabic first published in 1986 under the title, *Harem
Years: The Memoirs of An Egyptian Feminist*, translated, edited and
introduced by Margot Badran (1986). The memoirs were published in Arabic edited by Abd al-Hamid Fahmi Mursi with an
introduction by Amina Said in 1981 under the title *Mudhakirrat
Raida al-Mara al-Arabiyya al-Haditha* (Memoirs of a Modern Arab
Woman Pioneer).

Farewell, Betrothal and Wedding

c. 1945

❧

Childhood Companions and the Farewell

From the time we were very small, my brother and I shared the same friends, nearly all boys, most of whom were the children of our neighbours. The boys remained my companions until I grew up – that is, until I was about eleven – when suddenly I was required to restrict myself to the company of girls and women. I felt a stranger in their world – their habits and notions startled me. Being separated from the companions of my childhood was a painful experience. Their ways left a mark on me.

Betrothal to My Cousin

One day when I was dozing while recovering from an illness, I was suddenly roused by excited voices coming from the far end of the room. My mother and 'Aunt' Gazbiyya Hanim, were talking. Gazbiyya Hanim said, 'I have heard that the Khedive's family is going to ask for her and if that happens you will have to bow to their will.' She continued, 'However, if necessary, we could arrange a marriage with her cousin [Ali Shaarawi].'

My mother said angrily, 'It would be shameful for her to marry a man with children of his own who are older than she is.'

Gazbiyya Hanim replied, 'He is the son of her father's sister and "lord and master" of all.' My mother answered, 'We shall see what happens.'

The room began to spin and the remarks of the nurses and slaves came echoing back whenever my cousin called. After announcing his arrival in the routine manner, they would add, 'Go and greet your husband.' It angered me but I dismissed it as a mischievous taunt. When the truth behind it became apparent, I wept long and hard, and the shock caused my illness to worsen and persist for a long time afterwards.

My cousin began to come to Cairo with greater frequency and passed many hours in the company of my mother. At times, I feared they were about to reach an agreement over my future but my forebodings vanished when I detected anger in my mother's speech. Gradually I paid less attention to the matter and it eventually slipped from my mind altogether.

One day, when my mother summoned me, I found a casket of jewels lying open in front of her; she asked me to select some pieces in fulfilment of a vow she had made for the recovery of my illness. I chose a splendid diamond necklace and bracelet and rushed to show them to Umm Kabira so she could share my joy.

Not long after that, Umm Kabira died. Profoundly saddened by her death, I put on the ring she had given me for memorising the Quran and have never removed it since. If she had not passed away, I might have discovered certain truths but, as it was, there was no one to explain things I could not understand on my own.

After the forty days of mourning passed, I noticed that when friends came to call on my mother, Fatanat would fetch the jewels to show the guests. When this was repeated a number of times, I became dismayed and remarked people would begin to think we were *nouveau riche* and had never before seen such things. The maid scowled but said nothing. I later observed Fatanat and the slaves embroidering squares of silk with silver and gold thread, and learned that *shurs*, as they were called, were customarily presented to friends and relations at the signing of a marriage contract. When I inquired who was getting married, I was told it was the daughter of a pasha in whose household my mother's maid had once been employed.

Not long after that, repairs began on our house. During that time my mother decided to pass the winter months in Helwan and so she took a small villa east of the *jabal*, where the sanitarium is now, but which at that time was still a barren stretch leading to the rocky escarpment. When we left for Helwan, I was still ignorant of what was happening.

I marvelled at Helwan, which owed its splendour to Khedive Tawfiq, who had adopted it as his winter retreat. Immediately afterwards, other royalty and aristocratic families began to flock there during the winter season or for short outings. It became a pleasant haven from the capital. People frequented the theatre and casino and the garden pavilions where Shaikh Salama Hijazi performed theatricals. Music played and swaying lanterns illuminated the night. The theatre and concerts gave me great pleasure. In the days when women were still veiled, Helwan offered a more relaxed atmosphere in place of their routine seclusion in Cairo.

After we were there for some time one of my friends came to spend a few days with us. One afternoon as I was taking her on a promenade to show her the delightful sights, we were startled by the appearance of Said Agha, who was accompanying some gentlemen. 'Where are you going?' he scowled. 'Return to the house at once!' We submitted to his command and retraced our steps. Upon entering the house I was surprised to find that the woman who had instructed me in Turkish had arrived in our absence. She was standing in the hall, still wearing her *tarha* and carrying another one in her hand. When she handed me a Quran I grew perplexed. Said Agha entered escorting Ali Pasha Fahmi, the husband of a second cousin, and Saad al-Din Bey, an officer in the Palace Guard, who later married Gazbiyya Hanim. When they came towards me, I hastened to my room thoroughly bewildered, but they followed and I retreated to the window, where I stood with my back to them. To my utter astonishment, Ali Pasha Fahmi announced, 'The son of your father's sister wants your hand in marriage and we are here on his behalf.'

Only then did I understand the reason for the various preparations underway in the house, as well as a number of other mysteries. With my back to the men, I cried without speaking or moving. I stood sobbing by the window for nearly three hours. Occasionally passers-by glanced up sympathetically. Eventually Ali Pasha Fahmi and Said Agha whispered in my ear, 'Do you wish to disgrace the name of your father and destroy your poor mother who might not survive the shock of your refusal?' Upon hearing these words, which pierced my heart, I replied, 'Do whatever you want,' and rushed immediately to my mother's room scraping my head on a nail on the side of the door in my haste. Bleeding and about to faint, I must have been a pitiful sight. My friend and others around me wept.

My spirit was broken and I spent the rest of my stay in Helwan with my eyes full of tears. I began to stroll on the lonely escarpment instead of in the gardens with their concert pavilions and theatres. My two young companions used to accompany me, but I often left them to wander off in the distance alone, while I pondered how I could avoid the marriage. When I shared my thoughts with my companions, the elder, who believed in sorcery, said a magic spell would be cast upon me so I would accept tomorrow what I rejected today. I tried in vain to disabuse her of this.

When we returned to Cairo, I discovered great changes. The house had been repainted and the furniture redone. The dressmaker had begun work on my wedding gown but I did not let her try it on me. I ignored the other endless preparations, right up to the time the wedding day approached and strings of lights were hung in the garden. My mother, I noticed, was given to frequent outbursts of anger, the way she had been about the time of my betrothal, but I did not know the reason for her ill-temper and did not inquire.

I was deeply troubled by the idea of marrying my cousin whom I had always regarded as a father or older brother deserving my fear and respect (as I had been previously made to understand). I grew more upset when I thought of his wife and three daughters who were all older than me, who used to tease me saying, 'Good day, stepmother!' When my brother and I were small and our guardian-cousin called on us, I did not find him gentle. He was especially abrupt and curt with me, but treated my brother better. All of this alienated me from him.

My mother surprised me one day when she came to my room with a document which she asked me to read aloud to her, adding that my future husband had refused to sign it. It stipulated that my cousin, upon his marriage with me, would have no further relations with the mother of his children, nor would he ever take another wife. Until then, always mindful of his wife and children, I was certain that the marriage would not take place, but after reading the document reality struck home and I wept. My mother, thinking I was upset at my cousin's refusal to sign said, 'Everything has been done to secure his written consent but all efforts have failed. The preparations for the wedding have been completed and the invitations issued. It would be a disgrace to stop the wedding now. Accept things as they are for the moment, my daughter, and, God willing, in the future he will agree to these conditions. This is your destiny and God is your guide.'

I didn't utter a word, when my mother pressed me to speak, I said, 'Do as you please,' and left in tears.

I had known nothing of the rooms in the house prepared for me following my marriage until the day my mother, herself, took me to see them. I must confess, I had never before seen such sumptuous furnishings. I grew excited and I inquired if they were to be my very own. When my companion witnessed this she said triumphantly, 'Didn't I predict that you would be won over by magic?' Her remark plunged me into gloom not so much because I took it seriously, but because the beauty of the rooms had elevated my spirits for a fleeting moment.

The Wedding
The three nights of wedding festivities with their music and gaiety expelled my melancholy and kept me from thinking of what was to come. I laughed and was merry along with my friends, so much so, that the household interpreted my earlier behaviour as nothing more than the ordinary display of fears common to prospective brides.

On the night of the wedding ceremony, the rapt attention focused upon me, especially by my friends, increased my joy so that

I almost leaped with delight while I donned my wedding dress embroidered in thread of silver and gold. I was spellbound by the diamonds and other brilliant jewels that crowned my head and sparkled on my bodice and arms. All of this dazzled me and kept me from thinking of anything else. I was certain I would remain forever in this raiment, the centre of attention and admiration.

Presently, the singing girls appeared to escort me. My attendants supported me while the heavy jewels pressed down on my head and the wedding dress hung heavy on my small frame. I walked between rows of bright candles with rich scents wafting in the air, to the grand salon where I found a throng of women – Egyptians and Europeans – in elegant gowns with jewels glittering on their heads, bosoms, and arms. They all turned and looked at me with affection. When I raised my head to ease the heavy tiara back a little I heard a woman's voice whispering, 'My daughter lower your head and eyes.' I then sat down on the bridal throne surrounded by flickering candles and decorated with flowers, fancying I was in another world.

Some of the European guests placed bouquets of roses and other flowers in my hands or at my feet. I failed to understand the feelings of sympathy these women had for my marrying at such a tender age. A pair of maids brought the shawls presented to me by my mother's friends. Removing them from their velvet packets one by one, they unfolded the shawls and spread them out one after the other announcing the name of the donor, repeating in succession, 'May bounty be granted also to her.' After all had been laid in a great pile they were bundled and carried away.

Next, a dancer appeared and started to perform in front of me. She then made the rounds of the guests dancing in front of the women one at a time. They would take out coins, moisten them with their tongues and paste them on the dancer's forehead and cheeks.

Suddenly, a commotion erupted outside the great hall. The dancer rushed out emitting a string of *zaghrudas*, the tremulous trills hanging in the air after her. To the roll of drums the women hastened out of the room or slipped behind curtains while the eunuch announced the approach of the bridegroom.

In an instant, the delicious dream vanished and stark reality appeared. Faint and crying, I clung to the gown of a relation – the wife of Ahmad Bey Hijazi – who was trying to flee like the others and I pleaded, 'Don't abandon me here! Take me with you.' My French tutor who was at my side embraced me and cried along with me murmuring, 'Have courage, my daughter, have courage.' Mme. Richard, supporting me on the other side, wept as she tried to console me with tender words. Then a woman came and lowered a veil of silver thread over my head like a mask concealing the face of a condemned person approaching execution. At that moment, the bridegroom entered the room. After praying two *rakas* on a mat of red velvet embossed with silver he came to me and, lifting the veil from my face, kissed me on the forehead. He led me by the hand to the bridal throne and took his place beside me. All the while, I was trembling like a branch in a storm. The groom addressed a few words to me, but I understood nothing. When the customary goblets of red sorbet were offered, I was unable to taste the ritual drink. Finally, my new husband took me by the hand. In my daze I knew not where I was being led.

The next morning when I looked out my window, the big tent adorned with fine carpets and embroidered hangings was gone. Gone also were the bright lights that had enchanted me the night before. I had been certain they would all remain a long time. How desolate I was when I saw the work of the hand of destruction! Nothing remained on the grounds where the tent had been raised – not a single tree of the many trees I loved, all of which held special memories for me. Gone was the apricot tree that shaded me and bent low offering me its fruit. Its purple flowers gave the garden a special beauty perfuming the air all round, even in the house. Nothing remained of the orange trees whose blossoms wrapped the ground in a fleece of white flowers which we used for making perfumed garlands. Uprooted were the prune trees and the magnolia tree whose large white blooms I plucked for my mother the moment their petals unfolded. Nothing remained of the *dahn al-basha* (the pasha's beard), with its delicate tiny fruit we called *tuffah al-walida* (mother's apples). Gone were the Indian jasmine, the Arabian jasmine, the basil, and the pear trees, and the luisa trees whose leaves we crushed in our fingers to extract the lemony scent. Not even a *sitt al-mistihiyya* (the shy lady) was spared. Its leaves, curled up and closed whenever we touched them, shrinking from us with shyness, we thought.

I loved all those trees – the big and the small – and swung from their branches in my girlhood. They had been planted by my father who had loved them as I had, and who had cared for them and enjoyed eating their fruit. All had become lost remnants of grandeur. All were sacrificed at the call of a single night, a night I had fancied would last in all its beauty and majesty forever, a night when my sorrows and agonies had vanished. But it faded like an enchanting dream. Bitter reality followed. I wept for my trees. I wept for my childhood and for my freedom. I saw in this barren garden a picture of life – the life I would live cut off from everything that had delighted me and consoled me in my melancholy childhood. I turned from the window with a heavy heart and avoided the garden for a long, long time, unable to bear these aching reveries.

Translated from the Arabic
by Margot Badran

Shirley Saad

(1947–)

Shirley Saad was born in Cairo to a Lebanese father and a Polish-Rumanian mother. In a letter to Miriam Cooke she wrote:

'I was educated at St. Clare's College by Irish nuns and grew up to feel absolutely torn between my European heritage and education and my Arab origins and environment. Before Gamal Abdel Nasser took over, it was not "done" to speak Arabic. Even the Egyptian court spoke French, Turkish and Italian. I grew up speaking English, French and Italian and only studied Arabic for a few years after the 1952 revolution when it became mandatory in the schools, even the private ones.

'For a whole year, I missed school expecting to go to Lebanon any day. A friend of mine played hooky every Monday, and we went to the cinema in the morning and read Milton and Shakespeare in the afternoon. We never spoke Arabic at home. When we went to Lebanon in 1961, I found to my great surprise that the Lebanese all spoke Arabic, even the Christians. I learned easily enough, having heard it around me all my life but only felt the need to read it after meeting Hanan al-Shaikh. I wanted to be able to read her novels.

'I sat for my GCEs at the British Council in Beirut and later took a couple of classes at the University of California in San Diego, but I am largely self-taught.

'I started writing while I was living in Abu Dhabi and feeling very frustrated with the restrictions imposed on me by the weather and the local customs. Although most of the restrictions didn't really apply to foreigners, only to the local women, I met some of them and sympathised with their plight. Some of them were obviously content with their lot, but some were eager for more freedom, more education, more opportunities to achieve something other than children.

'This is basically what pushed me to write "Amina" and other stories as well. In my stories the women often end up killing themselves, which does happen in reality, as they see it as the only way out.

'In Paris, where I lived next, I wrote more short stories, but by then my heroines had become more aggressive; one of them killed the man in her life. We then moved to San Diego and now my totally liberated heroine goes jogging and takes a lover! I think a psychiatrist might find that interesting.

'I have found that being brought up as a Catholic in the Middle East is doubly inhibiting. Whatever isn't illegal is sure to be immoral. I've always fought for the right to do exactly as I pleased, even if it shocked the neighbours. It is a heady feeling to be in the United States where I can be my own boss and it is taken for granted.'

'Amina' was written in English, and is published here for the first time. It tells of the anxiety of a woman who gives birth to girls only.

Amina

1985

❦

Amina opened her eyes and for a moment wondered where she was. Then she remembered and a moan escaped her lips. The English nurse hurried over and bent down, 'Don't you worry now,' she said. 'You'll be fine and the baby is all right.'

Amina asked, not daring to hope, 'Is it a boy or a girl?'

'A girl,' replied the nurse cheerfully. 'A beautiful, bouncing, four kilograms girl. *Mabruk*, congratulations.'

'*Allah yi barek fi omrek,*' murmured Amina as she sank back on her pillows. Another girl!

What a catastrophe. What would happen to her now? She had brought four girls into the world, four girls in six years of marriage. She felt tears running down her cheeks, and remembered how happy and proud she had been when her mother told her that she was engaged to be married.

She had seen Hamid twice, once at her cousin's house when he arrived unexpectedly. The girls all scattered to their quarters to put on their masks and veils. The next time, he came with his father to ask for her hand in marriage. The houseboy serving the coffee told the Indian housegirl who in turn, ran and told her mistress. So, she had gone to peek through the partition between the men's and women's *majlis*. She saw Hamid and his father sipping coffee and being congratulated by all the men in the family. They embraced and rubbed noses, big smiles on everyone's faces.

Amina remembered her wedding, the noise and the bustle, her hennaed hands and feet, the whispers among the older women which frightened her and the anticipation. Finally, she found herself alone with this stranger, who had turned out to be very kind and gentle and considerate.

Well, there would be no henna and celebration for this girl. God, why couldn't she have a boy? Just one, that's all she wanted, just one little baby boy.

She wished the midwife hadn't told her when she had that miscarriage that it had been a boy. The only one in six years, and she had to go and lose it. It was her fault too. She had no business climbing a ladder at five months. She slipped and fell and the doctors kept her in the hospital for a week, then told her she was all right and could go home. But there was no movement, no life, so she went back to the hospital and after two weeks of tests and X-rays and hope and despair, they finally decided the baby was dead.

After that, she had two more girls, and now the fourth.

Would Hamid divorce her? Would he take a second wife? His older brother had been pressing for two years now, urging him to take a second wife. Hamid loved Amina and his daughters, but he was human. He did have all that money and the social and political position and no boy to leave it to.

Her mother came in, then her sisters-in-law. Each one kissed her and said 'Mabruk', but she could tell they were not really happy. Her mother was especially fearful for her daughter's future and felt that some of the disgrace fell on her and the family too. The sisters-in-law were secretly jubilant, because they had boys. Hamid's social status and half his fortune would revert to their own sons if he never had any boys of his own. Of course, he was still young and he and Amina might try again. But for the moment the in-laws left reassured and falsely commiserated with Amina on her bad luck.

'It is God's will,' they murmured, smiling under their masks. Their mouths were sad, but Amina could see the twinkle in their eyes. 'God's will be done.'

Friends started coming into the room. They kissed Amina and said 'Mabruk', then sat on the floor, cross-legged. Arranging their robes around them, they sipped coffee from little thimble cups, eating fruits and sweets.

Her cousin Huda came too. She wore a long, velvet dress, embroidered on the sides and bodice, loose and flowing, to conceal her belly. She was in her sixth month and looked radiantly serene. She sat on the carpet and sipped her coffee.

Amina thought bitterly, 'She already has two daughters and three sons. What does she need another baby for? She's not so young any more.'

As if she had read her thoughts, Huda said, 'This is my last baby. It will be the baby for my old age. The others are married or away at school all day. An empty house is a sad house. You need many sons and daughters to keep your husband happy. You are still young, Amina. God has given you four daughters, maybe the next four will be boys. God's will be done.'

'As God wills it, so be it,' murmured the other ladies smugly.

Hamid came in and the ladies all stood up, saluted him deferentially, and hastily went into the next room. The maid served them more coffee. Hamid looked at his wife, tried to smile and searched for something nice to say. He thought she must be tired, disappointed, ashamed of having failed him one more time and afraid of being repudiated.

He sat down near the bed and said, 'Well, mother of my children, we will just have to try again, won't we?'

Amina burst into tears of sorrow, shame and relief.

'Don't cry,' he said, distressed. 'The important thing is that you and the girls are in good health,' smiling. 'As long as we are young, we will try again, eh?'

Amina blushed under her mask and pulled her veil around her face. He patted her hand, got up, and left the room.

The ladies came rushing back in, like a flock of crows, eager for the news, good or bad.

Amina's mother said solicitously, 'What did he say, my daughter?'

'He said better luck next time, Mother!'

The mother let out a sigh of relief. They had another year's reprieve. The women congratulated Amina and left to spread the news.

Amina sank back on to her pillows and drifted off to sleep.

Samira Azzam

(c. 1928–1967)

Samira Azzam was born in Jaffa, Palestine. In 1948, her family moved to the West Bank. Like a number of young Palestinian women of the time, Samira Azzam decided to set out independently and by 1950 she had moved to Beirut. She became editor-in-chief at Franklin House, an independent publishing company where writers like Taufiq Saigh and Badr Shakir al-Sayyab produced translations of American works of fiction, and literary and art criticism into Arabic. She helped Palestinians who came to Beirut in search of work. Kamal Boullata recalls: 'I remember she could always find you a job. She found me two design jobs when I came to Beirut in 1965. She was a strong, assertive woman who had at the same time a great sense of gentleness and humour. She was widely read, and was very active in Lebanese and Palestinian cultural life. She published her short stories in a number of journals, including *Al-Adab*. She was friends with the Palestinian writer Ghassan al-Kanafani. In June 1967, she left Beirut. She wanted to go back to Palestine but she could not stay. On 7 June, she arrived at Allenby Bridge. There she learnt of the fall of Jerusalem. She had a heart attack and died on the bridge.'

Samira Azzam's short story collections include *Al-Saa wa al-Insan* (Time and Humanity, late 1950s) and *Al-Id min al-Nafidha al-Gharbiya* (The Feast from the Western Window, published posthumously in 1971) out of which 'The Protected One' is taken. In this story, a father anxiously awaits the birth of his son.

The Protected One

1967

❦

Whenever he saw his pregnant wife move heavily around the house and relax her swollen body against the sofa as she thought about motherhood, his heart began to beat. He wondered what the newborn would be. A female? That's fine. Let her have large eyes and a fair complexion like her mother. A male? Welcome! Let the little one roam around the house on his wobbly feet . . .

He was not expecting either of them to have a white complexion, he knew the rules of genetics, but he was free to choose a nice name to fit his son's or daughter's personality, a name that was not common or hollow, a name that really suited his son . . . his son and no one else's son. He thought of the names that people call their boys and they did not seem very distinct . . . Nabil? Samir? Wasim? These names were so common that it seemed that every child had to be named Samir or Wasim or Nabil . . .

Wouldn't descriptive names be embarrassing? Wouldn't it be funny for someone ugly to be called Beautiful, for a coward to carry a name that means bold or gallant? No. This he could not accept. Patiently he thought of a name that would not conflict with his son's looks or personality.

When he tired of thinking, he browsed through a dictionary and wrote down possible names. He came up with a long list . . . When he was not satisfied with the dictionary, he asked his friends to provide him with another list of suggested names. All he wanted was an original name.

Heavens! What an effort! None of these millions of names interested him, nor did they seem appropriate for this unborn child. Lists of names grew and accumulated in his pocket. To ease the process, he weeded out the unwanted names and started to catalogue the rest alphabetically. The As were in one list and the Rs in another. Male names were separated from the female names.

The names that appealed to him the most had a red mark . . . When the newborn arrived the name would be ready for him or her. He decided that the name should not be composed of letters that would be difficult for a foreigner to pronounce; his son would be intelligent and motivated to travel and learn abroad. There is nothing worse than a name mispronounced by foreigners. Yes indeed, its letters should be easy rolling in the mouth, smooth as water . . . not garbled.

But why was he so concerned about the name? Shouldn't he give priority to his wife? The intolerable pain of childbirth that she was undergoing cannot be described. Wasn't her well-being more important to him than these names? . . . The lists are ready . . . They are spread out on the desk in front of him. He is waiting. As soon as he hears, he will rush to her and give her the name. Then she will give him the baby and relieve him of this dilemma and this waiting.

He stands up in anxiety and starts to walk around. He sits. Finally the phone rings and his heart leaps, his hands shake as they hold the phone. He controls himself and hears his mother's voice roaring down the other side saying: 'Congratulations, Abu Salih (Father of Salih)'.

Salih . . . Salih! How had he forgotten? How had he overlooked that his first son must carry his father's name . . . How stupid of him. He laughs . . . and laughs loudly. He takes the long lists of names and throws them into the wastebasket.

Translated from the Arabic
by May Ibrahim and Miriam Cooke

Ulfa Idelbi

(1912–)

Ulfa Idelbi was born in Damascus, Syria. She was an only daughter
with four brothers. She loved to read, and with her father, she read
all the Arabic classics as well as works by Taha Husayn, Mikhail
Nuaimi, Gibran Khalil Gibran, Shakespeare, Chekov, and Mau-
passant. At seventeen, she was married before she could get the
baccalaureate. In the 1950s the BBC organised a competition for
short stories in the Arab world. She sent in a story and won third
prize. She is the author of four volumes of short stories, including
Pisas Shamiyya (Damascene Stories), 1960 and *Wadaan ya Dimashq*
(Goodbye, Damascus), 1963, three collections of literary articles,
including *Nazra fi Adabina al-Shabi* (An Examination of Our Popular Literature) 1974, and a novel, *Dimashq, ya Dasmat al-Huzn*
(Damascus, Smile of Sorrow), 1981.

'Seventy Years Later' is from the collection *Wa Yadhak al-Shaitan*
(When the Devil Laughs) Damascus, 1970. Like most of her fiction,
this story presents a society in transition from an upper class older
woman's perspective.

Seventy Years Later

1970

୧୨୬

That charity organisation held a ball as a fund raising event for its activities at the beginning of each year. It was customary that a 'surprise' be announced at the ball to attract people to support the organisation.

That year the surprise was exquisite and entertaining. Twenty young girls were asked to wear a dress that had belonged to their grandmothers at their age. This was not too difficult a demand as a great number of older women kept their favourite dresses as a souvenir. A committee from among the guests was elected to choose the most beautiful garment worn by the most beautiful girl to whom the organisation would give a precious prize.

When the moment for the competition came, the twenty young girls paraded their antique dresses to the guests. There was laughter and merriment. Some young men joked and even made fun of the dresses, which had faded or had been damaged by time. One of the young girls was wearing a robe which looked as if it had never been worn before. It was so perfectly intact that the audience was filled with admiration. It was a superb dress in the style worn by nineteenth century European princesses. It was of a precious silvery velvet embroidered with glowing golden flowers. The embroidery was magnificent. It was a ceremonial dress which left the lovely neck and the round shoulders bare. The sleeves narrowed to the wrists, making the shape of the arms beautiful and smooth. The dress showed off the graceful waist under a large golden belt. It flew out in front barely touching the floor, and at the back it spread into a long embroidered tail like that of a peacock. All of this gave its wearer the air of a princess promenading in a vast palace. As soon as the committee was formed, the wearer was given the first prize and the audience applauded enthusiastically.

The mother of the winner was sitting with her friends at one of the tables, looking at her daughter with a tenderness and pride that seemed to be mixed with sorrow and grief. One of her friends asked, 'Why are you sitting silent and sorry as if you were not the winner's mother. Why are your eyes so close to tears? No doubt, they are tears of joy?' The mother of the prize-winner smiled and replied, 'It is joy that provokes my tears. Yet, the dress has awakened a very painful memory. I recall my mother, its owner. I wish that she were alive to see this cherished, forbidden garment of hers come out in the open at last to be admired above all the other dresses at an important social event like this. It remained hidden in her chest for seventy years. And now my daughter, her favourite and most beloved granddaughter, is wearing it.'

One of the friends said, 'This dress must have a strange story. Do tell us.'

The mother replied, 'It is a very sad story, but I will tell it to you so you will know how much our grandmothers and our poor mothers were prisoners of customs and habits unbelievable to us today.

'My mother was an only child of parents who showered her with love and care. At fourteen she was married to my father and moved from her father's house and her happy life there, to the house of her husband. It was the custom then for a young bride to live with her in-laws. Her husband's family was large. Besides his parents, he lived with his three unmarried sisters and four brothers with their own wives and many children. Her mother-in-law, who was my grandmother, was in charge of everything pertaining to the household. She took care of problems with great experience and ability. She was determined to be just and wise and to be fair in an absolute sense toward her daughters, her daughters-in-law, and her grandchildren. At the beginning of every summer and every winter, she provided each member of the family, and her daughters-in-laws, with a wardrobe. The young women had to accept her choice whether they liked it or not. She also assigned to each young woman a day to be in charge of the cleaning and good order of the house. The sons worked in their father's business. He alone had the right to dispose of the family fortune. He was responsible for the whole family, as was the rule in Damascus in those days.

'The family affairs went as smoothly as possible under such circumstances. Of course, there was no lack of problems and difficulties, as when jealousies erupted between the young women. They were soon ironed out, however, when the mother-in-law applied her authority, experience and care. Another custom of those days was for the daughter-in-law never to leave the house unless accompanied by her mother-in-law, and this only to weddings and funerals. Additionally, she could take her children to visit her own family once a month for three full days, a welcome relief from life with her in-laws.

'However, my poor mother was deprived of that pleasure when two years after her marriage, her parents left for Istanbul where her father was transferred. My mother could write and read perfectly, rare among women of her time. She wrote letters to her parents expressing her sadness at being parted from them and the bitterness of her solitude. She described all the things she had to put up with, all her joys and all her sorrows.

'One day she wrote to them telling them that the oldest of her husband's sisters was engaged and that a great wedding was being prepared. Her parents, whose hearts were forever grieving over their separation from their only child, wondered, "What can we send her that will bring her joy and lighten her loneliness?"

'They gave it considerable thought and finally their choice fell upon the dress you see tonight. It must have been the most precious and the most beautiful dress in all of Istanbul, then the capital of elegance and refinement throughout the Orient. My mother's father paid fifty golden pounds for it. He was not a rich man and had to borrow money to fulfil his wish to honour his daughter. He thought her dignity would be enhanced when her dress became the talk of all the women in town.

'My mother used to describe to us the joy that filled her heart when she received this lavish and unexpected gift. She called all the inhabitants of the house to show it to them. She started to worry, however, when she detected signs of displeasure on her mother-in-law's face.

'A few moments later, her mother-in-law summoned her to her private room and said, "My daughter, in no way can you wear this dress in our house. We are not able to provide the likes of it to my other daughters and daughters-in-law. You very well know that it is our custom that none of you is to be set above the others."

'My mother was stunned and said in awe, "How can it be possible for me not to wear it? It is a gift from my father, and I have none more beautiful! . . ."

'The other answered, "Have I not given you a beautiful dress made of golden threads for the wedding night? Isn't it the most expensive material available in Damascus this year? Don't you want to be like the other women of the family?"

'For the first time my mother dared to rebel against her and said firmly, "I swear by God that I will not wear any other dress no matter what you say . . . And where do you want me to wear it if I don't wear it the night of the wedding . . ."

'She answered, "You can wear it in your private chamber and in front of your husband only."

'My mother said, "But it is embroidered, and made for balls and grand occasions. My father did not send it for me to wear it in my room which is too small to even contain its train."

' "Thereupon her mother-in-law left her. She was very angry indeed. It was the first time she had met with rebellion in one of her daughters-in-law. She paced up and down the floor of the courtyard, waiting for her son to return from work to tell him about the problem before he could see his wife. She thought if he saw her and the gift she had received from her parents, he might be won over to his wife's side. As soon as he came home, she called him to her room and disclosed the problem, saying, "Would you like your wife to show that we are of a lesser station than her parents? Would you like, my son, to hear people criticise us saying that your wife's dress was more expensive than that of your sister on her wedding day? Would you accept, my son, would you countenance that your wife provoke the jealousy of your sisters-in-law and make the lives of your brothers more difficult?"

' "I have advised her to wear it in your private quarters only and for your benefit alone, so that we are spared problems we don't need, but she refuses to listen to my advice, and be persuaded by me, her mother-in-law and the eldest in the family! She swears she is going to wear it for the wedding because it is a gift from her parents . . . She is arrogant and stubborn. God help you with her! But you can handle the matter, I have brought you up to be a man . . ."

'My father had never refused anything to his mother before as he feared to arouse her wrath, for fear of God. He rose promptly full of anger against his wife and entered her room, as she was hastily putting on the magnificent dress in order to surprise him. Without even a look at the dress and cutting short any discussion he said, "I will declare you divorced three times if you ever wear this dress. I will never anger my mother for the sake of a dress given to you by your parents."

'My mother was seized with fear and nearly lost her mind under the blow but she said nothing. What could she do in the face of a divorce without recourse?

'So the young woman of sixteen years threw herself on the splendid dress, crying and kissing it passionately until midnight came. Then she arose, forced to admit defeat. She folded the dress and threw it at the bottom of a chest and sat in front of it, crying and wailing as she would have done had she been sitting before the coffin of a loved one . . .

'All her life she wished she could have worn it at least once. She also used to say to me when recounting the story, "How many times did I wish to shred it to pieces but a devilish thought stopped me. I used to tell myself: I will keep this dress in a safe, unreachable place and if, one day, this man, your father becomes unbearable to me, I will have an easy recourse. All I shall need to do is to wear this dress and I will be divorced in an instant." '

One of the friends said, 'If the story you tell had happened to me, I would have worn the dress immediately.'

The story-teller answered, 'My mother lived peacefully with my father for seventy years and never had to confront him by wearing the dress. But, we often saw her take the dress out of the chest and gaze at it for a long time. She would take great care of it, exposing it to the sun and the air so that the moths wouldn't eat it. She would also tell its story with pain and passion to anyone around her as if it had happened only the day before. She would have liked one of us, her three daughters, to wear it but none of us fulfilled her wish. It was out of fashion when we grew up and there were no events like this in our time.

'That is why I feel sad and weep. I wish she was alive to see at least her beloved dress getting the appreciation it deserved in a grand ballroom and winning a first prize after having been buried in the depths of her chest for seventy years . . .'

Translated from the Arabic
by Simone Fattal

Zainaba

(c. 1930–)

❦

Elizabeth Oram served as a Peace Corps volunteer in Mauritania, West Africa from 1985 to 1987. She worked extensively with the Maure ethnic group in rural areas organising community health projects. She writes:

During my service as a volunteer in Mauritania, I worked to develop a project that would address the depressed health status of rural women in my region. With the help of a local nurse, Zainaba, I established a training programme for traditional midwives living in isolated communities. I felt it was important to train these midwives because most women in these outlying areas still prefer the midwives' traditional medicine to making the long journey to the hospital in town. Through the training, I hoped to improve the midwives' knowledge of basic hygiene and first aid so they could treat the women that came to them better.

As part of this training, Zainaba and I decided to include the topic of female circumcision. We knew at the outset how difficult it would be to discuss this subject because of these women's traditional mindset. But we also knew that female circumcision is a major health issue for these rural women because its practice is widespread and because the complications experienced by women who live so far from medical care can be severe. Zainaba proposed that she give a lecture to the midwives instructing them how to modify their practice of circumcision and how to avoid infections by using sterile techniques. The text of Zainaba's lecture on clitoridectomy to the midwives follows below.

Although Zainaba's lecture was primarily technical in aim, it is also important as an example of the development of an awareness about female circumcision and the power women have over the perpetuation of this practice. To better understand the importance of her lecture some background about the practice of female circumcision in Mauritania and the beliefs surrounding the practice must first be explained.

Of Mauritania's four ethnic groups (Maures, Pulaars, Soninkes and Wolofs) all except the Wolofs practice circumcision 100 per cent.[1] In the Maure group there is a further subdivision between the white Maures, the ancient conquerors of Mauritania (of Arab

Berber descent) and black Maures, their former slaves (negro-
African descent). Among the Maures,[2] clitoral circumcision takes
place seven days after birth, at the time of baptism. In general, it
seems white Maures prefer mutilation of the clitoris to excision.
Black Maures on the other hand tend to practice a more severe
form of clitoridectomy in which the entire clitoris, and often the
inner lips, are removed. It is important to note that all of the
midwives involved in the training were black Maures and that
Zainaba's lecture addresses this more severe form of circumcision.
The other ethnic groups (all of black-African descent) also tend to
prefer excision.

Whatever the severity of the circumcision, many children experience medical complications. These are the same complications
suffered wherever clitoridectomy is practised but because of the
scarcity of water and ignorance of personal hygiene, these complications are made even more severe. Infections with fevers are not
uncommon, although often the family's embarrassment keeps
them from bringing the child to the hospital until the fever is quite
high. Tetanus from using dirty razors is always a danger. Urinary
problems as the result of a careless operation or excessive amounts
of scar tissue are also fairly commonplace. In these cases, the child
will probably have been circumcised by a midwife who believed (as
many of them do) that females urinate from their vagina and that
during circumcision there is no danger of damaging other organs.
The effects of circumcision can manifest themselves throughout
puberty and adulthood, often causing difficulty in having sexual
relations and in childbirth.

The beliefs surrounding female circumcision are deeply
entrenched in the Mauritanian culture. Because the country has
remained physically and culturally isolated, even into the twentieth
century, these beliefs along with many other traditions have gone
unchallenged and remain quite strong. Whenever I asked Maure
women why they have their daughters circumcised, their first
response was almost always, 'No man would marry an uncircumcised woman.' They believe that if left intact, the clitoris greatly
arouses a woman and causes her to chase uncontrollably after any
man as soon as her husband's back is turned. Thus, they believe
that an uncircumcised woman's thoughts would constantly turn to
sex and that she would do anything necessary to satisfy her lust, a
behaviour completely unacceptable for a woman and yet, notably,
encouraged in Mauritanian men.

Many women also believe that circumcision must be performed
because if not, the clitoris could grow into a full size penis. In fact,
the word for clitoris in Hassaniya (the dialect of Arabic spoken by

Maures) is 'zaman' or penis. Maures seem to believe that the clitoris is directly connected to arousal and sexual desire and that these feelings are proper only to men. Further, one of the words for female circumcision in Hassaniya literally means 'to beautify'. Thus, circumcision is seen as a cleansing or beautification process; making a woman totally female by removing her clitoris, her 'male' part. Women rarely mention that they believe circumcision is important for religious reasons. And yet, many men believe that this is the most important reason for continuing the practice. Most of them also admitted that they would not marry an uncircumcised woman for fear that she would be unfaithful to him. All the women I asked said that circumcision ensures a woman's piety and fidelity.

Thus, among Maures, circumcision seems to be seen primarily as the removal of something unclean and foreign from the female. Perhaps this is why it is done at such an early age and not at puberty. It is not, as it is in so many societies, celebrated as a girl's entry into womanhood. There are no gifts, no feasts, no cries of encouragement and no ululations of victory as there are for the boys when they are circumcised at the age of six or seven.

In light of the fact that Maures believe so strongly in female circumcision, Zainaba's lecture presented the traditional midwives with a challenge. This challenge was made even more poignant because Zainaba is both a Maure and a woman. It was crucial that it was she and not I that gave the lecture. As a Maure, Zainaba is part of the culture that she is trying to change. She is a Muslim, herself circumcised. She is subject to the beliefs and pressures of Maure society just as the midwives are. As a result, Zainaba never tries to invalidate the practice of female circumcision or the beliefs surrounding it. Instead, she points out the immense power that the midwives have when they circumcise girls and that they must use this power responsibly. Zainaba emphasises that circumcision is not just a simple cut, but one that can mean the difference between life and death, both physically and emotionally.

During the course of her lecture, Zainaba awakens the midwives to the fact that they as women have complete authority over the way clitoridectomies are performed. It is women who perpetuate the practice and it is women who must also take the responsibility to regulate it. It is they who must ensure that infants are not brutally circumcised, creating as she says 'worthless, lifeless woman' who will have no ambition or drive and will be unable to work alongside men towards a common goal as God intended. Thus, not only is Zaibana teaching the midwives how to circumcise safely and hygienically, she is teaching them about power and responsibility.

From this point on, I will discuss clitoridectomy in the Maure culture only because I lived and worked with this group for two and a half years and have only a general knowledge of the practices of the other ethnic groups in Mauritania.

Lecture on Clitoridectomy
to the Midwives of Touil, Mauritania

1987

❦

Zainaba: Asalaam alaykum. Today we will be speaking about subjects that the government requires us to cover, one of which is female circumcision.[1] I will also speak to you about the manner in which a woman and a man, God willing, make babies. The man has, and I have not so far spoken to you about this so don't be embarrassed, the man has his 'friend' (penis) which in turn has its seed. The woman has her 'luggage' (sex organs): outer lips, inner lips, clitoris, urinary canal, vagina. The vagina has three functions: it is a passageway for birth, it is a passageway for the man and it is a passageway for the blood during the women's period. The vagina extends to the cervix and the cervix continues into the uterus. The uterus has 'horns' (Fallopian tubes) and in these 'horns' there are eggs. From the time a woman is born, these same eggs are inside her. From the age of eleven or twelve when a girl becomes a woman, she gets her period. Each month one of those eggs drops down and then the blood flows unless, God willing, she marries and sleeps with her husband. If, God willing, this happens and one of his seeds joins with her egg, it will remain in her uterus for nine months and will grow into a male child or a female child. Uhh . . .

Elizabeth: Who's there?[2]

Zainaba: It's only Fatma, my maid. And today I want to speak to you about female circumcision. The Way of the Prophet, Muhammad Rasul Allah, may peace be with him.

Midwives: May peace be with him always.

Zainaba: . . . tells us that women should be circumcised. It is not a sin if it is not done, but it is better if it is. In any case, it is said that the manner in which it should be performed is that one third of the clitoris should be cut off and two thirds should be left intact. One third should be removed, two thirds should be left. (*Speaking in an excited voice*) Someone who practically attacks a girl with a knife, cutting off everything, not even leaving the place the clitoris used to be in, is, in any case, going directly against the words of the Prophet, God grant him peace.[3]

Midwives: (*Disturbed chatter, 'I didn't know . . .', etc.*)

Zainaba: (*Again excited*) God created woman to be with man. He created her to be his wife so that they could help each other. It is

not right if only the man has feeling and the woman feels nothing.
That is a great sin. After all a man and his wife are from the same
tribe, aren't they, and people from the same tribe should always
work together and help each other, shouldn't they?

The woman has only her clitoris – it is this alone which allows her
to feel something. It is that which makes her a woman, it is that
which makes her desire a man. (*Emphatically*) If a woman's entire
clitoris is cut off, it leaves her cold, lazy, without desire, without
interest, humourless. Doing that is like killing her, it is a sin. That is
why the Prophet tells us that only one third should be taken off and
two thirds left. Those of you who are cutting off the whole clitoris
are clearly committing a sin.

And, you should know that near the clitoris there is an artery
that comes right from the heart. If you cut wildly with the razor
and hit this place, nothing sweet will come of it. You won't be able
to stop the bleeding and they can do nothing for you at the
dispensary. The blood will flow and flow until the girl is left lifeless,
like a piece of cardboard, and she dies . . . (*Excited*) Remember,
there is a dangerous artery there, there is a dangerous artery there,
there is a dangerous artery there! Those of you who are going to
circumcise, cut off one third and leave two thirds! Cut one third,
leave two thirds! You who circumcise, this woman for example
(*pointing at one of the midwives*) who cuts off every bit of the clitoris,
is dangerous to your daughters! And this woman (*pointing at
another*) who delivers babies and then brutally cuts out the baby's
inner lips and clitoris – she is dangerous!

Midwives: (*Nervous laughter*)

One of the midwives: I didn't know that I should leave part. Now
that you told me, I won't cut it all out.

Zainaba: Sss, ss, quiet! And above all that . . .

Midwives (*More nervous laughter*) I wouldn't want to do anything
sinful . . .

Zainaba: Above all that there is something called tetanus. You
know that all children and pregnant women should be vaccinated
against tetanus. You all must not, as is your custom, rush into a
family's tent when they call you to circumcise their daughter
saying, 'Give me the child, give me the razor blade and get my
payment ready!' First you must clean everything. Today we are
teaching you to be nurses – we will give each of you medication and
explain how to use it all. When you circumcise, you must clean your
patient with soap, your razor blade with alcohol and, when you're
done, apply antiseptic to your patient. Understand? Clean everything with antiseptic. And remember, before you even use your
medicine both you and the patient must be clean. If your patient is

clean, the medicine will be beneficial, if not, it will be useless. (*Excited*) I repeat, do not cut off the whole clitoris, do not cut off the whole clitoris . . .!

Midwives: (*Nervous chatter*) I remember she said that . . .

Zainaba: Cut off one third, leave two thirds. A woman with no clitoris is like a mud wall, a piece of cardboard, without spark, without goals, without desire. She becomes nothing – like a puddle of standing water. Cold, lifeless, her children are unhappy, her husband is unhappy – she makes nothing of her life. It is not to be all cut off! It must not be all cut off!

Midwives: We understand that very well now . . .

Zainaba: In any case essential in all this is cleanliness. Whether you are performing a circumcision or treating a cut or doing anything, you must wash your hands, make sure your instruments are clean and use only a new razor blade. And if you absolutely cannot find a new razor, take the best one you have, place it in the small metal dish in your kits, pour alcohol on it and light it to disinfect it. (*She demonstrates*) Understand?

Midwives: Yes, definitely.

Zainaba: The importance of cleanliness cannot be overstated. When you are clean, your hands and your comportment is clean, then you are worth something. When you are sloppy or dirty, you are shirking your duty and you are worthless. Your prayer itself is worthless because you are dirty. God loves that which is clean and organised. Someone like this will be admired by people. Clean people don't become sick. But people who are dirty, like you (*pointing to one of the midwives*) – her skirt is dirty, her head and veil are dirty – ugh, ugh – this person shall fall ill. This is not the behaviour of a nurse. Thus, those of you who are dirty, who smell – you cannot become nurses. You should not treat others. You shouldn't be given the responsibility to do anything. One who is clean is pleasing to God and an example to others. Remember: One's comportment on earth will be the same in the afterworld.[4] God overlooks nothing. When you go back to your villages, you have a duty. You must be an example of cleanliness and health to everyone, especially to other women.

Remember, you are becoming nurses of people, not animals. If a person is sick, you don't dawdle. If you deliver a child and there is something wrong with it, or a woman is having problems with her pregnancy that you don't understand, get up before the morning prayer and bring her to the dispensary. If you wait, the woman and/or the child may die in your care. You only bring problems upon yourself when you try to treat something that is beyond your capabilities.

For instance, if a woman has an abscess or sores on her female parts, send her to the dispensary to be treated. If she is not treated, when the child is born it could contract a type of conjunctivitis which may blind it. Or for example, if the child develops abscesses, it is not normal. It could be an outer sign of an inner illness. Or if the woman has a lot of white discharge, that too is an illness, send her to hospital. And, once again, the clitoris must not be completely cut off! Understand?

Midwives: Oh yes!

Zainaba: Do what the *Sharia* tells you – cut off one third, leave two thirds. A woman who is completely circumcised is like a wall, lazy, lifeless, with nothing sweet for herself or her husband. And all of you who circumcise, remember the importance of hygiene. Hey! What's the matter, can't you sit up straight!

Midwives: We're tired.

Zainaba: Understand? You must not cut it all off. And let me tell you one more thing. You are being trained to be nurses and we are providing you with medicine: aspirin, iron pills, vitamin A and *most importantly* with medicine to care for wounds. It is the rainy season, the planting season. Many people cut themselves with their planting tools. You have medicine – treat them. It is also the season when the men who circumcise boys come up from Mali to circumcise large groups in your villages. When these men come, don't pound up your Baobob leaves and camel dung to put on the wound.[5] You are nurses, treat the wounds of circumcision as any other, with antiseptic and antibiotic ointment. Boys and girls who have been circumcised must be treated every day with antiseptics. Do you understand all this? Do you know it by heart?

Midwives: Oh yes! (*Lots of discussion*)

Zainaba: Now I want each one of you to describe the female reproductive system to me to see whether you have understood everything I've told you. All right, Amina, tell us about the parts of the woman.

Amina: What do you mean? (*Nervous laughter*)

Zainaba: The woman's 'luggage'.

Amina: (*This time in a serious tone*) All right. *Bismallah*, this is her belly button, that's first. And this is her front and her lips and then her clitoris, her vagina and her uterus. The vagina is the place the man goes in when they sleep together. If, God willing, she sleeps with her husband when one of the eggs is ripe, she will get pregnant, if not she will get her period.

Zainaba: Very good! All right, you next!

Aisha: All right. Look, this is her stomach, this is her belly button, lips, clitoris, urinary tract and vagina. Above the vagina is the uterus and it has horns and in them are eggs. If she sleeps with her husband and God wants to give them a child, one of the eggs will fall into the uterus and will be fertilised. If not, she will get her period.

Zainaba: Very good! All right now you.

Lalla: I'm ashamed.[6] (*Nervous laughter*)

Midwives: There's no problem. Go on, go on!

Lalla: Well, this is her front and her lips and her clitoris and her urinary canal and vagina . . .

[Each of the midwives repeats this approximately, some with small additions, some timidly, some with confidence.]

Introduced, edited and translated from the Arabic
by Elizabeth Oram

NOTES

1 Zainaba used two words to refer to female circumcision, 'tizian' which means to make more beautiful and 'gaaad' which means to cut off and make even. The latter is also used to describe male circumcision.

2 The training was held in the administrative office in the middle of town since it was the only room in the village able to hold all of us. We held the lectures with the doors shut because the women were so uncomfortable – afraid that a man may overhear what we were talking about. Thus, every time I heard even a slight movement outside the door, I jumped to make sure no one would walk in on us and spoil the 'safe' atmosphere I was trying to create for the midwives.

4 A Mauritanian saying, '*Had sivtu vi diniya, hiya sivtu vi lakhra.*'

5 Traditional methods to stop bleeding include paste made from dried plants and animal dung. This mixture can cause both infections and tetanus. To discourage them from using it, Zainaba and I provided them with antiseptic and bandages and instructed them in their use.

6 Poor Lalla, she was the youngest midwife at the training and, as such, she was low woman on the totem pole of respect. Traditionally, you must never even say the words 'pregnant' in front of an older person – it would be disrespectful. Imagine her horror when asked to recite all the female organs in front of twelve women older than herself!!

Alifa Rifaat

(1930–)

Alifa Rifaat was born in Cairo, Egypt. Her father was an engineer who did not think that girls needed an education beyond the primary level. She wanted to attend art school, but instead she was married off to her cousin, a policeman, with whom she travelled all over provincial Egypt. She knows only Arabic and has been out of Egypt only three times: in 1980 on the Hajj or Pilgrimage to Mecca; in 1982 on the Umra (small pilgrimage) to Mecca and Medina; and in 1984 to London for the international Feminist Bookfair. She wrote her first short story when she was nine, but only published when she was seventeen. Her story 'My Secret World' attracted considerable attention which led her husband to forbid her from writing. She complied in that she did not publish her stories, but she continued to write them in the privacy of her bathroom. On his death in 1974, she published eighteen short stories, most of them in the literary journal *Al-Thaqafa al-Usbuiya*. The following year, her first volume of short stories, *Hawwa Taud bi-Adam* (Eve Brings Adam Back), appeared. In 1981, she published another collection entitled *Man Yakun al-Rajul?* (Who Will Be the Man?) In 1984, *Distant View of a Minaret*, a collection of stories translated into English, was published in London.

Her stories are both fantastic and natural, rural and urban, and are informed by a religious tone that tempers her stringent social criticism. She discloses the extent to which women are complicit in their own victimisation. She portrays the wistful worlds that women create when illusions about marriage have dissipated. Her women confront loveless marriages, joyless sex and husbands' sanctioned abuse with pained resignation.

The following quote from 'Bahiya's Eyes' encapsulates Rifaat's commentary on being a woman in Muslim society: 'Daughter, I'm not crying now because I'm fed up or regret that the Lord made me a woman. No, it's not that. It's just that I'm sad about my life and my youth that have come and gone without my knowing how to live them really and truly as a woman.' Jan Morris has called Rifaat's writing 'horrible, beautiful, comforting, divine and devilish all at the same time'.

These two stories, each of which has Bahiya as protagonist, are taken from the collection *Who Will Be the Man?* They follow Bahiya through clitoridectomy to its aftermath. Having been initiated into womanhood, she rouses everyone's fears about the safeguarding of her honour. The little girl is confused by the pain and unwelcome attention.

Who Will Be the Man?

1981

༖

Every day I wake up with the memory of that dreadful morning hovering over me. I'll try to describe my ordeal. It was a humid morning. Clouds of mist flooded the fields and transformed the four wild rose trees outside my window into little guardian angel birds. I awoke to their joyful chirping in celebration of life and looked down upon our fields stretching away into infinity.

I'm still confused. How could my mother abandon me to their coarse hands? How could she even let them into the house? I – Bahiya Hasan al-Kamawi – was the daughter of the *umda*, the headman of the village for generations. The villagers were riff-raff who could not hurt me, they could scarcely look me in the face. Whenever the village shaikh himself saw me skipping along on my two skinny legs, he would get off his donkey, close his umbrella and walk with head bowed, his hand raised in a respectful greeting. He did not ride again until I had passed.

That morning felt like every other morning and as usual I rushed to my window. I sensed the magic of the sunrise and sniffed the perfumes of the field and the breakfast baking in our oven. I watched Maruf the gardener who was in charge of the orchard and our vegetable garden. The animal pens and the chicken coop were nearby.

Every morning Maruf picked grapes from the tall trellis and shook the guava tree and picked ripe peaches, figs and mangos. He walked in the courtyard where my father, the umda, had his bench on which he settled village matters.

My window overlooked this scene. I shared a room with my sister Sophia who always slept until noon. Every morning I hurried to Maruf, stroked his dog and carefully chose the most delicious piece of fruit from his basket. I slipped into the green room where my grandmother slept. As quietly as possible, I pulled out her silver smoking box from under her pillow. I did everything just the way she did: I rolled cigarettes and licked the white paper to stick to the tobacco. Then I lit the end and blew slowly, shaping my lips to let out the smoke in circles.

That morning before I could look out of my window, coarse hands fell on me and my sister Sophia. They folded us into their black flea-ridden *gallabiyas* and carried us to the special parlour where men who are not allowed into other parts of the house are received. We only enter this room when we are invited to meet guests. Then we rush in, shake hands and rush off to our hiding places.

That morning the big carpet had been removed from the marble floor and replaced by a big wooden table. They put Sophia on it while Smuha held me in her powerful arms. The women surrounded my sister and pointed her legs into the air. The village midwife, Hajja Warad approached, reciting the *bismallah*. Her veined bony fingers dug around Sophia's soft flesh until she held a piece which she rubbed. I trembled anxiously as I watched this terrifying event. I felt faint. Smuha had to hold me up. Hajja Warad frowned as she announced:

'The girl, God bless her, is pure. She is the daughter of pure parents. The angels cleansed her. Her blossom did not wither in my hand.'

She left Sophia and rushed off to the entrance. She was surrounded by the women's ululations and praises and prayers to the Prophet.

My turn came and I advanced with calm steps. Freely I approached the table and let them do what they liked with my thin legs. For I, too, am the daughter of pure parents like Sophia. The only difference between us is that she is fat and I am thin; she is quietly withdrawn and introspective and I am chatty and inquisitive. Certainly the angels must have purified me also even though I didn't understand what purity meant at that time.

I felt the rough hand rub me. I saw the razor blade flash after they spilled alcohol on it. She lit it. Hajja wiped it with clean cotton. I saw it coming near me. I screamed. I screamed, and my shouts sounded like the shrieks of a slaughtered baby rabbit. I screamed as it burned and tore through my flesh. I screamed for mercy as Hajja poured alcohol on my wound and turned it into a raging fire. At that moment I saw the large body of my mother Hajja Zainuba. She was screaming, 'My friends! The girl is weak from losing blood! Hajja, she is bleeding too much!'

Hajja Warad cried out 'You there, Najya! Go get me some ground coffee right away.'

I stammered between my tears and wooziness, 'You're going to make coffee? Is he dead at last?'

My mother came close to me and wiped my sweat. She dried my tears with her handkerchief, and then asked, 'Who died, sweetheart?'

I wailed and the women around me laughed. I laughed with

them. I laughed and the pain disappeared. Hajja Warad treated
my wound with a handful of ground coffee beans. The bleeding
stopped.

As soon as Smuha had carried me to bed, streams of visitors
arrived. Coffee cups were passed around and the watchman fired
off bullets. The guests slipped gold gifts under my pillow. A
bedouin relative wearing a veil embroidered with gold coins
arrived. Spouting one oath after another, she said she would slip
one row of coins under my pillow. She ululated loudly and
melodiously, 'Get up, oh bride, let down your braids and take off
your silken gown. Perform half of your religious obligations and
come on the *hajj* with me.'

My heart fluttered with joy. I climbed out of bed. When I tried to
walk, I lurched and clapped my hands.

'Great! I'll go with you!'

The guests laughed and my mother said, 'Aren't you ashamed!
You want to marry before your sister?'

I laughed gleefully as I devoured a tray of rich and tasty food.

Darkness fell. My mosquito net was tied around me to ward off
the gnats and the night's humidity. Hajja Warad dabbed some
healing ointment on my wound. Najya raised the kerosene lamp to
light the bed. The fringes of the net caught fire. Around me the
bed flamed. The lamp fell and the kerosene flowed out onto the
only wooden floor in our house. Quickly the flames grew and
ululated around me. I stood amidst the noise and commotion.

I got up and ran through the dancing flames. I fell, got up, and
then fell again. Then a hidden hand reached out and led me.
Walking with it, I passed through the fire. Men were killing the
flames with water-filled cans. I left the fire safe as Abraham (peace
be upon him). The women shrieked in excitement as they surrounded me saying praises. My miracle was greater than Sophia's. The
angels had protected Sophia but God had protected me. Smuha
whispered, 'Najya lit the fire to steal your gold.'

But I didn't care. I was sure I had reached God even without the
pilgrimage. He was holding back spectres who, with hidden lust,
were forcing themselves into my body.

Smuha carried me to my mother and the rest of the family. On
the bottom floor, the door to the living room had been opened and
I was laid on a mattress and some blankets. My eyes wandered over
some Quranic verses carved in gold letters on the high walls above
the furniture. Ignoring the whine that was rising up from deep
within me, like the moan of a cracked flute, I asked, 'Why is that
room bolted?'

My mother replied curtly, 'That's none of your business.' But she saw the flash in my eyes. I pointed to a heavy wooden door, and asked, 'What's behind it?'

In silence, the adults exchanged alarmed and fearful glances. Assuring themselves the fire was out, they left. All was quiet in the middle of the night, except for me and my wound, my curiosity and my moaning. I got up, taking feeble steps to the door and I pressed its rusty latch with difficulty. It opened after I tried again. It opened into pitch darkness. I stood, confused, staring, trying to see. The door moved a bit and creaked lightly. My feet slipped on some wet mud and I crouched where I was, trying not to move. From the depths of the dark blazed a pair of luminous eyes. Then I felt it, long, slender, smooth on my body. It slid until it touched my wound and I felt a violent tremor of pain. I screamed. I kept screaming until they heard me, opened the door and pulled me out to where my mother sat.

From between her toothless lips, my grandmother said, 'Beat that cursed child.'

But my mother was content merely to pinch the inside of my thigh. That was how she always disciplined us.

Muttering, Smuha hurried to rescue me. 'Good thing she didn't fall into the well.'

'What do you mean well? Something in there scared me!' I shouted at them furiously.

My mother screamed, 'Oh God! The girl's been touched!!'

My grandmother yelled, 'Everything's fine, God willing. Bring her a cup of buttermilk.'

They brought me a silver container engraved with Quranic verses. I drank.

Finally, when I was overwhelmed by their concern, I blurted out, 'Since you love me, why did you sacrifice me?'

Hiding a smile Smuha answered, 'So that men will come running after you without your asking. And when your husband goes away for a long time, you won't suffer at all.'

From that instant a thorn grew in my heart and scratched me with the question:

'Who will be the man? Who will be the man?'

Translated from the Arabic
by Elise Goldwasser and Miriam Cooke

Honour

1981

❧

Sadness wrung my heart as my sister Sophia wailed through the night. Her feet and hands tied in white cloth until the henna dried, she cried out, 'Oh people have mercy on me. I don't want to marry Smain.'

I crept into her bed through the edge of the mosquito net tied around her and laid down by her side.

'What's wrong, darling? I hope to God it's not serious.'

She clung to me weeping, her braids drank the tears from her face which was buried in my chest. 'I don't want Smain to touch me. He will kill me, sister. Bahiya, he will hollow me out like an eggplant.'

I went on calming her, stroking her until she was quiet.

One late afternoon her father the *umda*, Hajji Hasan al-Kamawi, came to our room, followed by our mother, Hajja Zainuba who was full of joy. With a wide smile he announced, 'Congratulations, Sophia. We have read your *Fatiha* over Smain, son of my brother Shaikh Mujahid. The contract will be signed and your wedding will be soon. What do you think, Bahiya?'

I laughed in embarrassment as obscure spectres embraced each other in my imagination. Meanwhile, Sophia hid her face in her veil and my father laughed happily. Proudly, he twisted his moustache and grunted his frightening cough that made hearts jump. Then he left, followed by my mother, swinging her heavy buttocks coquettishly. Her trilling laughter resounded and was quickly answered by friends' ululations. Echoes of joy reverberated until they covered the entire village.

When the commotion died down and we were alone again, Sophia uncovered her face which was covered in tears. She slapped her cheeks shaking and moaning with grief. 'Oh Sophia, you miserable, ill-fated, hopeless girl. The evil eye is on me.'

I threw myself on her and hugged her. 'Sophia, may God protect you from Satan. What has happened?'

Wailing hoarsely, she replied, 'The boy Tariq Effendi, son of Namik. He kept charming me with his kind words and sweet eyes. He stood in front of me until I fell in love with him.' I shouted out in fear mixed with a secret thrill, 'Heavens! Where did you meet him?'

Through her tears Sophia burst into nervous laughter. Stretching out her arms and tightening her body sensuously, she whispered, 'At first I would watch him from afar, from our side of the garden. He was on the other side of the canal, riding his horse on his father's land. Whenever he saw me, I was embarrassed and ran away. Suddenly I found myself in love with him and unable to do anything. In the evening he motioned to me, "Wait until midnight." He swept me onto his horse and took me to the jasmine kiosk in the garden. I was happy when he kissed my hands and feet. He cried like a woman, saying, "Love has cast a magic spell on me. Cure me, I am melting from passion." He kept pouring fourth sweet words and I wanted him to go on forever.'

I shouted, unbelievingly, 'Shame on you. Did you make up this story? During the day your father isn't there. Fine, but at night where were your father's dogs and his watchmen?'

Shrugging her shoulders, 'Well, sister, the guards were sleeping on their rifles and the dogs know me so they don't bark when I slip away. What can I do, Bahiya? Love burns you and steals you away to a different world. He puts me on his horse and we plunge through the moonlit woods. We stay awake until the cock crows. My precious, without even feeling it, slowly, slowly, I became his woman.'

My head span, I beat my temples, 'Oh, what a disaster has befallen us! Sister, how could you have been robbed without feeling anything? Is it such a small thing? Honour is precious. It can cost lives. It's fine as long as he marries you. If not, we'll be disgraced.'

Her black eyes flashed and the tears were still wet on her face, 'Shaikha, you don't know anything about this. What do you know about love? Ignorant one, love has a different taste than marriage. I swear that if our father insists on marrying me to Smain against my will, I will run away to my true love.'

Angrily, I replied, 'Do you want to lead us to disaster? If your lover were sincere, he'd already be at the door.'

She said, 'Open up your benighted brain. Don't you understand? He's still a high school student.'

I shook my hands in despair 'Sophia, don't let disappointment mislead you. How could you fall for his honey-coated words? Those are the kinds of things boys say to girls all the time. Who is this light of your eyes? Only a deceitful, miserable student who took you for nothing!'

She said forcefully, 'Quiet, adviser. I am the daughter of honorable people. He brought me a fan from somewhere far away, the likes of which your father has never seen. My beauty melts him.'

I hugged her, 'Sister, dear one, tell him the terrible thing your father has done. He'll support you. Then you won't have to long for him.'

That night, when it was quiet and the lights were out, I could not sleep. I saw her from my net. A blurred shape wandering around and then escaping through the window. She was gone a long time. Anxiety crept into my soul. I prayed continuously for Sophia's protection until she returned at the first signs of dawn. She slipped quietly into her bed.

In the morning, her face was pale and her eyelids sore from crying all night. I spoke out in pain. 'So he left you, that son of a dog?'

Still sobbing, she said, 'Don't talk like that about him. I love him.'

Burning, I said, 'You're ignorant. His deceit has emerged, Shaikha. What did that rotten boy say to you?'

She answered through her tears, 'He said, "Did I force you? You came to me of your own accord. I cannot marry you but we will remain lovers forever."'

I stamped my feet, 'By the Prophet! If I were you I would put a stop to his sweet song and break his neck. I would spit on him and those like him.'

We stopped talking when our mother Hajja Zainuba, swaying her massive body and shaking an incense burner, entered our room. She had lit a mixture of incense and a plant called devil's eyes over ground corn cobs to protect us from envy, and melted a chunk of alum to recognise the hexer's form. She recited Quranic verses and prayers while she stared into the burner and muttered. Incense filled the air.

'By the life of the Prophet, the girl has been envied! I seek refuge in God from the evil eyes of the people and their harm. Her dowry will be the biggest in the area.'

Then she grabbed some scissors and a sheet of paper. She cut a human shape. With a pin, she poked out its eyes as she chanted, 'Hadaraja Badaraja from all evil eyes Zadaraja. I charmed you, I ask God to charm you against the evil eye of Bahana, and Shalabya and Tahiya and Insafa. Let them go their way! And from the eyes of your mother and your father and from the eyes of all who see you. May they not pray to the Prophet.' She tossed the paper doll into the incense burner. Sighing in relief, she prayed to the Prophet.

Sophia fell on my mother's hand, kissing it beseechingly, 'By the Prophet, Mother, I don't want to marry.'

My mother beat her chest in fear. 'Quiet girl, are you possessed? Watch out, don't become overbearing.'

Tears pouring down her face, Sophia insisted again, 'By the Prophet, Mother, I am asking for your mercy.'

Her fleshy cheeks quivering, Hajja Zainuba pinched the inside of Sophia's thigh and shook her angrily, 'You fool! What's wrong with Smain? He's a good man and he will weigh you down with gold and thousands of hopes. Wretched one, do you want to break your father's word and put our heads in the mud? For other girls this would be a golden opportunity.'

Sophia shook as if she had been killed, her body broke out in sweat. Hajja Zainuba became gentle again, stroking Sophia's silky braids and asking, 'Are you feeling well, darling? Do you want to see the doctor, precious?'

Suddenly Sophia said, 'No! I want to see Hajja Warad.'

I was paralysed with fear at the mention of the midwife's name and my mother cried out, 'Oh fateful day! Why her? Hajja Warad is involved in scandals, children! What will the people say? We have always been an honourable household.'

My voice shaking, I came to my sister's support, 'No, Mother. It's nothing much, just a stomach ache but Sophia's afraid to take off her clothes in front of the doctor.'

Hajja Zainuba laughed as she said, 'I was afraid for nothing.' Carrying her incense burner, she left.

Hajja Warad came that evening. She saw Sophia alone, while we waited in the courtyard. Finally, the door opened and we ran in as my mother shouted, 'God willing, Hajja, everything is fine, yes?'

Glancing sideways at Sophia, Hajja Warad replied, 'Fine, Hajja. She has only a bit of a cold. Wake up Smuha and make Sophia a cup of warm milk. God willing, we will present her to the groom in a few days.'

Laughing, my mother and Hajja Warad left the room. Then I ran to my sister and whispered, 'What happened?'

Smiling and shaking her head coquettishly so that her long earrings shook, she said, 'Calm down, sister. Their honour is safe. On the wedding night Hajja will bring some powdered glass to smear in me. She is my salvation, God bless her. I gave her a gold bracelet so she is satisfied. She's been paid.'

Every night I sat up in bed while the lovesick spectre wandered away without fear, and returned only when the cock crowed. That lasted until the night of henna when the lanterns and green flags dangled from the palm trees. They burned in the heart of the dark until dawn when the animals were slaughtered. The cook stayed up preparing the wedding banquet. Trays of fermenting henna came with candles and scattered with basil. Sophia, in her glittery pink gown, sat between rows of girls who danced and sang while we dipped our hands and feet into the henna. Afterwards we tied them with pieces of cloth and went to sleep on our couches. Then Sophia let out a frightful scream, 'Come here, Bahiya. That boy Smain will kill me. He will hollow me out like an eggplant.'

Although I felt numb, I tried to encourage her, 'Sister, aren't you the one who said, "I want Hajja Warad"? And you were happy with her work? You're strange.'

She calmed down a bit and murmured, 'There's no other solution.'

I said: 'Don't be afraid. You'll fool him one hundred per cent.'

She laughed and then quieted down. Colour returned to her cheeks and we slept until morning.

The next morning, they took Sophia to the public bath. The bride's bath involves special rituals. Shalabya, the bath house attendant came with her equipment to perform them. She brought ashes from the stove, sugar, lemon, scented soap and an abundant supply of containers filled with warm water, all of which are applied to the bride's body so she will be smooth and hairless. During the process, Shalabya whispered words of guidance into the bride's ear to prepare her for the night. Amidst the singing and cries of joy the bride let Shalabya decorate her with red and white dyes. Then we combed her hair.

No sooner had the sun set between the palm fronds and wild rose bushes than we heard bullets announcing that the bridal procession was beginning. The sounds of the drums and tambourines rose as the dancers danced in the courtyard. After the evening prayers the contract was signed and the men sat down to eat sweets and to drink.

Ululations resounded in the house, and the bride sat like a clay statue, not moving her red arms nor her velvet shawl. She looked like an idol smeared with colours. Her feet were submerged in copper trays full of water and purslane.

She sat there, staring dully at the girls who were dancing around her in time with the boys' fiery chanting. Together, their passion increased and they approached her, pinching her knees, inviting her to join them. Then they sat around trays piled with meat, rice and couscous until cups of cinnamon were passed around. The drums continued and the ululations grew louder and songs echoed in return. My father, the *umda*, entered twisting his moustache impressively. He led the bride outside to where a camel bearing a howdah painted and decorated with palm leaves stood. She disappeared inside it.

The girls volunteered to carry the bride's trousseau from the red clothing boxes to the trays of food and new pots and pans. The procession advanced with the boys in front dancing to a flute until we reached the couple's house. Smain, the groom, a slender dark young man with strong sinewed arms and a twisted moustache plunged boldly into the howdah and carried off his bride amidst ululations and bullets. The tambourines were beaten harder and harder. He disappeared with his precious burden into his house where Hajja Warad was waiting. The wooden door closed. The boys gathered in a group and shouted loudly. One group yelled, 'Toro Toro.' The other replied shouting 'Tear down the house.' Meanwhile the girls in their bright dresses stood in a circle, clapping their hands feverishly with an excited sparkle in their eyes. Then the loud shouts that everyone was expecting came and tore their hearts. Everyone grew quiet to listen to the shouts mixed with pride and elation.

Then the blood throbbed in everyone's veins until the door opened and the face of Hajja Warad tensed with joy, appeared as she handed my father, the *umda*, the bloodstained silk handkerchief and clutched the sweet reward of good news in her palm. My father placed the handkerchief on the tip of his cane as he proclaimed loudly: '*Mabruk*, pure one. You have brightened our faces and lengthened our necks.' Raising his cane very high, he walked in a circle with it, showing off the honour. Male cousins grabbed the cane and danced with it. The laughter, bullets and music resumed. The girls, clapping their hands in fervour and stamping their feet so that their breasts and buttocks swung in view of the boys, dreamt of their own wedding nights.

I ran to see my sister inside the house. Exhausted and haemorrhaging she had thrown herself on the bed. Smiling victoriously, despite her terrible pain, she whispered happily, 'You should have seen it, Bahiya. Hajja Warad was screaming at Smain and peering at him as she said, "Are you a baby? What's going on you pitiful thing?" until he got confused and fumbled. He didn't know his head from his elbow. So, finally, she helped him and they did it.'

Amused, I started to laugh and clapped my hands. 'You're lucky. A bullet hit you and only left a scar on your eye. *Mabruk Arusa!*' For the first time my heart beat with joy. I raised my hand to my lips and shouted joyfully from the window in the bride's room.

Translated from the Arabic
by Elise Goldwasser and Miriam Cooke

Khairiya Saqqaf

(1951–)

Khairiya Saqqaf was born in Mecca, Saudi Arabia. In 1973, she earned a BA in Arabic Literature from the Girls' University College of King Saud University. Three years later, she gained an MA from the University of Missouri. In the early 1980s she worked as editor of the women's section of the national daily newspaper *Riyad*, which she left after receiving her doctorate. She devoted herself to teaching at the Girls' University College. She is currently Academic Director of the University Centre for Women Students, and curriculum co-ordinator at King Saud University. She gives radio talks as well as public lectures at women's instititions in Saudi Arabia.

'I Saw Her and That's Enough' and 'In a Contemporary House' are short stories taken from her collection, *An Tubhir Nahwa al-Abad* 1981, (Taking Off into the Distance). They tell of the anxiety of young girls at not being considered fully human and of their resentment towards their fathers. 'In a Contemporary House' vividly evokes the suffocating confinement of home.

I Saw Her and That's Enough

1981

❀

She had jumped in fear . . . When she veiled her face, she veiled her inside . . .

Caverns of silence, sadness and darkness. Before her is a strange and desolate world of mystery . . . Spiders of silence, terror and fear wove it; steps of the past and present shaped it; she sent it screaming; a long suffering . . .

She collided into everything cruel . . . rocky . . . that doesn't shatter like a boulder . . .

The whole moon disappeared in her eyebrows, a shyness that never speaks . . .

Were it not for some touches like pieces of clouds wandering over her face . . . and her short black hair covering her temples like two hands holding a frame. The past and present scream from above the tip of her nose . . .

She was shivering . . . jumping in fright sometimes like a wild animal . . . and then quickly darting looks like arrows saying, 'What is happening to me?'

For a few minutes, she was still afraid . . . terrified, proud . . . and then a few moments passed, and she is looking for stability in what she sees and feels. She started to cry and said: 'At this moment, my age will be revealed to my observer. I present it willingly on this desk in front of me . . .

'How cruel it is for us to expose our age on the palm of our hand. It is painful because it arises out of fear and necessity and not out of solution in a moment of satisfaction.'

Each tear imprisoned in her eyes was a stick that whipped the past and the future.

She was anxious to gain a moment, how bitter is confession! How cruel is the confession of a father who is my father?

She was standing in front of the woman at the desk. A student . . . She had moved away from her family and became an exile, how difficult is exile . . . It is the time of separation even when one feels that one is in one's country and with one's own people . . .!

The one sitting behind the desk was the school director. *The happening*: a moment of fear, discovery, embarrassment and realisation . . .

'Madam: I am confessing my sin but . . . (oh, if you only knew).'

'You will not be spared the punishment as long as you do not say everything.'

'If only they knew that the female at school is a human . . .'

'Why aren't you talking?'

'Oh . . . Madam, if only you knew how aware I am that you are torn between your emotions and your responsibilities . . .'

'Why are you quiet, young girl?'

'Oh young girl . . . you are saying my girl . . . you are indeed a human madam, and I also, a human! . . .'

'My little girl, talk! Why did you do what you did?'

'I must be more courageous . . . The woman in front of me is of flesh and blood . . . there is no barrier between me and her . . . I must talk, be the first to say something . . .'

'I . . . I am . . . oh Mad . . . am . . .,' I stutter. And suddenly, 'Madam, did you talk to my father? Tell me, did you talk to him . . . did you???'

'I wonder what separates her from her father? There is mystery in her eyes . . . caverns of mystery . . . Loneliness and sadness. As if illusory spiders had woven threads of fear before her, and . . . I remember her coming to us as an orphan . . . She seems to have a father . . .'

'No, my little one . . . I have not yet talked to your father . . .'

She sobbed . . . and wept . . . the imprisoned tears started falling from her eyelids and . . . the trail of tears were a bridge between the girl's heart and that of the director . . .

Oh Madam, Oh . . .

I was standing waiting for the bus, not knowing that I was on the path of what will be . . . It was hard for me to wake up early in the morning . . .

Had I known that I would sacrifice half of my life standing at this moment . . . and all of it on your desk . . . I would have placed dozens of pillows on my head without moving . . . without braiding my hair . . . without decorating it with silky ribbons that take me to a paradise filled with flowers, perfume and songs of the nightingales . . .

The director sympathises with the student.

A piece of paper suddenly fell . . . The director reached out and held it up:

Father, Remember those spring days during which I was like a butterfly flitting happily and spreading the perfume of youth and joy? You used to embrace me, making my sister Lamis angry and my brother Alaa cry with jealousy . . . The adults including Ahmad used to complain, 'You are spoiling her, Daddy. She is greedy, stubborn and a trouble maker . . .' But Muhammad was the most reserved and moderate. He responded to their protests saying, 'Raha will grow up and be the song of the rain . . .' He liked al-Saib . . . and the Song of the Rain . . .

That damp evening your voice woke us up. You were arguing with my mother . . . It was a dreary night . . . portentous . . . Our hearts trembled. Our ribs stretched out fine, transparent, moist threads that hung on the mist and they had tongues and it seemed that they had voices.

Our beautiful evenings became filled with weeping . . . and weeping is a means . . . whenever desire emerges it gets stuck in our throats. Do you remember that evening . . . You were threatening my mother: 'I will divorce you . . . I am divorcing you . . .?!' Divorce . . . death . . . suicide . . . darkness . . . failure . . . isolation . . . loneliness . . . I catch my breath: Terror and fear, something vague, deep emerges out of the unknown and wraps itself around our necks . . .

In the morning we got up not having slept. The creaking of the door still scared us; you closed it forcefully, after carrying your luggage . . . we clung to you, desperately trying to stop you from leaving. We held on to your neck, to your clothes. Your neck became a strong elastic spring, but your clothes were unable to resist us . . .

You spat on the floor, part of your spit caught part of my hand, until today I have not dried it . . .

Can I dry your sin, Father?

The helpless woman was lying on the floor overwhelmed by sickness and your cruelty . . .

She was not from your family, nor from your country. She took her identity card and left . . .

On that day, both of you conspired to tear us apart . . .

Until today we are ignorant of the motives . . . You got used to letting us feel the separation and when it took place you conspired to tear us apart!

Alone, I was torn . . . It did not affect any of my brothers; because I was the light butterfly, you cut my wings, and so I fell to the earth, crashed into the mud and sin!

Neither of you was beside me . . . I did not then, and still do not know the reason . . . A few days passed . . .

That day I was reading a newspaper abandoned underneath a dirty chair. Mother was not at home. Lamis was stronger than me to confront . . .

I read the newspaper and a boarding school for orphans attracted my attention. It welcomed all who have neither father nor mother! I did not have either!

I went to it . . . I became one of the students. I know what it was to be an orphan. I had tasted its bitterness . . .

That day I forgot to carry with me, my father's identity card . . . It contained a list of names . . .

Abd-al Majid Abd-Allah	Employee Married
Maami Ahmad	Wife (from the Gulf)
Lamis	Daughter
Ahmad	Son
Fuad	Son
Muhammad	Son
Samir	Son
Raha	Daughter

It became the song of the orphanage!

The Gulf: it was my identity . . . its ocean was that gorgeous world that had begotten my mother, she ate its fishes, adorned herself with its pearls, pouring its love, its taste and eternal adoration into us.

Her heart was a pearl . . . Her eyes were two forests of palm trees! I have never forgotten this identity.

I tried to forget my father. I tried to forget you, since you had tried to forget me. My brothers, the oldest particularly, insisted on carrying my bag to school. At the door, Ahmad said to me, 'Don't forget that you are not an orphan!'

But Mohammed told me, 'Raha, you became an orphan before we died!'

In this house, Oh! father . . .

I felt dreams accumulating, then freezing into a dot on the palms of my hands . . .

I was condensed, concentrated and buried between my toes . . . My whole being, father, shrank and shrank becoming an illusion. Then I stopped.

Father, I still long for a time when I can embrace you and for another when I can sleep in the lap of the woman who is escaping from us . . .

Why did you desert me with the whirlwind, lost, living in darkness?!

Why weren't you a perfect model of two loving, kind parents?

You were heaven; but heaven was not on earth; no human is able

to enjoy it . . . Heaven is far from human conception; deeper than
surmise . . .

Father, I wish I could have carried your faults and hers . . . I
wish I could have been a sponge to erase the depths to gather the
remains of bitterness that had spilled on the earth and with which
you had nurtured my heart . . . and the earth . . . the word . . .
and . . . time . . .

Can I be stronger than sin? Stronger than darkness?
She decided one day to escape from the school to see her
mother . . . a hard hand extended to her shoulder and touched
her . . . the voice behind her said, 'Go back to the school' . . . Oh . . .
what . . . How . . . A vortex of confusion . . . Do you have a
solution? . . .'
No sooner did she utter a word than the words backed into her
mouth. In her eyes was a strong world of mystery . . . cares of
silence . . . sadness . . . darkness . . .
Her life was shrivelling . . . Her name was melting . . . Spiders
around her were weaving a fence protecting her from dissipa-
tion . . . words, meanings, pictures and signs accumulate . . . She
spits on the floor . . . she screams out in stubbornness and help-
lessness saying, 'Madam, do as you wish . . . I saw my mother and
that is enough . . .'

She had jumped in fear. During her escape, she had lifted the veil
from her face . . . she couldn't remove it from herself . . .
Your father will not know . . .
That is . . . whether he knows or not . . . half of his life is
shattered . . . one quarter of it . . . all of it . . . was sacrificed about
the rocks; the light of his eyes was crushed on the rocks, was
shattered on the rocks . . . his life is a stick whipping the past and
future . . . that burns . . . 'I appear to be more courageous . . .
No . . . my reality is not that . . . I fear him . . . I will melt if he
knows . . . I shall die if he knows . . . he will kill me if he knows . . .'
The phone rings; the director picks up the receiver. Pointing to
her, she says, 'Go, young woman, no one will know your secret.'
Raha walks . . .
'Hello . . .'
'This is Raha's Father . . . I am coming to see her . . .'
'Raha . . . you . . . her father is coming to her!!'
She froze on the spot.

Translated from the Arabic
by May Ibrahim and Miriam Cooke

In a Contemporary House

1981

❧

Everything around her was quiet . . .

The curtains are shiny, smooth . . . the walls velvety, the utensils and furniture crystal, glass and gold. The noise of the air conditioner rumbles protesting about continuous suffering . . .

'This cold is in my veins . . . turn it off . . .' She shivered from the cool . . . her extremities were like ice . . . her eyes protruded in their search for the shiny things around her . . .

It is night . . . I do not know . . .

Or is it day? Maybe . . .

It could be any time except that which I am able to know or clearly define . . .

In such an environment, she is unable to define clearly the time in which she now breathes . . . incapable even of knowing its secret . . . she became depressed.

She felt an overwhelming weight on her chest, on her throat, paralysing the movement of her breathing . . . rising with a pain that spreads to some parts of her head, then, falling to convulse her intestines . . . her extremities tremble . . .

What is this nausea . . . this boredom . . . this fatigue descending on my remains and paralysing me?

The curtains are shiny . . . with a crystal background . . . all the bright things around her smell of roses and they cannot move . . . the silence is dreadful . . .

She got up suddenly . . . some power travelled through her veins . . . where did it come from? How did it reach her? How did it control her nerves?

She opened the windows impatiently. She tore the curtains . . . she threw the crystals on the floor . . . with haste she took the glasses, one by one and threw them on the floor, and they broke . . . were shattered . . . around her, everything was nothing . . . inspiring murder . . .

Suddenly . . . the noise of the air conditioner stopped . . . its protesting rumbles disappeared . . . after she had extended her hands to it and stopped it . . .

The room began to warm up and was filled with fresh air . . .

The sun appeared at the corner of the window . . .

She heard noises coming from outside . . .

Some life was entering it . . . life started coming in with the sunlight . . .

She came forward violently shaking her head to get rid of the vestiges of darkness . . .

Translated from the Arabic
by May Ibrahim and Miriam Cooke

Wadida Wassef

(1926–)

Wadida Wassef writes: I was born in Alexandria. It was not the fantastic creation of Mr Durrell, but a sane and sober city dominated at the time by a powerful European community. I grew up speaking Arabic, French, and Italian. When and how I learned these languages I don't know – I must have picked them up from my father, mother, and the nurse, respectively. All three were *lingua franca* in our house. I learned English formally at school. As a child I was sent to a government school because, contrary to common practice for families like ours, my father insisted I should start my education by acquiring a solid foundation in Arabic which only a government school could provide. Although parochial and language schools offered superior education, they neglected to teach Arabic. Students of these schools were more familiar with the language, history, and culture of the countries to which these schools belonged than with their own. Father also believed that as a Copt, living in the midst of a Muslim majority, it would not hurt me to become acquainted with the religion and culture of the majority. So I also attended classes of Islamic religion where I learned the Quran.

Later I joined the American Mission College in Cairo. Besides academic knowledge, this college stressed moral and cultural training and it prepared girls for life in the home and community. For several generations the college graduated leaders in all fields of national life.

Between graduation from school and marriage I was allowed, as a concession, to while away the time in the Faculty of Arts Department of English. For a while after that I taught English language and literature, and European history at Al-Nasr Girls College, formerly the English Girls College, and I loved my profession.

In later years, after marriage, I worked in translation, on the side, mainly for the American Research Centre where I contributed to volumes of Egyptian short stories, drama, and contemporary Egyptian thought, edited by Dr Louis Awad for the University of California. For UNESCO I translated *The Cheapest Nights*, a collection of short stories by Dr Yussif Idris, a very prominent Egyptian writer. I am still busy with a variety of other translations.

I started to write in the 1970s when I went with my husband to Shabin al-Kom, a town in the Nile delta where he was appointed chairman of a large textile mill. Alone, and locked in a flat for days on end, with nowhere to go, and no one to talk to, there was ample time to brood and meditate on things past and present. Vague and erratic though they were, I started to put down my thoughts on paper. Slowly they were taking shape, and so it all began. I don't know how it will end.

In 'Hasan's Wives' the patriarch of a shanty-household avails himself of the Quranically allowed plural wives, constantly shuffling them through divorce and remarriage. Wadida Wassef observed this family from her house in the Rushdi quarter of Alexandria. On the road leading up to her house, across from the British Embassy, were huts like Hasan's which intrigued the author as a young girl. In this story she reveals with a certain humour how the wives, collectively and individually, managed to get revenge on their husband by using the *zar*. The story was written in English.

Hasan's Wives

1970

❦

In bringing up her children my mother was governed by a strict set of taboos, like belly dancing, or drinking straight from the tap (we had a filter in the pantry) or out of each other's tumblers. Eating pickles too was taboo. But the most serious of these offences was to listen whenever a quarrel broke out in the Hasan ménage.

Hasan was a bedouin who had settled in our neighbourhood long before any of us. Tired of his nomad existence, he arrived on the site one day, hot and bedraggled, on the back of his rickety donkey. His shrewd eyes travelled over the desolate grounds, and summing up what he saw, he decided this was as good a place as any in which to settle. So he alighted, tied his donkey to a pole, and built himself a shack out of sheets of tin and planks of wood rescued from rubbish dumps, which he surrounded with barbed wire. When, after a couple of years he found that the law was still ignorant of his presence there, he grew a little bolder and expanded the limits of his enclosure a few feet on all sides, then lay low and waited. Still nothing happened and he remained unmolested on his small domain. A little later he took a headlong plunge and spread out some more, this time a couple of hundred feet. Now he was master of a sizeable piece of land and all that remained to make his happiness complete, were documents to prove he was the legal owner. These he had no trouble acquiring in those halcyon days, and for any who showed doubt he would dig into the folds of his *gallabiya* and come up with an impressive collection of documents, wrapped up in filthy rags, all adorned with the state seal.

With time, Hasan thrived and his possessions increased. They came to include cows, donkeys, chickens, goats, and the four wives conceded by the laws of God, all of which he accommodated within his enclosure. But in his haste to make his status known to his neighbours, it had slipped Hasan's mind that God had laid one condition to the blessings of polygamy: no favouritism, with the sad result that Hasan found it hard to maintain a state of peace in his house, for fights amongst his wives became a routine.

It was not unusual for the placid serenity of the area to be shattered by the sound of fearful screeching coming from Hasan's shack. That was the signal that a conflagration was about to start,

and we would shoot upstairs to the roof which had the double
benefit of giving us a bird's-eye-view of what was about to unfold,
and of discouraging fat Badriya from clambering all the way up to
get us away in the event of a quarrel breaking out at Hasan's. But
most of the time she made it, panting and spluttering. She had an
expert trick by which she got the three of us locked simultaneously
in her two fat paws so that it was impossible to break loose. Then
she would go spluttering back downstairs dragging us behind with
the force of a powerful locomotive. On lucky days, a bout of
lumbago, on top of her corpulence, rendered the climb impossible,
and we would be left to enjoy a scene, unmatched to this day in
sheer exhilaration.

Because of the narrow space within the hut, Hasan's wives
preferred to fight out of doors where nothing impeded their
movements. So that after the preliminary sounds of alarm, an
enormous mass of female bodies, tightly coiled in a savage scuffle
was propelled into the courtyard. They struggled and fought, now
rolling in the dust, now standing upright, kicking and screaming,
while their myriad offspring, scampering to the rescue, would take
their positions behind their respective mothers, and lustily give
their support. The commotion never failed to attract gardeners,
suffragis, and hangers-on from the entire neighbourhood who
joined in as peace-makers. They'd throw themselves on the wri-
thing bundle and try to reason with it, only to emerge with their
garments torn, their teeth missing, and their bodies streaked with
the bloody traces of female claws. Black veils flew high in the air,
together with tufts of hair and odd bits of apparel, while the
terrified chickens hopped about, madly flapping their wings, and a
volley of invective reached the sky.

Now was the climax: an avalanche of obscenities which far from
making us recoil in horror thrilled us to the core. Dirty word upon
dirty word shot to high heaven with the sparkling brilliance of
fireworks. We stood, tingling in every nerve, taut and motionless,
straining hard to pick up the whole treasury of smutty epithets
Hasan's wives were lavishing on one another. All this rhetoric was
sustained by lewd and vulgar gesticulations which gave the scene its
final touch. In an instant Hasan's wives had made a shambles of
mother's belaboured efforts to mould us into 'nice children'.

Overjoyed to be shedding that cumbersome virtue, up to the ears
in the sin of disobedience, and utterly charmed by the bawdy
demonstrations of Hasan's harem, the moment was one of unmiti-
gated bliss.

However, like all stolen joys, it was too short. For at this point,
Hasan, armed with his green-lined umbrella, would pounce on his

women, hacking wildly, roaring threats of divorce. The horrified women would immediately draw apart in a temporary truce. For the mere thought of that possibility drew them instinctively together to form a unified front in the face of that menace to their very existence. Finding themselves bound now by ties of common interest, unable to shake off their belligerent mood, they immediately joined forces and turned the tide of their fury on poor Hasan, who thus unwittingly had made himself the target of a new assault from which he emerged much battered but none the wiser.

Over the years a sort of peaceful co-existence has been worked out, and Hasan and his chattel have come to be regarded as part of the landscape. He proved invaluable to the new generation, easing them into their classless epoch. I can see him now as I look across the road, unchanging and timeless as the rock of ages, squatting on his wooden bench by his gate. He is drawing contentedly on his *shishah*, devoutly reciting the ninety-nine sublime names of God over his amber beads, while the cow-dung fumes of his yard rise above the jasmin vapours of my lawn and blow softly away in the twilight with the blue smoke of his pipe.

With time, the district became one of the most elegant in Alexandria. Gradually Hasan found himself hemmed in by the ostentatious villas and gardens of a thriving bourgeoisie. Much though his presence in their midst offended his neighbours, none succeeded in ousting him. No bribe, no threat, no amount of reasoning would induce Hasan to leave. For nothing equalled the satisfaction he derived from rubbing shoulders with the elite. And, not feeling the least bit out of place, Hasan stayed on with his goats and cows and current set of wives, for those were constantly changed according to Hasan's inconstant heart and fluctuating finances. Nor was it possible to ignore Hasan, for on hot days a fetid stench emanating from his shack offended the genteel nostrils of his neighbours, and many a time was their daily siesta disturbed by the frequent and noisy brawls of his household. But against it all they were quite powerless. Today, Hasan with his donkey, and his green-lined umbrella can still be seen, heading a procession of goats, cows, water buffalos, and all four wives, on their way to pasture. Twice a day they thread their way through elegant cars and the pampered charges of a few remaining uniformed nannies, the goats stopping here and there to nibble at neatly trimmed hedges, absent-mindedly littering the road with their droppings.

None was more pleased with Hasan's continued presence than Nadira, Sami and I. For there was never a dull moment with them around. Their incessant activities brightened up those dreary afternoons before television, when we used to sit and watch them furtively, with our noses flattened into three round buttons against the window pane. Although we were always betrayed by the mess of fingerprints and the mist our breathing left behind, watching the Hasans was well worth the scolding. Anyhow, mother knew she was beaten in advance where it concerned the Hasans. The scolding was only a stern reminder that we had been disobedient and that 'Mummy was very angry'. That made no difference.

In spite of their disturbing inclination to fight, the noisy Hasans were rather a gay lot of people. Festivities never ceased in the intervals between their fights. Landmarks in their day to day life were duly observed by the punctilious Hasan in a manner to impress his rich neighbours and poor relations alike. Circumcisions, weddings, the seventh day after the birth of a child, and funerals, were never allowed to pass unobserved. Considering the range and extent of his family, these events were uninterrupted the year round, as were the festivities incumbent on them. The clash of the belly dancers' cymbals, or the more heady beat of drums frequently pierced the silence as it drifted over with the various odours from their shack, particularly that of cow-dung when it warmed to the sun. It meant the Hasans were holding a *zar*, a ritual ceremony intended for casting out devils. For each of Hasan's wives, it appeared, was possessed of a devil, evidently of the stubborn kind, for even now, I hear periodic celebrations. Obviously they haven't departed yet. We still have hours of frenetic dancing and eerie chants to the persistent beating of drums, that last through the day, and if necessary well into the night.

It was Sayyida's devil, the youngest and naturally the favourite of Hasan's wives, who was discovered first.

She had begun to complain of undefined ailments which only grew with Hasan's solicitude. She had dizzy spells; she had a pain in her heart too, she said, pointing to her belly. The pain in her feet was such that she couldn't stand up, she wailed to Hasan from where she reclined in the shady coolness of the sycamore tree. Alarmed, Hasan applied all the known remedies. Nothing worked. Finally, it became clear this was a case for Hajj Tawfiq. Besides being the local herbalist, Hajj Tawfiq was reputed to be a wizard in the matter of obscure ailments. He immediately diagnosed an evil spirit. Sayyida was possessed of a devil, not of the benign variety to be placated by prayer and fasting, but such as required the sacrifice of a three-horned bull, a lame nightingale, and a blind toad. A *zar* was imperative. Meanwhile, Hajj Tawfiq advised Hasan, Sayyida's devil must be appeased by conceding to his every wish. Hajj Tawfiq volunteered to interpret the *afrit*'s cryptic messages, which Sayyida

communicated to him every day. He was found to have a voracious
appetite for rare meats and a predilection for gold ornaments.
Soon Sayyida was gorging on delicacies, and fairly glittering with
gold trinkets. And every other day a *zar* would be on, full blast. For
hours they sang and danced and swayed hysterically to the mad
beat of drums. Faster and faster, louder and louder, until Sayyida,
by then in a trance under the spell of her *afrit* rose for her solo
performance, as the central figure in whose honour the revels were
held. Slowly at first, then gradually more quickly, she swayed
uncontrollably to and fro, backwards and forwards, this way and
that, until worn out by frenzy she collapsed on the floor, a limp and
exhausted heap.

Not to be outdone, Hasan's other wives soon developed *afrits* of
their own, just as tenacious and no less demanding than Sayyida's.
So with all those devils to be cast out, and the ceaseless weddings,
and births, and funerals in the family, life in the vicinity of Hasan
was one long uninterrupted chain of loud celebrations.

But the long-suffering Hasan, despite his living in style like his
well-to-do neighbours, was beginning to buckle under the strain of
a household constantly on the increase. For his foursome of wives
were in the habit of getting themselves pregnant. If not one then
the other. Chasing Hasan into their beds was an aim they pursued
with unflinching determination.

There was never a closed season. The resulting infant, conceived
out of spite, was irrefutable proof of its mother's appeal to Hasan.
Too benighted to know that science could be trusted to balance
concupiscence with income, he allowed his household to grow at a
staggering rate. So did the cost of its upkeep. Feeding all these
infants, in addition to their mothers with their incessant demands,
to say nothing of those of their *afrits*, Hasan was starting to fray. He
needed to supplement his income in some way. So his livestock was
quickly conscripted and from then on our eggs and milk and
chickens came from Hasan's.

One or another of his wives brought them round. Subhiya
brought the milk everyday. She was wife number one and the least
attractive. It must be admitted to Hasan's credit that each successive wife was an improvement on her predecessor. To say that
Subhiya was the least attractive is, in fact, an understatement.
Actually, in form and substance she was all beef. Haunches and
haunches. Enormously fat, her skin was the colour of mud. A
strong odour of cow-dung clung stubbornly to the air wherever she
happened to be. Anyone who doubted had only to look at Subhiya
to recognise that a mother's surroundings had a powerful impact
on the foetus from the moment it was conceived. From too much

proximity to her cattle Subhiya's mother had their image printed on her subconscious, like a film negative, which in turn stamped itself on poor Subhiya while yet in the womb.

Her brains were no brighter than her looks. They sparkled when she tried to cheat on the measure. The milk came in a large tin urn-like container to which a large tin tumbler was chained. Twice the content of the tumbler equalled one *oke*, our daily ration of milk. The servants were instructed not to turn their backs on Subhiya while she poured. If mother happened to be around she took the extra precaution of looking for yellow bubbles floating on the surface, which meant Subhiya was diluting buffalo milk with cow milk, and buffalo milk was known to have more food value. There would follow a long harangue when Subhiya swore by the light of her eyes, and by all her dead relatives, and by God and the Prophet, while mother threatened to take her custom elsewhere. It all led to nothing. Subhiya continued to cheat when she could, and mother to shut one eye. And so it went on for twenty-five years, until we moved away. But cow or buffalo, it was good milk that had the flavour of milk which suffered no chemical detours before reaching us.

Wives two and three, Khadija and Amina, between them, brought the chickens, alive, in a large cage made of palm reeds, which they hauled on their heads alternately. We could hear them coming long before they appeared in the garden. Their wretched charges, squeezed in a cage intended to contain half their number, crazed by their airborne journey, tossing from Amina's head to Khadija's while their feet and their wings and their beaks got caught on one another, raised an infernal cackle which could be heard miles before they appeared. It did not stop even at their journey's end when they were finally deposited at mother's feet where she stood waiting for them in the back garden.

That was only the start of their ordeal. Abdallah, the cook, was called and he arrived with the big kitchen knife. With his hands on his hips and a look of contempt in greeting to Amina and Khadija, he would order them to open the cage and show him what they had. Then the examination began. Amina and Khadija, working in collaboration got one bird out at a time, twined its wings behind its back and proudly held it up for Abdallah to inspect. He poked a sceptical finger into the flesh, then felt the thickness of the breast, and then brushed the feathers the wrong way, to check for parasites. Every chicken we bought was reviewed in this manner. Then mother took over because at this point it was time to discuss the price. She generally took the line that those were miserable birds and that she was doing Amina and Khadija a favour by even consenting to look at them. Amina and Khadija replied in unison that if mother were to search the whole city she would never find fowls to match theirs. Those were not ordinary chickens they were selling. They were home grown. Wait till she got them on her table, roasted and sizzling, she will want to eat her fingers with them, and she will call blessings on Amina and Khadija with every morsel. By then they will have met half-way and concluded the deal.

The abomination that followed, barbarous beyond words, held us spellbound.

Abdallah handed the knife to Amina who rolled up her sleeves, while Khadija held the bird by the wings with one hand and folded the neck well back with the other for Amina to cut its throat in the name of God the Merciful, the Compassionate, according to the *Sharia*. Then she would fling the bird over her shoulder and reach for the next one. The unhappy creature gave out a strangled croak and staggered drunkenly around for a minute or two before it collapsed to the ground making a final appeal to life by a feeble flap of the wings every few seconds, which grew weaker and weaker until at last it was still. Rivers of blood flowed into the mud of the flower-beds. We stood there and watched that gory scene in a trance, drawn by the irresistible fascination of the horrible, without a flicker of revulsion.

The lighter chores were of course the privilege of the spoiled and pampered favourite, very aptly called Sayyida, which in Arabic means 'lady'. The meaning of her name, from long association, seems to have rubbed off on her person, the way she conducted herself. She would come tripping up the kitchen steps with the hem of her long gown caught between her teeth, ostensibly to keep her from stumbling but in reality to gratify the male staff with a glimpse of her ankles.

From the moment she appeared there would be as much traffic in the kitchen as in a public square. Abduh who goes upstairs suddenly remembers he has forgotten the duster and comes down to fetch it taking all day about it. Uthman who goes downstairs decides it is time for the master's coffee and takes forever making the water boil on a very low flame. The gardener who never brings the flowers unless he is repeatedly reminded, barges in with an armful and wiggling his eyebrows, throws voluble good mornings right and left, to Abduh and Uthman and 'the lovely ones'. Sayyida who was fully aware of what she was doing would keep her eyes bashfully averted while the devil looked out from beneath her drooping eyelids, heavily lined with kohl.

As for Abdallah, Sayyida could have been another frying pan for all he reacted to her presence. Neither her ankles, nor her alluring backside she so carefully placed in evidence, nor her languid looks and many sighs had the slightest effect on him. He glowered and muttered, his eyes darting fire, and his black stone face twisted into an expression of pure disgust.

With the sound of mother's footsteps the whole lot vanished in thin air. The duster was never found, and the coffee pot was left standing on the stove. The gardener after scampering out of sight would innocently put in a second appearance with the flowers, pretending he had just arrived.

There was no haggling over the eggs. Seven for two piasters, and mother usually bought the maximum divisible by seven. The remaining odd ones Saida left as a gift, and back she would trot to Hasan's fond embraces, and the plotting of her rival wives, and the merry-go-round of celebrations and brawls and reciprocated beatings when they all got caught in their vital struggle for survival.

Written in English

Nadia Guendouz

(c. 1940–)

Nadia Guendouz was born in Algeria, and witnessed the 1954–62 Algerian War of Independence from the French. It was the first war in which women's participation was publicly acknowledged. However, two years after the war, people were already forgetting military women. In 1968, she published *Amal* (Hope), an anthology of poetry. In 1974, she published her second anthology with the title *La Corde*. This is an angry collection that accuses Algerian society of turning its back on its women: 'I said shit to this society. It's hard to be a woman in Algeria.'

This poem from *Hope* was written on 1 May 1963 on the occasion of the first anniversary of Independence. The following anonymous contribution by a woman to *Liberation*, 18 October 1978, amplifies Guendouz's distress: 'I believe that here in Algeria many suffer from loneliness. There is a kind of iron curtain between men and women and between the generations . . . The celebrated notion of respect eliminates all possibility of a spontaneous relationship. Everyone is isolated, everyone waits. What for? No one knows. But waiting we suffocate. I'm suffocating. I feel completely depressed because I feel that I can't control the present because there are so many blocks . . . This famous solidarity of which we were so proud during the war is far away. Today, we – men and women – are prisoners of our sexual misery, of our prejudices.'

People

1963

❀

All I asked for was
A hug
A piece of bread
All these people
Are throwing me to the dogs . . .
Bread hug
I steal them
I feel guilty
To eat to love . . .
I steal guilt
I steal the right to live
I steal the right to love
I rape your freedom
Suffocating.

I saw the image for which
Until my death I shall struggle
An Algerian man, an Algerian woman
Hand in raised hand
Raised toward pride and liberty . . .
Yes!
So bring your sister
Yours, and not your neighbour's
And take her hand
Tomorrow is our May the First
Teach her to read
If she does not know how
Guide her hand
Next May the First
She'll write
She'll work
Algeria needs her
As much as it needs you.

Translated from the French
by Miriam Cooke

Marie-Aimée Helie-Lucas

(1939–)

Marie-Aimée Helie-Lucas was born in Algiers. In her own words, she claims descent 'from a lineage of feminists: grandmother, mother and maternal aunt were independent, self-sufficient working women', and her eldest daughter, Amina, is a feminist historian. Marie-Aimée Helie-Lucas was active during and after the national liberation struggle. Trained as a sociologist and social anthropologist, she taught for twelve years at the University of Algiers. She was a founding member of AAWORD, the Association of African Women for Research on Development. From 1983 to 1984, she was a research fellow at the Institute of Social Studies, Department of Women's Studies at the Hague, Holland. In 1984, she set up an Action Committee which became the Network of Women Living Under Muslim Laws. The Network actively assists Muslim women oppressed in the name of Muslim law.

This paper articulates a feminist awareness emerging from participation in and reflection on the national liberation struggle. Appearing a quarter of a century after Algerian independence, the paper deconstructs the national myth of women's militarisation and shows how the projects of socialism, nationalism and religion became 'tools for the elaboration of an anti-women state policy'. She warns against the dangers of silence.

This paper was presented to the International Symposium on Women and the Military System at Siunto Baths, Finland in 1987. Earlier versions of this paper were produced by the Peace Movement in Finland and Wheatsheaf Books of Brighton, England.

Women, Nationalism and Religion in the Algerian Liberation Struggle

1987

☙

The image that the outside world has formed of women in the Algerian liberation struggle is shaped by Frantz Fanon's books, a very widely distributed film called *The Battle of Algiers* and the true story of a few national heroines. From these sources, the Algerian woman appears as a freedom fighter who carried arms against French colonialism and its army, a 'terrorist' who planted bombs in the city during the Battle of Algiers, who was equal to men in the struggle and who shared decision-making both at the political and at the military levels.

These myths hardly match personal experience. They are now also challenged by Djamila Amrane, a freedom fighter from 1957 to 1962. Hers is the only serious study produced on women in the struggle since independence. As a registered veteran, she was allowed access to the Ministry of Veterans archives for her research.[1]

From her study one can question who was registered as a veteran by the Ministry. The request for registration had to be supported by a documented, stamped file of extensive testimonies. This cumbersome bureaucratic procedure made it difficult for poor and illiterate people to register. Amrane emphasises the added difficulty for peasant women who were not only illiterate but also sometimes veiled and secluded. Registration procured advantages: jobs, promotion, retirement benefits, etc. Hence, it did not benefit women, since only 2.1 per cent were employed. Few registered. Those who did represent only 3.25 per cent of the total number of veterans. Official agencies did not encourage women to register and there was a universal desire immediately after independence to have women back in the home. Hence statistical data derived from the archives of the Ministry of Veterans are not indicative of the number of women who participated in the Independence struggle.

From these statistics, one can also ask who is a fighter, a veteran? Most of the fighting took place in rural areas, little in the cities. The peasants helped the armed fighters in numerous ways: guiding, hiding, feeding, carrying messages, buying arms, observing the French army moves, taking over the arms of killed fighters.

Whereas a line can be drawn between fighter and civilian in the city, it is not so easily done in the country. Yet gender distinctions persisted. If a man carried food to the armed fighters at great personal risk, he was called a 'fighter'. A woman doing the same was called a 'helper'. If a man risked his life to hide armed fighters or wanted political leaders, he was called a 'fighter'. A woman doing the same was simply performing the female task of 'nurturing'. Nor was she considered a fighter when she collected fuel or food for the fighters, or carried their guns, or guided them through the mountains. She was merely helping the men. Only the French army acknowledged her action by imprisoning and torturing her in concentration camps and killing her. This explains why even fewer women are registered as veterans in the country. The official data is therefore even more biased and not representative of the reality, in which, in these types of guerrilla liberation struggles, the whole population is involved, if not by will, by force. Hence we can consider that most peasant women were involved in the Algerian revolution.

Out of 10,949 registered women 9,194 were designated as 'civilians' and 1,755 as 'military'. This means that 81 per cent worked for the Civil Organisation of the National Liberation Front (OCFLN) supporting guerrilla and urban terrorism: 19 per cent were part of the army and worked in the bush, 78 per cent of the women worked in the countryside, and 20 per cent in the cities. This corresponds to the male ratio. One out of five women were jailed, tortured or killed. They were from all age groups, from under twenty to over fifty, though 41.7 per cent were between thirty-one and fifty, all of the latter were married and mothers. In the civilian branch (OCFLN) 47.3 per cent were between thirty-one and fifty. These figures show the overall participation of women, their heavy repression and the involvement of mature women and mothers.

Amrane's study details women's civilian and military tasks. They were:

1. Supervision of hiding places and food collect (63 per cent in the civilian branch; 2.9 per cent in the military, i.e. only six women performed such tasks in the military.) Amrane remarks that several women worked together and that only one (the leader) was allowed to register as a veteran.
2. Liaison and guides (22.1 per cent civilian, none in military out of a total of 677 women).
3. Collection of funds and medicine and ammunition (9.3 per cent in civilian, i.e. 286 women, none in military).

4. Nursing (1.8 per cent in civilian, i.e. 56 women, 49.3 per cent in military, i.e. 101 women).
5. Cooking and washing (none in civilian, 44.4 per cent in military, i.e. 91 women).
6. Terrorists (2.1 per cent in civilian, i.e. 65 women, none in military).
7. Tailoring (0.6 per cent in civilian, i.e. 19 women, 1 in military).
8. Secretarial (0.7 per cent in civilian, i.e. 5 women, 0.4 per cent in military, i.e. 3 women).
9. Political commissaries (none in civilian, 1 per cent in military, i.e. 2 women).
10. Armed fighters (none in civilian, 0.5 per cent in military, i.e. 1 woman).

Although we know that many more women were in the struggle, these biased figures still give a fair idea of the fact that even in the hardest times of the struggle, women were oppressed, confined to tasks that would not disturb the social order in the future. Although these tasks were absolutely essential, they should not have absorbed all female energy. One woman bore arms, none was in a decision-making position! Sixty-five dealt with bombs in the urban sectors (probably carrying spare parts) and two political commissaires!

So much for Fanon's and others' myth of the Algerian woman liberated along with her country. These liberated women were in the kitchen, they were sewing clothes (or, flags?), carrying parcels, typing. Nevertheless, since there was 'no humble task in the revolution' we did not dispute the roles we had. It would have been mean to question the priority of liberating the country, since independence would surely bring an end to discrimination against women. What makes me angrier in retrospect is not women's confinement but the brainwashing that did not allow us young women even to think of questioning. What makes me angrier still is to witness the replication of this situation in other struggles for independence. It angers me to see women covering the misbehaviour of their fellow men and hiding, in the name of national solidarity and identity, crimes which will be perpetuated after independence.

This is the real harm which comes with liberation struggles. The overall task of women during liberation is seen as symbolic. Faced with colonisation the people have to build a national identity based on their own values, traditions, religion, language and culture. Women bear the heavy burden of safeguarding this threatened identity. And this burden exacts its price.

Probably most of the women present at this symposium take for granted that they belong to a country or a nation which does not have to prove its existence. For them, the concept of nation can be transcended and criticised. This is not true for Algeria nor for other decolonised or still colonised countries at war with imperialism. For us it is much more difficult to criticise the nation, and even the State which claims to represent the Nation.

One of the earliest slogans of nationalism in Algeria was promoted by the *ulama*, 'Arabic is our language. Islam is our religion. Algeria is our country.' Women were supposed to raise sons in the faith and preserve traditional moral standards and to teach the language of the forefathers.[2]

Women should be bound by tradition, while men had some access to modernity. Yet, it is now commonplace that tradition serves the purposes of those in power. Tradition is seen as ahistorical and immutable, modernity draws from the wealthy West – whatever that means.

Let us now discuss two examples of traditions as symbols of national identity during the Algerian struggle. The first is the veil, the second tobacco and alcohol.

Although there is no doubt that veiling women is a measure for control and oppression, it became for a time a symbol of national resistance to the French. During the war, French officials had insisted that Algerian women should be freed from the oppression of the veil. French army trucks had transported village women to urban areas. There these women were forced to unveil publicly thereby proving their renunciation of outworn traditions. Both Algerian men and women resented this symbolic public rape. In addition to its symbolic role, the veil was supposed to have a practical function. Fanon praised the revolutionary virtue of the veil – it allowed urban women freedom fighters to escape the control of the French army. They could hide their guns under their veils and travel incognito for underground purposes. How, therefore, could we take up the issue of the veil as oppressive to women without betraying both the *nation* and the *revolution*? Many young women, even those brought up in liberal families, chose to don the veil as a demonstration of their belonging to the oppressed Algerian people – in their lives and in their symbolic existence. The FLN (the National Liberation Front) encouraged such an attitude that emphasised women's modesty and could also be labelled 'fighting for the Cause'. More recently, we have seen another such example in Iran.

It is important to view this sexist program as part of another which denies the individual control over private matters. At the time of the Battle of Algiers, the FLN engaged in a campaign against tobacco and alcohol which they branded anti-revolutionary. Use of either could lead to a death sentence, or at least to the cutting off of the culprit's nose! The reasoning was that all Algerians were supposed to be Muslims, Islam forbids the consumption of tobacco and alcohol, those who consume are not true believers, and infidels are allies of colonialism. Similarly, the Ramadan fast became symbolic for Algerian identity, and it was universally enforced. Slowly and surely, the entwining of concepts as heterogeneous as nation, religion and ethnicity began to shape the future of independent Algeria.

I feel the need to remind us all that we women, we non-religious beings, we internationalists, did not raise our voices – it would have been difficult and dangerous – or our consciousness. We did not recognise the implications of such ideological confusion. We, too, were afraid to betray the people, the revolution and the nation. At no point did we see that a power structure, predicated on the control of private life and of women, was being built on our mental confusion. Obedience, morality and conformity were necessary to the revolution. In a struggle where secrecy is the basis for action, one cannot question the decisions of the comrades in charge. This leads to blind obedience. In a struggle that demanded anonymity, militants had to conform, to wear traditional clothes, even the veil. Soon the morality, particularly sexual, of the militants was controlled. Women were the first to be affected.

During this crucial period, women were assigned a place in society which could not be challenged without questioning both the past (as tradition) and the future (as revolution).

Immediately after independence, Algerian leaders evolved a discourse about Algeria which increasingly retreated from the lived experiences of the Algerian people. We used to elaborate on the discourse, and the discourse on the discourse became our reality. We talked endlessly of Algerian socialism, even though there was no attempted socialism.[3] State capitalism was in transition to private capitalism because there was no private, indigenous capital to be invested at the time of independence.[4] We talked about Algerian models of self-management, while self-management in industry was being converted into state-owned industries less than one year after independence, and self-managed farms were being converted into state-owned farms soon thereafter. We talked about democratic institutions while the police state and its army were daily gaining in strength. We denied the political use of religion and the growth of Islamic groups later to become powerful fundamentalists, since the socialism that was proclaimed shielded us from such evils. And of course we congratulated ourselves on the freedom that women had gained during the struggle. We were inside the myth talking about the myth.

In fact, what started during the war of liberation continued to unfold. Under the Constitution, as long as it conformed with the *Sharia*, women were equal to men. Later we were to learn what this meant. Minimum marriage age for girls was fixed at eighteen years, but the law was not enforced. Forces marriages still took place, sometimes followed by suicide. Women were beaten and secluded by their male relatives and they had no recourse.[5] Education for girls was compulsory, but there were not enough schools nor will there ever be enough schools for girls. Women's employment was legal, but there were no jobs, nor will there ever be enough jobs for women. Women could legally walk in the streets, but the men and the police harassed them: what was an honest woman doing outside her home? When men started to beat women in the streets, no one came to their rescue for fear of being questioned by the police: 'You sided with her. Do you know her? What were you doing there?' In the very summer of independence, the FLN army patrolled the streets of the capital, arresting men and women who were walking together in groups: 'Who is married to whom here? This one. Is she someone's sister or wife?' A valid marriage certificate had to be produced. People retreated into their homes in fear of the authorities and of denunciation by neighbours. More women veiled. We were free to be ourselves . . . but, beware of foreign ideologies. Ramadan was observed – police locked up those who did not fast. Hypocrisy grew as neighbours, colleagues, friends and even family members became informants: 'Mother must not know that I am not fasting'! 'Officially' people did not drink alcohol, or smoke in the presence of their fathers. A law was passed – and intermittently enforced – forbidding Algerians from buying alcohol. Those who denounced this state of affairs were persecuted by the authorities as traitors. We developed a split personality.

It is important to stress the role of what was officially called 'specific socialism' in the context of decreasing political liberties and growing religiosity that disadvantaged women in particular. Why specific? This differentiated it from 'scientific socialism', which was atheism, and it included Islam. Another trick by those in power to delude those who had given so much for national independence.

We were already silenced by fears of accusations of betrayal and by the nationalist myth. But this socialist label was the most effective silencer. We could not oppose the politics of this socialist

AWARENESS Marie-Aimée Helie-Lucas 111

state without opposing socialism. Because the people were in power, we could not oppose the regime without being anti-people. This rhetoric successfully silenced the left in most East European countries also.

It took years to dare to become a dissident. We knew that speaking out could be used by the right both in and outside Algeria to undermine socialist ideas that promised justice and equality. As long as we remained separate from the international left, from other dissident socialists, we were riddled with guilt.

Nationalism, socialism and religion were used as tools for the elaboration of anti-women state policy. At independence, Algeria was still under that old nationalist French law of 1920 which forbade not only the use but also all knowledge of contraception. Like other laws this one could not be immediately replaced, so there was 'tacit prorogation'. We women hoped that after independence we would have access to some means of contraception. But many men died during the struggle and the state policy was to replace them. Moreover, the concept of patriotic motherhood was still in force. Fortunately, if I may say so, the United States was at that time trying to enforce a brutal policy of birth control in the third world which culminated with their attempt to put pressure on governments to adopt their world plan, the 'fertility target', at the World Conference on Population at Bucharest.

Algeria as the champion of the liberation of Africa, as the champion of socialism, could not accept such a policy. As we all know population policies are not *the* way to develop. Could we women disapprove of that? Could we socialists not support the international policy of our government? No. We supported its views and did not protest when the natalist law was not changed. Although we managed to get statements from the highest Islamic authorities stating that contraceptive practices were not forbidden by religion, nothing was to change for a whole decade.

The anti-imperialist stand on birth policy suited the needs of those in power. Women had to pay a high price. In about ten years, the average number of children per woman was 7.9. The number of pregnancies ranged from fourteen to around twenty-one. We do not know about illegal abortions or maternal death. The population growth reached 3.5 per cent – one of the highest in the world. Within ten years a socialist bureaucracy became a conventional capitalism with the ruling classes nervous of the lumpen proletariat. Suddenly, birth control was legalised, contraception clinics were opened and their numbers increased rapidly. Therapeutic abortion was legalised. Population growth came down to 3.2 per cent within a few years. In January 1981, the law of finances suddenly penalised large families: the more the children, the higher the taxes. Women, however, had no say. Reproduction was in the hands of the state.

Although the Constitution guarantees equality, the Family Code is closer to the *Sharia*. From 1963, three projects were drafted: one under Ben Bella, the first president of Algeria, two under Boumedienne, the second president. Each project canonised women's inferiority and subjection to the authority of a man who had legal tutelage over her. In 1981, under President Chadili, a new, secret project was drafted. Ministers and deputees were allowed to read, though not to keep, a copy of the project during a special session. We never heard that any of them protested. Some women succeeded in getting hold of a copy. They demonstrated in the streets for the first time since independence. They stopped a law, labelled Quranic, which would have forbidden women the right to choice in marriage, to divorce, to work without permission from a male guardian, to a rightful share in inheritance. However, in May 1984, without warning or discussion, a family code, reproducing this fourth project with the exception of the right to work, was finally passed.

It is now a legal fact that women have lost many rights which were guaranteed by the Constitution on the grounds that these rights were anti-Islamic. Fundamentalist Muslims, known in Algeria as Muslim Brothers, are coming to the fore throughout the Arab world. In Algeria, the number of mosques has increased so that each housing block, each school and each university has at least one huge prayer room. These improvised mosques collect large numbers of young men who rule their female relatives according to the prescriptions of their leaders. Also, ministers of justice in the Arab world and in South Asia meet in attempts to regularise family codes in a way that is even more restrictive to women. One of the most striking elements of fundamentalist philosophy is a nationalism expressed as a 'going back to tradition', especially insofar as this relates to women, in the face of western imperialism. Muslims who believe that Islam mandates equality see no contradiction in the inequalities that Islamic laws force on women. They also claim that Islam demands of each believer to be fair to his women, and yet polygamy and repudiation are now legal in socialist Algeria.

During wars of liberation women are not to protest about women's rights. Nor are they allowed to before and after. It is never the right moment. Defending women's rights 'now' – this now being any historical moment – is always a betrayal of the people, the nation, the revolution, religion, national identity, cultural roots . . . Leftist Algerian men are the first to accuse us of betrayal, of adhering to 'imported ideologies', of Westernism. They use the same terminology that our government uses against the left at large. We are caught between two legitimacies: belonging to our people or identifying with other oppressed women.

It is difficult to persist in total isolation in denouncing regression in terms of the woman question on the part of so many once-revolutionary countries. We are prevented from speaking for women, from thinking, from dreaming. We are not even aware of the differences between one Muslim country and another. Let Muslim women step out of their national ghettos. Let them see that the clitoridectomy practised in Africa is unthinkable in Asia, that the veil worn in Arab countries is absent in sub-Saharan Africa, that none of these practices are based on religious precepts, but that religion everywhere backs such practices whenever they allow for greater control over women.

Let us dream of secular states. Let us dream of the separation of religion and state. Let us dream of the end of using nationalism to further oppress the already oppressed.

When I was in Pakistan recently, I heard comments about Iranian women in exile. Their detractors said details of their oppression should not be voiced in the West lest this be used as ammunition against the Iranian people, Muslim countries and Islam. But who are the Iranians? Are they those in power? Or, those who are oppressed? Were the Germans who denounced Hitler during the Second World War anti-German or anti-Nazi? Whom does silence benefit?

In Algeria, many, including myself, kept silent for a whole decade after independence. We gave those in power the time to strengthen and organise and to enforce discriminatory laws against women. Even now Algerian feminists are trying to analyse their oppression from within the Algerian context alone. They refuse to acknowledge the international aspect for fear of being accused of betrayal. And yet the same thing is happening throughout the Islamic world. In India, Muslim fundamentalists have persuaded Muslim women activists to stop their campaigns against the Muslim Personal Law in the face of Hindu fundamentalist riots and massacres. They claim that these campaigns may be used 'against the community'. Women must, therefore, suffer discrimination both from dominant Hindus and from their own Muslim com-munity.

We have everything to gain by being truly internationalist. We must exchange information and support one another. We must create such solidarity so that we will be able to retain control over our protest.

Recently we set up the Network of Women Living under Muslim Laws. Women and women's groups from seventeen countries or communities now communicate with each other through the Network, ask for documentation, compare so-called Muslim laws in different countries, send appeals for solidarity, inform each other about their strategies in very practical terms, for example, how to write marriage contracts. Through the Network we have learnt of projects of unification of family codes, both in Arab countries and in South Asia. We are learning how young fundamentalists are trained. We have been informed about progressive interpretations of Islam from the times of the Prophet until today, and about what happened to the courageous pioneers, both men and women, who spoke of an egalitarian interpretation of religion.

We have realised in concrete terms that most of our regimes leave no room for agnosticism or atheism and that religion is forced down our throats because of the constant ideological confusion between religion, culture and nationality. We must work towards a clear-cut definition of these concepts. We are supporting each other from within and are decrying discriminatory situations throughout the Islamic world. We are leaving less and less ground for nationalist justifications for silence. Internationalism must prevail over nationalism.

NOTES

1 Djamila Amrane, *La Femme Algérienne et la Guerre de Libération Nationale (1954–62)*, Actes du Colloque d'Oran, 1980.

2 We will not discuss here the legitimacy of Arabic in a country where the dominant ethnics are Berber and speak Berber languages.

3 Damien Helie, *L'Autogestion Industrielle*, thesis, Paris, 1967. (Socialism was simply a good recipe for the primitive accumulation of capital.)

4 Fadila Mrabet, *Les Algériennes*, Paris, Maspero, 1965; *La Femme Algérienne*, Paris, Maspero, 1967.

5 Tahar Benhourya, *Economie de l'Algérie*, Paris, Maspero, 1980.

Daisy al-Amir

(1935–)

Daisy al-Amir was born in Basra, Iraq. She earned her BA from the Teachers' Training College of Baghdad. In 1963, she went to Cambridge, England where she hoped to write a doctoral thesis on Arabic literature under the guidance of the orientalist A J Arberry. However, her father refused to pay the tuition. On her return to Iraq, she stopped in Lebanon. She got a job in the Iraqi embassy in Beirut as a secretary, and later as Assistant Press Attaché. When war broke out in Lebanon in 1975, she was appointed director of the Iraqi Cultural Centre. She returned to Iraq after the Israeli invasion of Lebanon in 1982. Her first collection of short stories, *Al-Balad al-Baid Alladhi Tuhibbuhu* (The Distant Country that You Love), appeared in 1964. In 1969, she published *Thumma Taudu al-Mawja* (Then the Wave Returns), a collection of short stories that she dedicated to the Palestinian woman writer Samira Azzam. Daisy al-Amir is a Beirut Decentrist and she has published two short story collections on the Lebanese Civil War: *Fi Dawwamat al-Hubb wa al-Karahiya*, (In the Vortex of Love and Hate, 1979) and *Wuud li-al-bay* (Promises for Sale, 1981).

'The Eyes in the Mirrors' was published in the *Promises for Sale* collection. It describes the anguish of a professional woman compelled to eat alone in a dining room full of men.

The Eyes in the Mirror

1981

❦

I called the hotel's headwaiter to send dinner up to my room. He was silent, before saying that the hotel administration did not allow food to be eaten in the rooms. Didn't allow! That's the first time I've ever heard that food is forbidden in rooms.

Whenever I'm alone in a restaurant, I eat breakfast early and in a hurry and never feel relaxed. How would I feel at dinner?

However, I had to obey the orders. Would I be able to sit in the corner I had chosen for myself? I convinced myself that it was nothing, and hunger insisted, so I had to obey its demands.

Nine p.m. and the hotel restaurant was packed . . . packed with men. I looked at all the tables and could not see a single woman. Were hotels created for men? I looked for a remote table that was tucked away in a corner without lights. I sat down and turned my back on the dining hall. Suddenly I saw a group of men around me. How did they manage to surround me? A sea of eyes staring at me. I raised my eyes and saw mirrors covering the restaurant walls. The restaurant grew and the number of men increased and the staring became more intense as they speculated about this strange bird.

A woman in a hotel restaurant dining alone? What is this crime? What is this sin?

The hotel administration does not allow food to be eaten in the rooms, so what crime had I committed to be obeying their orders?

I thought about leaving the dining room before the waiter came. The staring eyes made me forget my hunger, but the waiter's arrival reminded me of my growling stomach. I took the first dish that he recommended. It was crucial that the food come quickly, that I eat it quickly and leave the restaurant quickly.

But I had a long wait. The minutes refused to pass, my watch refused to move. The clock hanging on the wall disappointed me, it kept up with my watch which I had hoped was out of order. I stared at the ground. I guessed the number of colours there were in the carpet, the kind of designs, I even began to count the number of knots. When I looked up toward the kitchen door I did not see the waiter but I saw the eyes that had increased in number and intensity. I shrank back into myself and looked for something else that I might count.

I wished that the waiter would bring my order before anyone else's. I wished that I were not hungry and could just escape to my room.

Suddenly the dining hall was filled with an uproar, voices and loud music bearing down from loud speakers and scattering noise in all directions.

At home there was silence, a beautiful silence to which I listened with pleasure. I put my hands over my ears and imagined myself there but the mirrors surrounding me assured me that dreams are useless.

I am alone in a hotel and curious eyes are staring at me with strange doubts. I wished that I were a snail carrying its home on its back, a home into which it can enter whenever it wants and then close the doors behind it.

I wished that the staring eyes knew who I was. I wished that I could talk to them to tell them that I had come here to do a job and that I was shy.

My clothes are modest . . . I am not beautiful . . . I am not lost . . . I am not a refugee. Remove your accusing glances. What is my sin? To be the only woman in a hotel restaurant teeming with men?

Is hunger a disgrace? Again I looked up toward the door leading to the kitchen.

He had not yet come out. I fixed my eyes on the door. Finally the shadow emerged carrying a tray piled high with food and drink and placed it on another table and then retraced its steps.

I returned to the carpet to consider its colours, designs and knots and . . . and . . . who will give me a vanishing cap? Now I knew why that fairytale had been invented. Had the inventor been in something like my situation or was he perhaps a sinner?

Criminals want to vanish. I am not a sinner. I swear by all that is holy that my stomach knotted in hunger is the cause and that I shall pay the restaurant price and that I will have won the price by the sweat of my brow. I am a good citizen and I . . . and I . . . What's the use of telling all this to myself. What if I were to stand up and shout this all out? Everyone would laugh and think I was crazy to be answering questions that had not been asked. But the eyes that filled the mirrors asked a thousand questions so how should I answer?

How should I pull myself together while sitting on a chair at a table in a hotel restaurant? How could I hide these facts? Whenever I looked up I saw herds of eyes. How could I remove their stabbing? How could I remove the mirrors from the walls? How could I stop the hunger pangs? A thousand hows, so how could I have no answer . . .

I went on waiting and counting the colours, designs and knots of the carpet. Then . . . then and with a voluntary action I stood up, ordered my stomach to stop demanding and walked deliberately, head high and looking forward. Before reaching the door I saw the waiter carrying a tray of food.

I didn't look at the contents nor at any of the tables.

I turned the key in the lock of my door and then locked it behind me. Then I filled my stomach that was burning with rage and hunger with cups of water. Tomorrow the sun will rise and I shall have breakfast early before the restaurant is teeming with curious eyes and then I'll escape to the conference hall.

There they know who I am. There . . . there I am a model woman explaining and trying to solve their problems. Yes, I deal with women's problems, take care of their circumstances and help them overcome their obstacles. So who will solve my problem of eating dinner in a hotel restaurant whose walls are filled with eyes?

Translated from the Arabic
by Miriam Cooke

Noha Radwan

(1968–)

Noha Radwan was born in Cairo. She attended Ramses College for Girls and then went to the American University in Cairo where she is presently studying Economics. She has published short stories on women, working children, and Palestinian children in the Egyptian magazine, *Sabah al-Khir*. A self-declared feminist, she has been a member of the Arab Women's Solidarity Association for two years.

This short story, Radwan says explicitly, is about marital rape. 'It is a story based on my imagination of what a real situation is like. I have often heard women say how they have stayed with their husbands for the sake of their children. It surprised me to see my mother's reaction to this story. She hated it to the point of never wanting to see it in print.' The story is taken from a collection of short stories by Egyptian women being published by the Arab Women's Solidarity Association Publishing House in Cairo.

The Silk Bands

1988

She pulls up her eyelids and struggles with them while her eyes wander around the room for a few minutes before they come down again. Everything around her suggests that she is in a bedroom which she has seen at least once before. The gold metallic curtains on the window, the tall mirror and the large wooden wardrobe with its monstrous ormolu do not seem unfamiliar. Once more she struggles with her eyelids and, startled, sees two eyes staring at her. It takes her a few seconds to realise that she is looking at herself in the mirror and that the naked body lying on the bed is actually hers. She lingers on the bed with its carefully embroidered sheets before she comes upon the naked body lying next to her. She closes her eyes, gasps for breath and tries to put herself back to sleep again but a heavy stream of nausea surges within her. The events of the last night force themselves upon her as she desperately presses her eyelids together. The scenes mercilessly follow until she sees what makes her whole body shudder. The scene is occupied by the same man lying by her side now breathing tediously. Did this actually happen last night? How did she allow herself to be raped? Why didn't she resist? She could have at least screamed for help. She remembers that she had been screaming but is not quite sure anybody had heard her. She sees the little children who have wrapped the silk bands around her wrists and ankles and even around her neck. They smile sweetly as they look into her face but their hands are busy tying her to the bed and she cannot move.

She presses her lips tightly together, overcome by a strong impulse to vomit. She wants to stop the fetid air of the room from going into her lungs. She puts her hand to her mouth; nausea makes her want to throw up, to let her insides come out, to be cast beyond the borders of her being and herself.

There is a knocking inside her head tormenting her until she fears it will explode. She knows she cannot go back to sleep. The knocking intensifies. It sounds as if there is a knocking at the door. She lifts her head and puts her feet on the ground looking for something to put on. She pulls a sheet over the naked body before she walks to the door.

At the door she freezes and stares at the little boy with his raised fist. Is it possible that she is still dreaming? The cold floor under her bare feet affirms that she is not. But she is sure she sees one of the children who had tied her to the bed. With the same innocent smile on his face of the night before he says, 'Good morning, Mommy. Is something the matter?' When she doesn't answer he enters the room. 'I just wanted to ask Daddy for a little extra pocket money.'

Translated from the Arabic
by the author

REJECTION

She did not know
Nor her family knew
But the bridegroom
Was a Ghoul
They sang and sang . . .
'He'll feed you
Fatten you
And on your wedding day
Will eat you . . .'

They sang and sang
She wept and wept
And then sang
'I don't want. I don't want.
I'm no fool
He's a ghoul
Wed? To a ghostly host? Am I?
Fed? His bridal-roast? Am I?'
She wept and wept alnight
'He was alright except

At night he was a goat'
They sang . . . Alweddingnight
She wept and sang and wept and sang
Alweddingnight
At dawn he slept
At last she crept. Away
She went. Away. Unwed.
They sang, resang . . .
Unwed . . . She left . . . Away . . .
They sang . . .

Nadia Sururi, 'Female Contractions' (Jordan, 1975)

Aisha Ismat al-Taimuriya

(1840–1902)

Aisha Ismat al-Taimuriya was born in Cairo, Egypt. She was the daughter of a Circassian concubine and Ismail Pasha Taimur, a Turkish aristocrat and high government official said to have known six languages. Aisha received a traditional, and thorough, Islamic education in the arts of rhetoric and composition, based on close study of the Quran. She learned Arabic, Turkish, and Persian, and composed poetry in all three languages.

In 1854, she was married to Mahmud Bey al-Islambuli, another member of the Turkish aristocracy; the pressures of home and family cut off her literary pursuits. After the death of her father and husband she returned to her studies. She received instruction in the art of verse composition from two women professors, Fatima al-Azhariya and Sitita al-Tablawiya. The death of her daughter Tawhida and an inflammation of her eyes combined to interrupt preparations to publish her poetry in three collections (Arabic, Turkish, and Farsi); subsequently, at least two have been published. She died in 1902.

Her published prose includes an allegorical tale, *Nataij al-Ahwal fi al-Aqwal wa-al-Afal* (The Results of Circumstances in Words and Deeds) from which the first selection below is taken, and the treatise *Mirat al-Taamul fi al-Umur* (The Mirror of Contemplation on Things), on the relationship of men and women in society, published some time between 1892 and her death ten years later. She is also known to have corresponded with other women intellectuals, notably the Syrian poet Warda al-Yaziji (1838–1924). Mai Ziyada states that Aisha al-Taimuriya was the first, among both men and women, to advocate 'equality' between the sexes.

The second selection is an article first published in *Al-Adab* newspaper, 11 February 1889 under the title 'Asr al-Maarif' (The Age of Education). It is republished as 'La Tuslahu al-Ailat illa bi-Tarbiyat al-Banat' (Families only Prosper Through Girls' Education) in Zainab Fawwaz's *Al-Durr al-Manthur fi Tabaqat Rabbat al-Khudur* (Pearls Scattered Through the Women's Quarters).

Introduction to
The Results of Circumstances in Words and Deeds

1887/8

৩১৯

Says the one with the broken wing, Aisha Ismat daughter of Ismail
Pasha Taimur: Ever since my cradle cushion was rolled up, and my
foot roved the carpet of the world, ever since I became aware of
where enticements and reason dwelt for me, and I grew conscious
of the inviolable space around my father and grandfather – ever
since that time, my fledgling aim was to nurse eagerly on tales of
the nations of old. I aged while still young trying to get to the root
of the words of those who have gone before. I used to be infatuated
with the evening chatter of the elderly women, wanting to listen to
the choicest stories. From those anecdotes, I gleaned the marvels of
destiny. To the best of my ability and efforts, I pondered all that
was repeated to me, both serious matters and those said in jest.
From the fruits of those evening chats, I plucked what the vessel of
my awareness could hold, to the point where I had no capacity for
anything but such listening and could not find it in myself to enjoy
anything but this sort of pleasure.

When my mental faculties were prepared for learning, and my
powers of understanding had reached a state of receptivity, there
came to me the mistress of compassion and probity, the treas-
urehouse of knowledge and wonders that amaze – my mother, may
God protect her with His grace and forgiveness. Bearing the
instruments of embroidery and weaving, she began to work
seriously on my education, striving to instill in me cleverness and
comprehension. But I was incapable of learning, and I had no
desire or readiness to become refined in the occupations of women.
I used to flee from her as the prey escapes the net, rushing
headlong into the assemblages of writers, with no sense of embarrassment. And I found the screech of pen on paper the most
inviting of melodies. I was certain that to become one of this group
of people would be the most perfect and complete of blessings.

In my yearnings, I used to entreat pieces of paper and the small
reeds of used pens. I secluded myself, withdrawing from the
people around me. I imitated the writers with my own writing, so
that I could delight in hearing that screech.

And my mother would come to me, reprimanding me harshly
and threatening me. But I flourished only at showing aversion and

flying away, while in the craft of embroidery I showed only my shortcomings. My father – may God shield him with forgiveness and make the chambers of Paradise his refuge – came and said to my mother: 'Leave this little girl to me, leave her to her pen and paper. You have her sister, so train that one in whatever forms of wisdom you wish.'

Then he grasped my hand and took me out to where the writers were gathered. He arranged two professors for me: one to teach me the language of Farsi, and the other to instruct me in the sciences of Arabic. And he, himself, began to listen every evening to what I had learnt in my lessons, until little by little I had acquired a trained mind. I discovered in myself an inclination for poetry composition; the first poetry I composed was in Farsi. Then I worked hard at my education, letting not a day go by and never ceasing to work, until I grew to appreciate the sweet taste of reciting the ancient Word of God. Begging that this be opened to me, I began my recitation with the bismallah, 'In the name of God the Merciful and Compassionate.' And God, who opens all paths, granted me success in opening the beehive to reveal the honey-comb of that pure honey; he allowed me to quench my thirst at that noble and salutary pool. I continued to acquire the light of learned understanding from the lamps of Quran recitation, seeking the sweetness of right guidance from the bowls which hold the cream of that goodness. I studied until I became mentally capable of perusing the legends of old and comprehending fully the imports which the usages of rhetoric convey.

I was not qualified to acquire that merchandise, nor to appreciate the gem of this craftsmanship. Nevertheless, the Creator had accustomed his creature to obtaining blessings and nobleminded-ness; 'He taught humankind what it does not know.' (Quran 96:5) So I studied the histories to the best of my ability, and to the extent that my dull mind could understand them – since it was not possible for me to enter the assemblages of the learned scholars and since the sessions of the erudite were not expanded to include me. How my chest was inflamed with the fire of longing to enter the paradise of their gatherings! How my eyelids overflowed with tears because I was deprived of harvesting the fruits of their beneficial learning! What hindered me from realising this hope was the tentlike screen of an all-enveloping wrap. And the lock on the private quarters of femaleness hid and secluded me from the radiance of those celestial moons. The ally of burdens and griefs kept me in the prison of ignorance. Whoever may censure me for lapses in that which I write must see that this seclusion is the greatest of excuses.

So do not reproach a woman hidden and secluded – O assemblage of the erudite – and do not toy with a grieved prisoner. For had I been able to pluck the blooms of educated refinement from the gardens of knowledge, then my mind would have produced the finest honey of scrutiny. I came away with knowledge and understanding, content and gratified by what I am able to recite from tales of the people of old. I drank at the watering pool of their stories as one drinks who has ladled copiously and then has acknowledged it. I have surveyed the destinies of those to follow; I have pondered the course of nations and have become convinced that both good fortune and misfortune are dependent upon what has been preordained. I have witnessed, by God, the truth of this statement in myself. With my bad luck, I have suffered that which is most disastrous and bitter to the taste, and I have suffered this in the cave of isolation.

Compassion for all people who have encountered what I have encountered, and who have been struck by the same blows, has led me to fashion a tale which would distract them from their cares when thoughts crowd in, and would entertain them, drawing them far from the grief they feel in the exile of solitude, which is harder to bear than exile from home's homeland. It is a story which will set them in gardens of wonderful fruit, and will create for them a path which is the pleasantest of ways and the straightest of roads. For only this pathway gives pleasant distraction to the thoughts of one alone, and only these roads obtain camaraderie for the stranger. I have called this tale *The Results of Circumstances in Words and Deeds*.

Translated from the Arabic
by Marilyn Booth

Family Reform
Comes Only Through The Education of Girls

1894/5

❀

Perhaps I am not qualified to speak in this sphere, and I admit to my limited powers of grasping the subject at hand – for I am secluded by the tent of an enveloping wrap. Yet, across its borders, I perceive that programmes of education are treasure chests, and I see that the paths of refinement hold, at their ends, the keys to every gem that lies hidden. It is the duty of every noble soul to favour strongly those splendid ways and to urge all who are dear to him to graze in their rich pasturelands, so as to acquire these unparalleled jewels.

However, I note that eastern society looks only to immediate interests, and concerns itself solely with those; were it to consider and examine what comes after the day at hand, then it would be wringing its hands in chagrin over what it has let slip away through neglect. But by taking note of the judicious dominion of the Shaper of Souls and the Originator of Beings – beings who are the marvellous craftshops of the Divine, and the original edifices of nature – eastern society would discover that the populousness and wealth of this world turn upon the pair, male and female.

Were it possible for either male or female to exist in isolation, then the Knower of Secrets would have distinguished one to the exclusion of the other, and would not have put the favoured one in need of the other. Contemplation of the primordial matter of the cosmos would have made the male establishment see their obligation to concern themselves with the education of girls and the refinement of families, for the fruits of dominion return to them. Take the situation of a man overcome by a perplexing situation – his wife draws him to her with her delicate fingertips, calms a burning brand, and torments him with her fine management. In spite of that, he strives to conceal her merit among the members of society, and is wary of announcing her worth, fearing that it will be said she is an educated woman, and fearing that his tranquil existence will be put into turmoil.

This situation is contrary to that in the western nation-state. How regrettable is a society which has not examined the west's admirable arrangement with respect to men and women, and has made no effort to strive for the elevated dignity which this arrangement confers. How astounding is a civilisation infatuated with adorning its young women in costume jewellery, one which resorts to exhibiting their comeliness through the ornamentation of metals and stones, fancying that such embellishment greatly enhances their beauty and coquetry. But in fact this civilisation has cast those girls into the pit of evil; they have derived nothing from those trinkets but self-admiration and vanity, qualities which lead them into the vastness of utter devil-may-care and dissolution. This happens because these girls' powers of understanding have been suspended, and because they fail to work with the results of conditions and the outcomes of things:

> A white-blazoned brow was embellished with pearls
> And bedecked with a veil of black ignorance
> Enclasped by a necklace which made its goodness beautiful
> While ignorance darkens all more glorious virtues.

If the male authorities strove for the improvement of these girls' behaviour through their education and attracted them with the evidences of civilisation to the exquisite novelties of study, these belles would then find themselves crowned with the rubies of knowledge and adorned with necklaces strung with pearls of learned understanding. The older they grow, the more accustomed would their step become to the paths of comprehension; they would come to understand the merit of their real jewels. They would make brilliant their jewels, and would become clever in making its value rise. They would load this jewellery copiously with splendours and radiance, and would find the lustre of its majesty sufficient, dispensing thus with the most elegant jewels – even if they were clothed only in cheap white muslin.

> Truly the sciences are a jewel, the basis of pride
> With which the value of the lowly is raised aloft and made honourable
> Its presence within the heart gives distinction
> To its possessor among human beings, and grants him the heights.

I beg your forgiveness – you of great minds – for what I have to say: we, the assemblage of females kept in seclusion, are more knowledgeable than you in the formation of the young, both boys and girls. It is well known that once the infant arrives on the midwife's palm, it begins its life by crying and then subsides for a moment, flagging from the wearying efforts it has faced, particularly in making the unprecedented effort of letting its voice go in screams. Then it begins to pay attention to its surroundings, swivelling its neck right and left, opening its mouth to demand nourishment. Its mother nurses it and it falls asleep as soon as it has taken its fill. You notice it smiling slightly in its sleep. This is an indication that our world is an abode of cares and a place of woes and anxiety, a place of much roughness and little tranquillity.

As the child begins to develop, reaching five months, his first mark of intelligence comes in recognising his mother, and then his father. Then, he learns to grasp an object – for it is offered by his mother – and to put it in his mouth. You may contemplate the construction of this trivial sign, this gentle expression.

Then, as the baby's nerves grow stronger, as his limbs become firmer, so his screams grow louder. His mother rushes to him with melodies ready, to which he tries to listen. If his chest grows tight with pain, she treats it with all compassion, picking him up and carrying him from place to place until his grief is dispelled and his pain is eased. All the while, he believes that this tender easing, this pacification of his pain, is due to her ability. And she spends her night in worry and exhausted distress, the result of her maternal compassion.

When the child is restored to health, then his father – to the best of his ability – brings him whatever delights and cheers him. When the child grows to become a youth, and is bent on childish naughtiness, his mother invents means to distract him; she frightens him with made-up names which he imagines to bring terror. If he raises his voice, she reminds him of these names, and if he acts the devil she calls them down upon him. Thus, the child grows quiet. At times she reminds him of his father's presence, and frightens him with the spectre of punishment from an evil father. Thus, in his heart, the child anticipates something fearful from his father, thinking his father's power to be greater than it is, looking upon his father as larger than life, making his father's awesome countenance the core of his identity.

I wonder what the situation of this woman poor in the branches of knowledge can be! – when her hands are empty of what she deserves. Indeed, there is a wise saying in this respect:

> If you were to fill the lamps to overflowing with fat
> Their glow would point the way to every acquisition of knowledge
> And if their oil is wanting, their wicks go dry
> Where is the light of a thread not immersed?

How can such parental compassion be considered sound when it leads to mistreatment of the object of compassion? If our men – the easterners – in their paternal compassion, would take an interest in the education of their daughters, and would agree on instructing those girls in the fields of knowledge, then their daughters would achieve the highest distinction and would acquire the most beneficial seriousness of mind. These young women would be compensated for their state of nervous anxiety by the repose of educated understanding. With the supporting help of their knowledge, they would expand the narrow compass of their comportment, moving into the spacious arena of pliability and submission. They would undertake the duties of home management; they would concern themselves with maintaining the foundation of their acquired jewels and preserving them from destruction. Homes are laid waste after their inhabitants are sundered – this is natural, and what is natural is not harmful. Nevertheless, when the homes *do* exist, to destroy their noble roofs with pestilent ignorance is not only shameful but is also the road to fiery destruction. And it is a strange sight indeed, to see a planter of seedlings who neglects to prepare the ground properly and then expresses chagrin at the crookedness of the branch which represents the outcome of his planting the seedling. If men watered their seedlings from the vessel of knowledge and understanding, then at a time when they are enduring the load of heavy burdens, they could lean on firm, upright branches. These branches would help them to ascend to the highest levels, and to grasp hold of the strongest proofs of their own authority.

However, this society of ours has become great in the embellishment of superficial appearance, to the exclusion of refinement and education, on a pretext feebler than a spider's web: this excuse is that if females learn to read, they will become attached to infatuation and passionate flirtation, and will initiate exchanges with others.

Have not the ears of the men been struck by the narratives of the uneducated and the anecdotes of the ignorant?

Thus, O men of our homelands, O you who control our affairs, why have you left these females behind for no reason? Why have you neglected the benefits of the maxim: 'What you do today you will encounter tomorrow'? Since you have been miserly in extending to these females the true adornment of humanity, and since you have been content to pull them away and isolate them from its brilliant jewel (when they were under your authority, more pliable than a reed pen, when their submission to your control was famous indeed) then why do you raise your hands in confusion, like one who has lost the meanings of things in the hour of need? For you have mocked their situation, and you have made light of their sharing the work with you. You deemed it best to separate yourselves in every way. Now look: upon whom does the blame accrue?

I have wished these words of mine to see the light, but I found no support in this until the goal I sought was granted to me by the key to the drawer which the heart keeps locked and hidden. This is a letter from one of the women who regard the education of girls as an obligatory duty. And what a woman she is! In the darkness of nights, by the gleam of her attentiveness to this issue she has lit lamps. By the power of her understanding in this sphere, she has ascended many steps. The bloom of her able comprehension, with its fine scent, has cleft the minds of her listeners. The kohl of her counsel has adorned the eyes of the onlookers and revived their vision. This woman has deflected the spearheads of censure from womanhood, for she is expert and experienced in the abilities of women. I should congratulate the company of secluded females, thanks to the one mentioned above, who has delighted listening ears with her words. I see the stars of her esteemed lamps giving off light among educated men; giving guidance so that all who approach will heed her memorable praise; making every discerning person keen to take a bit of that light which will lead him onto the path of the destination intended. Peace be on the one who follows God's guidance.

Translated from the Arabic
by Marilyn Booth

Bahithat al-Badiya

(1886–1918)

Malak Hifni Nasif, the poet, writer, and feminist known by the pseudonym, Bahithat al-Badiya (seeker in the desert) was born in Cairo into a literary family. Her father, Hifni Nasif, had studied at Al-Azhar with the Muslim reformer, Shaikh Muhammad Abduh. He encouraged the learning of his daughter, the eldest of six children. She received her secondary school diploma from the first teacher training school for women, the Saniyya School in Cairo, where she later taught. She spoke on Fridays at the women's lectures at the Egyptian University and in the offices of the liberal paper, *Al-Jarida*. Her speeches and essays which appeared in *Al-Jarida* were published in 1910 under the title, *Al-Nisaiyat* (Feminist Pieces). The following year she sent feminist demands to the National Congress in Heliopolis. Her life took an abrupt turn when she married Abd al-Sattar al-Basil, chief of the bedouin tribe, al-Ramah of Fayyum. She gave up teaching, and went to live with him in the Faium oasis west of Cairo. She discovered he already had a wife (his cousin) and a daughter he expected her to tutor. Some of the sufferings she experienced and observed are expressed in her writings which include letters to Mai Ziyada. In 1918, at the age of thirty-two, she died of influenza. Huda Shaarawi delivered a public eulogy for her to an audience of women which became Shaarawi's first feminist speech. Bahithat al-Badiya's brother, Majd al-Din Hifni Nasif collected her writings and published them in 1962 in Cairo in a volume entitled, *Athar Bahithat al-Badiya, Malak Nasif* (The Heritage of Bahithat al-Badiya: 1886–1918).

Bahithat al-Badiya was a strong advocate of rights for women within marriage. Married unwittingly to a man already a husband and father she was hostile towards the institution of polygamy. She stressed that Islam condoned multiple wives only when each received equal treatment, something the religion taught was nearly impossible. The real life account that follows serves as a first-hand indictment of this institution. This piece comes from her *Al-Nisaiyat*.

Bad Deeds of Men: Injustice

1909

✤

Some things leave an impact deep inside that will not go away. I shall speak of something that touched me profoundly.

Once when I was visiting a friend, I asked her about a woman I had known a long time ago. She sighed and answered me in a sad voice saying that the woman had experienced great sorrow causing her to fall ill. The reason for this was that her husband had contracted to marry another woman and would consummate the marriage soon. I was amazed to hear this. My friend noticed my reaction and asked: 'Isn't this a common occurrence?' I said, 'Yes, I am not surprised because it happened, but because it happened to her. She was among the finest of women in character, beauty, and education. I used to hear from her that she was living in comfort with her husband and I saw her with my own eyes working in her home which was clean and well organised. She had young children. What more does a man need than a wife with education, a good mind, fine character, beauty, and children?'

My friend said that the two children had died within the same month and her husband then started to look for another wife. He became engaged to a woman the same month he lost his children and while his first wife was pregnant. How cruel the man was. Was it her fault that the two children died? Was it not enough that she was grieving over her loss, that he should not shoot another poison arrow into her broken heart? Did he discover a letter from her to the angel of death asking him to come and take her two children away? Were these children only hers and not his? Man is stronger in his will than woman and can endure more misfortune than her. If he endured misfortune would this make him forget kindness and mercy? Oh God, you do not condone this treatment.

If a woman needs kindness and consideration at any time it is in dark days. Is there any day darker than the day she loses two children? In time of great sadness when people far and near extend sympathy is it fitting that her own husband would abandon her to grief? The grieving woman is his wife and those who have departed are his children. If she were grieving for a brother or another relative it would have been his duty to share this grief with her even if only externally. But, if it is their child, who would lessen the pain if he does not? If he, himself, were not saddened and did not console her why then didn't he leave her be? A poet once said, 'I have considered you a strong fortress to protect me from the enemies' arrows but you became their archer. If you cannot protect me, be neither for me nor against me.'

When he married the other woman he broke the heart of his first wife and did something whose outcome he could not control. Is it not possible that his new wife will be barren or that she will give him children who will die like the first children of his first wife? Fate cannot be opposed nor averted. Birth, life, and death are in the hands of God. We do not know when He will grant life or take it. This woman does not have room for both the fetus and sadness. Isn't her husband condemning her and condemning his new child if sadness is its companion and it is born dead? This cruel husband is criminal under the rule of law, decency, humanity, and kindness.

This painful incident reminds me of a similar one. An eminent man began to dislike his wife because all his children were girls. He divorced her and married another woman in the hope of having boys, but his new wife gave him a girl, then another, and still another. God refused to grant except that which He willed. The man got more girls as if he were replacing one set of daughters for another. He lost the love of a good woman and wrought change in the hearts of his first daughters. He thought that he had gained the love of another woman, but he was deluded.

If we think that giving birth to girls is something undesirable as some of us do, is it the decision of the woman to do so? Why isn't the man blamed as the woman is blamed? Why doesn't the woman ask for a divorce and marry another man so that she can bear boys? If one of the spouses clings to this fallacy, it could be that the other would adhere to it as well. They are equally able to be right or wrong in this matter. In our home life there is much to concern us. We have archaic practices that shout for reform. Men should not occupy our time and thoughts complaining about their work. I think they are subject to the injustice of the government on the one hand, and the difficulty of making ends meet on the other. They find no one to take revenge upon except us. I do not believe that there is any opponent who is weaker in weaponry than us, and less vengeful. Oh God, inspire the men of our government to do right because their injustice to the nation has many repercussions on us. It seems that we have not received anything more than men receive except pain. This reverses the Quranic verse that says, 'One man's share shall equal two women's shares.'

Translated from the Arabic
by Margot Badran and Ali Badran

Ghada Samman

(1942–)

Ghada Samman was born in al-Shamiya, Syria. Her father was Rector of the University of Damascus and Minister of Education. She went to Beirut in 1964 where she graduated from the American University in Beirut. She earned her MA from the University of London. She began to write in the early 1960s. Her works often deal with the problems women in the Arab world confront). Her first collection of short stories, *Ainak Qadari*, (Your Eyes are my Destiny) was published in 1962. It is read throughout the Arab world. She has written extensively about the Arab national struggle against imperialism, and been attacked by critics for the outspoken nature of her social and political commentary. To be able to continue publishing what she wanted she founded her own publishing house. Her nine short story collections include *La Bahra fi Bairut* (There's No Sea in Beirut, 1965), and *Lail Al-Ghuraba* (The Night of Strangers, 1966). Collections of essays, published in the 1960s and 1970s, include *Al-Sibaha fi Buhairat al-Shaitan* (Swimming in the Devil's Lake, 1979). Her novels include a fictional recounting of the hotels battle of October and November 1975 entitled *Kawabis Bairut* (Beirut Nightmares, 1980). Her poetry includes the anthology *Itiqal Lahza Hariba* (To Catch a Fleeting Moment, 1979). She has also published a collection of interviews that she has entitled *Al-Qabila Tawtajwib al-Qatila* (The Tribe Interrogates the Killed Woman, 1981).

The following article appeared in *Jaridat al-Nasr al-Suriya* in November 1961. Ghada Samman did not publish these articles in any of her collections because she only came across them recently. She wrote to Miriam Cooke in a letter dated 10 May 1989, 'At that time I was having a fight with Shaikh Ali al-Tantawi. He thought I was representative of a "woman whom our society rejects". I decided to travel to become independent in my struggle, and not have to modify my tone in honour of my father . . . In Beirut, I spoke completely freely [her dialogue with Samir Sayigh in the magazine *Mawaqif* in 1969 was translated into English in Elizabeth Warnock Fernea and Basima Bezirgan's *Middle Eastern Muslim*

Women Speak, 1977]. The gap between the two dates of writing explains a difference in frankness, openness and style. At that time I was living in a hotel in East Beirut called Alexandre. I was working and living alone and free. I was responsible to myself alone for what I wrote.'

Our Constitution – We the Liberated Women

1961

೧౫౩

It's a Crime for the Slave to Love her Bonds
Let us pray
For the slave who loves her bonds
For the slave who is whipped

We don't know in which cave she got used to being whipped, but we hear her tearful, moaning submission. We threw her ropes on which she spat. She melted her chains. She reunited them for a master to re-tie her because she's afraid to live, because she is too cowardly to bear the responsibility of living. We gave her our voting rights, the right to participate in the running of the country and to decide its future, the right to struggle in the path of God and country, the right to toil and to bear responsibility.

Yesterday I read a protest in some newspaper signed by some sisters in Hama (these women had refused suffrage). They were protesting the acquisition of the right to live and to fight and the honour of responsibility and struggle. What can I say?

Millions of women have moaned, aeons of sadness have settled in our hearts like a heavy fog. Generations have longed to participate in humanity along with men. Now the authorities honour us and invite us to practise our humanity. They grant us the honour of duties and responsibilities. So, shall we refuse? What can I say? Only the coward refuses to live. Some sisters from Hama are refusing the call of the country so as to escape responsibility while shouting 'Islam'.

Islam is women's honour. They escape from our country's battles out of weakness and resignation, shouting 'Islam'. Aisha fought when it became necessary. They are afraid of mixing with men and of what people will suspect. Aisha was suspected once. God honoured Aisha with a verse that revealed her innocence and that of all women who dare to be human in a society that insists that women remain colourful mummy/slaves whose existence revolves around the household, make-up and stupid stories.

I shall not respond to Professor Ali Tantawi (a shaikh and president of a religious group who published a pamphlet against the feminist revolution). He has the right to his personal opinion as long as he remains true to himself. Some day we may convince him that his fears are unfounded and that women, these sweet gentle creatures whom no one has described as exquisitely as our great Shaikh, are also strong human beings capable of sharing men's responsibilities. Professor Ali Tantawi's opposition to us is not treachery. It is a noble challenge that increases the violence of the noble response.

As for our Hama sisters and the treachery among the ranks of us, women of this country, this is the treachery of the eyelashes to the eye, of the fingernail to the finger, of the hand to the arm. What can I say? What can half of me say if I choose for the other half to be paralysed when the enemy is all around?

Let us pray.

For the cancer which is us. Let us pray because we shall amputate the arm if it betrays.

Palestine is moaning while we twist in the cocoons of our time and our defeat. Algeria is crucified every dawn and there are still some of our women who do not know who Jamila (Bouhired, an Algerian heroine) is. The world is in competition to get to the moon and they are drawing a veil over their hearts and chains over their existence. All Jewish women are fighters, why not also Muslim women as in the past?

Let us pray.

For those who accuse Islam of denigrating them, whereas it is Islam that delivered us from the deserts where we were being buried like cadavers. Our heads only touched the clouds when eagles snatched us up and flew with us to the caves of terror and disgrace. Islam forbade us to be dolls decorating tables and playthings for the god of petrol, and butterflies around the coloured lamps of vanities.

Let us pray.

For the butterflies who refuse to break out of their cocoons and to confront the storm. They have become used to being jailed worms.

Let us pray.

For those who refuse winter's toil and summer's harvest. They have condemned themselves to the suicide of silence and defeatism. Today suicide is the ultimate cowardice because our lives are not ours alone they belong to our past, to our destiny and to the future of our country and we are compelled to live.

Our Constitution – We the Liberated Women
The liberated woman is a person who believes that she is as human as a man. At the same time she acknowledges that she is female and he is male and that the difference between them is how, not how

much. Since they are equally human they must have equal human rights.

The liberated woman is not, as some think, that modern doll who wears make-up and tasteless clothes. That woman has only liberated herself from her clothes, her humanity and self-respect.

The liberated woman today is a reality and part of the intellectual awakening of Arab society. She wants to free herself from some of the inherited social laws and traditional attitudes which contain no human meaning and which disfigure her humanity. It is a revolution of honour by the thinking woman against the doll woman and a fervent cry to affirm existence and dignity and to become free from delusions, uncertainty, guilt and to reach the sun of truth, thought and reality. The liberated woman believes that as a human being she has the right to be responsible for herself and her society. She insists on the right to responsibility because responsibility is what distinguishes humans from animals.

Responsibility is one of the outcomes of freedom. That is why the liberated woman insists on having complete freedom and to assume complete responsibility after receiving sufficient education, culture, age and stability.

She does not insist on her freedom so as to abuse it. She needs it to make of it a virtue. She believes that forced virtue is a habit, not a human victory and not a virtue. The woman who is not allowed to go out and to exercise freedom of action is not by nature sinful or virtuous. She is nothing because she has chosen nothing. We are not responsible for anything we have been forced to do. In other words, we cannot obey any moral code when we do not have the freedom to choose what to do. Choice is the one thing which produces responsibility and the one thing that gives a moral code its true value.

The liberated woman believes that because she is human she may make mistakes. She is sorry about that, but she continues to insist that her mistakes are no more evil than those of men, that there is not a male mistake that is forgiven and a female mistake that is not.

The liberated woman has decided to liberate her mind from traditional stagnation and to conduct her life, that concerns her alone after full, deep and balanced reflection. For example, she refused to be priced for marriage as were her mother and grandmother. She refuses to sell herself because she insists on being a friend not a pampered slave. She insists on sharing his life and destiny not just his table. The liberated woman refuses this negative situation of being like a can of preserves that is unaware of its customers. She considers men to have intrinsic value in what they may become not in what they possess.

This is the woman they have decided to crush in the name of religion. Why? For whose good? Is this good for a religion whose primary goal was the organisation of human activities into the virtuous society? Is the elimination of these fruitful activities in its name good for religion, when it was the religion that was the first to honour and value her?

They Will Not Plant Us In Cocoons of Fog After Today
I said: These are the principles of the liberated woman, person. They said: Your words are fine . . . but she's a doll . . . were she conscious like her Scandinavian and German friend we would be pleased with her.

They said this with the spite of the enemy not the tenderness of the searcher.

They have decided that the Scandinavian and German women have succeeded in the experiment with freedom and then they say that the Arab woman has failed and she must return to her rules!

In fact, I see no reason to say that the Arab woman is less intelligent and energetic and sincere than the western woman. She does not want to create an anarchic society in which the family has lost its status, sanctity and beauty as has happened in Sweden.

She wants to create an Arab society in which she can act virtuously in full consciousness and have a noble life, and can participate in the building of assets and in setting limits. She is a wonderful person. It is better that we investigate the reasons for her backwardness instead of returning her to her chains in the cave and saying that she is only fit for its darkness.

Let us ask with the gentleness of a doctor and not the spite of the enemy: why do some women spend their time gossiping, at the hairdresser and at the seamstress? Does this mean that they really are dolls? But they are not by nature dolls! They are doing in shops and hairdressers' today what their grandmothers did in the harem. This is the modern version of life in the harem. Men share in the responsibility for this stupid life. I am surprised that they share my contempt for the life of the harem in this modern aspect and yet try to save women from it by throwing them into the world of the ancient harem. If only they could understand the real reason. If only they could say with me in kindness and sincerity: men have had 3000 years of freedom, the Arab woman has not even had a quarter of a century. She is not yet mature. She has not yet cleansed herself from her defects or liberated herself from false steps.

For 3000 years man has been free to build for himself his human civilisation. So what did he build? What if not a civilisation of destruction, O Hiroshima? Is a hairdresser any less destructive than the manufacturer of rockets and atom bombs?

They say: she's failed.

I say: she's not failed. She has the right to live through the moment of overwhelming confusion after her intellectual awakening. Why do they blame the eyes which have grown accustomed to the dark when in the first instant they cannot rightly choose their way in life?

Why do they blame her for bowing her head in the beginning and they forget that Plato's cave had a low ceiling and for ages she bowed her head to its cruelty? Does that mean that God created her from the beginning with her head bowed?

Let them curse the processions of mummies, let them explode in newspaper columns. From today they will no longer plant us as worms in cocoons of fog. They say: education is an evil colonialism brought.

I say that this is dangerous talk, really dangerous. It is not so dangerous for the woman as it is for the nation as a whole. I absolutely do not expect reactionarism to drive them to the point of glorifying the colonial system and its concern for women's education because it is known that the colonial plan was to preserve ignorance, poverty and degradation.

Women's education flourished during the period of our freedom and renaissance. A simple check in the records of the Ministry of Education will reveal that the number of girls studying has multiplied twenty times from what it was immediately after the expulsion of the French colonisers.

Let them think well of the Arab woman.

Let them remember that we betray our country if we turn our existence into a cemetery in which human causes die.

Let them curse the processions of mummies, let them explode in newspaper columns. From today they will no longer plant us as worms in cocoons of fog.

We have not yet had a quarter century of freedom.

For 3000 years man has been free to create himself his human civilisation. What is it but a civilisation of destruction, O Hiroshima.

Translated from the Arabic
by Miriam Cooke

Emily Nasrallah

(1938–)

Emily Nasrallah was born in Kfeir, South Lebanon. When she was nine years old, she asked an uncle who had emigrated to America to send her to boarding school in Shwaifat. She studied for her BA at the American University at Beirut and Beirut College for Women (now, Beirut University College). She worked her way through university by writing for the press. In 1962, she published her first novel *Tuyur Ailul* (September Birds). This novel has been assigned as a high school text and has been reprinted six times. Her novels include: *Shajarat al-Difla* (The Oleander Tree, 1968); *Al-Rahina* (The Pawn, 1973); *Tilka al-Dhikrayat* (Those Memories, 1980). She considers her most recent novel *Al-Iqla aks al-Zaman* (Flight Against Time, 1981) to be the sequel to *September Birds*. This novel was translated into English in 1987. Her collections of short stories include: *Jazirat al-Wahm* (The Island of Illusion, 1973) and *Al-Yanbu* (The Source, 1978). She has published two collections on the Lebanese Civil War: *Al-Mara fi 17 Qissa* (Women in 17 Stories, 1983); and *Al-Tahuna al-Daia* (The Lost Mill, 1985). Between 1981 and 1987, she contributed a regular column on famous women's lives to the women's magazine *Fairuz*. These articles were anthologised in two volumes entitled *Nisa Raidat Min al-Sharq wa min al-Gharb* (Pioneer Women from East and West, 1986). Of all the Beirut Decentrists she is one of the very few to remain in Beirut, 'The only place I can write.'

The following extracts are from *September Birds*. Muna, a village girl, has rejected her destiny which is to wait like Laila for an emigrant to return and marry her. She has sought her fortune in the city of Beirut. These chapters are reminiscences of her village childhood.

September Birds

1962

☙☙☙

Winter surprised the village early that year. The olives were still piled up in the largest room of our house. My mother had not yet finished preparing the winter provisions, so she did not leave the stove, her hand constantly over the boiling kettle.

Mother! She was always concocting such wonderful things.

I joined Hanna, Najla and the other neighbours and helped to pick out the plump, black, delicious olives.

The women in the village wait for the seasons which bring them together. They work together in groups, hands touching, tongues embellishing the latest gossip.

Harvest is a season.

Gathering the olives is a season.

Sifting the *bulgar*, rolling the *kishk*, and the weddings . . .

I remember the young girls sitting around the piles of grain in our courtyard. My father appears and greets them joyfully. He teases the pretty girls, or tells wonderful stories to encourage them in their work.

My brother Samir looks through the door shyly, with dreams and questions in his eyes. The girls' presence throws him into confusion. His hands are becoming tough and a few hesitant hairs are appearing on his upper lip.

Samir escapes from the door. I can still see him; his escape confirming his desire to stay.

Then my mother returns with delicious sweets and hot cardamom-spiced coffee for the girls. 'Take a break, girls.'

Mother! Your face comforts me as I wander through the roads of my exile.

How did you learn this art, Mother?

How were you able to knead life between your hands, making it as delicious, good, and uncomplicated as the coffee, and the quince and fig jams?

The girls rest; the air is filled with their joking and merriment. Empty cups are turned upside down on the tray, hands reach out eagerly, and all eyes are on Hanna.

'Read my fortune, Hanna. What do you say? Am I going to get married?'

Hanna's already serious expression becomes more serious. She reaches for each cup by turn and starts to disclose its secrets . . .

She continues her round, tearing away the veils of the unknown from the pretty blossoms and making their dreams come true. It's my turn . . . Hanna, how entertaining your conversations were! Yet, they tortured me, tormented my soul.

Hanna's words were delicious, enticing, I drank them in ravenously. Oh, tomorrow! How alluring the thought of tomorrow! How we longed for it.

'Listen, Muna! You're preoccupied; you're confused . . . A stranger . . . it could be a relative . . .' And Hanna stops to stare meaningfully at my mother, then she continues, 'You're confused, Muna. But your confusion will end well. You will be happy and have lots of money.'

That was Hanna's role in our lives. Then she turns to my mother. 'So, Umm Samir, have I said too much? There's no point in hiding anything. The whole village knows.'

My mother bites her tongue and tries to hide a sudden smile and to appear serious. 'As God wishes. Everyone has his fate. If that is fate, then let it be.'

Hanna won't stop. She keeps stinging me with the prick of her tongue. 'Muna, do yourself up. Tidy up your eyebrows. Sprinkle a little powder . . .' Then she turns to my mother. 'Doesn't Muna wear a bra, Umm Samir? Don't be bashful, Muna. Why are you blushing? Do you see how Najla keeps up with the latest fashion . . . And you, you have a reason . . .'

Her voice drones on. I drew a heavy curtain between us through which no sound can pass.

You have a reason!

How can she understand? How can she soar up with me to a world I have created, whose walls I have built with my own hands and in which I have established my own paradise?

How can she understand that my eyes are wandering to faraway horizons . . . far from the boundaries of the village? And that my feet are preparing to escape to a place where others will no longer plan my future?

Mother! This is what I want! I want to decide my tomorrow, and with these slender fingers, I want to build my own life. I want to remove the thorns with my own hands. I want to stumble over piles of stones on deserted paths and then get up again.

But do you hear, Mother? You were silent yesterday when that old man, whom Abu Elias was dragging along, visited us.

'An American . . . and rich. What more do you want?' That was Abu Elias's introduction, and I almost burst out laughing as I tried to think of what these two men reminded me. Abu Elias was manipulating the poor old man like a monkey trainer.

I felt sick listening to the 'American' trying to ingratiate himself with me. 'Come here, you pretty little thing.'

My shyness and the manners you taught me, Mother, kept me from kicking him.

How can you understand? How can Hanna understand this?

He went on chewing his stupid words, jabbering in a jumble of broken Arabic and ugly American. I sat in a corner, swallowing my rage and calming my nausea, trying to remain the little girl of whom her parents could be proud.

When he left us, I stood by the door in agony. Then, I lost consciousness. It was the only time I'd ever fainted. When I came to, you were near me, Mother. Your trembling fingers were stroking my forehead and my mouth. I noticed my father pacing about the room and wringing his hands. He repeated words I didn't understand. Then he came closer to me and knelt by my bed. 'It's all over, my darling. Come back to us. No one will talk to you about these things again.'

Thank you, Father.

And where is your hand, Mother, so that I may kiss it and rub my cheek against it and moisten it with my tears?

I was absolutely exhausted.

Yesterday, I walked among the people in the city streets. The verve and the energy in my steps had died. People were staring at my worn-out glances and at the exhausted self-questioning on my lips, as though puzzled that I should be wandering through this tumultous ocean.

People rushed through the narrow streets, their bodies dwarfed by the giant buildings. The rain pelted the ground angrily and violently. The city was like a hungry fish, opening and closing its mouth. With terror on their faces people pass in and out of the opening and closing mouth. Their shrunken faces vie to be reflected in the mirror of my soul. They are in search of answers to their questions.

From time to time, I noticed parts of their bodies seep out from under a heavy veil. 'They've gone. You'll not find them after today.'

The pen is still moving. I hear its scraping as it records their memories and the beautiful fleeting images of those who are coming down to the opening of the valley.

In my loneliness, I remember the vow I made to my pen on the day I waved my handkerchief to my dear village and knelt to kiss its earth farewell.

The storm was raging that night. The warm fireplace embraced us as though we were a band of refugees that had fled from a war of annihilation.

This is where nature has its primeval power; people laugh with the sun; they tremble with the thunder; their bodies crumble into dust storms; they cleanse their hearts with the purity of snow.

My father was awaiting his visitors that night; he was losing patience. Visits have a special scent on stormy nights. The violence of nature is moving, it gathers people together as though to pray for safety and the force to combat the elements.

I opened the door and went out into the storm. The silent snow flakes falling on the trees, on the roofs, and in the alleyways kissed me. The land was a sheet of light, reflecting against the rebellious mist that had shrouded it.

I invited the frost to enter the warm corners of my breast . . . I invited it to trace its simple white script on me.

My father's voice rang out in protest, as the storm penetrated the room, driving away the warmth that it had held onto throughout the day. 'What are you thinking about, Muna? You look grave, upset. Why? Are you thinking of someone?'

I smiled to erase any doubt from my father's mind as I shut the door firmly. Then I began to leaf through a book.

My father continued, 'What are you reading? Are you looking into your future? Are you searching for tomorrow between the pages of that book?'

'Yes, Dad. I am looking for the future.'

I was always looking for it anxiously and in confusion. That was why I had gone out into the storm. Perhaps it would lift me in the vortex of its violence.

When I told my grandmother some of my strange dreams, she would say, 'Don't be afraid, my child . . . Not all dreams come true . . .'

One morning, I told her one of these dreams: 'I was standing near a river, watching its warm waters and the meadows stretching away from its banks. I lived unreal moments of intoxication. Suddenly, I had wings and I began to fly up as though intoxicated. Then I fell into the waking world. I opened my eyes and the dream had gone. Yet its traces remained in the beats of my heart.'

My grandmother patted my shoulder with her warm hand, 'Dreams don't mean a thing. Don't be scared, my child.'

I came closer to the hearth, and pushed our black cat away to take its place in the warm corner. The cat jumped up and curled cosily in my lap, breathing gently.

This was the only time I felt close to my father. Thereafter, he distanced himself. He returned to his theories, his rules and his philosophies on 'Society, Education, Relations Between Boys and Girls' and their roles in life.

I wished I had used that moment to ask him lots of things: 'Are you afraid of them, Father? Who do you think I am? Who am I? A woman, a burden, a problem, the curse of weakness?'

I knew that you loved me very, very much . . . So what? So many questions disturbed my sleep, and I longed to ask them. Yet the timidity of childhood held me back as I hid behind an imaginary veil. I continued to live in an anguish of confusion.

The guests didn't allow me time for even one of my questions. I heard their footsteps in the courtyard, then on the doorstep. Intermittent sounds and sighs from the storm preceded them. There followed the calm of jumbled conversations and crude jokes.

My mother had prepared for the visit all day: delicious desserts, dried fruits and spiced coffee; the sole means of amusement in village gatherings at night. This was Simon's and his bride's first visit to our family.

Before he left the village, his name was Siman. The fields, the vineyards and the hilltops knew him . . . That was how those who shared his life so long ago remembered him.

He was seventeen, brawny, handsome; the echoes of his youth reverberated through the twists of the valley. He sat cross-legged on an ageless rock, guarding the flock and dreaming of the future.

Siman used to serve at Sunday mass. He loved the simple life and he had never dreamt of travelling or becoming a wealthy emigrant.

But this 'Simon' who visited us that evening did not evoke any memories. He was almost fifty. His jowls dangled and his eyes had sunk deep into the cavities of anxiety and fear. His obesity was evident in his fleshy fingers, luxurious paunch, and his slow, lethargic movements. The years had not spared his hair, which covered him with a faded veil blotting out part of his features.

'Simon' was well-known in the world of finance. His reputation preceded him across the ocean to the little house that had held him as an unknown youth. When Siman moved away, he left behind an old father and mother. When his father died, the widow survived on the remnants of a dream nurtured by brief letters from 'over there' which were received with tears.

How often Umm Siman had asked me to write a letter for her:

'Your mother will die soon, my son. Make her heart happy and come.'

'My darling, young girls in the village await you. I have chosen a lovely bride for you.'

'My son, I can smell you in the letter. I hide it in the folds of my dress, between my breasts, on my heart.'

'Oh darling of your mother, Siman, the absence has been long and the separation cruel . . .'

Siman was finally convinced, and he sent a cable informing his mother of the date of his arrival. The youths prepared to meet him. The village brought out the old and young to welcome her son after his long absence. Umm Siman was in the crowd leaning on her cane. Happiness had brought back the beauty of her youth, and she seemed stronger and more vivacious.

When the sleek car pulled up, the woman lost her balance as she danced and ululated and wept and laughed. She forgot her cane in the flurry of excitement and rushed forward with open arms, unveiling her head, welcoming her only son.

But when she embraced him, the fire in her eyes died. No one noticed as she stared at the stout, older man in front of her. She was trying to convince herself that this was her son Siman the seventeen-year-old who had once held her in his strong arms and left a farewell kiss on her cheeks.

'Siman plans to marry. I wonder whom,' Hanna said the following morning. And a day later, Hanna walked past proudly. 'Siman is going to propose to Laila, daughter of Abu Farhud.'

The courtship didn't last more than a few days, while the marriage arrangements were completed.

'Laila is lucky. Her happiness has come to her on a golden platter.' This is what Saada repeated as she sat on the bench and tried to find good fortune for her two ugly daughters.

Najla passed her hand through her chestnut hair. 'So, how about the money?'

The village youths, who wander through the narrow alleyways talked all week about the new event.

'Dollars, brother, are what count nowadays. They take the most beautiful girls in the village. By God, Rajji is right. The best thing to do is to leave!'

The echoes of jealousy, reproach, and malice faded into the splendid wedding which Siman planned for his bride.

I can't remember what Laila was like before that time. I can still see her standing motionless in a circle of village girls, listening to the trills of joy and moving her head back and forward according to the demands of her hairdresser.

Hanna came closer, establishing her presence as always. 'Cover her in necklaces, bracelets and earrings. Put two necklaces here. You are a bride, my darling.'

Najla pleaded with her, saying, 'Where is your taste, Miss

Hanna? She should have a necklace to go with each outfit . . . Let's go, people are waiting for the bride.'

I watched her elegant fingers adorn the bride. They were like steel, moving mechanically. Every one of the women used Laila's face and body to prove her skill with cosmetics.

'There's too little eyeliner. The rouge doesn't match the dress. Let her hair down to her shoulders. Where is the perfume? Dab a little on, Hanna. It smells good!'

The groom seemed concerned about every woman at the celebration, except the bride. Laila was in a strange faraway world. She was distracted, incapable of thinking amidst the fast current which dragged her to a single point. Her pleading glances shifted to me. She realised what was happening: she was to be sacrificed to save her family from poverty.

Her words pierced my heart and constricted my soul, 'What do you think, Muna? Will I be happy?'

I looked for something to hold on to and leaned against it. 'If that's what you want . . .'

Then, she fled from me wiping a tear from her eyes. She was about to spoil the colourful veil which young women are supposed to wear over their faces.

Why did you do this, Laila? For whom?

I entered the boudoir where the bride in her wedding dress was seated on some pillows and an ottoman like a pigeon. The white veil hung down over her face and shoulders.

I was reminded of an ancient legend about a hungry dragon and a king's beautiful, young daughter. The lot fell to the beautiful princess to wait on the beach for the dragon who once a year devoured the most beautiful girl of the village. The maiden waited, her hands on her breast, her eyes lowered in resignation.

She remained submissive as the dragon crept towards her . . .

I looked around, searching for someone to destroy the dragon and take the beautiful maiden out of its jaws and plunge a sharp spear into its neck . . . but the hero whose picture hung at the front of the church, did not enter the room. He left Laila for the dragon.

It was as though Laila had sensed the creaking of my thoughts and when our glances met she burst into tears. I fled from her to a remote corner in which Mirsal was sitting.

Mirsal had been looking for a drug to make her forget reality (her lover was about to emigrate) and heal the cruel agony in her breast. At that moment, I heard the ululating ring out from her throat like the screams of a person drowning in a stormy ocean. Her voice continues to echo between the walls of silence in my heart. We stood together, bidding Laila farewell, and gazing at her as she lifted her trembling hand to take the arm of the groom.

The next morning, life in the village resumed its normal tranquility. Everyone went to work. In front of the tiny bedroom where Laila spent the first night with her husband, her mother stood and raised between her hands, 'the gown' stained with blood. She smiled proudly. 'Come, Umm Siman, come and kiss your daughter-in-law.'

I remember that spring day. Its air was perfumed and its sounds trilled in my ears. The cock crowed, the chickens cackled as they prepared to lay eggs. The cows lowed in the nearby square where they were gathering before being hastened off to pasture. The donkey brayed under the window.

For a long time the storms of cold winter obscured the 'morning symphony' and my voice, on those long, rainy days, was muffled. Spring extended its fingers, pushed aside the veil, and blood pumped through the arteries.

I smelt the aroma of spiced coffee, and jumped out of bed full of joyous energy, 'I love life, Mother; it is our greatest blessing, we are connected with the universe whose sweet refreshing drops we drink.'

My mother ignored my philosophising and gave me a cup of coffee. Then we sat on the bench, breathing in the morning breezes. I gazed at my mother's face, at the silent, tranquil features. Disturbing wrinkles began to appear and challenge her artless attempts to hide them.

Every morning, my mother and father and the neighbours were there, surrounding me, pushing me on, controlling my breaths.

And that morning, I wanted to do something to break the circle. I needed to be free, independent, to escape from the group.

I laugh now when I think how serious I was at that time. I hitched my entire future on that moment.

I escaped from the house without informing my mother. It was my first attempt at independence to prove to myself that it was possible for me to close the door of the house without asking anyone's permission.

I didn't know where I was going. I decided to walk along the vineyard path, picking up little pebbles with which I played or which I threw at a nearby tree.

I continued walking, my footsteps on the pebbles accompanied me. The birds' calls reverberated amongst the olive trees. I climbed up to the terraces of the village, to the big Qirqar rock where the villagers go on their days off.

Since when did the rock have that name? No one remembers. Abu Elias once told me the legend of 'Qirqar' who had lived in the village hundreds of years ago. He was a recluse living in a little hut, far from people. He would sit on his doorstep, reading an old book. As the inhabitants passed, they greeted him or brought him plates of food and loaves of bread, and he would keep them in a little cupboard so they would dry out or spoil before he ate them.

He would respond to the greeting with a nod of the head or a wave of the hand.

No one had heard Qirqar's voice or speech. The villagers were used to seeing him every night, carrying his book, making for the rock, sitting on it and contemplating nature. He loosened his tongue to repeat the words over and over again like the beads of the rosary. Some boys discovered his secret and told it to the villagers. The next day, when a group of them tried to discover the recluse's secret, they found no trace. No one knew how the recluse disappeared, and the rock has carried his name to this day.

The legend has been passed down through the generations like so many others in the village: The door of the 'Sakra' whence Abu Khalil, my great great grandfather, saw the beautiful genie combing her hair with a golden comb, is one of them.

The most delightful legend is of Abu Nawwaf, the mill owner. Every night after the customers had left he would meet with a gang of genies who chose the mill for their weddings.

Legends and genies and charms . . . One time my grandmother burnt a handful of incense to scare away the evil spirits from the house. Angelina's place was 'haunted' before she called the priest to pray in it. Genies were living there. Umm Elias swore that she would light a dozen candles for the Virgin if she found the table cloth the genie had borrowed for a wedding.

The evil eye! The milk dried up in the udder of the cow. Umm Salim hurried to Saada and asked her to drive away the evil eye. This was one of Saada's talents. It was known that she kept magic charms. Women rushed to her in hard times: 'The children are sick', 'Burn some salt', 'Melt some lead'.

Saada assured the group that she had been given the power to see the possessor of the evil eye, she could see it in molten lead, but she was not allowed to speak about him or say his name.

The villagers pointed at the possessors of the evil eyes. And the mothers fled with their babies from their path. And the dairy cows were not permitted to be touched by their looks.

I took off my shoes to climb on the giant rock which overlooked the valleys, hills and homes of the village. It was a gigantic fortress, its top was level allowing little girls to hold their meetings on it. I leaned over to touch the sharp edges on the face of the rock. Then I sat on it, extended my leg and lifted my arms in an attempt to fly. A strange feeling seized me, as though I had been liberated from gravity. This feeling lasted an instant and I thought: 'If only the whole of life could be gathered into these moments of rare elation!' I floated on a pool of warm multicoloured sunlight.

I forgot the rock, its edges rough against my leg. I forgot the powerful smooth iciness of the spring sun. I felt as though my body were ether able to fly up freed of all shackles.

The village grew smaller, its colours changed until I could no longer make it out; it was finally as small as a spider. I saw its roads scattered in every direction. I saw them move and circulate, connecting its arteries with those of the world beyond the horizon.

I was as ignorant of that world as I am today of the hereafter. Hidden, mysterious strings still connect me to it, and I see it through books and the gossip of strangers who visited the village in summer, and the conversations of Shamal the merchant who brought us new gadgets.

The sizes continued to diminish, and the objects changed until the cawing of a raven circling near me over the corpse of a donkey returned me to reality. Many plains extended in front of me. And in a furrow of the plains nestled our village, the only spring to extend life to the land.

The village and its cemetery were life and death . . . then the land stretched out barren red, or fertile and green or pregnant with olive and almond trees swelling with pebbles of hard rock.

Behind every valley is a man who emigrates. And in every branch is a longing for the strong brown arms plowing up the soil and pruning the trees, and returning youth to the land.

The branches disappear. Handkerchiefs wave from the windows of cars speeding away, escaping along roads without frontiers.

The fields continue to groan their barrenness. The roots dry out in the fertile vineyard. The desiccation reaches the press, and the pressers wash their hands and legs, then they lock the doors or they smash them as they follow those who are leaving.

The contagion of the drought moves on to the plump cows' udders and to the young mothers' breasts, to the souls of the youths groping through the empty alleys.

I wiped away these disturbing thoughts and looked lovingly at the fields and longed to remain suspended there in that detached existence, living with the rock and the ghosts of ancient legends.

Translated from the Arabic
by Mona Yacoubian and Miriam Cooke

Hanan al-Shaikh

(1945–)

Hanan al-Shaikh was born in Beirut, Lebanon. She attended a traditional Muslim girls primary school and then the fashionable Ahliya school. In 1963, she went to Cairo to study at the American College for Girls. During her four years in Egypt, she wrote her first novel *Intihar Rajul Mayyit* (The Suicide of a Dead Man). In 1967, she returned to Beirut where she worked as a journalist. She has spent considerable time in the Arabian Peninsula and now lives in London. Her entire oeuvre has been produced outside Lebanon, yet she is considered one of the Beirut Decentrists. In addition to *The Suicide of a Dead Man*, her novels include *Faras al-Shaitan* (Praying Mantis, 1971), *Hikayat Zahra* (The Story of Zahra, 1980, translated into English in 1986) and *Misk al-Ghazal* (The Musk of the Gazelles, 1988). She has also published a collection of short stories entitled *Wardat al-Sahra* (Desert Rose, 1982).

'A Girl Called Apple' was published in the *Wardat al-Sahra* collection. It tells of a bedouin girl's resistance to tribal customs for the arrangement of marriage. She wants to marry and to have children, but she refuses to be commodified. Her rejection is total, it is also painful.

A Girl Called Apple

1981

❦

Apple had not married. She was almost forty and she had not yet married. Her dark skin was not the reason (many girls with her colour had married) nor was it her name. That is the least important matter in marriage, and anyhow oasis girls are sometimes called by the names of fruit: her girl friend Banana had married last year.

Fate? Accident? Or was it Apple's obstinacy which had refused and continued to refuse to raise the wedding flag on the roof? Even though its hoisting upon the occasion of the girl's first menses was customary in the oasis. But Apple had refused. She had begged and cried, hiding her face, saying to her father, 'Daddy, please don't. I don't want it.' Her mother had thought that Apple was embarrassed that everyone – old and young in the oasis – should learn that she had reached womanhood. So she shook her head at her husband, who understood and left Apple alone.

A month later when the matter was forgotten, her father was about to plant the red flag in an earth-filled container. But Apple ran up to him, begging him with tears streaming from her eyes, 'Daddy, I don't want it.' And he didn't understand. He asked her in obvious confusion, 'You mean that you don't want to get married?'

And when she answered, he did not understand what she meant despite the fact that he heard her say, 'I want to get married, but I don't want the flag.' And her weeping increased.

Her father clapped his hands together and repeated, 'There is no power and no strength save in God.' How was it possible? Her grandmother, her mother, all her aunts, and every woman born in this oasis had been married by means of the flag. The importance of raising the flag had not been explained to them, but they knew as well as they knew their own faces that the flag was probably the only way to get married. Indeed, this oasis was the only one that had not relied on the services of a matchmaker for generations – in fact, not from the time of Hind, who separated more than she brought together, and who used to describe every bride as a model of virtue, every groom as the moon of his age, a cavalier. The girl was said to be an enchanting dark-skinned innocent and the groom owned ten camels. The families would agree quickly to these descriptions, and Hind would swear solemnly that this was the truth. And on the wedding night the screams could be heard. Moreover, many strangers came to this oasis. They would halt their caravans, letting their camels drink for a couple of hours. Surely the idea of marriage would not occur to anyone in such a short period, and yet the flags fluttering above the roofs would tickle the men's hearts, enticing them to marry in this oasis.

Apple refused the red flag, although her father had tried to plant it in some sand in a can whose shiny surface rust had dulled. He tried to hoist the flag without her knowing. But Apple did not let the night pass with the stars guarding her flag. She pulled it down, and then she knelt and kissed her father's feet, weeping and saying, 'I don't want it.' Her father could not understand the secret of her refusal, but believed that an evil fortune had chosen his daughter, Apple, to be this generation's oasis spinster.

Scandal tried to whisper to her mother, but how? For Apple, like all the girls of the oasis, never left her home, day or night. And if ever these girls did leave their homes, they would be enveloped in *abayas*, their faces covered and they would be accompanied by someone. Days passed and Apple continued to help her father dye the sheep skins at home, bring water from the well, sweep and cook. Then she sat at her loom and with her woollen threads wove a carpet of camel hair. She thought about herself and wondered why it was that she refused despite her ardent desire to get married and to have a house of her own. And she loved children. She wanted to have lots of them. When she had really asked herself the reason, she discovered that the answer was easy: she was mortified at the thought of the flag and its fluttering on the roof. When she said this to her father, his wrinkles smoothed out and his hopes rose. Without further ado he got up and set off to plant the flag on the roof of the house of her bachelor uncle, after saying to her happily, 'Rejoice, for whoever knocks at your uncle's door will be sent here.' And to her amazement she found herself refusing adamantly. She was surprised by her refusal, especially since the red flag, the one that was used for the under-twenties, was about to pass her by; the blue one was good until age thirty, and then finally came the yellow one. Apple thought: 'God willing, I shall marry under the shadow of the blue flag.'

But she did not. The days passed, never to return, and the blue flag was about to disappear with her years. And Apple refused to let the flag flutter over the roof. And whenever she passed by the mud houses of the oasis and saw the coloured flags playing with the breeze, she laughed to herself and said, 'Crazy, stupid women.' And yet Apple envied the bride when she dyed her hands with henna in preparation for the wedding, choking whenever she saw her sitting like a princess, surrounded by singing and dancing in her honour. Whenever she heard the cry of the newborn babe she would run to the house, pick up the infant, put kohl in its eyes, and bathe it in oil, wishing that it were of her own flesh and blood.

The red flag flew away, and then the blue one, as she jumped past thirty. And although Apple shrugged her shoulders as though she did not care, she began to know depression. She had never before found herself grumbling about helping her father and doing the housework. She sat behind her loom, pulling the threads through and tying them nervously and in annoyance. She kept asking herself, 'Why do I refuse marriage? I long for a husband to be the crown on my head, and for children to skip around me. I am hiding the beautiful clothes and the turquoise stones and the heavy rugs until the day of my marriage.' She turned and saw the shadow of a date branch on the wall of the living room. She saw her mother's dress next to the prayer garment, and suddenly she was filled with tenderness for everything she saw, and she felt that this time she had found the answer. And she said out loud, 'I don't want to leave this oasis.' And she hurried to her father and said, 'I don't want to leave you or the oasis.'

And her father's wrinkles smoothed out: 'May you never leave my sight, Apple. If the man who marries you is a stranger to the oasis, I shall give him three camels and I shall build you a house in our oasis.'

He got up and, stretching under the bed, dragged out a palm leaf basket that Apple had made. When part of the yellow flag appeared, Apple ran to her father and kissed his hands, weeping and crying, and her head was almost rent from her body to fling itself against the walls. And she sighed and wept for herself because she had refused, because she could not control her obstinacy.

The following day after a sleepless night, she compelled herself to accept, and she hurried to tell her father the news, having seen with pity the grief and sorrow which had inscribed themselves in his wrinkles. But no sooner did she see the yellow flag in her father's trembling hand than she fell to his feet, once again begging his pardon and again refusing the flag.

Apple changed as though the black sickness had hit her. She began to frown much more, becoming thin and sad. She was annoyed by her mother when she wished her good morning and by her father when he wished her good evening. But she never let her annoyance cross the bridge to her inside.

One evening, she was holding the thread in her hand and was asking herself the question that she had thought about every moment of her life when she held her breath and heaved a deep sigh. And this time she grasped the true answer and it was so simple: the flag might flutter for months on end, and no one might come. I would be like mutton or old dates for sale. And she found herself for the first time coming to grips with her fear: 'Maybe no one will come. And everyone in the oasis will see the flag wherever they go, and they will feel so sorry for me because I am unsaleable merchandise.' Again she blamed herself, defeated: 'But why was this simple, clear reason so hard to find before age forty?' Apple found herself leaning under the bed and carefully dragging out the basket, making sure not to wake up her mother. She took out the flag that no house in the oasis needed, and she climbed the stairs up to the roof while her mother and father and the oasis were sound asleep. And this after everyone was sure that marriage had passed Apple by forever, because it would not be long before even the yellow flag would be gone, and then no one would open the path of marriage to her. Indeed, it was felt that this was already the case.

In the starlight, Apple raised her face to the heavens and called upon God to be her witness. Then she knelt and fixed the flag in the container, thinking all the while that the oasis was small, that there were few men and that there was no matchmaker. She went downstairs and, sighing, sat down to await a knock at the door.

Translated from the Arabic
by Miriam Cooke

Ihsan Assal

(1921–)

Ihsan Assal was born in Cairo. She was educated into the third grade of primary school. She is a member of numerous writers' associations in Cairo, and was a founding member of the Council for the Administration of Children's Culture. Her novels include: *Al-Amaq al-Baida* (The Distant Depths, serialised in *Al-Idha a wa al-Tilivizyun* between 1960 and 1961); *Al-Ghaiba* (The Absent One, 1963); *Al-Husa wa al-Jabal* (Pebbles and the Mountain, 1966). *Satr Maghlut* (A Mistaken Line) was written in collaboration with Huda Jad and Ihsan Kamal, in 1971.

Bait al-Taa (House of Obedience, 1962) is her only collection from which this story is taken. *Bait al-taa* is a provision within Islamic law whereby a wife who has left home against the wishes of her husband can be accused of *nushaz* – disobedience – and forcibly returned by the order of a *qadi*. *Bait al-taa* has been incorporated into statutory law in many Arab countries. In 1928, Ihsan al-Kousi in a lecture at the American University at Beirut said: 'Sirs, the *bait al-taa* is more dangerous than prisons for criminals: the prisoners are guarded by men invested with authority by the law. They are not driven by hate or animosity to take revenge or to trangress the bounds of legally bestowed authority. The husband is clearly an involved guard. No one controls him. To whom can the poor woman condemned to obey him have recourse? He can claim that his incarcerated wife has disobeyed him, so he can insult her and hit her and the courts will not consider this behaviour to be outside his legal rights. All these injustices are committed even though the state has a public legislation order that punishes anyone who hurts someone else. All citizens enjoy the protection of this legislation, that is all except for this poor woman. Worst of all, these injustices are committed in the name of a religion that says: 'Do not take revenge on your women' and 'Be gentle with them or leave them respectfully.'

The House of Obedience

1962

৵৹

'Never, Uncle, that's a lie!'

Just like that my voice rang out in the courtroom, exonerating my father of the charge of having induced me to leave my husband's house.

There was a roar of laughter in the courtroom . . . The judge smiled and looked down. The persons on his right and left turned toward me, and the three of them whispered together. The case was adjourned to another time.

The next time my father approached the jury. He held out a piece of paper. Quietly, he said:

'This is my daughter's birth certificate. Fortunately I found it.'

It was discovered that Nabila was only fifteen!

The judge took the paper from my father and studied it. Then . . . the case was rejected. My father was not punished for having married me off when I was a legal minor. He said happily:

'Let's hope we'll be given a break from these court cases this year.'

But a few months before the year was up we were surprised to hear that the case had been revived. My husband announced that I had completed my sixteenth year by the Hijra calendar. Now I had to obey him.

At sundown less than a week after receiving this notice my youngest sister rushed in, shouting:

'Hide, Nabila. Hide at once. There's a police officer with a soldier and a woman in a *milaya* asking about you.'

I did not know what to do. I sat in a corner between the chest-of-drawers and the wall and wept in suppressed convulsions. I was terrified.

My father came in, smiling reassuringly.

'Hey, little one, that's enough. There's no need for all that. Come on. Get dressed, and I'll come with you.'

Calmly we left our house with the police officer and the soldier.

In one of the taxis . . . I found my husband. He welcomed me with a broad, sarcastic smile.

I didn't pay him any attention until we reached the police station. When the legal proceedings were completed, they handed me over to him. At that moment, I could not control myself. I looked at him with defiance in my eyes.

He responded with a look filled with contempt and defiance: 'We'll see.'

My father asked the police officer if he could accompany me with my husband, and he agreed. Then I entered the house of obedience!

In the living room I was greeted by a sofa that was more like a swing. On either side was a cane chair, and in front was a small table.

I rushed into the bedroom to check out the rest of the furniture . . . a wooden bed, a large cupboard, a clothes peg.

For a moment I gazed at all this. Then I felt the blood go to my head as I exploded: 'I can't ever live here. Is this the legal house? It's not possible.'

Maybe my father pretended to be calm for my sake, or maybe he just pretended so as to assure my husband that we would not get excited. At all events, he patted me on the back affectionately. Then with a smile that I felt was forced on to his face, he said:

'Take it easy, daughter. Calm down. This is the legal house and there's someone supervising it.' He added, 'I'm going to reassure your mother. I'll bring you a small suitcase with everything you need.'

My father left. My husband followed close behind without uttering a sound. Then I heard the key turn in the lock.

I didn't cry. I didn't collapse into a chair. I swore that I'd never weaken whatever happened to me.

I hurried into the bedroom where I found two covers. I took one of them and a pillow. Then I returned to the living room, where I used the sofa as a bed.

I was happy to sleep. All I had to do was to consider my situation carefully. I was not far from Cairo prison. The house of obedience looked out on to its large square. I smiled to myself.

Lazily I threw myself on to the bed, and went over all the events of the day. Then I heard a light knock on the apartment door. I got up quickly. It was my father. With a sneer, I said, 'It's locked.'

My father whispered deeply, 'Never mind. I'll sit on the stairs until someone comes.'

For quite a while my father and I conversed through the closed door. Then my husband came and opened up without any apologies. Without waiting my father handed over what he had brought. He charged me, in front of my husband, to look after the house of obedience.

My husband locked the door from inside.

I shook my head silently and threw myself into some books I had asked my father to bring. I only raised my head out of these books when darkness had enveloped the place and I had to light the living room gas lamp.

I went on reading without bothering to respond to my husband's repeated attempts to talk. But my absorption in my reading did not succeed in calming my nerves and making me forget what was going on around me. I pretended to sleep so as to be able to think better. Very quietly, I closed my book and put it by my side. I lowered the lamp and then stretched out on the sofa after having wrapped myself well in the cover.

I closed my eyes to save myself from my husband's piercing glances. But then I heard his slow steps coming towards me. It was not long before he had sat down beside me and put his arm around my waist over the cover. Despite my agitation and revolt, I remained still until I felt him bend over my mouth and his heavy breath brushed me. I could not stand it any longer. I moved away quickly and said angrily, 'Adil, go away!'

But he didn't go away. His advances became more violent and harsh. I struggled obstinately until he left me.

The lamp lit his face as he turned his burning glances toward me and stormed, 'Get up.'

I sat up defiantly, 'Excuse me, Sir . . .'

'Do you not know who you are to me?'

'What do you mean, not know . . . I am your wife in the eyes of the law, Sir.'

'Is that why you push me away?'

Very, very calmly and slowly I answered quietly, 'Because I don't want you.'

He smiled haughtily and sarcastically, 'Never?'

Confidently, 'Of course. You think that the obedience verdict means that I have to give myself to you against my will? Adil, whatever you do I shall never in my whole life be yours.'

He responded with the same confidence. 'I shall never divorce you.'

He left me in a great fury. But I was delighted at my deliverance from the first battle. I slept like a log.

It seems that he thought that if he did not give me breakfast that would be suitable punishment. He didn't know that I had a lovely morning.

After getting up I observed my colleagues behind their walls. I sent them morning greetings, although I knew that they could not see me behind my prison window. Nevertheless, I felt that there was a strong link that bound us together.

I refused the lunch that my husband brought. I affected not to
be aware of his presence and not to be upset to be in his house.
Unfortunately, I did not continue with my abstinence. My mother
came after a bit, and before I knew it I was in her arms and our
tears were embracing.

When I had calmed down, I ate the food my mother had
brought. In front of her, my husband tried to say some nice things
to me. But I didn't answer. He got angry and threatened me. When
my mother left, he followed her.

Again, I heard the key turn in the lock.

Despite the quiet night and the peace that lay over everything, I
was in a state of anxiety about the coming battle. But he did not
approach my room when he returned at midnight. He left me to
rage until dawn when I fell asleep weeping.

A week passed in like manner with some nocturnal battles. One
morning my mother-in-law's servant came to wash our clothes and
when she went up to hang out the laundry she didn't lock the door.
This was the first time that I found myself unlocked. Before you
could say 'knife' I was in the tram going to Kubri Limun. People
were looking in amazement at a girl tripping over a black *milaya*.

I only relaxed when I got out of the tram at the Kubri Al-Qubba
station.

My mother laughed merrily when she saw me in the *milaya*. But
my father's joy at my return did not last. When he heard of my
escape, the lawyer told my father. 'He will do it again. And on the
third time *nushuz* is declared. I think that's what he wants. She will
be neither married nor divorced.'

It was not a week before I was sent back. The only difference
from the previous time was the number of battles that broke out
when my husband extinguished the gas lamp.

I was tempted by the thought of escape once again. I seized the
opportunity of my husband's midday nap without locking the door.

Those were beautiful days that I spent in my father's house. I
convinced myself that my husband would not try to get me back
once again. But one day when I was in the bathroom I was
surprised by a clamour in the house, my mother's voice denying
that I was in the house and my husband's voice demanding that the
house be searched. Then . . . light knocks on the door and my
mother whispering:

'It's no use . . . Get dressed at once!'

I don't know how I put the clothes on my quaking body. I went
with him in misery, I had lost all hope of getting rid of this man.

This time he knew how to get his revenge. After about two
months imprisonment in the house of obedience, I felt that the

space would suffocate me, that I could not stand any more of this. Then I made a decision that allowed me to sleep peacefully.

Early in the morning I entered his room. Breathing with difficulty, I said quietly, 'Do you want *nushuz*?' Firmly, I added, 'Don't go to work today. Let's go to the court and I'll tell them that I'm recalcitrant. Come on, give me the papers and get me out of this house.'

Then I sat down and struggled to catch my breath.

Gleefully, he said, 'So you're coming to your senses.'

He added, gallantly, 'Whenever you want to come back to me I'll take you as my wife.'

He didn't lock the door after him this time, and I didn't escape. I calmed myself and told my father about the agreement my husband and I had reached.

Sighing deeply, he replied, 'That's the best solution now. Later, I'll offer him a few more pennies to divorce you and we'll finish with the matter.'

He added like someone who has washed his hands of the matter. 'As long as you have decided that you don't want to be with him I shall not force you.'

Among the papers that my husband brought was one that certified that I was disobedient to my husband and that I had no right to a divorce or to alimony for the rest of my life. My only right was to leave the house of obedience.

I agreed to these conditions. All that was left to do was to sign the papers the following day in the court house. Then I could relax forever.

In the afternoon he left me to copy the papers, and I was left alone for the last time.

The calm was total. The magical sunset drew me to the window. I floated far away beyond Muqattam. In my dark purple gown I floated, completely at peace despite the darkness that enveloped my married life. Despite the glow of the sunset I preferred the night, the time of rest, whatever its price.

When I left the room I noticed my husband's jacket on the clothes peg. Quickly I searched the pockets. I found what I wanted, all of the legal papers that if I got hold of would prevent him from seeking another judgement for a year. I shuddered with delight. I was torn between wanting to steal my freedom papers and wanting to enjoy my victory to the end. I left the papers where they were and crept out of the room. The arrival of my mother and father saved me from my quandary.

I calmed my nerves, and showed my joy at the prospect of leaving for freedom. I didn't tell them where the papers were.

After a while the husband came, but with another paper. This one registered my *nushuz* for the rest of my life with the stipulation of his right to impose obedience whenever he felt like it. He merely promised that he would not enforce the paper. All he was doing was obeying the law.

The room whirled around me. Then I went stealthily into the other room and in a flash the papers were flying through the air in tiny pieces. Then I returned to them having closed the window without a sound. My father was begging the two of us, my husband and me, to forget our differences and to resume our married life.

I pretended to be submissive until my husband should agree to a truce. Very early in the morning I changed my clothes half way down the stairs and left my husband snoring. I closed the door behind me.

I was the only woman in the still lit tram. Under my arm was a robe and inside it was a pair of slippers.

My family's amazement at my presence did not last long. My husband very soon appeared looking ridiculous; his clothes were unbuttoned, his shoes untied, his hair unkempt. Smiling, he said, 'Nabila, is this how you let me come out?'

Then looking at me he said tenderly, 'I know perfectly well that you don't want me. So I'm going to divorce you today. Happy? Come on, change your dress. Give me a comb and a tie. After breakfast my uncle will come with us to some *maazun*.'

He waited till we were ready to leave. Then he drew me aside and whispered, 'Bring the papers with you.'

'Papers? Which papers?'

'The court papers.'

Coldly and sarcastically, I answered, 'Oh, the papers that will send me to the police station. The verdict of obedience with which you want to suffocate me for the rest of my life.'

He was overcome by an indescribable fury. He left, swearing that he would revive the case however much money and effort it cost.

I knew he would come back. In fact, he returned the same day and tried to trick me into coming out with him for one last time. But I refused. The house of obedience had taught me to be afraid of being alone with my husband.

When we were with the *maazun* I was shocked when my husband got up, left us and then called me from the door of a neighbouring room.

I didn't respond and looked fearfully at my father, who said quietly, 'See what he wants.'

Trembling with fear, I went to him. He drew me into the room and I was sure I was going to die at once. But he held me to his chest tenderly and kissed my forehead and then sighing deeply and weeping, he said:

'Good bye, Nabila. I had wanted you to be with me forever. It looks as though I didn't know how.'

I started to cry when I heard the vow of divorce, as though a dagger was plunged into my heart.

When I walked out into the street my husband's last words still rang in my ears.

The last sentence despite its simplicity was the only nice thing he had said to me throughout our married life. I felt some regret, for I had discovered suddenly that he really loved me. Nevertheless, I absolutely refused to return to him when he wanted me to come to him once again.

The shadow of the house of obedience had estranged me from him . . . forever.

Translated from the Arabic
by Miriam Cooke

Evelyne Accad

(1943–)

Evelyne Accad was born in Beirut, Lebanon. She began her studies at the Beirut College for Women (now known as Beirut University College). In 1973, she received her Ph.D. in Comparative Literature from the University of Illinois where she has been teaching French and Comparative Literature since 1974. She has published extensively on women in the literatures of the Middle East, Sub-Saharan and North Africa. Her major work is *Veil of Shame: The Role of Women in the Contemporary Fiction of North Africa and the Arab World* (1978). She has written some fiction, including the novel, *L'Excisée* (1982) and *Coquelicot du Massacre* (1988).

The following passages are taken from *L'Excisée*. They describe a woman's initiation into strict tribal life. This woman is led through initial submission to outright rejection: 'Woman refuse this hold on you. Woman make your voice heard.'

The Excised

1982

❀

She throws the cigarette butt into the sea, sadly watching it
disappear over the waves. Presentiment? Mirror? Reflections? Echo
of one soul in search of another, in search of communication, of
understanding, of a departure over the walls, partitions and veils.
Furiously she lights another cigarette. Her eyes are lost on the
horizon, her brow knitted, her neck tense. Her mouth is bitterly
tight, her hands tremble. She turns once again towards E. (the
novel's protagonist) as though hesitating to say something to her.
She stares at her for a while. Then she blurts it out, as though
anxious to get rid of a burden she had been carrying ever since she
boarded the ship.

'Do you know what they do to women over there when they
reach puberty, or even before, or just before marriage if they had
by mischance escaped the old women's vigil? Do you know the
suffering of the flesh, the burning, the tearing, the removal of this
delicate and sensitive organ between the legs, excision, the ablation
of the nerve called the clitoris, this button of desire, and the small
lips and the large lips are also cut, mutilated, excised, and the
wound that bleeds and bleeds and bleeds without end, and the days
and weeks of immobility in the dark, legs bound together with
rope, the body torn by spasms, and the feeling of shame, of a
terrible shame, the cries of the women, the piercing pain that will
not let up when you know that your body will never be the same
again, when you feel that something has been taken from you that
allowed you to throb, to palpitate, when you are afraid of dying
because of all the blood that has escaped out of your body, that you
have already been raped, that they have taken part of your life and
instead have sewn you, tied you up, closed you up so that you will
never again be able to breathe, to open yourself up to life, to
tenderness, to the dew of desert mornings. And the women scream
and scream and scream happy to avenge themselves of that which
life has deprived them, happy to see the blood continue and that
suffering had not been limited to their bodies, but that the internal
cycle perpetuates itself and turns and turns and turns . . . What are
you doing? Why don't you break the cycle like I did? Why do you
not revolt before it's too late, before you too become an excised

woman? You have lived through the war (Lebanese Civil War). You have seen the horror of bloodshed on the streets, on the earth, outside yourself, but if you had to live this blood and this shame and these horrors that you have described to me, these mutilated bodies, these ripped out sex organs, these violated corpses, if you had to live all of this inside yourself, in your very flesh, what would you do?'

E. thinks that she's dealing with a lunatic. She doesn't understand the stranger's words very well. Sexuality had always been a taboo subject at home, and the young woman's descriptions make her feel vaguely sick. She anticipates a bitter move toward unknown regions whose violence exceeds that which she had already experienced. She is very alert and filled with contradictions. She is tense and does not know what to say. The stranger's look has taken on a sinister air. Her face is pale as death. All her movements seem to be concentrated on the cigarette which burns in its ash tip, red with purple and violet. She twitches spasmodically and uncontrollably. She looks around fearfully, like a little bird caught in a big net. Her large, black, sad eyes stare at her distractedly and wildly like someone who does not know where to go, to whom to turn. Then she disappears behind a rescue boat like a child who has just been whipped for something unfair, monstrous, devastating and who does not want to show her tears, and who does not want to let her chagrin show in front of a spectator or even in front of a mirror.

The following days she looks in vain for the stranger who seems to have disappeared. She goes up to the bridge, looks behind the rescue boats, but there is no trace of the Egyptian woman. Had she ever existed? Had she dreamt the whole scene? Then she remembers some of the stranger's words: 'Maybe one of my brothers has followed me.' And what if it were true? It's the kind of crime one finds all the time in her country. Wash honour in blood or in the sea. She leans over to look into the sea that has suddenly become dark and menacing. She is overwhelmed by an anxiety that chokes her. She would like to understand. She would like to find. She looks into the cabins through the portholes. She lifts the canvas that covers cars or boxes. She follows traces through the ropes. And always she returned to the sea that seemed impassive and cruel. Why did it not vomit up all its secrets?

(*The protagonist, a Lebanese Christian, is married to P., a Muslim Arab. The following section describes her thoughts as she is driven to the groom's village.*)

The woman pushed behind the veil
is forced into herself
She beats against the walls of her heart
And her hands hit the veil
Of her past, her present and her future
That are all in the same image
She cannot even cry
Because her invisible tears
Only mark her skin
Behind the veil
The look of the other is never her reflection.

The car continues over the dusty road. It is desert, sand that stretches out into infinity. She has wrapped herself in her veil and is silent, her head turned to the window through the veil. She no longer belongs to the world of men. Suddenly she has broken through the veil, gone through the partition and entered the world of silence, of mystery. She breathes with difficulty. Will she be able to stand this world of abnegation? She has been crushed. From childhood she has been crushed, stifled. Yet she has already hit, screamed, broken, shaken the Father's yoke . . .

In front, the two men are talking. She no longer understands what they are saying. The separation has been effected, their words no longer make sense, language has become a vehicle, like this car, an instrument of conventions, an instrument of power, a money-making machine, violins screeching discordantly . . . And they talk, they talk . . . They talk work, they talk money, they talk authority.

Behind she is no longer anything, an abandoned object, a black mountain that one drags around that one has to return home, that one must penetrate through the easiest orifices, so that the mountain should produce little ones, lots of little ones, between the mountain and P., between their dream and . . .

The serpent hisses
The woman scratches the wall with her nails, with her palms
she hits and she hits
only the echo responds
She wants to see the sea, she wants to find its issue
The serpent is very close to the child's head
The child cries and the woman gets up
and hides it in her torn veil and dress
Her hands and nails are bleeding, her feet torn up
The serpent hisses along the wall
And the woman is afraid

The car enters the village. A crowd of neighbours, friends, relatives and children await them inside their new home. The house consists of a rectangular courtyard surrounded by low buildings. The buildings are juxtaposed next to each other: closed buildings, courtyard surrounded by walls, walls surrounded by more walls. There are lots of children watching her wide-eyed. The looks move her. These are the same looks that she had felt when she had visited the Palestinian camp: inquisitor's look, the fresh look of childhood, the look of hope, looks which try to understand, looks which cut.

What could she represent for them? A black mountain that moves around, the new arrival, the Christian, the stranger? Where were the dreams they had as they looked out over the sea and into the infinite skies, when he held her hand gently and told her of all those children for whom they would build a new world? What kind of a message can she bring them, woman become shape, secluded woman, enveloped woman, woman-envelope, sewn-up woman, woman stopped by the veil.

She looks at all these children and stretches out her hands to them in a gesture of despair and anguish, she wants to reach out, to understand and transform, she wants to grow branches, to go out, to blossom. But nobody sees that gesture and nobody understands her anguish.

> Marry as you wish, two, three or four women.
> But if you fear that you cannot be fair then take one woman or war captives
>
> (Quran, 4:3).

Ever since she no longer satisfies his nocturnal ardour, ever since he has sown the seed and the seed has taken and she has nailed herself to her bed, sick of the heat and of fear at this new life that she feels in herself, he has abandoned her. He goes elsewhere now. Shouldn't that be a relief? Why this fear?

The period of waiting for pregnant women ends with childbirth. God has made things easy for those who fear Him.

She feels terribly alone in this Damascene room with its violet bed. It is worse than the bedroom with the nailed shutters and the double-locked door, because outside there is nothing, not even the hope of a promise, not even the sea with its infinite horizons.

Her stomach is beginning to grow and spread like the flowers in the desert which open on a single day, large flowers with brilliantly coloured petals, and only live that single day. She looks at her smooth stomach and the shivering of the skin when the child moves. She drinks a lot, she drinks all the time. She wishes that the

water might fill her and fill her and create a new life in her, a
different life, a child that would know how to shout out what she
had to keep silent. This child would have to talk, this child at least
must communicate the vision aborted because it was muted. They
want me to accept, to be silent, to suppress the revolt in me. Fine.
So I shall shout it out through the child. I shall communicate to it
that breath that they are trying to stifle in me. She drinks and eats
dates. That this water, these fruits weave in her a real life, a life that
will cry out justice, truth and liberty.

> And the child will leave the tent for the desert
> And the child will look for the path of the river
> And the child will light flowers of flame
> And the child will give the birds grains of sun
> And the wind will sweep everything away
> And the dust will rise up blinding the child, drying out the
>   fruits and the flowers
> And the child will walk in the river as far as the sea
> He will cry against the mother who gave him birth
> The man does not come back. The man stays in the town to
>   feed his aspirations, his ambitions, his pride, his narcissism.
> The man runs to his business, to money, to women whom he
>   buys with his prestige and power.

Woman, rise up from behind your veil
Woman refuse this hold on you
This force that annihilates you
Woman, make your voice which is only the hint of a trembling
    heard
Because, for the moment, your voice is like a violin of desert nights
It must unite with other voices of veils
With other morning hands
And all these hands and all these voices shall take up the sword and
    transform it into a rose, into earth and into a garden

Translated from the French by
Miriam Cooke

Andrée Chedid

(1921–)

Andrée Chedid was born in Cairo. She was educated in French schools and at the American University in Cairo from which she graduated in 1942. Following her marriage, she lived in Lebanon from 1942 to 1946. Afterwards she went to Paris where she has lived ever since, returning periodically to the Middle East. In 1988 she received an honorary doctorate from the American University in Cairo. Following an interview in Cairo with Elizabeth Rodenbeck the latter wrote, 'Her cross-cultural links and influences have sharpened and enriched her sensibilities . . . and made her more open to a breadth of human understanding, able to sympathise with people, particularly women, caught up in traumatic situations as varied as the Lebanese civil war, an earthquake in Algeria, or the pain and loneliness of a loveless marriage.'

Her 1960 novel, *Le Sixième Jour*, set in the 1947 cholera epidemic in Egypt, made into the award-winning film, *Al-Yaum al-Sadis*, by Yusuf Shaheen, was shown at the Cairo Film Festival in 1987. She has published nineteen poetry anthologies which include: *Textes Pour une Figure*, 1949; *Terre et Poesie*, 1956; *Terre Regardée*, 1957; *Seul, le Visage*, 1960; *Lubies*, 1962; *Double Pays*, 1965; *Fraternité de la Parole*, 1972; and *Ceremonial de la Violence*, 1976; Her seven novels include: *Heart on Holiday*, Cairo 1943; *Le Sommeil Délivré*, 1957 (From Sleep Unbound, 1978); and *La Maison sans Racines*, 1985 on the Lebanese war. In addition to five plays, she has also published two collections of short stories entitled *L'Etroite Peau*, 1965, and *Le Corps et le Temps*, 1978. She has gained numerous literary prizes: in 1972, she was awarded the Aigle d'Or for poetry; in 1975, the Royal Belgian Academy's Grand Prix for French literature; in 1976, both the Louis Lapier and the Mallarmé Awards for poetry.

'House of Arrest' was published in *L'Etroite Peau*. It tells a story very similar to that of *Le Sommeil Délivré*. A wife is driven to distraction by her oppressive husband and she determines to kill him. Whereas the protagonist of *Le Sommeil Délivré* succeeds, this protagonist does not. Her husband has control of her innermost thoughts. She cannot liberate herself from him in any way.

House of Arrest

1965

❦

When the earth is changed into a humid hideaway
Where hope, like a bat,
Flies around knocking the walls with its timid wings
The rotten ceilings with its head

Baudelaire

That was how she had had the idea.

She had seen him sleeping on his back, his arms spread-eagle, his legs together, his chest full of snores.

Slow, thick smoke left his mouth, heavily encircling his chin and his brushy moustache (she noticed that it was made of the same bits of straw that animals use for sleeping) and suddenly setting it alight.

The fire caught the straw of the moustache, took the straw of the eyebrows, ate the straw of the hair, the straw of the mattress, and everything blazed in silence.

Of the extended man all that was left was a grey, straight streak that disappeared through the hole in the ceiling that served as a chimney.

She had seen it all without being moved.

Then it occurred to her that she should remove the black-haired cat that had slipped into her corset. She felt its claws against her skin. But her nervous fingers only brought out a leaf that drifted drily to the ground. A brown, dead leaf. With her foot she crushed it with indifference.

How well she breathes now! How the house has expanded. Slowly, she walks toward the door, opens it. And, facing the night, she prepares to wait.

That was how she had had the idea. Just like that, because of a dream.

She would do it that night.

When the streets are alone with the moon, straight as a young girl, she would do it.

It would be enough to pull hard on the trigger. Once, twice. Her hands must not tremble. She must calm her sixty year-old heart and her wandering thoughts. She must put an end to this hate, to this host of memories. Put an end to this presence, this body, this voice and this scratching of the neck which is always the same and which makes you feel like crushing, destroying.

She couldn't stand this presence any longer. Foreign and familiar at the same time. She wished that the Nile would flood and remove this man. Engulf him, the house and her also, if necessary! But rivers, like people, don't think of helping you.

Everything gets mixed up, eddies, disappears before the words can attach themselves. Yet, out of the blue and after forty years of resignation, something snapped. She who had never thought of leaving, whom the habit of boredom and the terror of customs had nailed to the spot, suddenly, here she was no longer accepting anything.

A crazy hope made her hold her head high, a blade was being sharpened that would cut through her fear.

She had to put an end, 'put an end.' The phrase returned like the beating of wings. She had to put an end. So as to wait for what? . . . Death?

That wouldn't change anything. That's what life had been, one long wait.

She had dug herself further and further in, without surprise, between childbirth, work recommenced, the emptiness of silence, the words: those hollow balls that bounce off the walls.

The man stretched, yawned noisily, rubbed his eyes. His siesta had just ended. He propped himself up on his elbow:

'I want my tea,' he said.

She nodded. The water was boiling. She took the white iron box that she put in the corner. Bending made her always cry out in pain because of a pinched muscle, yet it had never occurred to her to put the box within easy reach. The house, at a distance from the village, was less miserable than the others, but it was not cared for.

'Pick up my clothes and give me my slippers,' said the man.

He was seated on the bed, his legs dangling, his feet bare and the large toes spread. She put the box on the step-ladder, approached him and knelt to look for the slippers – he always kicked them off under the mattress – her back was about to break, but she stifled her cry.

Still on her knees, she put the slippers on his feet. He then indicated that she should go away, and he dragged himself groaning to the door.

As he did every evening, he crossed the threshold and sat on the single stair. There, he kicked off his slippers so that 'his feet could breathe'. Then, with his mouth half open, his arms folded, he waited for time to pass.

'Since you wear your slippers so little, why don't you give them to one of your sons?' she had often begged.

He would shrug his shoulders without deigning to reply.

The tea was ready. She poured it into a glass, after having moistened her lips with it to make sure that it tasted good. Then she handed it to him.

The first swallow was to rinse his mouth. He passed it from one cheek to another, moving his tongue, and then he spat it high into the air splashing his clothes and the slippers. The yellow leather had finally acquired a halo of indelible spots.

'Do give them to your son,' she would say. 'They're obviously of no use to you and you're spoiling them.'

Again, he would shrug his shoulders. She had given up trying to make herself understood.

'The tea's never strong enough. Never strong enough! When will you learn how to make my tea the way I like it?'

She didn't listen to him. She had given that up also.

Some moist leaves remained at the bottom of the pot. She scooped them out with her hand and chewed on them.

As twilight fell, she began to be agitated. She went to the unmade bed to adjust the covers.

'Leave my bed alone!' he shouted.

When she hesitated, taken aback, he repeated, 'Leave my bed alone. Come and sit.'

She walked toward the door, looking at the man's back as though seeing it for the first time. It was a wide, fat back. There would be plenty of room to deposit some bullets in it.

'When he's at the edge of the bed. When he undresses, when he pulls the long shirt over his head, when his head is caught in his shirt like a fish . . .'

She crouched by his side on the stair. Now their elbows were touching; on the dust of the road their feet were lined up tidily.

'When his head is caught in his shirt like a fish. I'll pull on the trigger, once, twice.'

The rifle was under the mattress, she knew its contours by heart. She had practised putting it in the hollow of her shoulder. She would pull hard. With all her might. She tried to imagine what he would look like when it was all over. 'The same head, but he won't be there any more.'

They were seated side by side, their black clothes blended together. One could have scarcely slipped a pin between their shoulders.

Some labourers coming back from the fields greeted them in
passing, 'May you have a long life!'

They responded with the same smile, he raised his hand to his
forehead and she bowed her head.

'Woman, it's getting cold. Go and get my cap and prepare my
bed.' Then, immediately, 'I'll go myself. Stay where you are. I tell
you, I'll do it myself.'

He had never stood up to do anything himself! He went to the
bed, took out the cap from under the pillow and stuck it on his
skull: 'Why are you looking like that? Can't I do anything without
you staring like a toad?'

'Soon,' she murmured, 'Soon, you'll not see my toad eyes!'

A few seconds later, he had resumed his place by her side.
Together, they watched night fall.

The last people returning from the fields had disappeared.
Peace enveloped all the alleyways. Some delayed crows took flight,
the branches played with the breeze. Now and then, the cry of an
animal or of a child rose up from an enclosed shack.

Shortly, the moon's crescent would place itself to the right of the
minaret. One would have to think about sleeping again.

The room was lit by a gas lamp with a tentative flame. The two beds
faced each other; the woman's was a mattress on the floor.

The man undressed, scattering his clothes; then he kicked the
slippers under the bed. The woman ground her teeth and kept
staring at him. Now, he was turning his back to her and his
movements became slower and slower. She had all the time to do
what she wanted.

He bent over to pick up the tail of his shirt. Soon the shirt would
cover his head, that would be the moment.

She turned swiftly, bent down to slip her hands under the
mattress. The wood of the rifle was warm like a living thing. She
thought of a bird's chest with bullets for a heart.

Soon would be the moment. She did not tremble. Her eye, her
arm were young. She knew what she had to do, she couldn't go
wrong. She would have to spin around, aim, count till three and
shoot.

An explosion tore through the air. Then, a second. A burning
pain pierced her back, drowning her cry. Turning, the victim
reeled, collapsed, her face on the mud floor.

The man approaches, looks. Next to the inert woman, he drops his
rifle, and does not notice the other weapon partially hidden under
his clothes.

How well he breathes now! How the house has expanded.
Slowly, he walks to the door, opens it. And, facing the night, he prepares to wait.

Translated from the French
by Miriam Cooke

May Muzaffar

(1948–)

May Muzaffar was born in Baghdad, Iraq. She is the author of two volumes of short stories, a novel and a collection of poetry.

'Personal Papers' is from a collection of short stories *Al Baja* (The Swan), Baghdad, 1973. The narrator knows very well the rules of her society, she has heard her brother's disgusted description of contemporary women's behaviour.

Personal Papers

1973

❧

Thursday

Since I have known you, words have been overflowing from me; I gather them and study them and confide them secretly to these small sheets of paper until they are filled. I cherish them. I am experiencing here a freedom I have never known before. I talk to you on these pages all the time, and I talk just as I please. I spend with you my most beautiful hours without outside supervision . . . I ask you questions without shame and I tell you my dreams, leaving out nothing, with no interruptions and when I am done I hide these papers under lock and key as I hide my thoughts.

Saturday

It was a pleasurable dream. I saw in it that I was in a strange place I had never seen before. My room was full of light and I had in front of me a wide window overlooking a big round tree; its leaves were small and I could see lilac flowers through them. A scent, similar to sandalwood mingled with rose water, was rising from it. A scent like the night before a wedding, when you can smell henna and jasmine mixed with candles in a noisy, busy joy. I could see the bride sitting there alone on her isolated throne, her two feet in a bucket of water, covered with jasmine, and her hand drowned in henna; as for her face it hesitated between joy and fear.

My dream was in colour. I keep recalling it in order to forget domestic chores and the sadness of an evening without a friend.

Wednesday

Came back from our outing filled with despair, the result of that terrible event near the river. You were marvellous; you tried to catch that unfortunate bird, but it got frightened and fled. At that moment those evil youths encircled it, held it and started to torture it with great delight, and made a guillotine with a nylon thread and killed it right in front of us. We stood on the wooden bench, I was silent and your face was sombre; you cursed the moment you intended to catch the bird.

Friday
Guests came to our house. It was one of those visits that provoke a
tempest of fear and threats. They came to ask for the hand of the
only remaining sister (the first two had married one after the other
without discussion or resistance). I stayed in my room refusing to
see them. My mother tried all her customary rites on me. First she
argued, then she shouted, then she beat her head, breast and
cheeks. But she did not leave my room without recomposing
herself and getting back her calm so as not to anger my brother
anymore.

   She went to him and told him all the details of the conversation,
gently trying to put down the groom and his family, hoping to
provoke a refusal instead of an acceptance. But nothing could bend
the rigidity of his determination to marry me off at any price in
order to get rid of his responsibility to me, as he put it. He flew up
in anger and started to beat my door with his fists shouting and
cursing. Then, after he calmed down, I heard him repeat, 'May
God have mercy upon you, my Father, you have spoiled this girl
with love!'

Sunday
Here I am breathing the smell of freedom. I extend my hand and I
touch a solid reality: your face, your dimples, your black eyes. We
walked together, away from the menacing crowd. We took a
streetcar, then another, no one crossing our path. The music was
coming out from every corner as if the whole earth had been
planted with it, for each time I put my foot down, a song sprang up
and its echo was repeated and filled the whole atmosphere. I was
seeing every thing you had talked to me about: the gardens, the
streets, the cafés on the sidewalks, but there was something else
that nobody had told me before, and that was that these trees that
were planted on both sides of the boulevard, and were spreading
their shadows over big spaces, had pink flowers on their tops; on
the top of the terraces, everywhere, and were wafting a scent warm
as a summer breeze.

Monday
Your colour changed when I told you that my brother had slapped
me on the face when he stumbled across this novel by an Arab
writer. He threatened to confine me at home and keep me from
pursuing my studies, should he ever find another book of this kind,
'for the reading of novels spoils morality', as he put it. And so I now
cover the books with the special paper I use for my textbooks and I
hide the novels in their midst. Another secret endeavour. Do you

know that I have become a brilliant expert on such undertakings? It is only in so doing that I can find a way out of my problems. Since he has hit me, I use the word slapped, for you to bear it more easily, and also because I am ashamed of it. He did not only slap me but he grabbed me by the hair and threw me on the floor and walked on my head and shouted that he would smash my brains in if I did not stop answering him back . . . so I am saying that since that day I understood that a direct confrontation does not work, for his brutal force frightens me and his abuse, both verbal and physical, kills in me all interest in life, and fills me with bitterness and humiliates me.

I havë stood a lot of that abuse with great endurance and I feel with each blow that my resolution grows stronger and with each humiliation I sever myself some more from them and in my heart is growing a flower just recently sprung: you.

Thursday

I am in revolt against the reins but since I cannot cut them, I slip between the holes. And I reach you. With the help of a thousand and one excuses I steal an hour out of that closed world to walk with you by the river where the vegetation hides our shadows for I do not want to be slain like a goat or crucified like a fly. I want to live and I want to use some of my rights to know myself without any control.

I still feel your palm on my shoulder and it has great strength. Oh what peace of mind I experience under its warm pressure! This is our world, where people and nature can live in harmony. How I wish that this green branch falling in the river could create a world of its own where relationships can grow with ease and happiness, where it is possible for birds to be among people's feet and for women to walk without fear.

Saturday

Yesterday I listened to my brother talking to my mother. I was in the kitchen preparing his dinner and his voice travelled the distance between us. He was telling her how the new generation is misbehaving and the young are carefree . . . I listened, trying to get the gist of what he was saying; his voice kept going up and down, sometimes only whispering, and I heard only phrases. Then my heart started to beat hard and strong. I heard him say: 'They were walking in the street hand in hand . . . The women have their faces painted with bright rouge and their heels are like daggers.' His voice would lower and then become clearer: 'The women of this generation are like the black plague, they are everywhere, I see them anywhere I go. They have pushed themselves into every place. Open your eyes well, for I do not want a terrible fate to befall your daughter.'

I could hear him pacing up and down nervously and he clapped his hands and said, 'We will have to marry the girl very soon.'

Fear overcame me and I was unable to sleep. I will not tell about this incident next week when I meet you. I can see you already changing colour and worrying. And the road in front of us is very long. I will try to bear this alone. I have the strength I need for this battle.

Monday

Let them come to the summit of this mountain and hunt us down . . . You and I are on this summit covered with ice. I am walking with you; behind us we have left an ancient history delineated by an abandoned sidewalk and ancient towers. We are not afraid any more of the evil eyes and we do not take refuge among the trees so that they may protect us . . . We do not have to shorten the minutes of happiness in order to avoid the howling of scandal.

You told me once that ice could bring warmth. Why is it that I am shivering with cold? You are wrapping your woollen jacket around me but I am still cold to the bone. You propose that we run; I try to run but my feet are deep in the snow. Your face blackens. We are in the season when the snow should be melting; the earth has started to mellow. It could fail us any minute. You pushed me toward a rock where we felt the earth to be hard enough and we sat.

The sun is bright above our heads. The sun is playing with me and warming me up. Your woollen jacket talks to my heart and the earth is white. I must say I do not like the ice and I do not like the white space. This whiteness reflects the things out of the earth and propels them far away. It is not like when you look at the desert and you see that in it are hidden secrets, and the setting sun on the sand dunes forms signs of an unknown world. I feel that this icy mountain is blocking my eyes and is forbidding them to enter.

Suddenly the dream changed and another image came. Another place. I felt the sound of water and the smell of incense. I turned around and I did not see you any more but I saw my mother opening her arms to me and kissing me with joy.

That is how I lived my dream.

At 11 o'clock on one autumn morning they were walking together hand in hand. Holding their books tight to their chests, lazily following the river bank. The day was uncertain but the sun was conquering the sky with candour and purity. They were heading south, with the flow of the water, talking to each other in rapid short sentences, like the movement of a rippling current. Everything seemed tranquil and easy.

A hundred metres away from them a young man was walking. His face was troubled and his looks sombre. He was walking slowly and he kept touching his side as if to make sure he had not lost a part of his body.

When the road became clearer and there were fewer people around, the three figures and their movements appeared as a simple scene on the theatre of destiny.

The young man hurried forward and made up the distance between them so that there were no more than two metres left. At that moment, a bullet was fired, then two, and three. The young girl fell and her books scattered on the sidewalk. Her companion froze. He stood petrified with fear at first, then he started moving, raising his arms. But a threatening movement of the revolver pointed toward his face stopped him. And the man shouted: 'Get away from here, or else . . .'

The young man stepped back and left.

The man sat on a wooden bench and dropped his arms. He lit a cigarette and drew a long breath, the revolver still in his hand, the body of the young girl still bleeding.

Near the site of the incident the books were scattered and one was covered with brown paper. On it were written these words in very fine print: 'Personal Papers.'

Translated from the Arabic
by Simone Fattal

Fadhma Amrouche

(1882–1967)

Fadhma Amrouche was born in Taourirth-Moussa-ou-Amar, the Algerian Kabyle. Her family converted to Christianity. Many members of her family were traditional singers and Fadhma enjoyed telling folk tales and chanting traditional songs. In 1913, they emigrated to Tunisia. She is the mother of the writer Marguerite Taos Amrouche and the poet Jean Amrouche. She died in 1967.

This selection is taken from *Histoire de Ma Vie* which she wrote in August 1946, in Mula-Rades. She dedicated the story to her son Jean, and the epilogue to her daughter, Marguerite Taos. A year after her death Taos published these memoirs with Maspero in Paris. This story tells of the oppressive bonds of a Kabyle extended family. The elder Mansour Amrouche opposed publication of these memoirs. As long as he lived the text could not be published.

My Mother

1946

❧

My mother was originally from Taourirth-Moussa-ou-Amar, several miles away from Tizi-Hibel, my village. She came from a very good family, the Aith Larbi-ou-Said. She was married very young to a husband who was almost an old man; he had a daughter older than my mother.

My mother never complained about this man who loved her in his way. She bore him two sons, my brothers Muhand and Lamara. This man had a much younger brother who had no children. The latter wanted to make a will leaving his possessions to his wife. Before he could do so, his elder brother ambushed him and the next day he was found dead on a haystack, in a deserted place outside the village called Sibala, where all the villagers piled their hay. They never discovered his murderer and the affair was closed.

My mother told me that from that day a curse was on her husband. He came down with a terrible sickness: his entire body was covered with pustules full of water, and this yellow water would run down his legs.

'The year he died,' said my mother, 'there was a miraculous crop. In human memory the fig trees had never been so laden with fruit, the arbours with grapes, nor the ears of wheat so beautiful.

'When we went to the fields, he would say as he lifted the branches, "Look, wife, look at all the wealth God has given us!"

'And I would answer softly, "*Ma ne der!* (if we live!)"

'One day when I answered him again that way, he was seized by a sudden rage and began to shake me and yell:

"We shall live, wife! We shall live!"

'He was not to see the figs nor the grapes ripen. The harvest was hardly in when he died.'

Her husband had not yet been put into the ground when my maternal uncle, Kaci Aith-Lârbi-ou-Said, came to get my mother and ordered, 'Leave this house. Bring your children and come to live with us. Our mother will raise them. And you, you will remarry.'

'I will stay with my children, in my house,' she answered, thus braving both her brother and the customs. My uncle, who was very tall, snatched a tile off the roof and threw it at her, fortunately without hitting her. He went straight to the *taimat,* and taking those there as witnesses, he declared, 'From this day forward, I repudiate my sister Aini. She is excluded from our family. Whatever she does, whatever becomes of her, we have no further interest in her lot. She is a stranger to us.'

He went back to his village and never again, after that day, did my mother see her father's house.

She occupied herself burying her husband as custom dictated. With money borrowed against her grape harvest, she bought a pair of oxen which she had sacrificed for the repose of the dead man's soul. The meat was distributed to the whole village. Each family had its share, a piece per person. In addition, a funeral feast was served at the *tajmâat* especially for the poor who get their fill of couscous in this way.

My mother was left alone at twenty-two or twenty-three, with two children, the older who was five or six, and the younger three. My mother was very beautiful: her skin was fair and rosy, with blue-green eyes; a bit stocky, solid, with wide shoulders, a wilful chin, and a low, stubborn forehead. She set to work courageously. She did her housework, carried water, ground her grain for the day, prepared her meals at night. During the day, she worked in the fields.

When she needed a man's help, she had to pay for it dearly.

But she was young and impetuous. In her own courtyard lived a young man from the same family as her late husband. He loved her. She loved him. And the inevitable happened.

She became pregnant and the man denied that he was the father of the baby.

Kabyle customs are terrible. When a woman has gone wrong, she must disappear, no longer be seen, so that the shame does not touch her family. Before the French domination, justice was swift; the relatives would lead the wrong-doer into a field where they would beat her, and then bury her in the embankment.

But at that time, French justice was combatting these harsh customs. And my mother turned to it.

The night I was born, my mother was lying alone with her two little ones; no one was nearby to help her. She gave birth alone and cut the umbilical cord with her teeth. Only one old woman came the next day with a little food.

The ninth day after my birth, my mother held me to her bosom for it had snowed, took each of her children by the hand and went to swear out a complaint against my father to the Procurer of the

Republic. She wanted my father to recognise me and give me his name. He refused, for he was engaged to a girl in the village, who belonged to a powerful family, and they threatened to kill him if he abandoned this girl. She was afraid!

The case lasted three years. During all that time, my mother through heat and cold, returned to plead and nag the judges. All the witnesses said that he was certainly my father, for I was his spitting image. At the end of three years, he was condemned to damages with interest – three hundred francs! – which my mother refused, but the law forbade paternity suits in that time. He could not be forced to recognise me. I wore on my forehead the stamp of shame.

In despair, my mother plunged me into an icy spring. But I did not die.

My mother pursued her usual tasks without any aid, by night as by day: washing, combing, spinning and weaving wool, ploughing the fields, gathering figs, grapes, olives, caring for her house, cooking, winnowing and grinding her grain, barley, or acorns, hauling water and carrying wood.

When I was very little, she left me asleep until she came back. When I was a bit bigger, she placed a little pitcher of water and a saucer with a little pile of couscous next to me.

When I awoke, I found the little pile, I took the grains and ate them, then when I had finished the couscous, I drank from the little pitcher which had a little spout.

I sucked the water and went back to sleep until my mother returned. Sometimes, when she had come back late, a kind neighbour agreed to keep me for a while, but that was rare.

The world is ugly, and it is the 'child of sin' who becomes the martyr of society, especially in Kabyle. How many blows, shoves, and pains I endured! It happened that when I went into the street, I would be knocked down and stepped on.

The first picture I have before my eyes is a summer's day, with a leaden sun on a steep, dusty road; I see a young boy of about ten driving animals in front of him, then a child, almost a baby, pink and white with blond, curly hair who runs after him crying, '*d'haha! d'haha!* – my big brother! my big brother!' Then there was silence.

Immediately after comes another picture; a house with an open doorway through which comes a square of sunlight. In this light, a woman is bent over the naked body of a child; hot tears fall on the suffering flesh, while the woman pulls thorns one by one from the child's body.

Later I knew that the child was me. I had followed my brother who was leading the oxen to the watering trough, and a cruel boy had pushed me into a hedge of prickly pears. My mother grew frightened. What should she do with me? How could she save me from the wickedness of men? She could not always keep me shut up, and if I went out of the house, she was afraid that someone might kill me and the fault would be hers in the eyes of the law.

She learned that there were White Sisters in the Ouadhias who accepted little girls and took care of them. She thought she would rest easier on my account if she entrusted me to these nuns. Still, she resisted a long time for she loved me, I was her child. She had refused to give me to the Justice of the Peace's wife, who had no child and had wanted to adopt me after the incident of the cactus hedge, and seeing that I was still the butt of bad treatment, she decided to appeal to the White Sisters.

Translated from the French
by Patricia Francis Cholakian

Samar Attar

(1940–)

Samar Attar was born in Damascus. Her mother, Masara Azam, was from an old feudal family whose ancestors had been Ottoman governors in Syria. Her father, Faiik Attar, a surgeon, was from a family of scholars. She is the youngest of six children, five of whom are girls. An older sister who had a great influence on her used to give her Russian, German, French and English novels in translation for her birthdays. Samar Attar's feminist consciousness was awakened early by an often repeated family story about her birth. When one of her aunts vacationing at a summer resort heard that her mother had had another girl, she sent a telegram saying that the news of the Second World War was less shocking. This, Samar Attar says, came from liberal people who never discriminated between women and men.

At fifteen, Attar published her first poems in *Al-Dunya*, a literary weekly. Throughout high school and college she published in *Al-Ayyam*, a daily newspaper, *Al-Adab*, and in *Al-Maqasid*, a Lebanese magazine. She contributed a short story every week to *Laila*, a political, social, and literary magazine.

While in high school she performed in radio plays. Later as a student at the University of Damascus she had a daily radio programme called 'Open the Window to the Sun.' She also acted on stage and television.

Attar studied English and Arabic literature at Damascus University. She received an MA from Dalhousie University in Halifax and a Ph.D. from the State University of New York at Binghampton. She has taught Arabic and English literature in the United States, Algeria, Germany, and Australia and is now at the University of Sydney.

Her recent publications include the novels *Laila* and *Al-Bait fi Sahat Arnus* (The House at Arnus Square) and poems in *Women of the Fertile Crescent* and *The Penguin Book of Women Poets*. She has also written a radio play, 'Australia Day', 1988. She currently teaches at the University of Sydney.

Now she returns to Syria only for visits. On one of these visits she
decided to write about her family house and her family's life there.
Exploring and confronting her past, she wrote the novel *Al-Bait fi
Sahat Arnus*. 'Rima' is a chapter from this book.

When Samar Attar was born, the veil was still worn by urban
women in Syria. Even in the sixties, as she says, the country was
more conservative than Egypt and Lebanon. Rima of the novel was
caught in limbo. She absorbed new ideas from books she read,
from her university education, and from political discussions with
her leftist friends. Choosing not to marry, she got a job and
continued to live in the family house. The story of Rima is a
stunning portrayal of the trap of partial rebellion. By remaining in
the family house – as unmarried women and men were supposed
to do – she escaped marriage but not domesticity and confinement.

Rima

1988

❀

'Rima Hanim wants to make us sell the house,' Fatum said to me while pounding the garlic in the brass mortar one rainy morning.

'But Bahiya and I won't leave this place until they carry us out in a box,' she assured me rolling her small black eyes.

'Does anybody wish to buy it?' I asked her cautiously.

'No one wants to pay very much. But Mr Hasan, our relative, may God mend his ways, told her he could demolish it. He wants to build shops and offices in its place. From that time, she has been jumping up and down. Houses at Al-Maza, at the end of the earth, nothing like our house, are worth millions. May I die, God willing, before I see her sell the house and turn us into refugees,' Fatum murmured. I saw her put the pestle in the sink and take hold of the tap for a moment as if she were afraid of losing her balance.

Unlike Fatum, Rima was dissatisfied with her life and she had to find something to vent her anger on and didn't find anything but our house. She wasn't unusual in that. All of us look for a scapegoat now and then. But she had become almost crazy, and with the passing of years, our big house in her eyes became a symbol of all that is repulsive and hateful − a prison preventing her from attaining knowledge, and a tomb burying her alive in her youth. She didn't wish to repair anything in it. True, she wasn't able to paint the walls from the outside nor to plug the big holes that started to appear in the front because the wages of the plasterer and the painter were very high, as Bahiya said. But I felt during my visit that Rima, without realising it, wished the house would crumble one day, maybe over Bahiya and Fatum, so that she could escape even though she did not know exactly where.

I wasn't able to speak with Rima about our Damascus house. She would always get angry with me whenever I tried to say something about it. I had left it forever and, in her opinion, I had no right to criticise. She knew that I would not stay long in Damascus. I was a foreign visitor, even in the opinion of others, and did not love my house enough, as she said to me, for if I had loved it I wouldn't have left.

No. Rima didn't find it necessary to repair our old house and restore it to its past glory because she was not convinced it deserved to be saved. The great old Damascus houses were being torn down and nobody objected, as she told me. Our house was not a great old house in her view. It had no river passing by. Branches of jasmine did not hang down over its windows nor were the walls in the main rooms covered with mosaic tiles.

I should have seen how my friend Nadia's house fell apart. Nadia told me with contempt how the fig trees had been cut down, and also the cherry trees, and how the Yazid River filled up with earth and no one ever objected. Her voice trembled slightly. They had left Nadia's house till the end. They demolished the other houses first.

When Nadia returned to Damascus after being away for years she discovered a stranger living alone in her house. How many rooms were there? She couldn't even remember. She had knocked cautiously at the door. Around her were nothing but decaying houses, and when the face of a man appeared in the small door she didn't know what to say to him. From the corner of her eye she saw the fountain in the inner court dancing under the sunlight. 'You are at the wrong place, my sister,' said the man with a slight cough. 'The house is destined to be demolished. Nobody is living here now.' Before she could object and before she could tell him she had lived in that house for more than twenty-five years he had shut the door in her face.

In Nadia's garden there had been masses of rose bushes and trees which the Arabs had known for centuries and which they had taken with them to Spain, Italy, and Malta. What's the use now, nobody objected when the trees were cut down and the fountains were covered over with dirt and the house decayed. Rima asked if I knew that the antique dealers were sending their men to houses that were being demolished to find bits of tile or the remains of painted walls with intricate designs. No. No. Our house is not like Nadia's house, she assured me swallowing hard as though she herself were not convinced of what she was saying. Anyway, I could stay in the house if I was so interested in it, she said to me mockingly and left me alone in the sitting room.

Rima was usually reasonable about everything, and we could argue calmly with her on various topics – all of us five children, regardless of the differences in our age, education, and views on politics and social matters. We used to take refuge with her during times of difficulty and she would find solutions to our problems and mediate among us when we disagreed. She didn't have enemies inside or outside the house. Really, I don't know how she managed it. She did not go along with those who disagreed with her in their political or social views. She would call a spade a spade, but disagreements with others would not prevent her from being friends with them. She was liked. She had friends who were communists, others who were right-wingers, and others who were socialists. Whenever I looked at her in astonishment, she would laugh like a child and say, 'Gentleness is the key to everything in life.'

However, since the death of my mother in the seventies Rima had started to change little by little; and without wishing it, it became necessary for her to play the role of the man in the house. She could not travel outside Damascus for any length of time. She had two women on her hands who were minors – never mind that they were close to sixty – and who were dependent on her for everything. She managed their financial matters. She bought their daily necessities from the government shops. She was the one who took them now and then to the resorts near Damascus on Fridays or official holidays. Rima didn't like her new responsibilities. Preferring not to marry and have children she had decided to work and be a free woman. However, she had not left our house for a house of her own. Maybe because that was not customary in our milieu – women or men who are not married stay with their families until they die. But, most likely, in Rima's case, apartments in town were not widely available and rents were extremely high. And it was convenient for Rima to live in our house and find her breakfast, lunch, and dinner always ready. She tried to counter my views, saying, 'I eat very little. I don't care about eating.' Her room used to be cleaned everyday and the dust removed from the books on her shelves. The mirror of her dressing table and her windows were sparkling clean and the small pinewood table polished. The Persian carpet was swept. The bed was made. The floor tiles were washed with soap and water. But, Rima preferred that nobody enter her room; Bahiya, as she claimed, broke the French perfume bottles when dusting or rearranging the books on the shelves. Rima closed the door of her room sometimes before leaving the house at quarter to eight so that Bahiya couldn't enter the room. But often she forgot, so that when she returned home at about three in the afternoon she would find something to complain about: Bahiya had taken her pen from next to the telephone (there were two telephones in our house, one for Rima and one for the rest of us); Bahiya had washed her shirt that should have been dry-cleaned; Bahiya had broken her jar of Christian Dior skin cream.

With the passing of years, her mania grew: her mania about Bahiya, her obsession with the house. Rima was no longer always reasonable. She became impatient. She would get angry for the smallest reasons. One idea returned to her day and night. She spoke about nothing except selling the house or dividing it into apartments or shops. In her mind, our house (the house where all of us had been brought up except Afaf who got married at an early age) changed into a dreadful animal that did not let her sleep and made her life hell.

Maybe it was the daily monotony that pushed her to hate our house. For twenty-five years, after her graduation from the University of Damascus, she set the alarm of the old clock we bought in the forties for a quarter to seven. She put the clock outside her room and closed the door. She couldn't sleep at night with the clock in the same room. Its ticking was loud, her sleep was light and her nerves were always on edge. During a visit to Europe a few years ago Rima bought a small clock radio. The clock didn't have any tick nor emit any sound and at a quarter to seven Rima would be awakened to the sound of classical music. A few minutes later Bahiya would open the door to her room with a coffee tray which she put down next to the white telephone. Then she would open the door to the balcony and the rays of the sun would slowly enter the room. Rima used to get up lethargically. She would put her pillow behind her head. Then she would cautiously extend her hand to lift the little cup of coffee. 'What a good morning,' Bahiya would say to her and sit down on the long grey chaise longue to pour another cup of coffee for herself (was it the third or fourth? I don't know because she used to get up at five-thirty or six in the morning) and before she finished drinking her coffee she would say to Rima, 'May God be pleased with you. Don't forget the oranges today and if there are bananas at the government shop buy a few kilos for us.' Then she would pour another cup for Rima and take the tray and leave the room.

Sometimes, I drank coffee with them. Never once did I dare to sit on the edge of Rima's bed. She never liked anybody to touch her American linen or the white woollen bedcover she had bought in Algeria a few years ago. All of us used to speak with amusement about her eccentric behaviour that increased with advancing age. For instance, we knew that Rima never liked any of us to sit on her bed or on her long grey chaise longue, especially during our monthly periods. We could not discuss this issue with her. She was not reasonable when the subject of 'cleanliness' was being discussed and whenever we wanted to make her angry and hear her 'chirping' – as we agreed to call her screaming which differed from Bahiya's – we would go to her room and sit on the edge of her bed. I believe if Rima could have boiled us with our clothes on, she would have. We would go – in her view – into the street, we rode on buses and in taxis and brushed against people and carried their smells and dirt with us. She didn't want the germs to be transported to her room.

Of course, I would be lying if I said Rima was the only neurotic person in our house. All of us were neurotic one way or another. However, Rima's neurosis on the question of 'cleanliness' exceeded all limits. Whenever I recalled her image to mind I would see her running between her room and the bathroom to wash her hands, or to stand under the shower for half an hour everyday, or to soak her clothes in soap and water. The men in her office smoked non-stop and, as she said to me, had a bad smell.

I laughed with Bahiya when I knew the secret of the agreement between her and Rima about using the western toilet and the two Arab toilets in our house. (One toilet was for Fatum alone and one for the guests. Bahiya sat on the seat of the western toilet and Rima lifted the seat as men do.) But, I clenched my teeth in anger when I heard that Rima did not allow anybody to put their underwear in the washing machine. Fatum had to boil the underwear separately.

Sometimes we would laugh at Rima and make jokes about her stories, and she would join in our laughter. With the passing of time, however, she became impatient and couldn't bear any criticism from us. She would say that she was tired of her responsibilities as the family caretaker and that she would soon resign from a position that she had not chosen of her own free will and that one of us would have to take over and help out with the house. We all listened to her in silence. None of us dared to laugh in her face or discuss anything with her.

In our opinion, there was a simple explanation. Rima hadn't married, and in a society like ours that meant that she would live in the house in which she was brought up until she died. For different reasons Rima did not revolt completely against her environment. She rejected many things, but she agreed – though with reluctance – to limit her freedom and continue to live in the house she hated to call home. Loneliness pushed her to create a special world of her own. Her room was different from the other rooms in the house in its furniture and arrangement. There was nothing in it that indicated that its owner was an Arab woman nor that she had lived most of her life in Damascus. This was not because all the furniture was European – most people nowadays bought imported furniture; and not because the books on the shelves were by Sartre, Simone de Beauvoir, Camus, Nabokov, Dostoyevsky, and D. H. Lawrence, since educated Arabs read western literature in translation or in the original. It was because of the special touches – the flower vases in the corners or the Greek statues among the books or the prints on the walls and above all because of the stereo

equipment and the masses of classical records from Bach to
Beethoven and from Vivaldi to Chopin. Rima did not use the
reception room when someone visited her. Her room was a
different world – not just from the other rooms in our house but
from the entire town. In this room she received her guests, men
and women. With some she drank a glass of whisky or champagne,
and she smoked Lord Extra cigarettes, and listened to Mozart or
Rimsky-Korsakov and spoke with them about politics, literature,
and economics.

Because a young woman like this was rare in our town some
people misunderstood her, but she quickly changed their miscon-
ceptions because of her sharp intelligence and natural gentility.
Even my mother, when she was still alive, had accepted Rima's
actions as if they were natural and pushed aside the opinions of a
woman who used to phone her from time to time whispering in a
voice filled with hatred, 'Water runs beneath your feet, and you
don't know that your daughters are pregnant.' My mother did not
give up under pressure. There was also my sister Afaf and her
husband who valued people's opinions. 'Nobody used to be able to
point a finger at us,' Afaf would say in anger as if she were
desperately trying to change my mother's views. 'The rat is
learning from her,' she would say pointing at me in mockery.
Despite this my mother was not hard on Rima or me. She was a
clever woman and she realised that the world around her was
changing and that the position of women could not remain
stagnant forever.

No. My sister Rima did not get pregnant as the hateful woman
said. Men came and went from our house. Even after twenty years
I didn't know if Rima had loved any of them or kissed them on the
lips. We never spoke about sex; in our house – like other Syrian
houses – sex was a forbidden subject. Even the cultured and the
liberated Rima did not wish to say anything about the subject when
I asked her simply, 'Did you love anyone?'

I knew that she had been the friend of an educated young man
while I was away from Damascus. I thought that they had been in
love but she insisted that the relationship was no more than
friendship. She was in her late twenties at the time and he was in his
early thirties. Like a western woman (but without her sexual
freedom, I believe) Rima went everywhere in town with her friend
where people could see and hear them. That was in the early sixties
in a society that had not yet opened up and did not easily accept
friendship between the two sexes however innocent it was. When I
returned to Damascus after twenty years I was surprised that my
sister's friend had married a teenage girl whose father was said to

be extremely rich. Rima didn't want to talk about it. In her view, men were trivial.

This bitter experience did not push her to remove herself from the world. She continued to be friendly with people who had different inclinations and interests, something which amazed all of us. Some like Afaf would remark mockingly, 'She accepts anything and gets along with everybody.' But, personally I used to envy her. All her friends loved her in a way that was not possessive or domineering. Maybe for this reason alone she did not find a suitable man in our town. Our men do not understand the relation of equal to equal, especially in marriage. Born out of time and place, Rima was a different woman from the women of the town. Regardless of this she did not choose isolation even in her political life. She joined a leftist party when she was not more than twenty. She decided not to support anybody after she saw her friends one after the other die in prison or in exile. But, these bitter experiences did not leave scars, I believe. She always remained optimistic, and perhaps it was this that made her survive. She wasn't able to stay angry for long even when she spoke about our house which she hated so much. She would laugh heartily whenever anyone reminded her of her unfounded fears about cleanliness, and sometimes – if she were in the right mood – she volunteered funny stories about herself.

No. Rima did not completely revolt against her society. Maybe because luck did not help her. Will alone is not enough. During her fifty years only a few chances came her way and with her sharp intelligence she recognised them and did not let them pass by. She was twenty-one years old when she left for Cairo to complete her higher education. Being away from the family was a chance to establish her independence as a woman. But the environment of Cairo was not greatly different from that of Damascus. Just a few months passed when she returned to our house. She made excuses, and found reasons to speak scornfully about the Egyptian universities and the Egyptians she met; she said her stay in Cairo was a black spot in her life. At that time none of us understood why she went to Egypt nor why she returned. But my mother tried to lessen the weight on Rima, saying that many chances were still in front of her. Thirty years passed – during which my mother died – and not one chance, veiled or unveiled, appeared before Rima.

She was awakened everyday, except on Fridays and official holidays, at quarter to seven. She drank her coffee in bed and then took her shower listening to the news from London or Monte Carlo. She quickly put on her Parisian clothes, drank a glass of warm milk, ate a small piece of Arab bread with yoghurt, brushed her teeth for the second time, gargled with Odol, examined her face, and lastly put some shadow on her green eyes, not forgetting the jasmine perfume by Dior. At quarter to eight she rushed out of the house driving her car to her office through the swarms of cars that started honking early in the morning. She returned around three in the afternoon. And, when the working hours changed in her organisation, she had to go back to the office after four o'clock to work for a few hours longer.

For thirty years Rima did the same work everyday. She was promoted and reached the highest ranks, but in the opinion of those in positions of responsibility because she was a woman, it wasn't reasonable for her to become the director of the organisation. The director's job was a political job and only a few could reach it. Sometimes, her male colleagues, those who graduated the same year or later, became directors in her department or even in the economics organisation. Rima would protest openly and behind the scenes, but that would not lead to anything, and in the end she had to shut up.

Nobody could make her laugh except Afaf's husband. He sat with us during our monotonous evenings with his belly hanging between his legs and his jowls shaking without stopping. 'Come on, be happy,' he would say to her in his laughing voice. 'It is very simple. In the twenties they used to throw silver nitrate in the faces of unveiled women. Had you lived at that time you wouldn't have gotten a job or anything.' It wasn't Afaf's husband alone who used to try to tease Rima. All of us would make comments and we would laugh until late in the night.

No. In our country a person who takes things to heart dies in grief, Rima said to me once. And maybe that was why we would laugh whenever Afaf's husband spoke to us about men who blamed all the natural and unnatural calamities in Damascus on the over-made-up women. He had countless stories and would begin one and go on to the next, like Scheherezade in the Thousand and One Nights. He would illustrate with lines of poetry and make up Quranic verses and sayings of the Prophet to assure Rima that equality between man and woman was impossible. My brother's wife sometimes aided him in that and added some salt and pepper to his stories or reminded him of ones he had forgotten.

'Who brought locusts from the desert to Syria long ago?' she would ask squinting her brown eyes and trying to hide her laugh. 'Who else but women? Salome the dancer, has anyone forgotten her? They hanged her. Constantinople gave the order. Had you lived at that time (she was directing her talk to Rima then) they would have said that you were the cause of everything: locusts, earthquakes, fires and strange diseases.'

I couldn't laugh but my sister Afaf used to laugh until she cried. Many times she would be forced to rush to the bathroom and Bahiya would follow her and, almost whispering, say to her, 'May God be pleased with you. If you want to go to the bathroom you know which one is for the guests.' And Afaf at that moment would lean against the wall, holding herself, and laugh hysterically.

Rima didn't suffer from a sense of inferiority, she was wiser than that. Chances were not abundant in a country like ours for men or women. People were born, grew up, and died without seeing luck face to face, without having at their disposal the means of choice. She knew well that she was lucky compared to many other men or women but deep down she felt resentful because she was born out of her time and place. She did not show her resentment to others. She always smiled and rarely did we see her frown for long. If she had given a personal interpretation of the political events she had lived through for fifty years she would not have smiled or experienced tranquillity for a single day. She always separated the private world from the public world and didn't allow the one to influence the other except in particular instances. Maybe this was the key to her relative happiness. How many military coups had she witnessed since she was fifteen years old? Seven? Nine? She no longer remembered nor was she interested in remembering. Men alone are the ones who fight to rule, and they are the ones who kill each other by shooting. Perhaps for that reason she didn't feel the maternal instinct a single day and never chose to give birth to a child in a world drowning in blood.

'Oh my, oh my,' Fatum said to me one day while she was rubbing my back in the Arab bathroom, 'What grief! Rima Hanim can no longer give birth to children.'

From the corner of my eye I saw her wiping the tears with her left arm. When I laughed out loud, saying that I didn't know Rima had wanted to have a child, she interrupted me sharply; 'No. No. It is not that. Seven years ago they removed her womb. She had an operation in the hospital.'

'But Rima didn't write to me about that,' I said to Fatum.

'Eh. What would she write? Where would she start? What grief! She stayed a week in the hospital. They didn't remove the stitches for forty-five days. She couldn't drive her car or carry anything heavy.'

'Was there someone she could have had children with?' I said to Fatum, mischievously.

'Never mind,' she said in a low voice. 'Who knows? This is life and its ways.'

She stopped rubbing my back for some time to wipe the sweat from her forehead with the back of her hand. Then I heard her murmuring as if she were speaking to herself: 'What's the use of a woman who has no womb?'

I didn't want to laugh so as not to hurt Fatum's feelings. She thought, like everybody else in our town, that women are chickens who lay eggs. And when she stops she is of no use. Fatum, Fatum of all women, never loved a man in her life and didn't lay even one egg. She never went out of our house, the tomb, into the big world.

'And Rima? Was she sad like you, Fatum?' I asked her affectionately.

'You know her. Rima Hanim's mind is a little loose. She wasn't sad because they removed her womb. She said it is better without a period. But she was sad about something else,' she said and she giggled like a child.

Her observation aroused my curiosity. At that moment she was rubbing my leg while I was standing behind the big stone basin. I looked at her and helped her up saying, 'What was she sad about, Fatum?'

With her small laughing eyes she said, 'A woman working with her thought she had the same problem. The woman's relatives said to her, 'May the evil be far away.' When her ladyship heard the story she was very sad. 'What's the matter, am I not normal?' she said to the woman. 'Do you want me to be frank? You are not normal. A woman without a womb . . .'

Fatum started to laugh like a young girl, then I saw her thrust some twigs into the furnace, open the door of the bathroom and disappear down the hallway.

Translated from the Arabic by
Ali Badran and Margot Badran

Nawal al-Saadawi

(1931–)

Nawal al-Saadawi was born in the village of Kafr Tahla in Qalu-
biyya Province in the Egyptian Delta. She is a leading feminist,
writer and activist, and president of the Arab Women's Solidarity
Association. In 1955, she graduated from the Faculty of Medicine
at Cairo University; she has reflected upon her experiences there
in her book *Imraatan fi Imraa* (Two Women in One, published in
Beirut, 1975 and in English, 1985). She practised general medicine
and psychiatry in both the countryside and city. These experiences
have informed much of her writing.

She became Director-General of Health Education in Egypt. She
founded the Association for Health Education, and was the editor
of a popular magazine on health information. She was the first
feminist to publicly confront sexual issues such as prostitution,
sexual diseases, clitoridectomy, incest, and various forms of sexual
exploitation. For her daring writings on gender and sexuality, most
notably *Al-Mara wa al-Jins* (Woman and Sex, 1972) she was
dismissed from her job in the Ministry of Health. Her courage was
applied equally to her private life; she left two oppressive husbands. In 1981, she was imprisoned for her writings and outspoken
speech by Sadat. She has written about this experience in *Mudhakkirat fi Sijn al-Nisa* (Memoirs from the Women's Prison, Cairo, 1984
translated into French in 1984 as *Douze Femmes Dans Kanater*, and
into English, 1987). Also inspired by this experience is her play,
Al-Insan (The Human, Cairo, 1983). Her books have been translated into English, French, German, Dutch, Danish, Swedish,
Norwegian, Italian, Portuguese, and Persian.

Her twenty-four books include: *Mudhakkirat Tabiba* (Memoirs of
a Woman Doctor, Cairo 1960); *Al-Untha Hiya al-Asl* (Female is the
Origin, Beirut, 1974); *Al-Rajul wa-Jins* (Man and Sex, 1975); *Imraa
Inda Nuqtat al-Sifr* (Woman at Point Zero, 1975); *Al-Mara wa al-Sira
al-Nafsi* (Woman and Psychological Struggle, Beirut, 1976); *Al-
Wajh al-Ari Lil Mara al-Arabiya*, 1977 (translated into English as *The
Hidden Face of Eve*, 1980); *Ughniyat al-Atfal al-Dairiyat* (Children's
Songs, 1978).

'Eyes' tells the story of an Egyptian man who is very strict with his daughter, only permitting her to work outside the home on the condition that she is completely isolated from men. The daughter finds that 'ideal' job. Many months later, in the spring of 1988, this same man brings his veiled daughter to the office of Nawal al-Saadawi to see her in her capacity as a psychiatrist. 'Eyes' is based on the young woman's story. Egyptian Television wanted to produce a film based on this story – on condition that the protagonist was not a veiled woman, as she had been in real life. Nawal al-Saadawi refused.

Eyes

1988

❦

A few days ago a young woman came to me. She told me her story and asked me to write a prescription. I didn't prescribe any medication. I don't believe that pills can cure this young woman. The problem seemed to be psychological and social. This is why I would like the readers to share their opinions with me on this case.

For a year the young woman has been staring into space at night without sleeping. When she falls asleep, she sees a flood inundating the land and the Prophet Noah embarking on his ship and leaving her behind. She finds herself in life after death walking on a narrow path with an inferno below her. Her feet are bleeding and her body, off balance, is about to fall. She opens her eyes and finds herself asleep in bed under the blankets drowning in her own sweat. She reads the opening *sura* of the Quran and thanks God that she hasn't yet died and has a chance to repent. She goes to the bathroom and washes five times. She dresses herself in a long loose robe and wraps her head with a thick cloth. After she prays she sits with God's book in her lap, reading, and asks God's forgiveness for her grave sin. There is nothing in her life except that sin. Since she was born she has gone to bed hearing the voice of her father reciting the Quran. Since infancy her face has not been seen by a stranger. During her student years she never talked to anyone. After graduation she went to work in a place where there was no one other than herself – a storeroom in the basement of a small museum never visited by anyone. She would sit at her desk with an inventory in front of her recording the number of mummies that came in to be stored, or registering the ones already there. She dusts the mummies with a small yellow cloth. She counts them and records them in the inventory. She closes the inventory and puts it into a drawer. Then she opens up God's book and reads until the time the employees leave work. She covers the distance with a steady, controlled pace, no movement of her body discernible under her thick robe.

Her head wrapped in the black cloth is inclined towards the ground. In the heat and cold she walks the distance twice a day, back and forth. She doesn't ride the bus so that no one should brush against her from behind. She doesn't take a taxi alone with an unknown driver. At home she washes off the dust from the road performing her ablutions and praying before she eats. After she eats, she goes to sleep with God's book under her pillow. She wakes to the sound of her father's voice calling her to fix his food. After he eats, he prays and asks God to protect his daughter from the devil. If it weren't for the forty-seven pounds every month he wouldn't have let her leave the house. He's an old man without an income and she has no husband to support her. Nobody approached him for her hand in marriage except the son of his sister who is penniless. If God had sent her a husband in sound financial condition she wouldn't have left the house. In her room, she moves up and down in prayer. She does not ask God to send her a husband. She has dismissed the idea of marriage since childhood. Her mother died haemorrhaging when her husband hit her after she had gone to bed. Death is inevitable but she wants to die in a different way, not by being beaten. There is no man in her life. She doesn't know anything about the other sex. If she hears the sound of music or singing coming from the neighbours she plugs her ears with her fingers and shuts the windows and doors.

That day came last April when she was sitting as usual at her desk. She had finished counting the mummies and statues, when she discovered a statue that was not there the day before. She looked back over the entries in the register, closed it and put it back in the drawer. She opened God's book and started to read without a sound, her head bound. While she was reading her eyes peered through the two narrow holes of the black cloth and moved around the mummies and statues. They became fixed on the face of that statue. The features were carved in a strange way. The strangest of all were the eyes. They were looking at her with a movement in the pupils that she had never seen before in any other statue. She asked God's forgiveness. She asked God to protect her from the devil. She bowed her head to continue reading, but her eyes moved involuntarily towards the statue, smaller than the other statues. The dust covered it as if it had been neglected for years in the storeroom. She dusted the statue and put it near the window. She returned to reading God's book but her eyes peered through the two small holes attracted by the statue and its eyes. The eyes were slanted slightly upwards like ancient Egyptians' eyes. She held the statue in her black gloved hand and started looking for a symbol or for letters that might reveal the name of the person or the time in which he had lived. But there was nothing definite. She put the statue back and returned to her seat behind the desk. Her eyes settled on the lines in God's book.

No other person worked in the museum except the old woman

who was the manager. She would come down to her from time to time to inspect the entries in the inventory and pass her eyes over the statues one after the other. She might stop at one that drew her attention. That day her eyes passed over the small statue without being attracted by anything. The woman was puzzled. Why hadn't the director seen the movement in the eyes of the statue? The same question nagged her every day. As soon as she enters the office and sits down, her eyes settle on the face of the statue. The movement in his eyes is still there. He doesn't look anywhere with these eyes except at her. Since seeing it for the first time, she never stops looking at it. If she turns her head away or leaves the office his eyes are always before her continually looking at her with the same expression as if he were alive now, not several thousand years ago. In his gaze there is no arrogance of the Pharaoh gods nor the humility of the slaves. What is in it? She doesn't know. Everyday she's overcome by her desire to know. This grows day after day into a sinful desire. Whenever she sits at her desk she looks around her afraid that the director might suddenly appear and catch her looking into his eyes. What she fears most is that an order would be issued to transfer him to another storeroom. When she goes to bed she is unable to sleep. What would happen if she returned to her office in the morning and didn't see him? Since finding him, she walks to her office with a faster pace. When she opens the door and enters, her eyes peer through the two holes looking for his face among the faces of other statues. When she sees the movement in his eyes, her closed lips underneath the black cloth, part with a faint sigh.

One day she entered her office and she didn't find him. She searched all over the storeroom, in every corner, below the legs of the large statues, over the floor where hundreds of small statues were lying. He wasn't there. She returned to her desk to sit down. She couldn't write anything in the inventory and she couldn't read a single line in God's book. Her head is bent and her heart is heavy. Where did he go? His place next to the window is vacant. The whole universe is empty. There is nothing in her whole life. Nothing at all. Her hand in the black glove is cold and the blood in her veins has stopped. All around her she sees nothing but death in the shape of stone statues. Sitting at her desk she, too, is dying.

She lifted her eyes with an abrupt movement the same way air rushes out of the chest before the last breath and saw him hiding behind the windowpane. The director wouldn't have understood what happened if she had appeared at this moment. Her outward appearance was the same. She is sitting in her chair behind her desk with the inventory in front of her. Her head is bent and nothing in her moves except the black pupils through the two holes and the rushing movement of hot blood in the veins under her skin.

Before leaving that day she hid him in her handbag to take him home with her. In the morning she brought him back to his place. The director did not notice his absence and reappearance. At home her father didn't notice that he was inside her wardrobe. At night after her father sleeps she takes him out of the wardrobe and places him in front of her and doesn't stop looking at his face. She sleeps with her eyes fixed on his eyes. In her dream she sees him standing while a flood inundates the earth. She sees him standing in front of her in flesh and blood. And the flood inundating the land and the Prophet Noah climbing into his ark and leaving without him. Could it be that he is the son of the Prophet Noah who did not get into the ark and was drowned. Could it be that he is a sinner who followed the devil and not a believer who followed God? And more important, is it possible for him to come back alive after dying about seven thousand years ago? In the morning when she opens her eyes, the question whirls around her head. She walks down the street to her office her head bent, afraid to raise her eyes. Afraid she would see him in front of her in flesh and blood as she saw him in her dream. Through the two small holes in the black cloth her eyes start to move, to rise slowly glancing cautiously into the faces of the passers-by. Perhaps, among these human beings there is a face that resembles his? Or eyes with the same look?

Two months pass and she does not stop thinking. Her eyes do not stop stealing a look at the faces of people on the street as she moves back and forth between her home and office. Two months pass and among the faces she doesn't see a single one that looks like his, nor among the eyes any that have his look. She sleeps restlessly at night and while she sleeps the dream recurs. She sees the earth inundated in a sea of water and herself standing at the entrance to the city and suddenly she sees him in front of her. Now he does not notice her presence. He walks calmly forward, then turns around and looks at her. In his eyes is the same unchanging look. The water covers him from all sides. He keeps looking at her until he disappears under the water. His eyes are the last to disappear.

In the morning she opens her eyes, the roaring of the water still in her ears. The voices screaming for help are muffled by the sound of the crashing waters. In the moment between wakefulness and sleep, the dream appears as the destruction of her town seven thousand years ago which she had seen with her own eyes. He was drowned seven thousand years ago along with those God took in the flood. She continues lying on her bed. It is late for getting to the office. She rises up with a heavy body and in the mirror sees her eyes red and full of tears. She knows she was weeping over his drowning. What made her weep most was that he was not a follower of God; that he was a follower of the devil. No matter. Tears continue to gush from her eyes as she stands in front of the mirror. It seems as if he had died at that very moment, not thousands of years ago.

On her way to the office that morning as she stopped at an intersection, she lifted her eyes to look at the traffic lights – suddenly she saw him among the people crossing the street. The face was his face – the ancient Egyptian features. The eyes were his eyes. Involuntarily her body lunged towards him. She was about to grab him by the hand but she stopped at the last moment. Her closed lips parted under the black cloth crying, 'You?!'

The street was crowded with people rushing along their way. They stopped amazed at the scene. They saw her rushing towards him and him fleeing from her. She, a young woman, and he, a young man, walking in the street. It isn't normal for a young woman to rush towards a man that she doesn't know. And she was not just any young woman. She was a creature from whose being nothing appears except two small holes in a black cloth. The scene appeared to the onlookers as both strange and amusing.

Their laughter rang in her ears and she shrank under her thick clothing. She continued to shrink all day long sitting at her desk, the inventory in front of her. Only her eyes move towards the window where he stands in his place. His face is the same face and his eyes have the same movement and a look more human than that in the eyes of the people in the street even though he died several thousand years ago with those who drowned in the flood. She wept for his death. Every human being dies, but the stone statue lives seven thousand years. Is stone more permanent than human beings? The question turns around in her head without an answer. Now she has a friend made of stone. She feels his presence more than the presence of any other human being with a body. The word 'body' escaped from between her closed lips without a sound. The word produces a shiver in her own body. Through the two holes from under the thick cloth her eyes steal a look at her body. In her chest there is a heart that beats. In her head there are veins through which blood flows hot as air. Her mind understands that her friend is nothing but a statue of stone. But she sees in his eyes the look of one about to speak.

Is it possible he will speak? And in what language? In Arabic or ancient Egyptian? Is it fantasy or reality? And if it is fantasy from where does it come? Does her imagination mix with the blood in her veins and head? The question turns in her head like a whirlpool in the sea. And the water drowns her like a flood and he is standing in front of her and in his eyes there is a human look. Deep inside herself she is sure he is human – more human than all the people in the universe. He cannot be an evil person. She can swear in full consciousness that he is a follower of God and not of the devil.

She was fully conscious. If anyone saw her they would have no doubt about this. Her father sees her the same way he sees her every day modestly veiled going to her office and returning home on time. The director of the museum sees her sitting conscientiously with the inventory in front of her and when she finishes the inventory there is nothing in front of her except the book of God. On the road she walks in her measured step with her head lowered.

One day while she was walking she turned her eyes through the two holes and saw him step out of the door of a house and cross the street with calm steps mindless of the screaming horns. She saw him. The same person. She could not mistake him after all these days.

Her feet were frozen to the ground. Her hand inside the black glove was raised over her heart. He was standing in the middle of the street. Around him the cars were rushing like the flood. She thought he would fall and be drowned under the wheels but he did not fall. He continued walking calmly towards Nile Street. She recognised that he was a phantom and not a reality. But she sees him with her eyes. As long as she sees him with her eyes she doesn't care whether he is a phantom or reality. She walks behind him. In her ears she hears the sound of his shoes on the pavement. He's only a few steps ahead of her. If she speaks to him it's possible he'll hear her. She doesn't know what to call him. He doesn't have a name. Her sealed lips under the thick cloth parted with a sound: 'You.' She sees him turn around and look at her face to face. She recognises that it is him. The eyes are his eyes and the expression his expression. She hears him say, 'Who are you?' His surprise silences her. She stops. He is speaking in Arabic not ancient Egyptian. She thought he knew her as she knew him. How could she have known him all this time and yet hear him ask, 'Who are you?' She stands looking at him without moving. Then she looks down for a long time, shrunk in shame inside herself. After all this he asks her who she is. She looks up once more to be sure what is happening but he has disappeared in the crowd.

The second day on the way to her office her head was lowered as usual but her eyes were moving like two bees inside the two holes looking at the faces of the people. Her mind says to her that he is no longer living, that he had lived about seven thousand years ago, but her eyes never stop searching. Her mind tells her he exists. She has seen him. As long as he exists she can see him again. She is overtaken by the wish to see him in any shape. Let him be made of flesh and blood or of spirit without body. What's important is that she sees him.

She waited in the same place where she had met him yesterday. He appeared in the street. It was him. Nothing had changed except for a black moustache that had grown over his upper lip. Her closed lips parted underneath the thick cloth emitting a word without a sound, 'Male!' Never before had she uttered that word. She thought he was simply a human being without sex but this moustache meant that he was . . . her feet remained frozen to the ground, her hand inside the black glove rose up to cover the two small holes in the thick cloth.

When she lifted her hand from her eyes the street was still crowded with people and he was no longer standing in front of her. Under her shoulder in the cavity between her arm and chest was her leather handbag. It protruded through the thick cloth next to her left breast. She feels the touch as if it were electricity. Her mind recognises that it is only a leather handbag with nothing inside it except her purse and the small stone statue. But the touch continued to run through her left breast like electricity. Without opening it she threw it in a large dump. She didn't take anything from it. She even left her purse inside. She imagined that if she opened it she would see him. She had become afraid of seeing him. She didn't know why she was afraid. But she started to shake with fear. The fear accompanied her all the way home. She lay down on her bed. She realised that the handbag was no longer with her. She thought that the fear would leave her but next morning it was still there. On the second day the fear continued to accompany her in the street, in the office, in the house, everywhere. It accompanied her like the trembling of a feverish person. One night her father heard her moaning in a low voice. Her body shook with trembling like a person wracked with malaria. Her father took her to a doctor. She took medicine for thirty days but the fever remained. At night her father heard her speaking to somebody as she said her prayers. He thought she was speaking to God asking His forgiveness. But her voice became louder and her words became clearer. She was not talking to God. She was cursing the devil in words that could never come from the lips of a pure young woman. He believed that she had committed a sin that she was keeping to herself not daring to reveal to anyone. He took her to a holy man. But, after her repentance the fever continued. Again the pills the doctor prescribed failed. When the director of the museum visited her she said she was not suffering from malaria but from a psychological condition. That's how she came to me.

Translated from the Arabic
by Ali Badran and Margot Badran

ACTIVISM

❧

This pearl
Was a gift of my grandmother
   that great lady
   to my mother
   and my mother gave it to me
And now I hand it on to you
The three of you and this pearl
Have one thing in common
   simplicity and truth
I give it with my love
and with the fullness of heart
   you excel in

The girls of Arabia will soon grow
   to full stature
They will look about and say:
'Salma has passed by this road'*
and point to the place of sunrise
and the heart's direction.

Fawziya Abu Khalid, 'A Pearl' (Saudi Arabia, 1985)

Translated from the Arabic
by Salwa Jahsheh and John Heath-Stubbs

*This poem was written for Salma Khadra Jayyusi

Hind Nawfal

(*c.* 1860–1920)

The Arabic press in Egypt was flourishing by the 1890s and included a number of monthlies as well as magazines which appeared less regularly. Some journals like *Al-Muqtataf* (founded by Syrians) were devoted mostly to science. Others, like *Al-Hilal* (also founded by a Syrian) discussed literature. On November 20, 1892 the first Arabic monthly designed specifically for women appeared in Alexandria. Called *Al-Fatah* (The Young Girl) it was also owned and edited by a woman – Hind Nawfal.

A Syrian Christian, Hind came from a family of writer-journalists from Tripoli. Her mother, Maryam, had written a biographical dictionary on women which was published in the 1870s. They migrated to Alexandria in the last quarter of the 19th century. There, her father, Nasim Nawfal, helped her start a magazine.

In its forty-eight pages, *Al-Fatah* combined elements of form from the European women's press and the contemporary Arabic men's press. This included: biographies of famous Arab and European women, news, travel announcements, book and magazine notices, letters, poems, awards, and articles on fashion, housekeeping, health, and morality. The pages also reflected the debates on women's rights and responsibilities widespread in the press at that time.

Al-Fatah received acknowledgement and support from colleagues at *Lisan al-Hai, Al-Hilal, Al-Muqtataf* as well as letters of praise from literary figures. Those who contributed included Zainab Fawwaz and Aisha al-Taimuriya. Articles and agents came from throughout Egypt, the Ottoman Empire, indeed, the Mediterranean – Tanta, Alexandria, Cairo, Jaffa, Beirut, Tripoli and Lyon, France – reflecting a great range of circulation if not great numbers of readers.

In the seventh issue of the first year of *Al-Fatah*, Nasim Nawfal announced Hind's engagement to Habib Dabanam. The magazine continued to appear through March 1894 at which time it contained a lengthy description of a wedding, probably Hind's, after which the magazine stopped publication.

The selection given here is the introduction to the first issue, 20 November 1892. The original is quite flowery, reflecting the pen of Hind and the style of the time. Though journalistic prose became more simplified by the end of the century, *Al-Fatah* had established a precedent for a new genre as Arabic women's magazines appeared in great number with varieties of orientations.

The Dawn of the Arabic Women's Press

1892

⤷⧉⤶

The Maker of the world and Arranger of beings created the elements. He then created from them a huge world made of countless and innumerable suns, moons, stars, constellations. He filled the land with varieties of vegetation and species of animals, reflecting the utmost order and wisest arrangement. And thus began the cradle of man, the throne of his glory and seat of his power. And God gave him favourable characteristics, above all complete, rational power, and made the male and female, to grow and develop.

And He distinguished man from woman by the strength of his courage, zeal and boldness; and woman from man by her gentleness, compassion of heart and sweetness of speech. He joined them by natural attraction and innate love so that each of them would be helped by the other – earning money, managing the house, raising the children and taking care of things. He gave them the opportunity to discover natural mysteries and secrets of being and made the happiness of one linked to the happiness of the other.

When woman stepped out from behind the veil, refined and cultured, man saw her as an angel in the garb of humans. And the source of her dazzling beauty was reflected in the sparkle of her wit and the rays of her perception. Then man said, 'Bless Him who cloaked her with divine delight and made her a shining light in society.'

We learn from history how many a deadly lion has emerged from the harem and how many hennaed hands have held the reigns of kingdoms . . . And how many daughters, educated by wealth and cultured by poverty, have become heads of the harem and directed its affairs. And how many women were noted for intelligence and perfection, whose learning was not dependent on that of men. How many courageous women were like Joan of Arc, philosophers like Hypatia and poets like al-Khansa. And still, how many thousands of women made thinking their guide, diligence their motto, courage their principle, modesty their master and contemplation their companion. And there are others who showed the hidden jewels of their thoughts with the power of their speech, praising and glorifying the Creator.

As evidence of this, we point to their journals and their speeches, which show their talent to their readers and listeners. They even write poetry which delights the ear and compose prose which is magical.

No wonder *Al-Fatah* appears at this point in time! It seeks shade in the shadow of the al-Hamidi banner of our lord Sultan Abd al-Hamid Khan al-Ghazi, may God help him rule forever. Its appearance in the first year of the reign of his eminence, our great Khedive Abbas Hilmi II, a young man in the flower of youth who has surpassed seniors in intelligence and scholars in wisdom and comprehension, is a signal of the future success of the magazine, God willing.

With pride and wonder *Al-Fatah* finds itself on Egyptian soil. This is the land in which Egyptian women of Pharaonic times, for a period of two thousand years, showed extreme gentleness and refinement and demonstrated achievements and perfection which women of the west have not yet reached.

Al-Fatah is a scientific, historical, literary, humoristic magazine concerned with sex, the first of its kind under the eastern sky. It has no goal in political matters, no aim in religious controversies, no objective in researching subjects which are of no benefit to women, and no desire in discussions except what is relevant to the culture of al-Hifa and merits of al-Hasna.

It was founded to mirror the charms of the elegant and the beauty of the young. It will adorn its pages with flowings from the pens of women and gems of women writers' thoughts, with scientific subjects, historical episodes, literary selections and amusing anecdotes. Its sole principle is to defend the rights of the deprived and draw attention to the obligations due.

And it will discuss in serials – with one volume following another – the condition of woman and her natural place in ancient times, the middle ages and this period, a period of civilisation and culture. Topics include science and literature, character and morality, clothes and dress, childraising and good management, and all that is necessary for her in sewing, tailoring, threading, inscribing, drawing, painting and needlework.

We ask the gracious and learned ladies to consider *Al-Fatah* their newspaper in the east. It will express their ideas, probe the hidden contents of their breasts, defend their rights, review their literature and knowledge, and take pride in publishing the best of their work. But do not imagine that a woman who writes in a journal is compromised in modesty or violates her purity and good behaviour. No! The greatest of European women in science and literature and the highest in nobility are writers in journals.

Among those who have published in newspapers, we mention Mrs Carver, who writes in the *Daily News* of Paris and is counted among the most famous journalists . . .

It was not our intention by mentioning these great journals, renowned for their knowledge, culture, value, importance, and competence, to put *Al-Fatah* on a par. Rather, the digression was for the purpose of informing the reader that *Al-Fatah*, with the support of the gracious and cultured ladies, will grow, by the grace of God, to have years of success.

Why should it not succeed, if it is in the presence of the virtuous of the nation, our ruler, mother of our High Lord, of wide understanding and great merit? It compels us to raise the girl of our times in Egypt to her honourable position, to take pride in publishing her exploits and immortalising her deeds, with what was not told to Samiramis and Bilqis.[1] May Allah prolong her life and that of her daughters, who possess virtues of modesty and purity. They are a sun in the sky of splendour surrounded by moons in the constellation of the Alawi family. May God protect the desert winds in the celestial body of happiness, and the nightingales that sing in the garden of grace.

Translated from the Arabic
by Beth Baron

[1] Samiramis was queen of Assyria and Bilquis queen of Sheba.

Zainab Fawwaz

(1860–1914)

Zainab Fawwaz was born in Tibnin in southern Lebanon. In 1870, she emigrated to Alexandria with the family for whom she worked. She began to study the art of rhetoric with several local men of letters – Muhammad Shibli, Muhyi al-Din al-Nabahani, and Hasan Husni Pasha al-Tuwairani, founder and proprietor of *Al-Nil* news-paper, in which the article translated here first appeared. *Al-Nil* was founded on 17 December 1891, six months before 'Fair and Equal Treatment' was published.

She turned to the composition of poetry, and then began to publish prose essays in various periodicals of Alexandria and Cairo. Her book *Al-Rasail al-Zainabiyya* (Zainab's Letters) focused on the issue of women's rights to education and employment outside the home. She also wrote three novels: *Al-Malik Ursh* (King Ursh), a historical allegory, *Husn al-Awaqib* (Good Consequences), and *Al-Hawa wa-al-Wafa* (Passion and Loyalty). In 1894–5 she published her tome of women's biography, *al-Durr al-Manthur fi Tabaqat Rabbat al-Khudur* (Pearls Scattered Throughout the Women's Quarters), a compendium of biographies of famous Arab and European women. She died in Cairo in 1914.

This article is taken from *Al-Nil*, 18, Dhu al-Hugga, 1892. Zainab Fawwaz urges the recognition of women's abilities, their equal treatment and the rejection of essentialism.

Fair And Equal Treatment

1891

❧

The esteemed newspaper *Lubnan* published an article entitled
'Woman and Politics' by the distinguished woman of letters Hana
Kawrani. This writer is truly sincere in striving for her goals and is
to be marvelled at for her keenly sensitive powers of expression –
except that she has strayed in her judgment and has shown strong
disapproval of the young people of her sex. She has imposed
confinement to the home upon them and has worked to prevent
them from becoming involved in all outside activities pertaining to
the occupations of men. To quote:

> Woman, ignorant of the honourable nature of her position,
> thinks that her equality with men will be achieved only
> through her participation in the same kinds of work. How-
> ever, woman cannot perform work outside the home while at
> the same time fulfilling the duties incumbent upon her to
> serve her husband and children.

And about this programme – that is, homemaking as a way of life
– she says it is a natural one for women which they cannot properly
overstep, since it is a path of conduct marked out for them by God.
And if women exceed this path, the system of the universe will be
altered and the laws of nature will be transformed. Should human
beings attempt to change those laws, she says, their hopes will be
dashed and their efforts will fail, for altering these laws and
changing their *raison d'être* is impossible to achieve without destruction and ruin, whether in the short or long run.

The esteemed writer says that no one has really tried yet, as they
should, to understand what it is to be a woman and what it is to be a
man. Rather, she sees those who strive for women's equality trying
to equalise man and woman merely through the kinds of work they
perform. This, she says, is a false way to proceed. It will bring evil
consequences on the female sex in general, inevitably causing great
distress and heavy misfortune – for nature recompenses those who
transgress its system with grief and pain. She goes on in this vein
directing censure at the women of England for having demanded
participation in politics. This is the demand which – as is well
known to the honourable readers – embraces the issue of the

election bill which was a specific part of the women's demand for political participation. Noting how Mr Gladstone thwarted the bill in the British Parliament, the distinguished writer accuses the women of England of making a mistake in putting forth this demand. The esteemed man of letters who heads the newspaper *Lisan al-Hal* agrees with her in this respect.

In expressing my own thoughts on this subject, I want to begin with the following line of poetry:

> Your remedy is within you, and you do not see
> Your illness is from you, and you do not feel

Sage reader, contemplate how the human being is small in body, yet great in the world; weak in the true state of things, yet strong by deed. Coming upon difficulty, a person overcomes it through the power of human intelligence; when one assails problems with zeal, they yield in ready obedience. All creatures have submitted to the human being due to his good management and the strength of his determination. Nothing diverts his resolute will when he has settled on a demand that he desires to obtain and attain. Were it not for human determination, civilisation would not have flourished to become what it is today. Nor would the rights of knowledge and understanding have shone out, nor would the banners of progress have risen fluttering in this age. Europe would not have acquired its splendid palaces and magnificent edifices, its railroads and telegraph lines. Were it not for determination and undaunted initiative, Europe would not have emerged from behind the fog of its original, primitive state. Inventions and discoveries could proliferate only after humankind plunged into the treacherous torrents of destiny – after the human being took it upon himself to suffer perils and menaces. Were it not for the firmness of the human being's will then the slightest stumble would have forced a retreat from his aims, and the tiniest shock would have barred him from following the road to attainment of his goal. Without human will, it would not have been decreed that the human leave behind the noose of a primitive state of existence in favour of the arena of civilisation. Had he reckoned every misstep on the way as a failure and been defeated by it – retreating backward, dragging himself in shame and succumbing to disappointment and failure – then the universe would not have been populated or made prosperous. You would see nothing of the mind-boggling wonders that we witness today: it is through the grace of human intrepidity that conquests have been made and countries have flourished.

Of nations through which the illness of laziness has spread and the disease of indolence and apathy has seeped, there exists not a single one that has not been destroyed by these maladies – ills which have demolished the cornerstones of that nation's, fortitude and devastated the fortresses of its civilisation. What substantiates this precept for us is the greater progress of the West as compared to the East in the present era. The peoples of the West have been treated for their illnesses; their bodies have been cured of the disease of laziness and torpitude so that today the West has flourished to a greater extent than in any era. This age surpasses all others, to the point where the women of the western societies compete with the men and participate equally with them in work – since the great majority of people in the West agree that man and woman are equal in mental capacity and are two members of one social body, both of which are equally indispensable.

What objection, then, can be raised about woman's participation in the occupations of men and her pursuit of work in political or other spheres when she is capable of performing what she has been delegated to do? Otherwise, what benefit is derived from educating the western woman in all the branches of knowledge which men study – philosophy, law, mathematics, engineering? Or, why does she study the laws of politics if she is not then going to work in accordance with them, serving humankind and being considered one of the members of the ruling group?

For woman was not created in order to remain within the household sphere, never to emerge. Woman was not created to become involved in work outside the home *only* when it is directly necessary for household management, childrearing, cooking, kneading bread, and other occupations of the same sort, as the distinguished writer quoted above believes she should do. No, upon my life! Rather, the practices to which women are accustomed permit them to acquire and work in all arts and skills. As for household management and childrearing, these are natural and instinctive aptitudes in women, needing no lesson or education or code of practice or established guidelines. Indeed, whoever wants to learn the laws of household management and childrearing can gain this knowledge from women without much difficulty, whether those women are in a state of primitiveness or not, for even primitive women manage their households and raise their children to the best of their abilities and circumstances.

With regards to the esteemed writer's statement that if woman exceeds her presently defined place then the system of the universe will be altered and the laws of nature transformed: yes, existence does have a basic nature which cannot be changed, and God in His creation has set laws whose transformation cannot be decreed. But this transformation would not occur through employing women in

men's occupations or men in women's occupations as the honourable writer imagines. For such a change in practices is not in the
realm of what human beings *cannot* bring to pass, nor is it one of
those matters which would rock the tranquillity of the race, as the
writer supposes. She expresses her presumptions thus: 'Just as it is
impossible for humankind to transform vapour into gold or iron,
so it does not behoove woman to leave her household sphere.' But
the fact is that we have not seen any of the divinely ordered systems
of law, or any law from among the corpus of religious law (in
Islam), ruling that woman is to be prohibited from involvement in
the occupations of men. Nature has nothing to do with this: I do
not think that if this were to happen the sun would change its path,
nor would the water of the seas become sweet. But woman is a
human being as man is, with complete mental faculties and
acumen, and equivalent parts, capable of performing according to
her own abilities and distinguishing among times and places. How
many a woman has ruled over men, conducted the business of
state, determined statutes of law and behaviour, recruited soldiers,
gone forth into battle, and carried out wars – like the queens who
ran their kingdoms superbly, those who have preceded us, about
whom history has informed us. Among them are the likes of
Cleopatra, Zenobia, Queen of Palmyra, Elizabeth, and others who
have come before us. We see that their involvement in the business
of men did not violate the system of nature or detract from these
individuals' ability to manage their households. Rather, the family
structure remains as it was in their day.

But it is as if the writer is already opposing my words in advance
with her own, when she says: 'Those women were queens and able
to perform their household and administrative functions (both).'
However, to this I respond: Yes, and history has told us also about
the women of the Arab Bedouin: how they participated with the
men in work and wars, how they exposed themselves to danger,
how they suffered great tribulation and difficulties even though
they were wives and mothers. How many men have emerged into
adulthood from the nests of these women – and what men they
were! Men who came to rule the world in its entirety. And their
wives and mothers did not violate the system of the world: rather
they helped the men to populate the world and to organise society
properly.

Another piece of evidence from this age of ours: if a man passes
through the streets of any of the well-known major cities of
Europe, he will find its warehouses crammed with European
women carrying out commercial occupations – with their requisite
bookkeeping – and performing the handiwork of craftsmanship –

with its requisite perfection – according to the way things ought to be done. All of them are wives and mothers who manage both their household affairs and their work outside the home in consummate organised fashion. Then, if we were to regard the poor women we have in Cairo, Alexandria, and all parts of Egypt, we would find most of them pursuing work just like the men. Among these women are merchants, crafts workers, and those working with male labourers in construction and in other spheres through which men gain their livelihoods as is demanded of them. We find that in a family composed of man, woman, and children, the man directs himself to his occupation and the woman to her vocation – if she is a merchant, for example, then she goes to her shop – after she has looked to the well-being of her household and has provided what her children need, whether it be cooking, kneading bread, doing laundry, or something similar.

Thus, we find that the markets are full of women vying with men in business transactions, in giving and taking and in other such activities. And if we were to move our gaze to the countryside, we would find that the fields and farmlands are populated thickly by women – they are as numerous as the men or more so. All of them are helping their husbands and sons and running things as the men do: planting, weeding, harvesting, and other sorts of work particular to agriculture, which gives life to the whole world. Those women, too, have husbands and children. The intelligent person who inquires into the affairs of this world finds the two sexes equal. Yet careless neglect, and that alone, has dictated that women be held back.

I do not charge the women of England with wrongdoing for involving themselves in political affairs and demanding the right to participate in elections. Rather I say: Yes, they have a right to request this way of life as long as they are capable of carrying out their obligations as men do.

For it is well known that one does not take up the business of politics until after studying the laws of politics and striving to acquire knowledge of the science of administration as well as other related sciences necessary for this important sort of work. In the West, there is no difference between women and men in the study of the branches of knowledge. Women learn all that men must learn, in the fields of political science, commerce, crafts of production, and other areas crucial to the workings of the human world. Why should she not demand employment in politics just as she works in commerce, manufacturing, and other spheres needed by the human being in this earthly life?

The blockage of the bill which the women of England presented, including that demand for electoral participation, is not an event which calls for censure and violent attack. No, upon my life, for in the process of attaining one's goal, one cannot avoid encountering deterrants which hinder one's progress. There is no blame or reproach attached to this. I must strive, but in striving it is not necessary that I succeed. If it were not for the opposition of those who hold power in their hands, like Mr Gladstone and others, then the women's bill would not have run into the sort of opposition it encountered. It was not stopped for any reason which would indicate a degree of incapability on the part of the women or a need for caution about the outcome of such a bill's passage. No, upon my life, rather, this happened because the men regarded the bill with the eye of rancour and thought it represented militancy concerning political rights. Thus, the uproar grew, the unfounded chatter increased, the issue got out of hand, the crisis came to a head – and what happened, happened.

This is not the first such matter to encounter resistance. Indeed such resistance is God's way in His creation. In any issue broached for the first time, this resistance is a customary procedure sanctioned by time. This is well known to anyone who has perused the history of nations. Since the participation of women in politics is the first topic of discussion in this sphere to come up, then anyone who does not know the essence of the issue (especially if this person is a grudging sort) will certainly exaggerate its importance.

As for the women who approve rejection of this bill: they are the ones who – and pardon me – are more deserving of censure than are the others, for they have chosen isolation and sloth. They have given preference to idleness and unemployment over work; they have been content with showiness and with dragging their hems on the carpet of lethargy. If they were to put out some effort as their sisters have done, then they would have accomplished what their obligations require. They would then confirm that they are beings of determination who desire to serve humanity and the nation – as would be more appropriate for them than their present attitude – even if they are not to achieve success. In any case, the persistence of woman in demanding advancement until she obtains her rights is not to be considered a crime. Rather, posterity will glorify her, and she will be remembered with words of gratitude for opening the door of success to her sisters.

Translated from the Arabic
by Marilyn Booth

Bahithat al-Badiya

(1886–1918)

This was one of the first 'public' lectures in a series begun by and
for women only in Cairo in 1909. It was published the following
year in *Al-Nisaiyat* announcing that it had been given 'in the
presence of hundreds of women'. Bahithat al-Badiya and others
who gave talks to hundreds of women were school-educated
women of the middle and upper middle classes while their audience was full of upper class women. Bahithat al-Badiya's arguments for women's education at school and university and for new
work opportunities were made in front of women who had
received home tuition and whose daughters were being given the
same privileges. She also addressed the issue of changing modes of
women's dress and the decline of the old, stricter practices of
covering head and body, found among some of the newer generations of upper class women. This lecture (like the writing of her
contemporary, Nabawiya Musa), touching upon the most sensitive
social issues of the day for women and men alike, pointed to class
differences in behaviours and introduced a gender dimension to
the nationalist debates. Bahithat al-Badiya ended her talk with a
programme for change, the kernel of the more extensive set of
demands she sent two years later to the Egyptian Congress in
Heliopolis, a meeting of (male) nationalists.

A Lecture in the Club of the Umma Party

1909

༺ஓ༻

Ladies, I greet you as a sister who feels what you feel, suffers what you suffer and rejoices in what you rejoice. I applaud your kindness in accepting the invitation to this talk where I seek reform. I hope to succeed but if I fail remember I am one of you and that as human beings we both succeed and fail. Anyone who differs with me or wishes to make a comment is welcome to express her views at the end of my talk.

Our meeting today is not simply for getting acquainted or for displaying our finery but it is a serious meeting. I wish to seek agreement on an approach we can take and to examine our shortcomings in order to correct them. Complaints about both women and men are rife. Which side is right? Complaints and grumbling are not reform. I don't believe a sick person is cured by continual moaning. An Arab proverb says there is no smoke without fire. The English philosopher, Herbert Spencer, says that opinions that appear erroneous to us are not totally wrong but there must be an element of truth in them. There is some truth in our claims and in those of men. At the moment there is a semi-feud between us and men because of the low level of agreement between us. Men blame the discord on our poor upbringing and haphazard education while we claim it is due to men's arrogance and pride. This mutual blame which has deepened the antagonism between the sexes is something to be regretted and feared. God did not create man and woman to hate each other but to love each other and to live together so the world would be populated. If men live alone in one part of the world and women are isolated in another both will vanish in time.

Men say when we become educated we shall push them out of work and abandon the role for which God has created us. But, isn't it rather men who have pushed women out of work? Before, women used to spin and to weave cloth for clothes for themselves and their children, but men invented machines for spinning and weaving and put women out of work. In the past, women sewed clothes for themselves and their households but men invented the sewing machine. The iron for these machines is mined by men and the machines themselves are made by men. Then men took up the profession of tailoring and began to make clothes for our men and children. Before women winnowed the wheat and ground flour on grinding stones for the bread they used to make with their own hands, sifting flour and kneading dough. Then men established bakeries employing men. They gave us rest but at the same time pushed us out of work. We or our female servants, used to sweep our houses with straw brooms and then men invented machines to clean that could be operated by a young male servant. Poor women and servants used to fetch water for their homes or the homes of employers but men invented pipes and faucets to carry water into houses. Would reasonable women seeing water pumped into a neighbour's house be content to fetch water from the river which might be far away? Is it reasonable for any civilised woman seeing bread from the bakery, clean and soft, costing her nothing more than a little money, go and winnow wheat and knead dough? She might be weak and unable to trouble herself to prepare the wheat and dough or she might be poor and unable to hire servants or to work alone without help. I think if men were in our place they would have done what we did. No woman can do all this work now except women in the villages where civilisation has not arrived. Even those women go to a mill instead of crushing wheat on the grinding stones. Instead of collecting water from the river they have pumps in their houses.

By what I have just said, I do not mean to denigrate these useful inventions which do a lot of our work. Nor do I mean to imply that they do not satisfy our needs. But, I simply wanted to show that men are the ones who started to push us out of work and that if we were to edge them out today we would only be doing what they have already done to us.

The question of monopolising the workplace comes down to individual freedom. One man wishes to become a doctor, another a merchant. Is it right to tell a doctor he must quit his profession and become a merchant or vice versa? No. Each has the freedom to do as he wishes. Since male inventors and workers have taken away a lot of our work should we waste our time in idleness or seek other work to occupy us? Of course, we should do the latter. Work at home now does not occupy more than half the day. We must pursue an education in order to occupy the other half of the day but that is what men wish to prevent us from doing under the pretext of taking their jobs away. Obviously, I am not urging women to neglect their home and children to go out and become lawyers or judges or railway engineers. But if any of us wish to work in such professions our personal freedom should not be infringed. It might be argued that pregnancy causes women to

leave work, but there are unmarried women, others who are
barren or have lost their husbands or are widowed or divorced or
those whose husbands need their help in supporting the family. It
is not right that they should be forced into lowly jobs. These
women might like to become teachers or doctors with the same
academic qualifications. Is it just to prevent women from doing
what they believe is good for themselves and their support? If
pregnancy impedes work outside the house it also impedes work
inside the house. Furthermore, how many able-bodied men have
not become sick from time to time and have had to stop work?

Men say to us categorically, 'You women have been created for
the house and we have been created to be breadwinners.' Is this a
God-given dictate? How are we to know this since no holy book has
spelled it out? Political economy calls for a division of labour but if
women enter the learned professions it does not upset the system.
The division of labour is merely a human creation. We still witness
people like the Nubians whose men sew clothes for themselves and
the household while the women work in the fields. Some women
even climb palm trees to harvest the dates. Women in villages in
both Upper and Lower Egypt help their men till the land and plant
crops. Some women do the fertilising, haul crops, lead animals,
draw water for irrigation, and other chores. You may have
observed that women in the villages work as hard as the strongest
men and we see that their children are strong and healthy.

Specialised work for each sex is a matter of convention. It is not
mandatory. We women are now unable to do hard work because
we have not been accustomed to it. If the city woman had not been
prevented from doing hard work she would have been as strong as
the man. Isn't the country woman like her city sister? Why then is
the former in better health and stronger than the latter? Do you
have any doubt that a woman from Minufiya (a town in the Delta)
would be able to beat the strongest man from al-Ghuriya (a section
of Cairo) in a wrestling match? If men say to us that we have been
created weak we say to them, 'No it is you who made us weak
through the path you made us follow.' After long centuries of
enslavement by men, our minds rusted and our bodies weakened.
Is it right that they accuse us of being created weaker than them in
mind and body? Women may not have to their credit great
inventions but women have excelled in learning and the arts and
politics. Some have exceeded men in courage and valour, such as
Hawla bint al-Azwar al-Kindi who impressed Umar ibn al-Khattab
with her bravery and skill in fighting when she went to Syria to free
her brother held captive by the Byzantines. Joan of Arc who led the
French army after its defeat by the English encouraged the French

to continue fighting and valiantly waged war against those who fought her nation. I am not giving examples of women who became queens and were adept in politics such as Catherine, Queen of Russia; Isabel, Queen of Spain; Elizabeth, Queen of England; Cleopatra; Shajarat al-Durr, the mother of Turan Shah, who governed Egypt. Our opponents may say that their rule was carried out by their ministers who are men but while that might be true under constitutional rule it is not true under absolute monarchies.

When someone says to us that's enough education it discourages us and pushes us backwards. We are still new at educating our daughters. While there is no fear now of our competing with men because we are still in the first stage of education and our oriental habits still do not allow us to pursue much study, men can rest assured in their jobs. As long as they see seats in the schools of law, engineering, medicine, and at university unoccupied by us, men can relax because what they fear is distant. If one of us shows eagerness to complete her education in one of these schools I am sure she will not be given a job. She is doing that to satisfy her desire for learning or for recognition. As long as we do not work in law or become employed by the government would our only distraction from raising children be reading a book or writing a letter? I think that is impossible. No matter how much a mother has been educated or in whatever profession she works this would not cause her to forget her children nor to lose her maternal instinct. On the contrary, the more enlightened she becomes the more aware she is of her responsibilities. Haven't you seen ignorant women and peasant women ignore their crying child for hours? Were these women also occupied in preparing legal cases or in reading and writing.

Nothing irritates me more than when men caim they do not wish us to work because they wish to spare us the burden. We do not want condescension, we want respect. They should replace the first with the second.

Men blame any shortcomings we may have on our education, but in fact our upbringing is to blame. Learning and upbringing are two separate things – only in religion are the two connected. This is demonstrated by the fact that many men and women who are well educated are lacking in morals. Some people think that good upbringing means kissing the hands of women and standing with arms properly crossed. Good upbringing means helping people respect themselves and others. Education has not spoiled the morals of our girls, but poor upbringing, which is the duty of the home not the school, has done this. We have to redouble our efforts to reform ourselves and the young. This cannot happen in a minute as some might think. It is unfair to put the blame on the schools. The problem lies with the family. We must improve this situation.

One of our shortcomings is our reluctance to take advice from each other. When someone says something, jealousy and scorn usually come into play. We also are too quick to ridicule and criticise each other over nothing, and we are vain and arrogant.

Men criticise the way we dress in the street. They have a point because we have exceeded the bounds of custom and propriety. We claim we are veiling but we are neither properly covered nor unveiled. I do not advocate a return to the veils of our grand-mothers because it can rightly be called being buried alive, not *hijab*, correct covering. The woman used to spend her whole life within the walls of her house not going out into the street except when she was carried to her grave. I do not, on the other hand, advocate unveiling, like Europeans, and mixing with men, because they are harmful to us.

Nowadays the lower half of our attire is a skirt that does not conform to our standards of modesty (*hijab*) while the upper half like age, the more it advances the more it is shortened. Our former garment was one piece. When the woman wrapped herself in it her figure was totally hidden. The wrap shrunk little by little but it was still wide enough to conceal the whole body. Then we artfully began to shrink the waist and lower the neck and finally two sleeves were added and the garment clung to the back and was worn only with a corset. We tied back our headgear so that more than half the head including the ears were visible and the flowers and ribbons ornamenting the hair could be seen. Finally, the face veil became more transparent than an infant's heart. The purpose of the *izar* is to cover the body as well as our dress and jewellery underneath, which God has commanded us not to display. Does our present *izar*, which has virtually become 'a dress' showing the bosom, waist, and derrière, conform with this precept? Moreover, some women have started wearing it in colours – blue, brown and red. In my opinion we should call it a dress with a clown's cap which in fact it is. I think going out without it is more modest because at least eyes are not attracted to it.

Imams have differed on the question of *hijab*. If the getups of some women are meant to be a way to leave the home without the *izar* it would be all right if they unveiled their faces but covered their hair and their bodies. I believe the best practice for outdoors is to cover the head with a scarf and the body with a dress of the kind Europeans call *cache poussière*, a dust coat, to cover the body right down to the heels, and with sleeves long enough to reach the wrist. This is being done now in Istanbul, as I am told, when Turkish women go out to neighbourhood shops. But who will guarantee that we will not shorten it and tighten it until we transform it into another dress? In that instance, the road to reform would narrow in front of us.

If we had been raised from childhood to go unveiled and if our men were ready for it I would approve of unveiling for those who want it. But the nation is not ready for it now. Some of our prudent women do not fear to mix with men, but we have to place limits on those who are less prudent because we are quick to imitate and seldom find our authenticity in the veil. Don't you see that diamond tiaras were originally meant for queens and princesses and now they are worn by singers and dancers.

If the change that some women have made in the *izar* is in order to shed it when they go out that would be all right if these women would only uncover their faces but keep their hair and figures concealed. I think the most appropriate way to dress outside is to cover the head and wear a coat with long sleeves which touches the ground the way the European women do. I am told this is the way women in Istanbul dress when they go out shopping. But who can guarantee that we are not going to shorten it and tighten it until we transform it into something else?

The way we wear the *izar* now imitates the dress of Europeans, but we have outdone them in display (*tabarruj*). The European woman wears the simplest dress she has when she is outside and wears whatever she wishes at home or when invited to soirées. But our women are just the opposite. In front of her husband she wears a simple tunic and when she goes out she wears her best clothes, loads herself down with jewellery and pours bottles of perfume on herself . . . Not only this, but she makes a wall out of her face – a wall that she paints various colours. She walks swaying like bamboo in a way that entices passersby or at least they pretend to be enticed. I am sure that most of these showy women (*mutabarrajat*) do this without bad intentions, but how can the onlooker understand good intentions when appearances do not indicate it?

Veiling should not prevent us from breathing fresh air or going out to buy what we need if no one can buy it for us. It must not prevent us from gaining an education nor cause our health to deteriorate. When we have finished our work and feel restless and if our house does not have a spacious garden why shouldn't we go to the outskirts of the city and take the fresh air that God has created for everyone and not just put in boxes exclusively for men. But, we should be prudent and not take promenades alone and we should avoid gossip. We should not saunter moving our heads right and left. If my father or husband will not choose clothes I like and bring them to the house, why can't he take me with him to select what I need or let me buy what I want?

If I cannot find anyone but a man to teach me should I opt for ignorance or for unveiling in front of that man along with my sisters who are being educated? Nothing would force me to unveil in the presence of the teacher. I can remain veiled and still benefit from the teacher. Are we better in Islam than Sayyida Nafisa and Sayyida Sakina – God's blessings be upon them – who used to gather with *ulama* and poets. If illness causes me to consult a doctor and there is no woman doctor should I abandon myself to sickness, which might be light but could become complicated, through neglect or should I seek help from a doctor who could cure me?

The imprisonment in the home of the Egyptian woman of the past is detrimental while the current freedom of the Europeans is excessive. I cannot find a better model of today's Turkish woman. She falls between the two extremes and does not violate what Islam prescribes. She is a good example of decorum and modesty.

I have heard that some of our high officials are teaching their girls European dancing and acting. I consider both despicable – a detestable crossing of boundaries and a blind imitation of Europeans. Customs should not be abandoned except when they are harmful. European customs should not be taken up by Egyptians except when they are appropriate and practical. What good is there for us in women and men holding each other's waists dancing or daughters appearing on stage before audiences acting with bare bosoms in love scenes? This is contrary to Islam and a moral threat we must fight as much as we can. We must show our disdain for the few Muslim women who do these things, who otherwise would be encouraged by our silence to contaminate others.

On the subject of customs and veiling I would like to remind you of something that causes us great unhappiness – the question of engagement and marriage. Most sensible people in Egypt believe it is necessary for fiancés to meet and speak with each other before their marriage. It is wise and the Prophet himself, peace be upon him and his followers, did not do otherwise. It is a practice in all nations, including Egypt, except among city people. Some people advocate the European practice of allowing the engaged pair to get together for a period of time so that they can come to know each other, but I am opposed to this and am convinced this is rooted in fallacy. The result of this getting together is that they would come to love each other, but when someone loves another that person does not see the faults of that person and would not be able to evaluate that person's morals. The two get married on the basis of false love and without direction and soon they start to quarrel and the harmony evaporates. In my view, the two people should see each other and speak together after their engagement and before signing the marriage contract. The woman should be accompanied by her father, or an uncle or a brother and she should wear simple clothing. Some might protest that one or two or more meetings is not enough for the two persons to get to know each other's character, but it is enough to tell if they are attracted to each other. However, anyone with good intuition can detect a person's moral character in the eyes and in movements and repose and sense if a person is false, reckless and the like. As for a person's past and other things one should investigate by talking with acquaintances, neighbours, servants, and others. If we are afraid that immoral young men would use this opportunity to see young women without intending marriage her guardian should probe the behaviour of the man to ascertain how serious he is before allowing him to see his daughter or the young woman for whom he is responsible. What is the good of education if one cannot abandon a custom that is not rooted in religion and that is harmful. We have all seen family happiness destroyed because of this old betrothal practice.

By not allowing men to see their prospective wives following their engagement we cause Egyptian men to seek European women in marriage. They marry European servants and working class women thinking they would be happy with them rather than daughters of pashas and beys hidden away in 'a box of chance'. If we do not solve this problem we shall become subject to occupation by women of the West. We shall suffer double occupation, one by men and the other by women. The second will be worse than the first because the first occurred against our will but we shall have invited the second by our own actions. It is not improbable, as well, that these wives will bring their fathers, brothers, cousins and friends to live near them and they would close the doors of work in front of our men. Most Egyptian men who have married European women suffer from the foreign habits and extravagance of their wives. The European woman thinks she is of a superior race to the Egyptian and bosses her husband around after marriage. When the European woman marries an Egyptian she becomes a spendthrift while she would be thrifty if she were married to a westerner.

If the man thinks the upper class Egyptian wife is deficient and lacking in what her western sister has why doesn't the husband gently guide his wife? Husband and wife should do their utmost to please each other. When our young men go to Europe to study modern sciences it should be to the benefit, not the detriment, of Egypt. As these men get an education and profit themselves they should also bring benefit to their compatriots. They should bring to their country that which will profit it and dispense with whatever is foreign as much as possible. If a national manufacturer of silk visits the factories of Europe and admires their efficiency he should buy machinery that would do work rapidly rather than introduce the same European-made product because if he does he will endanger his own good product.

If we pursue everything western we shall destroy our own civilisation and a nation that has lost its civilisation grows weak and vanishes. Our youth claim that they bring European women home because they find them more sophisticated than Egyptian women. By the same token, they should bring European students and workers to Egypt because they are superior to our own. The reasoning is the same. What would be the result if this happens? If an Egyptian wife travels to Europe and sees the children there with better complexions and more beautiful than children in Egypt would it be right that she would leave her children and replace them with western children or would she do her best to make them beautiful and make them resemble as much as possible that which she admired in those other children? If the lowliest western woman marrying an Egyptian is disowned by her family shall we be content with her when she also takes the place of one of our best women and the husband becomes an example for other young men? I am the first to admire the activities of the western woman and her courage and I am the first to respect those among them who deserve respect, but respect for others should not make us over-look the good of the nation. Public interest is above admiration. In many of our ways we follow the views of our men. Let them show us what they want. We are ready to follow their views on condition that their views do not do injustice to us nor trespass on our rights.

Our beliefs and actions have been a great cause of the lesser respect that men accord us. How can a sensible man respect a woman who believes in magic, superstition, and the blessing of the dead and who allows women peddlars and washerwomen, or even devils, to have authority over her? Can he respect a woman who speaks only about the clothes of her neighbour and the jewellery of her friend and the furniture of a bride? This is added to the notion imprinted in a man's mind that woman is weaker and less intelli-gent than he is. If we fail to do something about this it means we think our condition is satisfactory. Is our condition satisfactory? If it is not, how can we better it in the eyes of men? Good upbringing and sound education would elevate us in the eyes of men. We should get a sound education, not merely acquire the trappings of a foreign language and rudiments of music. Our education should also include home management, healthcare, and childcare. If we eliminate immodest behaviour on the street and prove to our husbands through good behaviour and fulfilment of duties that we are human beings with feelings, no less human that they are, and we do not allow them under any condition to hurt our feelings or fail to respect us, if we do all this, how can a just man despise us? As for the unjust man, it would have been better for us not to accept marriage to him.

We shall advance when we give up idleness. The work of most of us at home is lounging on cushions all day or going out to visit other women. How does the woman who knows how to read occupy her leisure time? Only in reading novels. Has she read books about health or books through which she can profit herself and others? Being given over to idleness or luxury has given us weak constitutions and pale complexions. We have to find work to do at home. At a first glance one can see that the working classes have better health and more energy and more intelligent children. The children of the middle and lower classes are, almost all of them, in good health and have a strong constitution, while most of the children of the élite are sick or frail and prone to illness despite the care lavished on them by their parents. On the other hand, lower class children are greatly neglected by their parents. Work causes poisons to be eliminated from the blood and strengthens the muscles and gives energy.

Now I shall turn to the path we should follow. If I had the right to legislate I would decree:

1. Teaching girls the Quran and the correct Sunna.
2. Primary and secondary school education for girls, and compulsory preparatory school education for all.
3. Instruction for girls on the theory and practice of home economics, health, first aid, and childcare.
4. Setting a quota for females in medicine and education so they can serve the women of Egypt.
5. Allowing women to study any other advanced subjects they wish without restriction.
6. Upbringing for girls from infancy stressing patience, honesty, work and other virtues.
7. Adhering to the *Sharia* concerning betrothal and marriage, and not permitting any woman and man to marry without first meeting each other in the presence of the father or male relative of the bride.

8. Adopting the veil and outdoor dress of the Turkish women of Istanbul.
9. Maintaining the best interests of the country and dispensing with foreign goods and people as much as possible.
10. Make it encumbent upon our brothers, the men of Egypt, to implement this programme.

Translated from the Arabic by
Ali Badran and Margot Badran

May Ziyada

(1886–1941)

May Ziyada was born in Palestine. Her father was Palestinian and her mother Lebanese. 'May' – as she was widely known – was schooled in Nazareth and then in Ain Tura (Lebanon). She emigrated with her parents to Cairo in 1908, where her father became editor of the newspaper *Al-Mahrusah* in which some of her earliest writings were published. She lived in Cairo for the rest of her life except for a brief period in the late 1930s when relatives – convinced that she needed 'professional care' – had her put into an asylum in Beirut. After gaining her release, she returned to Cairo, where she died in 1941.

She was a prominent intellectual figure in the early part of the century in Egypt. A writer of prose and poetry, a sought-after public speaker and hostess of a salon which gathered together many of the leading intellectuals of the day, she was active in promoting women's access to education and employment outside the home. She wrote biographies of Bahithat al-Badiya (1920), Aisha al-Taimuriya (1924) and a speech about Warda al-Yaziji that was published in 1924 in *Al-Muqtataf*. She published widely in the Cairo and Beirut presses, and most of her prose works were collected during her lifetime in ten volumes, which have since been republished twice and most recently collected in a two-volume *Complete Works* (*Al-Muallafat al-Kamila: May Ziyada*, compiled by Salma al-Haffar al-Kuzbari, Beirut, 1982).

May Ziyada was one of the first Arab women to eulogise women colleagues. Such studies can be seen to constitute the foundation of a tradition of Arab women writers. In the following piece she points out the significance of correspondence between Arab women writers.

Warda al-Yaziji

1924

☙❧

This short piece was first given as a lecture at the YWCA in the middle of May 1924 and then published in *Al-Muqtataf.*

Warda al-Yaziji died at the beginning of this year in Alexandria. Salim Sarkis, whose style is elegant in prefacing certain subjects and in pointing out certain matters, one day published a letter of his to Warda al-Yaziji in heaven, and at the end he told her that I was planning to study her oeuvre in the same manner in which I have studied the works of Bahithat al-Badiya. This gave me encouragement and spurred me on. I wanted to do my duty by al-Yaziji even though I knew of the difficulty of her work because of its ambiguity, both in the poetry and in the prose, and its lack of personal detail. When I received the Association's invitation to give a lecture on any topic I wished, Sitt Warda's spirit was floating through my mind as I was browsing through her anthology, relishing its perfume.

I have only time to indicate in passing my esteem of what women from earlier generations have done to open up the way for us. I say: 'Open up the way', even though all they did was to put up a signpost at the threshhold of unknown territories. However, this signpost has value and use, especially when we remember when it was put up. It was left to us to uncover and register in existence the nature of the eastern woman, and to struggle thereafter to make sure that we help it to grow and that we polish it so that it appears the way it is in essence as a work of art, as a resource and as a treasure.

It seems that the goddess of wakefulness and activity wished to neglect the East for about half the last century, then there arose a group of learned women next to the men who were considered to be responsible for raising up the new East. Aisha Ismat al-Taimuriya was born in Egypt in 1840, and around that time Warda al-Turk lived in Syria as did Warda Kubba and Labiba Sidqa and others. Zainab Fawwaz the writer of the *Zainab Letters* and *Scattered Pearls* was born in Sidon in 1860. In that same year Fatima Aliya was born, the daughter of the Turkish historian Gaudat Pasha. Although she wrote in Turkish, she has the right to be mentioned along with Arab women writers because she knew their language and she was known in their lands and she lived long among them;

she had gone there as a three year old when her father took over the Aleppo region after having been Minister of Finance in the Ottoman State. In the year when Zainab Fawwaz and Fatima Aliya were born, that is in 1860, Warda al-Yaziji was 22, because she was born in 1838, the same year as Marianna Marash, the Aleppo poet.

Ladies, remember that geniuses are divided into two leading groups which are in turn multipally subdivided. The first group does not fit into its environment, and is before its time in understanding, perspicacity and creativity. The second group is a product of its environment and its time, and in it are contained the cognitions and the emotions of its society. This group talks to its society eloquently and clearly. (In the first group is Qasim Amin.)

The second group talks the language of its age and speaks of its needs and feels what it feels. As though they feed the people with that which helps them grow and leads step by step toward a future which will be shaped by members of the first group. Warda al-Yaziji is from this group.

(Ziyada tells of Warda's education)

Georges Baz, the poet's son-in-law and her most loyal assistant in Syria, said about *The Rose Garden* that it is the only anthology by a contemporary poet to have been printed three times. This is the only work of hers that is left to us. Clearly she must have taken the name of the anthology from her own. [Warda means rose.]

Among the most important of her prose writings was the correspondence with the Egyptian poet, Aisha Ismat al-Taimuriya. The latter praised her in the introduction to her anthology *Beautiful Embroidery* and then gave her a copy. Afterwards there was a delightful exchange of poetry and prose in which the poets competed in praising each other. Zainab Fawwaz published this correspondence in *Scattered Pearls*. In *The Rose Garden* we found poems by al-Yaziji for al-Taimuriya, such as this one in thanks for a gift:

> Time has returned Aisha to live the remnants of an
>   ancient knowledge
> My heart was enraptured at the sound and mentioning
>   her was my only pleasure and joy

In another poem she wrote about *The Results of Circumstances*:

> A young woman who has emblazoned the peaks with
>   pearls from the fresh jewels of literature
> I am enraptured by her from a distance, how would it
>   have been if the fates had allowed me to be close

We do not know if the two poets met after this correspondence. Warda al-Yaziji came to Egypt in 1899 three years before Aisha al-Taimuriya died.

We now turn to the dark roses, the roses of death and eulogy scattered on graves. Elegies make up more than half of this anthology. According to the custom of the time she wrote eulogies to the great, to scholars and to friends. These elegies begin with well-known proverbs about death and the impossibility of combating it and its lack of mercy to anyone.

She eulogised her six brothers, a sister, her father, her husband, two sons and a daughter (extracts from these and other elegies follow).

Ladies and young women, I see that you are weeping, and it is precious to me to know that I have brought you to tears. So I shall refrain from reciting to you her eulogy for her last brother.

At this point Miss Milia Badr, the superintendent of the American school for girls stood up and said:

'Is is your delivery that has made us weep. But do not cut your words short.'

'Despite the tears and these kerchiefs waving in our sisters' hands?'

'Yes. Despite the tears.'

'There's no harm in grief and weeping,' several voices said.

'All right, Ladies. You are right. There's no harm in weeping over the pains of others. Poetry needs grief and tears. Edgar Allen Poe, after many others, said that the poetic genius is sad in its essence and that those who reach this sadness and love it, approach that genius when they feel compassion for sadness and distress.'

Do not believe the accusation directed against her, and other women, that men write for her. She was the one who wrote her poetry. The greatest proof is that in the beginning they claimed that her father and brothers, Habib and Khalil, had composed it for her. Then they died and she eulogised them. So the people said: 'Shaikh Ibrahim is alive. He must be the one who composed the eulogies in her name.' Then Shaikh Ibrahim died and she eulogised him in verses that are among the most profound and sincere of anything she had ever written.

(*Ziyada introduces the section on prose by describing al-Yaziji's warning against unquestioning emulation of women of the West and her advocacy of education so that motherhood is not the only future women can anticipate.*)

I learned yesterday that the women of Beirut contributed to a portrait of Warda al-Yaziji and donated it to the pubic library in that city so that the poet's picture should hang next to those of the great men. That is in Beirut. That Egyptian and non-Egyptian women gathered to salute her is a sign of the respect in which she is held.

May you retain a memory that endures beyond this meeting. May housewives think of her because Warda of the Arabs was a blessed daughter, a judicious sister, a loyal wife, a good mother! May the school superintendents and teachers think of her because the poet was exemplary in her commitment to education and in her care for her siblings. May the students who will soon be finished with the end-of-year examinations think of her because al-Yaziji was an eager student. Even though, without their means, she continued learning throughout her life. May everyone be reminded by her that whatever good a woman does outlives her time and serves coming ages, like the grain of wheat in fertile soil that stores nutrients for the future.

May the women of Egypt remember Warda al-Yaziji and her emergent Syrian sisters just as the women of Syria remember Aisha al-Taimuriya and Bahithat al-Badiya and their emergent Egyptian sisters. May they be moved by her memory and her virtues just as the Syrian women are influenced and excited by the renaissance of the Egyptian woman.

I, the daughter of two continents, consider myself happy to have been able to draw the portrait, however pale, of an eastern woman for eastern sisters whose nationalism I admire. Like them I cry out enthusiastically and, following their model, I call for progress, understanding and the good of the nations!

Translated from the Arabic
by Miriam Cooke

Qut al-Qulub

(1898–1968)

Qut al-Qulub was born in 1898 in al-Mahamadi Palace in Cairo. Her father, Ahmad Abd al-Rahman al-Dimardash Pasha, was the head of the Dimardashiyya sufi order dating back to sixteenth century Anatolia that had headquarters at al-Mahamadi. Her mother was Zainab Taudi. Qut al-Qulub had a strict harem upbringing with tutors coming to the home. Her father arranged her marriage at twenty-five, old for her time, to Mustafa Bey Mukhtar, a lawyer and judge in the mixed courts with whom she had four sons and a daughter. She ended her marriage after seven years, kept her children and made sure that they carried her own family name, al-Dimardash, rather than their father's name as was customary. At her palace on the Nile between the Ministry of Foreign Affairs and the Qasr al-Nil Bridge, she received leading intellectuals, scholars, writers, and philanthropists from Egypt and abroad. She began publishing novels in French in 1935 depicting everyday life, especially life in the old aristocratic harems. Her books include: *Au Hasard de la Pensée* (1934), *Harem* (1937), *Les Trois Contes de l'Amour a la Mort* (1939), *Zenouba* (1946), *La Nuit de la Desinée* (1954), *Le Coffret l'Hindou* (1952), *Ramza* (1958), and *Hif-naoui le Magnifique* (1962).

Ramza, Qut al-Qulub's penultimate novel, was published in 1958. Set in turn-of-the-century Egypt, Ramza in her old age observes the freer behaviour of young people, especially girls, and reflects on her own life and times. Ramza, the daughter of a high official and a Serbian slave, after a privileged and circumspect upbringing typical of her class, rebelled against the convention of marrying a man of her family's choice in favour of a young middle class officer with whom she eloped. Much in *Ramza* is said to depict the life the author observed at close range in the harem in its final days, and the family stories she heard. Reproduced here are two chapters: 'The Elopement' and 'The Impossible Joy'. 'The Elopement' echoes the story of the marriage earlier in the century of the daughter of Said Abd al-Khaliq al-Sadat, the sufi leader, to Shaikh Ali Yusuf, the editor of the daily newspaper, *Al-Muayyad*. This caused a great political and social scandal in its day. We see Ramza's courage in marrying the man she loved in the face of her father's objections. In 'The Impossible Joy' which takes place after her father's death, she dissolves her marriage after it has become unworkable. It is she alone who has the courage and conviction to act. *Ramza* illustrates the tensions and contradictions produced by women's initiative within a social and economic order based upon controls upholding gender and class privilege.

The Elopement and the Impossible Joy

1958

❦

The next morning I went to see my father in the little drawing room adjoining the library where we usually met for breakfast. As I cracked open the door, much less confident of myself than I had been in my own room the night before, I could tell by his expression that nothing would go as I had planned. He had read my letter and before I could open my mouth he was already speaking: 'Ramza,' he said, 'once and for all I want no more said about this brother of Bahiga's. It's already a shame that he has seen you and spoken to you. He is a worthless fellow and has taken advantage of your friendship with his sister to seduce you.'

I looked at my father in horror and exclaimed before I knew what I was doing, 'Father, he didn't seduce me; I want to marry him. I've chosen him and I know his qualities.'

My father answered sharply, 'You miserable girl, you are my only daughter and I will not have you married to the son of a shopkeeper, a boy with no education, an insignificant army officer without a future. Do you see yourself tied to this man and following him from camp to camp, garrisoned in one town after another in the Sudan for the rest of your life? Is that your ambition?'

I was angry. I said, 'My ambition, Father, is to marry the man I have chosen freely, the man I have loved and not to be passed on like an inherited good from one member of Safwat Pasha's family to another.'

I saw my father's face soften and that expression of tender affection which he reserved for me come into his eyes. He smiled and said, 'I see that I've spoiled you, Ramza. I've allowed you to learn to reason and I am partly responsible for the state of things now. For this reason I feel I owe you an explanation for what I've done. We are easterners, Ramza. Here marriage is a family affair, not just a matter of falling in love with a handsome boy.'

I remained silent and he continued: 'You have a role to play in Egyptian society, my child. This role depends on your rank in society and that of your family. If I have accepted Safwat Pasha's request for your hand in marriage to his son, it is because his is one of the first families of Egypt. I also took into consideration what you are, Ramza, and did not want you to marry into a family that would be unsuitable for your tastes and education. I did not want to marry you to an old man, an idiot, a cripple or even a man overly attached to customs you would have deemed out of date, whatever his place in society. I thought of you when choosing Midhat, who has studied in Europe. He is broad-minded and modern and looks forward to a brilliant future in which you could play a part. Furthermore he is young, agreeable and nothing about him could be displeasing to you. He is a good mate for you, Ramza. You see I'm trying to persuade you as you would expect any European father to do. And you see, even if I wanted to refuse Safwat Pasha's request I could not. We are committed to that family.'

When he had finished I responded quietly trying to use logic with my father as he had done with me. 'Father,' I said, 'I understand what you are saying and I appreciate your reasoning, but I love Maher and cannot marry anyone else. I've given him my word.'

At this point my father grabbed my arm and began shaking me vigorously, the blood rising in his face and his eyes burning with horror. For a moment I thought he would hit or strangle me, but instead he shouted, 'That's enough. Go to your room and stay there. Tomorrow I'm taking you back to Cairo and I don't want to hear another word about that miserable rogue. You'll never see him again.' He went out slamming the door behind him.

I collapsed in tears. But soon enough came to my senses and began to hatch a plan. My father had left the house; Mademoiselle was still in church; Nargis would not have left her rooms yet. I would flee. I dressed quickly wearing black clothes, a black face veil and my black habara on top of it all. I made myself look as anonymous as possible. That dark costume was a perfect camouflage; nothing of an individual could come through its thicknesses. I then put my money in my purse and took all my jewellery. Near the kitchen I picked up a shopping basket to make me look like a woman from any popular quarter of the city and slipped out the service entrance without anyone being the wiser.

I had decided to go and find Maher and get married right away.

I had imagined that my father would give in before a *fait accompli* and would forgive me and give me his blessings. I was far from the truth. He had left Alexandria and returned to Cairo the day following my elopement. I was told that his fury had been terrible. He had reproached Nargis and Mademoiselle bitterly for their negligence and had sworn that he would kill me. He filed a law suit against Maher and me with the intention of declaring our marriage null and void. When Shaikh Abd al-Muti went to see him it was already too late. The affair had reached the courts.

The Shaikh reported to me that my father no longer thought of killing me and even authorised me to come home on condition that I stay clear of him. He did not want to set eyes on me. I was tempted by the idea, but remained in the harem of the Shaikh instead. Although I was not free to go and come as I pleased there, I felt I would be more independent than in our house. My father agreed to send Mademoiselle Hortense to me there, and her companionship during those difficult days was precious to me.

The struggle between my father and me began almost immediately and although I loved him and was miserable at the idea of making him so unhappy, I was as stubborn as he in fighting for my principles. I was also certain that his affections for me would not diminish as long as anger did not distort his thoughts which was not often during those weeks. The battle between us was long and painful but in our shared obstinacy neither would give in to the other.

I took on a lawyer whom the devoted Shaikh Abd al-Muti recommended. His name was Shaikh Mustafa al-Maghrabi; he was young and had already established a reputation for brilliance and a liberal point of view despite his Shaikh's turban and the kaftan he wore. He agreed to take up my cause and plead for me.

Meanwhile I grew more and more uneasy about Maher. Would his father persuade him to repudiate me after all? I think I would have died of shame had that happened. Shaikh Mustafa heard my plea and went to see Maher to ask him to stand up in his own defence and gave him advice on what to say.

News of my secret marriage soon spread and all Cairo was talking about it. I received letters from young girls in the harem congratulating me on my courage and pleading with me to carry on.

As the date of the hearing approached I grew increasingly worried. I had been carried along feverishly by the excitement of the fight and to tell the truth I had nearly forgotten that Maher was involved or that he was even the object of this campaign. I acquired law books, discussed endlessly the chances for our success with my lawyer, Shaikh Mustafa, who was so inspired by my ardour that he was as convinced as I was that we could not possibly lose our case. He warned me, however, that the presiding judge was not sympathetic to our cause. He had daughters and feared that I would set a precedent if I won.

I read and re-read the legal code of the *Sharia* and studied every intricacy of my case with Shaikh Mustafa. It seemed to us that there was not a loop hole we could not call the law to fill. Nothing there could prove that my marriage was not valid. The contract which we had signed before the *mazun* in Alexandria was unimpeachable. I had reached majority age and was in full possession of my mental faculties, and was therefore fit to sign a binding contract. Maher had paid a dowry of five hundred Egyptian pounds and endowed me with an equal amount to be paid after a certain lapse of time. All was conducted according to custom and the law. People could not accuse Maher of being an unworthy party. He had paid the dowry required for a person of my social standing and not a penny less. I was excited and confident.

Maher came to see me from time to time and we spent these rare moments mapping out our future. We took stock of our joint finances and decided we could manage very well. Beside the five hundred pounds which he had given me, I had two hundred pounds and all my mother's valuable jewellery. Maher owned a hundred or so acres of good land and a house in Shubra and had his pay from the army.

As we talked, we came to the conclusion that it would be best to get away for a while after the sentence was pronounced to let tempers cool before returning to Cairo. Maher said he would ask to be posted in the Sudan where we could remain a few years. After that everyone would have forgotten the whole affair and we would be accepted without question by our families and society. How eager I was for that time to come!

The day of the trial finally came. There was no question of course of my attending. Women did not go into court. But as the courthouse was not far from Shaikh Abd al-Muti's house, I made Shaikh Mustafa promise that he would come and tell me the verdict as soon as it was pronounced. I was sure that we could not fail and yet felt quite nervous about the proceedings. I remained posted at a window the entire time waiting for the Shaikh and Maher to appear. When I saw them finally, I knew from their expressions that we had lost. The Shaikh was indignant and cried, 'The judge didn't even listen to my pleas. His decision was made before he came to court. This judgment is iniquitous and I will make an appeal tomorrow.'

The whole experience had been deeply humiliating for Maher. He had been accused of every possible beastliness and my father's lawyer had claimed that a marriage between us was an aberration because we were not of the same social class. He had been dragged through the mud along with his family. He was livid with rage recounting to me how the lawyer had insulted him and his family calling them unworthy peasants and referring to their origins in the harshest possible terms.

'He damaged my father's reputation,' Maher cried and told me that the lawyer had referred to them as nothing better than worms.

The lawyer had continued saying that Maher was the son of a peasant whose recently acquired wealth was the result of penny pinching and avarice. 'As for me,' Maher said, 'I was treated as being nothing more than a lowly soldier who had been admitted to military school only because the army took in riff-raff for lack of anything better.' Sons of good families avoid the military, Maher recounted the lawyer's discourse.

Shaikh Mustafa tried to convince Maher that the words said in court were merely those of a lawyer trying to defend his client. Maher would have none of it and felt directly implicated. His pride was hurt and he had been deeply wounded. He was suffering and I suffered along with him. I would have done anything to erase the insults which had been inflicted upon him and his family. I felt at that moment that this unfortunate turn of events would always stand between us and would make Maher hate me.

According to Shaikh Mustafa, my father had obtained a decree from Sultan Abd al-Hamid establishing our family's descent from Imam Hussain, grandson of the Prophet. This put our family so high in the social order that my marriage to someone of inferior class would be considered null and void. My father had used this to annul our marriage and based his argument on the Quranic law which states that a Muslim girl is forbidden to marry below her station. In Shaikh Mustafa's opinion this difference in class had been over-emphasised in my case and Maher's and that it was far from being the real reason for the negative verdict pronounced by the judge. What the judge had wanted to condemn publicly was the freedom of choice of marriage partners by the younger generation. He wished to show that to defy one's family could only bring shame and unhappiness on a young couple.

The press took up the case and there was a violent exchange of opinion between those who supported the traditional order of things and the liberal elements who were for a modernisation of current practices regarding marriage and the status of women. This polemic went beyond us and beyond Egypt itself. It served as fuel for the existing conflict between Sultan Abd al-Hamid and his traditionalist policies and the more liberal Young Turks Party.

Every day some aspect of my case was discussed in the press and as I read the heated reports I realised that those for and against me reacted with an equal lack of restraint. Each was violent in his opinion. I was flattered in part by all this attention, but on the other hand, feared that all the publicity would compromise my chances of happiness. Maher and my father could only come out of this as eternally mortal enemies.

Despite the disappointing verdict, Shaikh Mustafa continued to feel optimistic and to encourage me. He had appealed the decision and felt sure that no judge would insist on upholding the verdict as public opinion was strongly in our favour. He told me one day, his eyes gleaming with pleasure, that the Khedive himself was on our side. That was surprising because I knew the Khedive to be a friend and admirer of my father's and that he would be reluctant to act in a way which would vex my father. He was young, however, only thirty years old then, and it was normal that he should hold views which were more liberal than those of his elders. Public opinion maintained however that Khedive's support was inspired by political motives. The Consul of Great Britain and Lord Cromer had intervened, it seemed, on my father's behalf and this was reason enough for the Khedive to take the opposing side. Of these two opposing factions, however, it was the Khedive's which was the most powerful. Discussions of freedom and national sovereignty followed Lord Cromer's intervention and opened the floodgates of interminable polemic in the nationalist press. From a simple girl fighting for the freedom to choose whomever she wished to marry, I had suddenly been propelled into the role of a national heroine fighting for Egyptian independence. Newspapers came out with sensational headlines such as: 'From slave mothers only slaves are born' or 'Let us free our mothers, wives and daughters so that they might give birth to free men.'

Suddenly, I found my feminist ideals taken up, magnified and embellished and found myself just as suddenly in the limelight, the heroine of a struggle for national as well as personal freedom. I must admit that I enjoyed the excitement which surrounded these issues and began to believe that I was truly a heroine with a great cause to uphold. Despite this, I was not completely at ease. What news I had of my father led me to believe that he had become even more inflexible than before. He was announcing publicly that he would marry me off to his steward, Salim Effendi, a man in his sixties. Rather than mollify me this fired my determination to fight on and to keep alive the struggle against servitude of any kind.

I grew increasingly unhappy however with Maher's weakness in a situation where I needed his support. His initial indignation gave way to fearful reticence in the face of authority. He could barely get up the courage to come and see me and he kept a cold front and anxious distance between us when he did come and we were allowed a few moments alone in Shaikh Abd al-Muti's office. Finally I asked him if he still loved me. He assured me that his love was stronger than ever and he was miserable when I suggested that I had my doubts and wondered if we had really gone through with our marriage or whether it had all been a dream. He could only murmur, 'What can I do? My father makes a scene whenever I come to see you.' I exploded and said to him, 'You mean to tell me you hesitate to choose between me and your father? I broke with my own father to marry you and you still succumb to the tyranny of yours? Can't you see how we are struggling to liberate women? Do we have to do the job for men as well?'

No sooner had I said this than I saw Maher go completely pale with confusion. I felt I might have pushed him too far and quickly tried to repair the situation by saying, 'Please try to understand that I love you, Maher. Nothing can keep me from being your wife and if you're afraid of living with me in Cairo let's go to the Sudan. Ask for a transfer. I'll follow you to the ends of the earth.' He could find no response save to implore me to be patient. Perhaps the appeal would bring results, our marriage would be valid and my father would take us back into the fold.

I felt then that Maher lacked the courage of his convictions and explained to him that my father would never concede and that his friends in court would act according to his wishes, not ours. 'My father has friends among the judges and the backing of the English who are masters here, as you know. What will you do if he forces a verdict for annulment? Only one thing can save us now, Maher, and that is to live together and have a child born of our union of which we would be proud.' I thought I had convinced him that day to leave his father's house and search for an apartment for us to live in. But the days passed and Maher did not reappear. I grew tired of living in Shaikh Abd al-Muti's home and although his wives and daughters were kind and generous, they were illiterate and their company wearisome. They understood nothing about what I was doing or what I stood for and from time to time would give me advice which amounted to little more than, 'Leave Maher and go back to your father's house.'

The Shaikh who at first had spared me now began to reproach me blaming me for the scandalous rumblings which filled the newspapers. He found the involvement of the press in such a personal matter shocking. One day when I answered back a little too briskly he cried out, 'Do you forget yourself, Ramza? Do you forget that you are living under my roof?'

I was taken aback and before I could stop myself answered or rather snapped back, 'Not for long.' Five minutes later, I had gathered my belongings and with Mademoiselle in tow left Shaikh Abd al-Muti's house forever. This house which had been a hospitable shelter for weeks had suddenly become a prison. I could not stay cloistered like the women of the harem, and I blamed myself bitterly for having remained there so long. What a fool I had been, championing women's rights and yet allowing myself to be shut up in a harem all the while. How absurd it all was, how ironic!

Mademoiselle listened quietly to all my reflections and outbursts as she had always done. We rode in the carriage to the outskirts of Abbasiya where I remembered that an old friend of my grand-mother's, Tahasin Hanim, lived. I found her house without difficulty but no one was there. I questioned the watchman who told me that Tahasin had become infirm and was living a hundred metres further down the street with her daughter. I went there and the old woman was pleased to see me. She agreed to rent me her house and give me a servant for the time being. She also found a way to send Nargis a message telling her my whereabouts. Nargis responded by sending me the daughter of my old wet nurse, Zuhaida, and her husband who would serve me. They brought along a small box containing two hundred pounds in gold coins from Nargis to help me through the difficult weeks ahead. Kind, kind Nargis! How I wished to see her now! In fact, I don't know what I would have done without this aid. The lawsuit had been costly and I was reduced to selling my jewellery to live.

Four days later I was surprised by a visit from Maher. Shaikh Abd al-Muti had told him that I had left and had not left an address. He had looked for me everywhere until he had found my traces. He burst in uttering nothing but blame and reproaching me for my decision to leave the Shaikh's house without consulting him first. I was rather pleased to see him so worked up and did not in the least bit regret the worry I had caused him. He had taken the trouble to look for me, and that was at least a sign of caring. But I did not let him see my pleasure. I continued working on the sewing I had in hand and answered his questions coldly.

This further exasperated him, and he cried out, 'Ramza, you are capricious. You do what you want without telling anyone and you act as if I didn't even exist.'

'I see so little of you anyway,' I replied coldly, 'I'm obliged to take decisions without consulting you.' He blushed, but seemed calmer and then changed the subject.

'You're certainly not planning to live alone in this godforsaken place, are you?' he said.

'Well, I have two servants to keep me company for lack of a husband,' I replied.

He shivered, but did not pursue the subject. Instead he began to look around him and complimented me on the way I had arranged this little villa in a matter of four days.

'I've been taught to keep house and to cook, you know,' I said.

He attempted to answer lightly, asking me if I would invite him to dinner.

'No,' I said dryly, 'I don't think you should linger here, you might compromise my reputation.' I told him that in fact he had better go right away and I began to leave the room as well.

He tried to hold me back saying, 'Ramza, you're being cruel. What have I done to deserve this?'

'Nothing at all,' I replied, 'You have been a paragon of prudence and wisdom. Go on, go back to your father. If he discovers you've been to see me he might take off his slipper and strike you.'

At this terrible insult he went white and tightening his fists said to me, 'Don't provoke me, Ramza, or I will be the one to strike you.'

He came toward me with a menacing look, but I answered him without flinching, 'And by what right do you think you can strike me or even speak to me in this way? Surely you don't consider yourself to be my husband!' He was furious. I had struck him where it hurt and he suddenly lunged forward, took me up in his arms and struggling carried me into my room. That was the moment I had longed for. I did not struggle long.

[The court pronounces their marriage null and void because of the difference in class. Maher urges Ramza to return to her father. But she escapes to him at Qina, an army barracks in the south. He is happy to see her, but insists that she remain hidden. When she appears at his office, he is furious and sends her back to Cairo. He assures her that they can never be married because both their fathers have cursed them.]

'Maher, answer me in all sincerity. Do you want me as your wife? Don't be afraid to say the truth.' Maher did not respond and during the pregnant silence that followed I reflected on what I had done. Everything was so clear. But love had made me blind to the truth and love had made it impossible for me to accept the evidence before me that Maher did not want me. After all, I had made him marry me in Alexandria. I had forced him to take me to Cairo. I had run after him to Qusair. Every step of the way the initiative had been mine. He had tried to run away. In the court case against my father, even, it had been me who had done all the pushing; Maher and his father kept well in the shadows and did not really want to win. They too were my opponents. That is why I had lost. Even here in the desert, he did not feel as if I were really his wife.

Despite this I was certain that Maher had loved me. Perhaps he still loved me, but his love was not enough to surmount the prejudices and the obstacles which assailed him. He was afraid of public opinion and his silence spoke louder than words could have done. He was vain and his pride had been hurt by the turn the verdict took. Even if I had won the case I would have always been the infamous wife to him. The one he would always feel ashamed of at the bottom of his heart and afraid of because of what she might do in the future. She did not possess the humility of the woman-servant nor the docility of the harem inmate.

Finally he got up the courage to say what was on his mind. He spoke nearly in a whisper, unable to look at me. 'You see, Ramza,' he said, 'while your father was still alive we could still hope to gain his approval and consequently my father's. Now we've killed him. He died cursing us. My father curses us also and will do so until his death.'

I knew from these words that Maher meant there was no hope for us. I knew exactly where I stood and what I must do.

'I understand your desire now, Maher. I won't stand in your way any longer. I'll disappear from your life altogether, but it will be of my own free will and not because of my father's instructions nor a verdict from the court. I'm declaring to you now that I no longer can be, nor wish to be, your wife. Please call out two witnesses and lets get on with a divorce.'

He recoiled in horror and, protesting, said, 'I'll never deal you such an affront, Ramza, and in any case there is no need of a divorce. We are not bound by any law since the court did not recognise our marriage.'

'I never recognised the verdict of the court,' I said coldly, 'and in any case those who have been united through love by God cannot be separated by men or their laws. Today, Maher, had it been possible to divorce you, in a world where women are only asked to submit and obey, I would have been the one to take the initiative. And you can be certain that my voice would not have trembled. So you go ahead and do it since I cannot.' I looked at him and despite my hard words, I tried to drink in his features, his face, everything about this man I loved, and print it forever on my mind. Then I covered my face with my hands and said to him, 'Go ahead, speak, deal the death blow.'

He tried to get away, tried to hide behind the irony saying, 'Come now, Ramza, enough of flowery prose. You'll miss your train.'

But I was dead serious and said to him, 'Maher, this is the last request I'll ever make of you. Strike like a soldier since this privilege is accorded you and not me. Or will you be a coward?'

Finally, in a whisper, he spoke the ritual formula for divorce: 'I repudiate you. You are no longer my wife. You have become like a sister and a mother to me.' This had to be repeated three times, but old Abdallah who was serving as witness intervened. 'That's enough,' he said hoarsely, 'Do you want to kill her.' I knew then, despite my pain, that even if Maher came back to me, this was the end. I would never take him back. I lowered my black veil and knew that Maher would never set eyes on my face again. A few hours later we were in Qina. Maher had disappeared and I forced myself not to look for him. Old Abdallah took me to the station, bought a ticket for me and settled me in the train and waited for it to pull out of the station.

I remained dry-eyed until dawn, then the tears came. I had been bruised and damaged by the battle but had emerged unbeaten. My heart was a shambles but I had not compromised my principles and I was undaunted. This fact gave me a sharp sense of satisfaction and I consoled myself with the idea that I had come through this struggle victorious.

As the train approached Cairo, I looked for my black veil. It lay crumpled beside me on the seat. I was tempted to toss it out the window and come out with my face uncovered for all to see. But the time for this liberation had not yet come. As the train drew into the station, I covered my face but swore that I would fight relentlessly until the day when women could emerge with faces exposed to the wind and their destinies governed by themselves and not by the despotism of jealous husbands and possessive fathers.

Translated from the French
by Nayra Atiya

Nabawiya Musa

(1890–1951)

Nabawiya Musa was born into a middle class Egyptian family in a village near Zigazig, Eastern Delta. She attended the Saniyya School, the first teacher training school for women in Egypt, and in 1907 was the first, and last, Egyptian woman to sit for the secondary school certificate until after Independence. She became a teacher in a state school for girls, a school principal and the first Egyptian woman inspector in The Ministry of Education. Later, after criticising the curriculum for girls she was fired. She established her own school, *Madrasat Banat al-Ashraf*, with a branch in Cairo and Alexandria.

In 1920, Musa published *Al-Mara wa al-Amal* (Woman and Work), adumbrating her life-long mission of promoting education and work for women. In 1922, she founded the Association for the Progress of Women to further these goals. She was a founding member of the Egyptian Feminist Union and a delegate to the International Woman Suffrage Alliance Conference in Rome in 1923, the first international meeting Egyptian feminists attended. She gave a speech on Egyptian women calling for education rights. Musa founded a journal called *Al-Fatah* (The Girl) and edited women's pages for *Al-Balagh al-Usbui* and *Al-Mará wa al-Amal*. Her decision not to marry in a society and at a time when this was rare showed her courage and determination to live life on her own terms. She dedicated her life to teaching, school administration, and writing. She died in 1951.

The following selections come from Nabawiya Musa's book, *Woman and Work*, published in 1920 while the national revolution was underway. Musa's feminist arguments, grounded in class and nationalist contexts, are based on her own close observation and experience of Egyptian society and women's lives.

In 'The Effect of Books and Novels on Morals', she turns the conventional argument that literacy for women will lead to their moral downfall on its head claiming that literacy would help women to guard their morality and reputation.

In 'The Difference between Men and Women and their Capacities for Work', Musa attacks biological determinism demonstrating the social construction of gender in Egyptian society.

The Effect of Books and Novels on Morals

1920

Knowing how to read and write is not to be considered an independent science. It is a mode of communication. When two people communicate while they are apart from one another, they do it through writing, which is like conversing as if they were near one another. A person who knows how to read and write is not considered educated except if he has taken it as a way to attain knowledge. Regrettably in Egypt we are ignorant of this and we automatically consider the woman who knows how to read and write to be an educated person. When she does something wrong we blame it on her education saying that education corrupted her morals. God knows that that woman is ignorant and committed wrong through her ignorance. She found a way to communicate with those outside her presence and expressed herself in this way revealing inappropriate thoughts coming to her through ignorance and arrogance. In this she is worse off than the woman who does not know how to read and write because she can record in her own hand something shameful that cannot be erased in the future. On the other hand, the woman who does not know how to read may say something improper, but it will be soon forgotten because it is not written down.

Knowing how to read and write is not knowledge, itself, but a door to knowledge we may enter, but if we leave it closed there is no way to reach knowledge. A person learns from reading useful books many times over what he can acquire in schools because the time for formal education is short and the subjects taught are limited. If a person limits himself to school education he will not attain complete knowledge. That is why we see that many men who were educated in the same school and attained the same degree differ in their levels of knowledge. We find one who is an expert scientist and another who is an ignorant and naïve person. That is because one of them was truly educated and therefore his mind developed and his knowledge increased, while the other limited himself to what he was taught at school and did not use his knowledge and therefore his mind became rusty and he forgot what he had learned.

The student learns at school from a limited number of teachers among whom there might not be anyone exceptional. But, in good books the student is directly exposed to the thoughts of gifted persons of different countries and different eras. Thus the student gains benefits from these books he cannot get from teachers because those gifted people have taken care in organising their thoughts and presenting them in a precise and clear way. People can also gain from reading newspapers. In reading the thoughts of his contemporaries, a person benefits much more than from those he meets face to face because writers do not speak with the same care and insight that informs their writing. In addition, the reader may come across the same idea expressed in different ways in different books and thus it becomes reinforced in his mind so he would not forget it no matter how much time passes. Reading has a good effect on morals and knowledge. The best schools are those that have teachers who work hard to develop a love of reading and intellectual curiosity in the minds of the young so that they will benefit from this when they grow up. Teachers cannot instruct the child in all that he needs. They do better when they guide the child towards reading and instil in him a love for books, inquiry, and discovery so he can attain whatever knowledge he desires. It is out of ignorance that we think that schools are sufficient to produce fully educated men and women. In fact, education in schools is only an introduction to what a person will acquire through his own effort after he leaves school.

Many educators in Europe and elsewhere have worked on persuading children to read. They have written tales and novels to attract them to books. A child naturally loves stories and reads storybooks eagerly and he reaps benefit in perfecting morals and understanding ideas which prepare him to appreciate useful books later on. These educators chose not to confront the child abruptly with books of knowledge and moral guidance because they feared the child would grow bored and his mind would be taxed and thus he would come to dislike books.

If novels are written by a gifted person who can portray morals and customs expressively they will attract the attention of children and youth and make them eager to read them. Novels can become like a magnifying glass through which they can look at virtues and vices in real life. Through them children and young people would come to love virtue and abhor vice. There are examples of excellence and glamour in novels that transcend the ordinary and the child marvels at this. Maybe these novels will inspire him to wish to be distinguished and make it easier for him to bear the burdens of attaining knowledge. Novels also teach children how to write better and how to discriminate in selecting expressions because the human being is a skilled imitator by nature, and especially the child who imitates what he reads and expresses it without realising that he is imitating. I do not look for criteria in selecting a novel except that the author is sound in mind and his writing reveals discrimination in his choice of subjects. The best novels are historical novels because they provide one with actual information even though it may be greatly enhanced. Romances are fine as long as their objective is to portray love and caution about its consequences because many of these novels end in scandal or sadness. In each case it is a warning to the reader if he has any sense or tendency towards virtue but if he is a stupid, evil person the warning would be reversed in his mind. Without a doubt, such a person is corrupt from the start and thus novels would have nothing to do with his corruption.

It is a big mistake for educators to think it good upbringing to keep a child ignorant of vice and never mention it in front of him. The educator who teaches the child how harmful vice is performs his duty towards his pupil. If the child insists upon courting danger while he is aware of the likely results he would have brought harm upon himself. On the other hand, if the ignorant person falls into danger because of his ignorance his teacher would be responsible, it is like a man walking down a path laden with dangers unbeknown to him. If someone who knows about these dangers does not warn him about them he might fall prey to them through his ignorance. He has an excuse because in this case the blame is on the person who did not warn him of the dangers before he met them.

The child has a great need to form his mind and strengthen his creative powers through reading, but he does not have the ability to be patient in persisting to read scientific or character-building books. He needs many books of the type I have mentioned – tales and novels – so that his intellectual and creative powers would be strengthened. We are at fault in preventing our children, especially our girls, from reading interesting books. They may quit reading altogether because other kinds of books are difficult and unattractive to them. This encourages bad habits to form so that when they grow up they will not be interested in seeking the treasures of learning found in books and magazines.

A person is able to expand his knowledge during his entire life if he becomes accustomed to reading. Reading becomes his greatest mentor, helping him to achieve his goals. That is why the Arabs are concerned that their children grow to love reading because it is the key to knowledge. While foreigners write novels and comedies in the everyday spoken language to attract children to read, we Arabic speakers have a far greater need to expend efforts in encouraging our children to read because our spoken language is different from our classical written language. The child enters school not knowing the classical language. We do not give enough attention to encouraging him to read outside school and helping him but rather give him lots of trivial rules of grammar. If the child is unable to express himself because of his lack of knowledge of classical Arabic, he directs himself towards reading novels in a foreign language. Thus, foreign languages become easier for him than classical Arabic because he does not read Arabic books.

The best way to promote classical Arabic now is to write, or to translate, useful stories and novels in an elegant and comprehensible style and to put them in school libraries and encourage pupils to read them. I am tired of seeing a student who has mastered grammar, but cannot express himself properly in good, classical Arabic because his vocabulary and style are limited. Niqula Effendi Rizq has done a service in creating his new series of novels (*Al-Riwayat al-Jadida*). I wonder why schools are still reluctant to add these books to their libraries for pupils to read as they read similar novels in foreign languages. We must encourage pupils to read books in good classical Arabic and at the same time discourage them from reading poorly written and unsuitable books. Unfortunately, many of the latter are widely circulated in Egypt. Rarely does one see a young student without one of these books written in a vernacular which is a hodgepodge of mistakes in classical Arabic and foreign languages. Expressions in these inferior books reveal the mediocrity of their authors. These books spread corruption in children and accustom them to a bad literary style. The schools should have confiscated such books. And, if the government had done the confiscation it would have been better for the nation than confiscating newspapers.

Pupils are attracted to such inferior books because there are not enough story books that are written in easy classical Arabic. The more pupils read inferior books the more they imitate their composition and style regardless of their teachers' efforts to teach them good writing. Whatever good teachers build these bad books destroy. If educators went to court asking for compensation from the authors of these books before an intelligent and just judge he would give them compensation because of the harm authors of these bad books have done to their profession.

Translated from the Arabic
by Ali Badran and Margot Badran

The Difference between Men and Women and Their Capacities for Work

1920

❦

Men have spoken so much of the differences between men and women that they would seem to be two separate species. With due respect for the views of men I would like to state my own to remind them of something they may have forgotten. Human beings are animals governed by the same rules of nature regarding reproduction, growth, decline, and death. The male animal is no different from the female except in reproduction. If it were true that the instincts of the male cat were different from the instincts of the female cat it would also be true that there would be a difference between man and woman in mental gifts. No scientist has claimed that the female cat likes to jump and play and devours mice while the male cat is reasonable, serious, and does not hurt a mouse or steal meat. Both male and female mice are said to have the same characteristics. Likewise, nobody has said that the male dog is honest and intelligent and the female dog dishonest and stupid. Both male cats and dogs have stronger muscles and larger bodies than female cats and dogs, but otherwise they are no different.

How then do we conclude that the woman is deceitful and cunning and the man is frank and truthful? The man quotes from God's words (the Quran): 'It is a snare of you women. Truly, mighty is your snare.'[1] This verse was spoken by God concerning a particular case. In other Quranic verses some men were described as connivers: 'And (the unbelievers) plotted and planned, and God too planned, and the best of planners is God.'[2] And, 'Mighty indeed were the plots which they made, but their plots were (well) within the sight of God, even though they were such as to shake the hills!'[3] Men have forgotten these verses and have not memorised but a single verse and have applied its meaning generally to all women.

Men have pointed out that the man has a larger body and stronger muscles than the woman and that his brain is larger than hers. Disregarding the rules of nature they have deduced from this all sorts of differences. The bull is larger in body and brain than the cow but no better equipped with intelligence. The bull does not know how to get its food any better than the cow. The cock is much larger and stronger than the hen. The lion is larger and stronger than the lioness. The male donkey is stronger than the female donkey. This is nature's way and it is linked to reproduction. It has also been observed that the strength in males is accompanied by rashness and attraction to females.

Nobody said that because the male dog is stronger than the female dog that he is more intelligent. Likewise, it is not true that the man is more intelligent than the woman because his body is larger and stronger. If this were true the geniuses and philosophers of this world would have had the largest bodies. In fact, the opposite is probably true.

From this, one could conclude that the woman is more intelligent than the man because of her smaller body but I don't want to exaggerate the way men do. I only wish to say that the woman and man are alike, the way animals are, as scientists confirm. They have not claimed that the male mouse is of one species and the female mouse of another. No one has asserted that because the male mouse is stronger than the female mouse, he should be her life guardian. The female mouse lives like the male mouse and does not depend on the male because nature did not make the female mouse more dependent on the male mouse than he is on her; they are simply equal. The same applies to the man and the woman. While she is smaller in size and strength she can take care of all her needs. She is independent of him and does not need him more than he needs her. She can do everything a man can, the way a short, slim man can do what a big, tall man does. Asserting that nature has destined the woman for the house because she is weaker than the man this is patently untrue.

Men claim they have superior intelligence saying there have been more men of genius than women. They forget that only when a people use their gifts do they develop. That is why poor men who have spent their lives as cooks or tailors have not excelled in the arts or sciences. How can we expect, therefore, to find women whose energies we have restricted to taking care of their homes and whose knowledge is confined to this sphere excelling as geniuses? If a woman does receive an education and has other pursuits she stops these after her marriage and devotes herself entirely to household activities. However, in countries with sound female education, a significant number of women have distinguished themselves proving they are no less endowed than men in natural abilities.

The woman is more tender-hearted and noble in her feelings than the man because she is more affected than he is. This convinces me that she is wiser than him and understands things better than he does. Insane people have no feelings at all. An insane woman would feel no pain if she saw her only child cut into pieces in front of her. She might even watch with a grin because she would not understand the meaning of compassion. If she had some feeling it would disappear immediately. Likewise, young children's feelings of pity and sorrow are not well developed because of their small brains, the way that savages in the past did not have feelings when they saw atrocities because their minds had not developed and become refined. In her tenderness the woman did not violate the rules of nature that apply to other animals. The lioness is tender towards her cubs and feeds them while the lion might not know his young. The same with the female cat who is tender and protective towards her kittens fearing that the male cat might eat them even though they are his own kittens. This is further proof of what I have said before that the female among the animals is generally weaker in body but wiser than the male. The male is stronger and more rash than the female and that is why he is less moved than her; he doesn't have feelings of tenderness coming from wisdom. By women's feelings I don't mean the screaming and crying of ignorant women. This is a habit related to ignorance. Educated women do not behave this way. They might be more composed than men when a calamity occurs; I speak of the tenderness of heart and compassion towards the weak which women possess more than men as an indication that women are very reasonable.

One need only look at the poor Egyptian peasant and his wife to see women's and men's similar natural abilities. Both have the same experience and know-how. The man frequently acknowledges his wife's superior insights and openly admits he does nothing important without consulting with her. She works side by side with him and she knows everything that is going on. When a man dies leaving children and property, perhaps half a *feddan* or a *feddan*, his wife takes over and by the time the children have grown their assets may well have multiplied.

It is unfair to compare the mind of an urban man with that of his wife. How can one compare the mind of a man of education and experience who has developed himself with that of a woman which has been neglected since infancy. Her mind became rusty through lack of use the same way iron implements rust through neglect. Her abilities were suppressed and she was sheltered from life's experiences before her mind could develop naturally. She is much worse off than the wife of a peasant who, although not educated at school, knows the struggles of real life. The urban woman is ignorant in both learning and life. Her life is more like a living death. If we compare the mind of the city woman with that of her educated and experienced husband it would be like comparing an old piece of cotton cloth left in a dusty abandoned shop with a beautiful piece of cotton one might suppose is silk because of its fine quality and brightness. Would this comparison indicate that the origin of the two pieces of cotton is different or would it prove the naïveté of the person making the comparison? We should not be deceived about men's and women's innate abilities when we know how differently they have been raised. We must educate both the same way.

Men and women when they are partners have found it expedient to divide the work between them. Each does their own tasks. People can decide upon this themselves; nature had nothing to do with it. I don't quarrel with this kind of sharing as long as the woman is married. However, if the woman cannot get married and remains a single person who has to earn her own living she must be prepared for this early in life so that she will not need to earn her living through menial jobs like being a servant or a street vendor. We should grasp these obvious truths. Isn't it strange that men write long articles about the definition of woman as if she were a weak insect about whom no one knows anything.

The respected writer, Farid Effendi Wajdi, said, 'The woman is a noble being created to increase the species and in this man cannot compete with her.' Is the woman alone able to procreate? Since man participates with woman in the creation of human life wouldn't it be more accurate to say that human beings are noble beings created for the purpose of multiplying the species like all other animals? Are men simply trying to create differences between the sexes? Their words on this subject make no sense. It is odd to speak of man's inability to compete with the woman in reproduction. The grinding of the wheat is done by two stones. The one does not compete with the other. If one is lost the whole operation stops.

The writer was distressed when he saw women in America standing in front of furnaces in factories. How odd that he notices things like this in America but does not see Egyptian women peddlars groaning under the heavy weight of their baskets of fruit and vegetables as they make their way down the streets enduring the bold stares and hands of insolent men. Doesn't he see Muslim women who have to earn their living laundering clothes in peoples' houses or in Egyptian and English military camps – in situations that threaten their chastity – doing backbreaking work in front of fires endlessly boiling water, causing their hands to bleed. Doesn't he see women workers burdened under the weight of earth and climbing scaffoldings. Doesn't he see women toiling in homes as servants exposed to men's desires while they do exhausting work?

The writer closes his eyes to all this noticing only the plight of women workers in America. What we are used to doesn't seem odd until we stop to think about it. Women suffer a lot in Egypt, but we don't feel it because we are so used to seeing it so we turn our attention to the misery of women in American factories who actually suffer less than our own women.

Egyptian women are not prevented from doing exhausting menial work but are forced to take tedious jobs requiring no education because we don't train them for better work. Egyptian and American women workers are equal in this misfortune. Only here, however, we prevent women from getting better work requiring training and experience such as writing, managing shops and educational institutions, practising medicine and law, and occupying positions in the higher ranks of government. By not allowing women these kinds of work we push them into hard, exhausting work that brings very little money. Is this justice and is this what a person claiming to be concerned for the comfort of women advocates?

If every woman were able to count on someone to support her and look after her comfort so she would never need to work I would be the first to advocate keeping women from work. I see women, out of necessity, forced to take up work that is draining and which exposes them to sexual exploitation. But, our good men insist that women should not be trained for work in which they could maintain their dignity and morality. So, they condemn women to misery.

Farid Effendi Wajdi says that if the Muslim woman does not find someone to support her there are alms institutions to help the needy. Where are these alms institutions? There are thousands of needy Muslim women before our very eyes. God forgive men who make declarations on the question of women that are not correct. Had they known the truth they would understand that they destroy the future of children with their own hands. There are many mothers of children who have lost their fathers. If these women could work they could give their children a proper upbringing so they could become productive persons in the future.

Wealthy and middle-class families in Egypt are often unable to maintain their status because they look at life with one eye – the eye of the man. If he is lost the family becomes blind. The whole family is endangered. The children lose status. The mother is unable to raise them properly for lack of money. The children, becoming unruly, are not prepared for an occupation. The ignorance of the mother causes the ignorance of children who become the future men of the nation. Western families look with two eyes. If one eye is lost the other guides the way down the right path. The education of women is a big reason in strengthening the families of a nation. In the case of Egyptians when the woman is widowed she is unable to raise her children and so upon the death of one person the whole family is doomed. Not only this but a widow and her children become a burden to her brother or other male relatives.

It is out of ignorance that people say Islam does not allow women to work. In the cities we see women of the lower and middle class families working as well as women from peasant families. Do we call them unbelievers? Our religion does not permit this. These families are the backbone of Egypt, the source of the country's wealth upon whom its advancement depends. If the women of these families were like the idle women of upper class families the whole nation would be lost. Why do we prevent upper class women from being prepared for work appropriate to their status if they find themselves in need while we allow poor women of the city and countryside to work? What does religion have to do with all this? It is better to leave religion out of the matter. We should admit what is at issue is custom so that we might then correctly assess the situation.

It is amazing to find that the men who are most opposed to training women for work are those who have been raised in the villages. They firmly oppose women doing higher forms of work in the towns and cities. At the same time, their own female relatives continue to do men's work in the countryside. These women of rural origins, in my view, are more modest in dress and behaviour than city women. Why do these men depart from the ideal ways of their mothers? Did they find something wrong with these ways or are they merely following city ways pretending to appear civilised and cultured? They fail to look into the pit into which they're being hurled by this corrupt civilisation. These men make their women discard their own peasant dress and natural walk, which are more respectable than the artificial city dress and the transparent veil, which stands for lies and deceit more than modesty and adherence to religion. Thus women of rural origin replace their natural manner which commands respect for the seductive appearance of the city woman.

Some obstinate people speak of corruption in the villages. I don't know if they claim there is no corruption in the cities. Corruption will not disappear except when the world disappears. It is every-where, but is more prevalent in the cities than in the villages. While the village man is ignorant he respects religion and makes a show of following it even if he is corrupt inside. In the villages women do not veil but there we do not see a man following a woman down the road to flirt. If he were to do this he would be killed instantly. Village men know women work outside their houses and that when they go out it is for work and not to flirt. But, men in the cities think that the woman has no work outside her house and if they see a woman in the street they think she has gone out to play. They are provoked by her dress and brush up against her. Work for women is a way to combat corruption not to encourage it.

If men considered all this they would see it as their duty to educate every single girl and equip her for work appropriate to her status in case she should need it. Thus, this way we do not condemn intelligent women of high status who find it necessary to earn a living in lowly jobs where they might be threatened by vice. Learning a profession does not prevent a woman from being a wife, happy to live at home without work if she finds a competent husband. Would anyone who has the opportunity to rest seek something else? This is clear in England, Switzerland, Germany, and in other countries where the woman works until she marries and then she stays at home becoming a disciplined and well-organised mother who takes care of her children and a good companion to her husband. When I speak of a woman going out of her house I do not mean to say that she should sit in cafés or just go strolling or interacting with men for no real purpose because I object more than anyone else to that. But, I say that the woman should be trained for work and allowed to do it. If she goes out she should go out for work and not for fun.

Translated from the Arabic
by Ali Badran and Margot Badran

NOTES
1 The Sura of Yusif (12), verse 28. Translation of the Quran by Abdullah Yusuf Ali, vol. 1, Hafner Publishing Co., New York, p. 560.
2 The Sura of Al-Imran (3), verse 54. Same translation, vol. 1, p. 197.
3 The Sura of Ibrahim (14), verse 46. Same translation, vol. 1, p. 633.

Nazira Zain al-Din

(*c.* 1905– ?)

Nazira Zain al-Din was born in Lebanon. Her father, a scholar of
Islamic religion and jurisprudence, and the first President of the
High Court of Appeals in Lebanon, greatly encouraged his daughter's education and intellectual development including religious
learning. In the house of her father, she met learned men,
especially religious scholars, with whom she debated and whom she
impressed by her keen mind and scholarship.

Nazira Zain al-Din was the first Arab woman to publish a lengthy
treatise which included her lectures on the subject announced in
the title of her book, *Unveiling and Veiling: Lectures and Views on the
Liberation of the Woman and Social Renewal in the Arab World*. The
book, dedicated to her father who guided her learning, especially
her religious learning, exposes patriarchal oppressions committed
in the name of Islam. The book is divided into four sections: a
general exposition of freedom, truth, religion, and reasoning;
rational evidence concerning unveiling, freedom and development; religious evidence on the same themes; and opposition and
responses. In 1927, while in her early twenties she completed her
book which took her a year to publish. In Lebanon, and the rest of
Greater Syria, veiling was still widespread, although in Egypt it was
well on the way to disappearing. Her book attracted hostile
criticism. Salah-Din Hamud claims that it attracted supporters as
well, including the Mufti of Lebanon and the Syrian Minister of
Education and Head of the Arabic Academy.

The pieces below from the second part include strong indict-
ments of veiling, unprecedented in their straightforwardness and
vigorous exposure of religious hypocrisy in men's social inter-
actions with women.

The outcry was swift and intense. Especially outspoken in attack
was Shaikh Mustafa Al-Ghalaini, the author of *Al-Islam Ruh al-
Madaniyya* (Islam, the Spirit of Civilisation) and *Nadharat* (Views),
who himself had disassociated face veiling from Islam. He accused
her of not having written the book and pandering to sectarian
sensibilities and colonialist presences. He alleged that the book was

written by missionaries and their followers, 'Muslims or Christians, with or without turbans.'

Later in 1928, in *Al-Fatah wa al-Shuyukh* (The Young Woman and the Shaikhs) Nazira Zain al-Din published some of the attacks against her and her responses to them.

Unveiling and Veiling:
on the Liberation of the Woman
and Social Renewal in the Islamic World

1928

⋙⋘

Two Views: One View on the Unveiled World and the Other on the Veiled World

Ladies and Gentlemen, in the beginning I compared opposites, the numbers of the veiled and the unveiled. I found that the veiled are not more than a few million Muslims living in towns. Those in the villages of the Islamic world and more than one thousand seven hundred million in other nations are not veiled. They have rejected the veil that they had previously worn. I have noticed that the nations that have given up the veil are the nations that have advanced in intellectual and material life. Such advancement is not equalled in the veiled nations. The unveiled nations are the ones that have discovered through research and study the secrets of nature and have brought the physical elements under their control as you see and know. But the veiled nations have not unearthed any secret and have not put any of the physical elements under their control but only sing the songs of a glorious past and ancient tradition. With such singing they sleep in stagnation.

I have seen many intellectuals of the nations where women are still veiled advocating unveiling, but I haven't seen anyone in the unveiled nations advocating or preferring the veil. That is, I haven't seen anyone who has tried unveiling and then has preferred the veil. Even if some westerner in his hypocritical words makes the veil appear in a favourable light, he is only pleased with the beauty of the oriental veil while at the same time he would reject the veiling of his mother, wife, sisters, and daughters because of the harm in the veil he favours for others.

I cannot imagine that in the advanced nations which have discovered the secrets of nature and harnessed its powers, which have not let anything pass without examining it to the fullest, where the struggle between right and wrong is continuous until right becomes victorious, nations which have produced works on social subjects we view as masterpieces of literature and sociology, have neglected to study veiling and unveiling to understand the benefits and disadvantages. I cannot think that our own ignorance can bring us any greater understanding of what honour is than the unveiled nations possess in learning nor that our conduct is superior to theirs, nor that their women going outside unveiled and enjoying their freedom is evidence of their lower conduct and corrupt morals.

Yes, I looked into all that and I could not but consider it evidence of their superior education and elevated conduct. When our esteemed ladies who wear the veil go to a western country, they take off the veil and the men accompanying them do not prevent them from doing this the way they do when they are at home or after they return. This is because we have more faith in the conduct of westerners than in our own conduct. The conduct of western men has been influenced by mingling with women and thus western men have based their habits and morals on logic and reason looking to benefits and positive results while our conduct and morals are based on our customs whatever they may be.

I shall never forget a conversation between an eastern man advocating the veil and an unveiled western woman who enjoyed her freedom and independence. The easterner said to the westerner, 'Our nature cannot accept your customs. Our customs are more noble than yours and our men support our women. The man according to his right walks in front of his wife but in your country the woman walks in front of the man as if she were the provider.'

The western woman said, 'If you really want to protect your wife please let her go in front of you so that you can watch out for her the way our men do, rather than letting her walk behind you so that she would misuse her freedom and get hurt.'

The eastern man paused and said, 'Truly, westerners ground their customs in reason. Reason alone should dictate custom.'

It is not fitting for us to say that we who are only a few million, most of whom are not advanced, are more honourable than the one and a half billion people (in the world) most of whom are more advanced than we are.

It is not honourable for us to deny our shortcomings and believe we are perfect and claim that our customs are the best customs for every time and place. This conceit and false presumption is a barrier to the reform we seek. When the nation feels its shortcomings that is the first step in its advancement.

It is inconceivable that we claim to be defenders of honour while the veil is our strongest shield. We must understand as everyone else does that honour is rooted in the heart and chastity comes from within and not from a piece of transparent material lowered over the face.

We have to realise, as the advanced unveiled world does, that good behaviour and honour come from sound upbringing grounded in noble principles and virtues. We are shortsighted if we think that the veil keeps evil away from women and that those in the rest of the world exceeding one and a half billion are all in the wrong while we are in the right.

He Who Bears Falsehood to the People Has to Provide Evidence to Them
I have mentioned the above, Ladies and Gentlemen, fearful that I might be confronted by someone who does not use logic and reasoning to make his points, but relies on untruths concerning the advanced unveiled nations. He may look where vice is but he does not wish to rise up to see where virtue resides. He might have seen their baser women and generalises from them, subsuming the noble and honourable in his generalisation, and hurls accusing arrows of untruths at them even though human beings should not be likes flies pouncing on tails (of animals) and ignoring their heads.

He does not dare to lord scientific and industrial knowledge over the unveiled nations because these are tangible matters. Therefore he accuses them of lack of morals and good conduct because these are not tangible. Thus he is overwhelming in this even though his accusation is false.

You know gentlemen, nations are like trees whose rotten fruits fall to the ground and vermin, humans and animals go after them. Those who are wise and advanced look only to the good and ripe fruits, by which the tree is identified.

My antagonist seems to be ignorant of that or is playing the role of the ignorant. He wants to know the tree by the fallen fruits he sees beneath it. Moreover, he does not want to recognise that in every nation, however advanced, there is a lower class overcome by corruption whose morals and conduct have deteriorated because they did not have the chance to be educated and to develop so that they could reach the higher level in the nation.

Gentlemen, we should do our best to see to it that the majority in our nation are able to have an education and the means to develop. Then it would be possible for us to be proud before our nations . . .'

We should not believe everything we hear and take our evidence from falsehood, especially evidence that brings great evil to the nation by obstructing reform and maintaining continual backwardness.

We should abstain from hurling lies and falsehoods at others, which is alien to morality and decent debate and only brings down those who lie. Instead we should subscribe to truth, sound reasoning, unbiased knowledge, and correct behaviour. In accordance with the will of God almighty and the will of His Prophet, may God bless him . . . (She quotes from the Quran and Hadith).

How Men Should Support Women
Gentlemen, you have heard the response of the western woman to the Eastern man who was proud to support his woman and to walk in front of her. Yes, let men support women in principle. Every man supports his own wife spending money on her, but he has no authority over any other woman. An *aya* from the Quran was sent by God about this in relation to Saad ibn al-Rabi from al-Naqba and his wife Habiba; the words are related specifically to husband and wife. Men should know that authority is limited by the benefit deriving from it. Therefore, men should attain high moral development as God wants and society requires. This would make women strong and self-dependent for when people have virtue, dignity, and honour they turn away from evil, not out of fear of punishment, nor because of reward, nor because of an immovable obstacle, but because evil is ugly and such a person would not allow herself to engage in lowly acts.

The Prophet, God bless him, said, 'I was sent to help you attain the highest morality.' Does not the highest morality come from the soul? Pieces of cloth over faces shall never be a measure of morality.

The Veil (niqab) *is an Insult to Men and Women*
It is not beneficial to men and women that men should just support women physically and financially, nor is it beneficial that man rule over those whom the *Sharia* did not give him the right. It greatly harms the two sexes that every man continues to insult his mother, daughter, wife, and sister, suspiciously accusing them of bad morals and keeping them confined to a cage, as the venerable Qasim Amin said, 'With their wings cut off, heads bent down, and eyes closed. For him (man) is freedom and for them (women) enslavement. For him is education and for them ignorance. For him is sound reasoning and for them inferior reasoning. For him is light and open space and for them darkness and imprisonment. For him are orders and for them obedience and patience. For him is everything in the universe and for them part of the whole he has captured.'

May God be merciful to Qasim and bless his pen about which

'The Poet of the Two Countries' has said, 'He tears down the ugly and builds the beautiful, returning to the Sunna of the Drawer. He sheds light even when he writes with the dark water of the night.'

Unfortunately, if the veil (*hijab*) implies the inability of the woman to protect herself without it, it also reveals that man, however well brought up and in spite of supporting the woman, is a traitor and a thief of honour; his evil should be feared and it is better that the woman escapes from him.

You, Man, the Supporter
If some women, because of the ignorance into which you have cast them, have not recognised the insult to them and to men by the veil, is it easy for you, the man who has kept himself free seeking perfection and good conduct, to bear this insult that comes to you and to your mother, daughter, wife, and sister?

Does the woman who escapes from you, or approaches you lowering the veil over her face, or turns her back on you, confirm your high status, as she might think and say and you might think and say, or is it a great insult? Does this constitute the woman's decorum, chastity and modesty? If so, then men should not be without these precious attributes; let them wear veils and let them meet each other and meet women lowering veils over their faces the way women do.

Translated from the Arabic
by Ali Badran and Margot Badran

The Young Woman and the Shaikhs

1928

❧

Dedication of the book to woman

Oh angel, I dedicated my first book, *Unveiling and Veiling,* to my father, but I dedicate the second book to you because the spirit of the mother is in you and because I believe that reform in the east is built on the foundation of your freedom and the struggle for right.

May God shed light on you and upon it.

I delivered my book straight to the nation from my room; why didn't the Shaikh do likewise and let those in society who are able, judge the two books. I know, Shaikh Ghalaini, that stirring up feelings against a book by a young woman like me is an easy matter for somebody like you because I don't have the chance to stand on the *minbar* (the mosque pulpit) that you stood on, or to speak to the communities that you spoke to to clarify right or condemn wrong.

The noble man is one who does not use a weapon another does not employ, either because he does not own it or because he deems it below his dignity to use it. There is a forum open to women and men in which to clarify the truth before important men and women of this nation by using the pen, rather than by creating distur-bances among the people through false speech.

Mr Shaikh, God has given you the gift of public speaking with a strong voice and an eloquent tongue. Fear God and use these gifts well in benefiting Islam. Don't use them merely as you fancy or as a weapon for hurting others or to take revenge.

Fear God, and you know that there is nothing more harmful to Muslims, or anything that has kept them from marching at the vanguard of the people of the world, than hypocrisy in religion and agitating the naïve instead of following the path taken by those women and men who abide by the truth.

Be sincere, in your words and deeds. The Messenger of God, may peace be upon Him, said, 'People are doomed except the learned, and the learned are doomed except for the strivers, and the strivers are doomed except for the sincere.'

I declare openly, gentlemen and ladies, Muslims, hear me when I declare that I wrote my book late at night and during the day alone

in a room in which I had no companion or assistance except pens
and ink pots, books and papers; in which there was no light except
that coming from electricity and from the Quran, the Sunna, and
from what the imams have said; in which I saw no missionary and
no one saw me except my father, who taught me the *Sharia*, and
sometimes my Arabic teacher who helped improve my language or
my argument without taking part in writing the book. No one took
part in writing the book whether he had an *imma*, a hat, or a *tarbush*
on his head. Nor did a missionary, nor an atheist, nor a teacher,
nor a lawyer, nor a Muslim geographer, nor a missionary agent: no
one assisted me in writing or printing my book with a single piaster.
I didn't give a man with an *imma*, a hat, or a *tarbush*, nor a
missionary, nor a layman, nor a Sunni Muslim nor a Shii Muslim,
nor a Druse, nor a Jew, nor a Christian a single piaster.

Mr Shaikh, your claim is false and God Almighty has said, 'If you
tell the truth, prove it.' Can the Shaikh prove what he has alleged
and declare openly that he did not receive financial assistance from
people in writing and printing his own book?

Didn't you, Mr Shaikh, receive financial assistance from people
saying you would spend it in defence of religion, and instead you
spent it in revenge against a young Muslim woman and in leading
Muslims to untruths? I said that to the Shaikh and others of the
opposition while their voices shouted, 'The missionaries and those
whom the missionaries have bought off are behind you.' They are
still uttering what the Shaikh said and the Shaikh still utters what
they have said.

Gentlemen, the missionaries and missionary-like people who
were said to be attacking us did not come to Beirut but went to
Cairo and Jerusalem and returned home nine months before I had
written my book and started to print it. But we did not see in the
missionaries in our midst – whether they be Americans or English,
monks or nuns, French or non-French – anything except fine
instruction to young Arabs, girls and boys. Yes, it was they who
established schools in our country and the largest institute of
learning. They educated us. Our noble Arab virtues, especially
sincerity, necessitates that we be grateful to them.

Ye, generous people – slingers of arrows – who are none other
than the sincere children of our nation – dignified, moral, educated, cultured, reforming, and progressive, in the name of God
stop your arrows. Do not throw them at your brothers in nationalism and your sisters in Islam. I said that in vain. The arrows are still
coming like heavy rain and the Shaikh is still fighting with lies.

Translated from the Arabic
by Ali Badran and Margot Badran

Saiza Nabarawi

(1897–1985)

Saiza Nabarawi was born Zainab Murad in 1897 at the Minshawi Palace outside Cairo. She was adopted by a distant relative, Adila Nabarawi, who took her to Paris. She was brought up like a French girl and educated at a convent school in Versailles and later at the Saint Germain des Près Institute in Paris. Her life took an abruptly different course when she was sent back to Egypt. Although she continued her education in a French school, Les Dames de Sion School in Alexandria, she was required to fit into a very different society. After her foster mother's suicide in Paris, her biological parents, modest people who spoke only Arabic, came to the school to claim her, announcing they were her real parents. But she rejected them and instead she went to Cairo to stay with her maternal grandparents. In her early teens, her late foster mother's friend, Huda Shaarawi, took an interest in her. When Nabarawi's grandfather insisted that she veil, she rebelled. Huda Shaarawi persuaded her to wear the veil for the time being. In 1923 Nabarawi and Shaarawi removed their veils in a public political act at the Cairo train station upon their return from the Conference of the International Women Suffrage Alliance in Rome as delegates of the Egyptian Feminist Union. Nabarawi dedicated her life to feminist activism. She edited *L'Egyptienne*, the newspaper of the Egyptian Feminist Union from 1925 to 1940, attended international feminist conferences, spoke widely and campaigned tirelessly for women's liberation, national liberation and peace until her death in 1985.

When the first parliament opened in 1924 following independence in Egypt, in the aftermath of the national revolution in which women had participated, women were not admitted to the inaugural ceremonies except as wives of ministers or other officials. This helped to politicise women into organised, public feminist activism. At the third convocation of parliament in March 1925, women were represented by Saiza Nabarawi, the editor-in-chief of *L'Egyptienne*, who was not allowed entry. She protested this exclusion in her article, 'Double Standard' in the April 1925 issue of the feminist journal.

Double Standard

1925

❦

Last Monday was the memorable day of the third convocation of
parliament, a parliament so short-lived that it lasted but a few
hours. Every man and woman on the eve of this great day
attempted to obtain access to this feared fortress by favour or by
right.

Like many others, I dared to make one timid request. But what
was I in this ocean of assembled greats! Wife of a minister? Wife of
an ambassador? I am far from having this importance (even
though I am not less than these). What title then might I have to
call upon those with the power to open sesame?

Friendly readers, in my innocence I had thought that my new
position as editor-in-chief of *L'Egyptienne* would allow me to pass
among the invited officialdom without offending the stern President of the Senate. But, what after all is *L'Egyptienne* but a humble
monthly magazine which has none of the privileges of a daily
newspaper! This is the least of what the Minister of the Interior
told me when this very kind minister, in order to make the pill
easier to swallow, let me know that not even *L'Egypte Nouvelle* had
been able to obtain an entry pass. Regretfully for the accuracy of
the information the Minister of Interior, I have to say that this,
unfortunately, was not the case. *L'Egypte Nouvelle* had been invited
to the opening ceremony of parliament and if the director of
L'Egypte Nouvelle himself was not in attendance, he at least sent a
representative in his stead. Probably more clever than I, he had
spoken directly with the dispenser of tickets.

In stating my complaint I by no means resent the presence of my
distinguished colleagues but simply wish to raise a voice against
unequal treatment. I should point out that representatives of the
local press are often less favoured than certain foreign women who
are readily given invitation cards for little more than calling
themselves press correspondents. A double standard! This will
always exist as long as men rule!

Allowing my humble person into such an honourable assembly
would signal that the state was honouring Egyptian women and
Egyptian men equally. The presence of the wives of ministers (who
appeared as spouses of high officials) does not signifiy representa-

tion of women. The Egyptian woman who constitutes half the nation was therefore totally forgotten. The names of presidents of women's organisations were not recognised and those of women journalists equally ignored! Why?

Could it be that the Egyptians in power, whose liberal views I praised recently in front of a European woman, resemble a poorly trained bear who during an entire day hid in his cave to escape the demands and solicitations of our abhorrent sex? Might those in power be hiding behind old habits and customs which excluded women from public meetings? But, how then do you explain the invitation to the wives of our ministers?

I racked my brains and found nothing, absolutely nothing, which could explain such a strange attitude. If I go back in memory and do a little psychological history, I recall that the president of the Feminist Union and the founder of *L'Egyptienne* turns out to be the same person who some time ago vehemently protested against a minister over the Sudan and today, in his new position, he is the holder of invitation cards! Perhaps this might explain the persistent ill-will directed against our magazine, its founder, and indirectly, its editor.

Is it just that in this Egyptian land, so hospitable to foreigners, our women should be the last to enjoy the rights and prerogatives accorded others, and that this should happen under a (Liberal Constitutional) ministry which proclaimed in its speech upon taking power that through higher education it hopes 'to place men and women on an equal footing in order to permit the latter to fulfil their duty in the national renaissance'?

I would like to hope that in taking our legitimate grievances into consideration the administration will do its duty to better reconcile its acts with the declarations of its statesmen and that it will not forget at the next opening of Parliament to invite *L'Egyptienne* to occupy its rightful place in the assembly of the representatives of the country.

Translated from the French
by Charlotte Petrey

Zoubeida Bittari

(1939–)

Zoubeida Bittari was born into a lower middle class family in Algeria. She attended a French-run school until the age of twelve when her family withdrew her from school to marry her off without her knowledge or consent. Her ignorance of her impending betrothal echoes that of Huda Shaarawi. Her narrative reveals the contradictions between a sense of being 'born to be free' and the inherited notion of 'family claims to have rights over me'; between her own modern francophile family and her traditional Arab family-in-law, but most of all her mother-in-law. Married at twelve, she was mother of a son at thirteen. She was repudiated at fourteen, and her son was taken away from her by her in-laws. The oppression of her painful experiences within her new family became a crucible of liberation.

When Zoubeida Bittari was twenty-five years old, she published *O, My Muslim Sisters, Weep*. Bittari seems to have written just this one book. The book, published in Paris two years after Algerian Independence, reconstructs her early life up to the 1950s when she went to work with a family in France. In the selection below, she expresses a sense of release and euphoria that comes with emergent consciousness and acts of defiance. Her earliest, most painful oppression was at the hands of her mother-in-law and husband, then from her father and brothers who sheltered her when she returned home a repudiated woman but who disapproved of and distrusted any movements outside the house. She realises that her efforts at acquiescence within the patriarchal family system are futile and that total rejection and rebellion are the only alternatives to total submission and loss of self. Her solution is to quit Algeria, to seek refuge in a place she believes offers a better life for women – France. This occurs at a time when the national struggle for liberation is in full force. Her narrative does not reflect a tension between loyalty to nation or self; her biggest struggle had been between family and self. Her memoirs reached out to her Muslim sisters in an effort to create solidarity through the hope of a better future to be gained through courage and struggle.

The Voice of Happiness

1964

৫৯৯

The beauty of life: what intoxication for me, a cloistered woman! I no longer wanted to be tied down by anything that would oblige me to do what all my Muslim sisters did because it had always been and would always be that way, since all of them accepted it without rebelling. So, I had to go on. It wasn't a fairy with a magic wand who was guiding me toward the gate of freedom, but the moral and physical anguish I had suffered during my son's absence. I was leaving the swamp where I had been bogged down for so long, without hope of ever seeing better days.

I shout myself hoarse. I scream. Yes, I almost howl! I want to tell everyone, both men and women, what I have learned at such great cost: today customs are free and so are ideas, so it is no sin to be independent, to rebel against ignoble servitude – a 'sweetie', to be displayed, flattered, congratulated, but not treated as a human being. A dog is happier than us cloistered women, because he is petted, he is given things, while we don't even have the right to say a word. I search for friendship once more, I refuse to accept compromise and innuendo. In our day civilisation is rich in support. We are in the twentieth century – let's live in our own time and not in the past. Woman was not born to be enslaved. She came into the world equal to man, to be united to him and not to become his plaything. Woman is man's moral support, for without her he would lack the best thing in life. Thinking back on my own past, I feel sorry for us all. One despairs, knowing that one is unhappy when happiness is within the reach of all people, men and women alike, with a little good humour and good sense. Now our men should no longer be ashamed of going out with their wives, fearing that their comrades will laugh at them. All of these prejudices are details that poison life. Claiming that he is stronger than his master, he daily transforms his home into a battlefield because someone tells him that his wife has done this or that, even if what she has done is only look out of the window or something of the sort – all the 'what will they say?' that the gossips have such a taste for.

Shame on them and on those who listen to them. It is no crime to look and to speak, because otherwise God himself would not have given us speech and sight. Then why have an arena at home, like boxers, to fight with someone who doesn't dare to, doesn't want to, and cannot defend herself? All these thoughts give me courage. I think of reaching the end of my journey, of soon scaling the barrier that separates me from my French sisters. My plans now seem to me to be full of promise, while before when I was a submissive wife I was very well aware that they were only the fruit of my imagination, but they allowed me to dream of the life I longed for. Now it is very different. I have faith in the future.

Convalescence

I was no longer thinking of anything but my future, of what I wanted to do. My son was going to school with my little brothers. I was unable to do anything at all because I was still in bed. I was recovering slowly but surely, and was hopeful for better days to come. After two months of convalescence, I was supposed to go and see the doctor at the hospital for a check-up. I was lucky that no one was available to go with me, so in a voice that I tried to make sincere and innocent, I suggested that I might go with my son, since it was Thursday. The request was granted to me by my family – my brothers, and my father. There was no hesitation. They simply advised me not to stroll in the streets and to take the direct bus so as not to be noticed or have any unfortunate encounters.

Ready at last, we left at about nine o'clock, my son and I, happy to be having a lovely excursion in the beautiful sunshine, with a warm light wind blowing across the bright blue sky. Then there was the arrival at the hospital, the entrance, the front desk, the waiting room, and finally the check-up when the doctor appeared, and then the diagnosis. I went back out of that hospital where so many people have cried out, wept, screamed with pain. Waiting for me I found the blue sky, the trees and the greenery, the streets, the people, the children, the cars, and all those trivial things that strike a woman with such force when she has been cloistered for a long time. Yes, that is the right word, I am using it correctly. Cloistered! After all, that was what had happened to me. Now I wanted to live. Everything was a novelty to me. A bicycle ridden by a child was a strangely attractive picture. I was more enthusiastic than my son, because I had been married too young and deprived of all these pleasures, so I looked at others with envy. I strolled. My son looked at the displays of toys on the sidewalk. He laughed at all these little creations, and so did I. Hours passed in this way, and I wasn't even aware of them . . . My return home was received very badly. I was forbidden to set foot out of the house again. What had I done? Why had they inflicted this further torture on me? Hadn't I endured enough of this? Well, I would show them!

The next day, when it was time for school, I decided to accompany my son, whether my family wanted me to or not. I did it. Remonstrances and insults did not make me change my mind. Then, on the following days, I did the same thing, and I was proud of it. I must not give in, not for anything. I had to achieve independence, but I couldn't do it too suddenly. I had to proceed carefully.

My parents scarcely said anything, and I realised that I had won the first round. The month of December came, then Christmas, January, and Lent. It was Ramadan. It was beginning, that month of fasting, and for me it was always the same routine. I went out to take my son to school. I went out often on an errand, something that was never done in my husband's family. According to them, I had become a girl of the streets, a p—. I'll omit the other words. I was not at all ashamed, because I had nothing to be ashamed of. I didn't pay any attention to what they said.

One day, during Ramadan, I had a terrible toothache. I went to the dentist in the quarter, accompanied by a neighbour who had herself been repudiated and who had removed her veil because she had a job in a post office. During Ramadan, Muslims never go to the dentist in the daytime, because in their eyes any contact, any medication, invalidates the fast. So even if he didn't drink a drop of water as he left the dentist's office, the patient would have to account for himself on high. To avoid all that, we went for a consultation in the evening. I made the arrangements. When I say the evening, that means after the cannon goes off at seven-thirty. We found about six people in the waiting room. I begged the dentist to let me in ahead of the others, explaining my fear. 'No special favours,' he kept repeating. I waited my turn with growing impatience. When it came, it was ten o'clock. Horribly late! My son must surely be asleep. He must have waited for me for a long time. My only thoughts during that long wait were of him.

After the dentist had put a dressing on my tooth, I hurried home, accompanied by my neighbour. I had the key to the door. Alas! when I got there I tried to open it, but it was bolted on the inside! It was impossible to get in! I rang several times: there was no sound except the barking of dogs in the distance. I called, softly at first, then louder. Still nothing, not a living soul responded in that house where a few hours earlier people had been swarming like ants on an anthill. I became angry and pounded on the door with all my might. My neighbour stayed with me to see what was going to happen.

My brother appeared, armed with a belt. He lashed me across the face as hard as he could, kicked me everywhere he could reach, called me a whore, and then, after this totally undeserved punishment, pushed me outside and closed the door behind me, saying, 'Go back where you came from! We don't want any women of the streets in our house! Go away!' I couldn't stop myself. This time it was too much. I didn't stop to think. I threw my veil on the ground, stamped on it, and ran like a madwoman to the neighbourhood police station, where I told my story. A police car took me home. This time it was my father who opened the door. He insulted me in front of the policemen, who asked to talk to him and he agreed. My brother had told my father that I had gone out with a man and that this man had brought me home. Such a thing was unheard of among Muslims. The policeman listened to me. I explained that I had gone to the dentist. They promised to verify my story the next day, and woe to me if I were lying! My father had not calmed down. He screamed that he was going to throw me out of his house, that he never wanted to see me again, and that if I were still there the next noon he would do something desperate. I wanted to know why, but in answer he spat in my face. Then I made up my mind to leave, but where would I go with no money? I didn't sleep all night. I thought and thought and finally decided to give my son to my husband so he would not be miserable here. Fate was set implacably against me. I no longer had a home or a room or a house where I could keep my son. At his father's he would have every comfort and would be cared for as lovingly as he had been with me. He would miss his mother, but at least he would have a real home. I would manage somehow.

The next morning, I didn't let my son see that anything was wrong. He didn't suspect anything. I got him ready. A few moments later, Papa knocked on my door, repeating to me that his was a respectable house and not a refuge for whores, and he told me to leave. I didn't have a cent to my name, but I had no choice. He was merciless.

'God is great,' I answered him.

I packed my son's suitcase and took the bus, which let me off near my husband's house. My arrival astonished them. No one was expecting to see me. I told them of my misadventure and informed them of my decision to leave my son with them. Their eyes were bright with joy, but my husband made me sign a paper saying that I had brought the child of my own free will. Here it is, just as I wrote it:

> I, the undersigned, Mme . . ., wife of . . ., do hereby declare that on this day, the 11th of February 1951, of my own free will, I have brought my son to my husband's house, no longer

having a home of my own, because my father has expelled me, for a sin that I did not commit, as I can prove. Having no other shelter for my son, I entrust him to his father. As soon as my situation improves, I will come for him. I have not disowned my son, but I do not want him to suffer because of me. Signed . . .

And that is how I gave up my son to my husband, because one of my brothers was angry at the liberties I was taking. My life was already ruined, my health almost destroyed, and now my only happiness was taken from me by slander. 'My God, how I suffer from all these punishments! Am I not your child? Have you created me only to watch the tears stream from my eyes?'

Work
I went to get a few things: some clothes, nothing more. I did not take much – not my radio, nor my jewellery, nor my other things. I took away nothing but a change of clothing, a pair of shoes, and a comb. I left everything there. I had not done anything to deserve the cruel fate of being thrown out and having to go off into the dangerous unknown. This was not the way I had dreamed of establishing my independence. Alas! This is the way it turned out to be. '*Maktub,*' the Arabs would say; I would say envy, jealousy, slander. So I left, but God was with me that day. The postman came to bring me the cheque for my food allowance! I refused my son's, because he was no longer there. I was honest; I didn't want to cheat. Then I left. I left my childhood home where I had lived very happily for a very long time, warmed by my mother's love. On the day I was thrown out, my heart was bruised, wounded by the loss of my son and by a relentless fate.

For a long time, in the street, with suitcase in hand, I paid no attention to anything. My only thought was of my little child whom I had voluntarily abandoned because I didn't want him to suffer or to become the victim of my future misery. I had been afraid for him. I thought he could have a normal home away from me. I had decided on my own to make him happy by giving him to his father. I believe that no woman, no man, no judge will condemn me for that.

Then I lifted my head and looked at the world. I had just turned the page of a frightful chapter in a grim novel. I was coming out of a long dark tunnel and still shaken I was looking into the unknown.

Carrying my suitcase, I went to get the bus. I got off at the parade ground in the centre of the city. I was no longer trying to think about what was happening to me. I was walking like an automaton. I went to see my lawyer and told him of my misadventure. He couldn't believe his ears. He had never imagined that my father would behave like that, and, since he was very kind, he undertook to ask at the employment bureau for a job for me, so I wouldn't have to be in the street. He made it clear to the person in charge of placement that I came from a very respectable family and that he, as my lawyer, would undertake to furnish the necessary references.

And so I hadn't even gone to a hotel, I hadn't even had time to bemoan my fate. My lawyer had taken pity on me and immediately found me a job in the home of an aristocratic French family in Algiers. He went with me himself to my employers' home and introduced me to them. First he had called the dental surgeon to find out if I had really been to his office, what time I had left, and whether I had been accompanied. While my lawyer was talking on the telephone, I could see by his expression that he believed me. I had not lied. Now he trusted me.

My employer, Mme. A., put me at my ease. She asked me what I could do and then told me that I would be the cook. A few moments later, she showed me my room. It wasn't big, but it was very clean and neat. There was a bed, toilet articles, some other furniture, and a rug. The room was near the kitchen, and I had every comfort. I hadn't had to suffer for very long, because God was with me, and that was a great comfort. My morale had risen, because I had just won the first battle. Only my heart bled when I thought of my son.

As for my family, they were told by the police, who had received the information from the dental surgeon, that I had not lied. It was too late. I had already gone. I learned that my father did everything he could to find me. My brother, who *had* lied, was punished in his turn, but I repeat, it was too late. My father paid a detective to find me. It hurt me to discover all this, but out of self-respect I refused to return to my father's house. What kind of future would I have had if I had gone back? And besides, I had suffered too much for five years. Five years of tears, of anguish. I had lived in fear of the next day. Now I was at peace with myself. My employers wanted me to make peace with my family, but I refused. The life I would lead in my father's house would not be a peaceful one, because I would have to return to old customs, to the demands of the family, to 'what will people say?' No, I didn't want to see any of them again. I didn't even want to go out. I was happy in this family that had welcomed me with kindness and consideration.

Now, having survived in spite of all my misadventures, in spite of the meanness of which I had been the victim, inflicted not by strangers but my own family, I told myself that I was guilty of nothing. It was simply that fate had set itself against me. Everything I had was destroyed. My life was now diminished.

Now none of my daily problems came from the painful past, but from my work. Now I could say, to hell with people's opinions, long live the kitchen! I wanted to forget everything, yes, everything in order to work, with joy in my heart, no more awful thoughts, no more waiting for a husband who only came home to reproach or beat me! I don't want to think about anyone, since no one ever thought about me. So I turn the page. Everyone took advantage of me. They took everything away from me and gave me nothing except perhaps a year of unforgettable memories. They hated me while I was asking for nothing except to love and be loved. I had been betrayed. Then the days spent in the hospital, my physical suffering, and my convalescence had given me the idea of doing what some of my fellow countrywomen had done. I wanted to forget the shattered life I had led for five years. The brutal shock of the second separation from my son would pass in time, perhaps. I knew that he would be happy and loved. Just thinking about having left him made me shudder, but it had been necessary so that he would not have to endure my sorrow, my innocent one, my beloved, my son, *waldi*. The day I gave him back to my husband, his look and his tears had broken my heart, and today torment seizes me again just at the thought of it.

My life at Mme. A.'s took a pleasant turn, something I had long wished for. I enjoyed my work. I was treated very considerately by the family. I prepared dinner for the most important guests. I also prepared cocktails and *hors d'oeuvres*. It was a pleasure to see all those elegant guests eating what I, a girl who had suffered so much, had made. Ladies came right into my kitchen to congratulate me. They were aristocrats or women of the world. Their compliments were simple and kind. They knew my story and wanted to see me. They were envious of my employer because I was in her service, and they asked me a lot of questions about my special recipes.

I knew that Mme. Y. or Mme. Z. had had no luck with their employees because, at idle moments during the day, my employer often came to chat with me and would tell me certain things in confidence. However, I was really indifferent to what her friends said to me, and to their flattery as well. I simply accepted their words with a smile of thanks. My only real joy would have been my son's presence. Alas, he was far away!

I thought of this family as my own. They had welcomed me in a time of distress when my real family had disowned me because of a simple lie. I applied myself to my work wholeheartedly, because I was very fond of my employers. I was no longer desperate. I pined for my son, and that was all.

I had been working for Mme. A. for almost ten months. Day by day my life was becoming more and more pleasant. Sometimes I wondered how I could possibly have come there, how I could have escaped the precipice, and I realised that only a miracle could have kept me from falling into the abyss.

Winter was coming to an end. Spring was visible everywhere. The little birds chirped from early morning, the flowers reappeared, daisies and cowslips. Spring flowers blossomed around the houses, and the geraniums turned red in the sunshine. All the trees were adorned with little green buds. I had never until this day observed nature with such joy in my heart. I watered a jasmine border with the hope of one day seeing it grow and watching its little white flowers bloom. My heart is joyful at the thought of this plant which is still here. Who will have the pleasure of seeing it blossom, of watering it so it will bloom? Others will look at it, will enjoy its fragrance, and will gather flowers from its branches. This plant is a living being. When it is little, it is like a little child. If it is watered and pruned it will grow, but if it is only cared for now and then, it will be burned in the fall with the brush from the garden . . .

My work wasn't hard at Mme. A.'s. She was very sweet to me, very understanding. I no longer talked to her about my personal life, ruined forever. The wounds were healing little by little; I was regaining my taste for life.

Peace reigned in this house. Never since my arrival had there been a scene, not even a few words exchanged in loud voices. Everyone was happy, and they had adopted me as their daughter; they seemed to forget that I was the maid, the cook.

I felt well. My morale was better, and my health was too. My employers were pleased with me. I didn't go out. I had no friends. I didn't talk to anyone, except my employer, because of my work. With her husband, who was an industrialist, and her sons, one of whom was a doctor and the other a student, my relationship was limited to 'good morning,' 'good evening,' or *'bon appetit'*. I never went out, not even to see my son, for that would have caused innumerable complications, and I was afraid, too, that someone from my family might meet me in the street.

I was not bored in that beautiful house with its plants, its valuable objects, its pictures. The radio was at my disposal, and that reminded me that my husband, out of spite, had forbidden me to listen to it. When he went to work, he had taunted me by removing the tube in front of me. Sometimes he was truly an infernal being. This harrassment was to make me understand that I was nothing at all in his home. Today, times had changed. Doors were opening to me: radio, television, records – all of that was offered to me by my employers. It was all new to me, and I was greatly delighted, like a child who is given a toy. Then the explosion of that great joy almost turned into bitterness . . . my son . . . the memory of my child came back to me . . . and I relived the day when my father threw me out. I had said to my father, 'God is great'. It's true, he really is! When the thought of my son came over me, I became nervous, I felt oppressed by a heavy weight. Then I confided in my employer, who consoled me as best she could.

My little child was far away. Perhaps he was living happily in a place where no one would say anything harsh to him. For example, when he broke something or committed some fault, he would not be scolded except for his own good. I knew that. Then I said to myself, '*Allah yastur waldi.*' (Allah, take care of my son.)

Summer was beginning. We experienced its heat – somewhat oppressive but bearable. No sooner had June arrived than people started to talk about vacations. They packed suitcases. They washed clothes and hung them in the closets with mothballs. Blankets and rugs were sent to the cleaners. Furs were put in storage so as not to risk unpleasant surprises. Our preparations weren't hurried. Every day, Mme. A. decided on tasks so we would not get overtired and I wouldn't feel pushed. Mme. A. was a model homemaker, because she organised her work to perfection and that allowed her time every day to take a well-earned rest.

With her I constantly learned new things. It was wonderful! And every day I admired this woman more and more. She was so full of youth, gaiety, and good humour. She undertook to do what was necessary for me, getting the papers I needed and signing the certificate of responsibility for me. She was taking me with her to France, she was broadening my horizons. All at once, like the wind, she was blowing away the frightful clouds from my sky to let it appear entirely blue.

She also decided to dress me in the French style. Algeria is a country where it isn't very cold in the winter, but it is very hot in summer. We had to prepare for a different climate in France. So she bought me two dresses of fine woollen material, two other light dresses, and a coat. She also gave me shoes. I didn't know how to express my gratitude to this woman who had welcomed me in my deepest distress. I didn't want to think of anything but my work and the beautiful outfits Mme. A. had just given me.

M. and Mme. A. took pleasure in watching me when they gave me all those treasures. I couldn't believe they were for me! Then, Mme. A. took me to her room and asked me to try on one of the dresses. I was then very thin. 'Our daughter,' she said, looking at me, 'has the figure of a model.' I was happy, happy! Suddenly, for a moment – I don't know why – I thought she might be making fun of me. Then I was ashamed and tears came to my eyes, tears of joy, tears of remembrance, and I took refuge in Mme. A.'s arms as I used to do in the distant days when my Maman was alive.

That evening, I was invited to their table. I was overwhelmed by their kind attention. Even today, I say, 'Thank you!' to them again.

European life broadened my horizons more each day. It was full of surprises. Every day my personality grew stronger, while my sisters continued to live in servitude. No new idea can reach them after the iron discipline of marriage is imposed upon them, and I suffered because of this.

How I would love them to know this level of civilisation where life is noble, full of support and new ideas!

(Years have passed; her husband wants her back)

My ex-husband was growing restless. He told me that he no longer recognised me, he who had never heard me answer back. I had always been ready to please him. He couldn't really take it in. He asked me again what day and what time would be convenient for him to come and get me. I replied that I had no free days, being fully occupied with my work, and that I didn't see how I could do it. He thought that I was making fun of him, and, turning to my father, he asked him to intercede for him so that his son should not be an orphan. My father didn't want to disappoint him. He asked me gently but firmly to restore my conjugal home. I replied that it was now no longer possible, after all that had happened. Furthermore, the operations I had undergone, and for which my husband had been responsible, required me to refuse. I no longer recognised him as my husband. Besides, six years had passed, and only now did he remember that he had a wife.

'No,' I said, 'I will not return, even if you try to force me. I am happy the way I am. If you truly want to live happily, my husband, let's be friends, nothing more. What you are asking is beyond my power. I will never be able to do it. Besides, we are very different from one another. We would be able to stand each other for a moment, and after that there would be the same endless arguments, the blows. I cannot believe in the happiness that you imagine you can provide for me but which is really only an illusion.

You want us to resume our life together, yet I think – in fact, I know – that you simply need a maid for your sick mother and father. Why are you trying to hide your real face?' I was getting irritated, I was talking loudly, but that was just nervousness.

'Never, do you understand? I will never come back to you. You have come here of your own accord, without my asking you, after I waited so long for you. Now, before my whole family gathered here and also before Mme. A., I am telling you everything that I have had in my heart to tell you. But you should know that I loved you, although that is an unusual thing in our society. I wept for you, I waited for you. But I had nothing but arguments from you. Now I live for my work. I want nothing from you. The only thing I want is my son.

'I will add, as thanks for the wonderful treatment I encountered at your house, this reflection. You will grow old with your looks gone, the gnawing worm of your spitefulness will hide all the charm of life from your eyes. Your soul was monstrously empty, empty like those of all who are full of themselves and scornful of others. By repudiating me, you ruined my life and destroyed my health, something I did not deserve. You took my child away from me and beat me, and then, by vile manoeuvring, you got everything you wanted. As for me, I fell into the void. However, I did love you, I gave you a son of whom you were very proud, and you thrust me aside like a mangy sheep, as if I had the plague. I, who saw the world only through your eyes! Today I have sworn to climb the slope again, in spite of all the difficulties and pitfalls, all for my little one whom I love and from whom I am separated. My suffering will be very long, for it has only just begun. Yes, my husband, you gave yourself the pleasure of seeing what frightful situation your repudiation would lead me to, and so now you are satisfied.'

After having spoken this way, I went over to him and grasped his hand, to demonstrate my friendship. I was trembling with nervousness.

Then he spoke to Mme. A., telling her that she must make me see reason. She replied briefly:

'I am not a member of the family, and besides, she is my employee. I can't dismiss her if she doesn't want to leave.'

I went into the courtyard to calm my nerves. I played ball with my little nephews and nieces, my brothers and sisters. I was young and pretty. I was just eighteen. My long hair, which was nicely arranged, and my suit which fitted me perfectly could make my husband fall in love once more. I was no longer the little girl of twelve and a half but a young woman who had matured, who knew how to conduct a conversation, who knew how to dress. You can't get over it, can you, my husband? So, look, I'm playing ball, almost forgetting that my uncle was buried just four hours ago. I am exciting, aren't I? Well, I will never be yours any more, no, it is over. You have talked big, and you have received your reward. Don't complain!

I went to say goodbye to him, to my husband, to the father of my little one.

'I would like to see my son again,' I said to him. 'If you really mean what you said, bring him tomorrow. I will be at my father's for three days.'

Then I went back out into the courtyard where the children were waiting for their mischievous sister and aunt. My ex-husband came there on his way out. He grasped my hand again. No one had come with him because they knew I was outside. He asked me to go out to the car with him, because he wanted to prove to me that he had changed. I didn't accept, but I went with him up the steps to the street. He squeezed my hand very hard and then, unable to restrain himself, he pulled me to him and kissed me on the mouth, promising me the moon, but I was only thinking of my son, and that was the only tie we had.

The next morning, my son arrived, accompanied by his grand-mother. He recognised me, but he was shy. He was very cute. He began to tell me little stories a few minutes after he got there. I embraced my former mother-in-law and led her into the house. I introduced her to Mme. A., and taking advantage of the embraces and *salam alaikums*, I escaped with my son into an adjoining room. How he had grown! How handsome he was! He was very talkative. He was so glad to see me. He told me stories, recited a poem for me, and sang *Au clair de la lune* and *Frère Jacques* for me. He was delighted when I sang with him, because, he explained, his grandmother only knew how to sing in Arabic. He unbraided my hair, and that amused him. I could see that he was happy. Then, a moment later, he asked me to come home. I told him that I would like to, but that I was very ill. I was overwhelmed by my child's request, but if I came back to him for his happiness, I would destroy not only my own moral existence, which I would have sacrificed to him in one hasty moment, I would be refusing to recognise the need and the right of our women to achieve independence, and that my conscience forbade.

So I began to sing him Schubert's *Trout*. He was delighted, because he didn't know it. He forgot what he had just asked of me.

When my mother-in-law was ready to go, I asked her to leave the child with me and to tell her son to come for him the next day. O joy! she left him with me without objecting in the least, but she did try to turn the conversation to my return home. I evaded the question.

After that, I saw my son from time to time. I went back to work. Mme. A. received letters from my ex-husband, asking her to put pressure on me, but she was not a woman who would act that way and she left me to make my own decisions.

My husband then suggested bringing me my son on my days off, but I didn't have any because I wanted it that way. He then suggested to Mme. A. that she make me go out, me, a Muslim woman! That was the limit! He had come to that!

I had no more happiness or joy, but I had the satisfaction of knowing that he really loved me – now that it was too late.

I do not want to return to slavery, no! No matter what happens, I will never do that.

I pity my Muslim sisters with all my heart, those who are still bent under the yoke. I hope the day may come when they too will emancipate themselves.

For myself, I have chosen liberty! I have had my share of tears, humiliation, physical and moral suffering. It is enough. I could not bear any more.

What do I want? To leave this land of Algeria, where I have suffered so much, and to go to France and earn my living honestly, to be free at last, as French women are, liberated from all the terrible servitude that oppresses Muslim women in Islamic lands.

And my son! My beloved son, my son who is everything to me, for I will never have another, I do not forget him, I will never forget him, the only person I love!

God grant that later, when he is a free man, we may find one another again. God willing!

Translated from the French
by Jane Blanchard

Farida Benlyazid

(1948–)

Farida Benlyazid was born in Tangiers, Morocco. After obtaining her secondary schooling in Morocco, she went to France where she attended the University of Paris VIII. In 1973, she was awarded her Licence en Lettres Modernes et Cinématographie. For two years, she pursued graduate studies in cinematography at the Ecole Supérieure des Etudes Cinématographiques, Paris. She directed her first film in 1977: 'Identités des Femmes', a short film about immigrant women in France. It was broadcast on French television in 1978. Between 1978 and 1979 she wrote the scenario for *Poupée de Roseau* which she produced in 1980 under the directorship of Jillali Ferhati. The film was widely acclaimed and it was chosen for participation in the 1981 Cannes Film Festival. Additionally, it was awarded numerous prizes, among them the 1981 Valencia Grand Prix du Cinéma Méditerranéen. She is currently involved in research into the life of Ito, the Berber heroine of the Middle Atlas who in the mid-1920s took up the arms of her dead father and led an army of women against the French.

The following extract is chosen from the script of her 1987 film *Bab al-Sama Maftuh* (The Gate of Heaven is Open). Nadia has returned from Paris to be at her father's bedside when he dies. Mourning heightens her Islamic consciousness and gradually she eschews her European values and way of life and allows herself to be guided by Kirana, the Quranic reciter. Her father left his palace in the heart of the Fez medina to his son and two daughters. According to Islamic law, a daughter inherits half of her brother's share. Nadia's brother who lives in Paris wants to sell the house claiming it is too big to maintain and that it is inconveniently situated: it cannot be reached by car. Nadia is dismayed and consults a woman lawyer. In this segment we see how a young woman against her brother's wishes contrives to save the family house through manipulation of popular Islamic practice. She converts the patriarchal house into a *zawiyya*, a religious retreat for women, a fairly common institution in North Africa. While men are kept out of this house of women, a *jinn*, a man in non-material form enters. Another man in the form of the spirit of a dead holy man entices another woman out to visit his shrine. The femininst consciousness expressed here is embedded in a popular Islamic/North African tradition. Patriarchal 'influences' in non-material forms penetrate the scene. But are they contained by the women? This segment, and the film itself, are provocative. Although the script was written in French, it is performed in Moroccan Arabic.

The Gate of Heaven is Open

1987

ഌ

This scene takes place in the office of Touria, the lawyer.

Touria and Nadia have been chatting for a while in a modern office. The lawyer reflects as she balances on a swivel chair.

NADIA: (*animatedly*)   What hurts is that we're getting rid of the best in our culture to retain the shell empty of its meaning. I'd like you to meet Kirana. She's an extraordinary woman. Through her I've discovered a world of which I had no idea. In Islam women are free to dispose of their fortune and of their time. The wealthiest financed *zawiyyas*, that is, refuges for women in need. You've got to understand: this kind of a house has always had a particular function in our society. It should not be lost.

TOURIA: (*nods with interest*) I understand. But it's going to be tough. The law is on your brother's side.

NADIA: (*shakes her head desperately*) I'm ready to fight to the end. This house must become a refuge.

TOURIA: Here's what we'll do. You're sure that you want to fill the house? You might lose it forever.

NADIA: (*impatiently*) I know what I want.

TOURIA: (*smiles*) I'm intrigued. First of all, we've got to gain time. I'll take care of the legal matters. So, open the doors and take in whomever you like. But, again, I'm warning you, if it works you'll never be able to get rid of them.

NADIA: Don't worry.

The next scene takes place in Nadia's palace in the Fez medina.

Ba Sassi (a jinn) leaves the painting and approaches Nadia. He is in the same clothes and is acting as he did in the flashback when he proposed to her. He smiles and speaks as though to a little girl.

BA SASSI: You mustn't be afraid of Ba Sassi. D'you remember? You agreed to be my wife.

Ba Sassi's wrinkled face gives way to that of a handsome black man. Nadia, asleep on her mattress, moves in her dream. She moans and Khaddouj, asleep next to her, awakes, looks at her and gets closer. She taps her on the shoulder to calm her.

KHADDOUJ: May God's name protect you.

N. opens her eyes and sits up. She looks at Ba Sassi's painting as though hallucinating. She speaks as though in her sleep and she points at the painting.

NADIA: Look. He wants to take me away. He says that we must prepare the wedding feast.

Khaddouj squints but sees nothing. Silently, she recites the Fatiha.

NADIA: (*looking at Khaddouj's swollen stomach*) He says you're going to have a son. You must call him Abdelhay.

Khaddouj continues to recite the only verse of the Quran she knows so as to overcome her fear.

KHADDOUJ: May God's name protect you. In the name of God, the Compassionate, the Merciful.

The muezzin's call to the dawn prayers seems to calm her.

Some time later Khaddouj is climbing with difficulty. In one hand she has her basket of food and in the other a bag with sewing materials. She stops at the cross road to rest.
   She turns to another steep road with steps on either side and sees Kirana. She watches her approach. Kirana looks up and sees her also. They smile at each other. Kirana hurries to her and they kiss each other.

KIRANA: Hello, Khaddouj. I was going to your place. How are you? This is great! You're walking. That's good for you in your state. But you shouldn't carry heavy things.

KHADDOUJ: (*shows her the basket and bag*) No. It's not so heavy. Just a sewing kit. I'm returning from class. It's small – just two of us.

KIRANA: (*grabs hold of the basket*) Let me have it since we're going together. Tell me, how are things going? I heard that Laila moved out. Aren't you afraid in that big house?

KHADDOUJ: (*nods and looks down a dark side street to the right*) I believe that Lalla Nadia has been bewitched. May God protect us.

KIRANA: Really? What's happened to her?

KHADDOUJ: (*overwhelmed*) Every night her screams wake me up. She says that she sees a *gnawi* who says that he wants to marry her and that the house must be turned into a *zawiyya*. To tell the truth I hear and see nothing. It's just what she tells me. The following day when I talk with her about it, it's I who seems to have dreamt. She remembers nothing. (*Khaddouj stops to catch her breath.*)

KIRANA: Have you spoken to Laila about this?

KHADDOUJ: (*nods unhappily*) Yes, I've spoken to Lalla Laila. She didn't believe me. I'd like someone to spend the night and then we'll see who's right.

In a room on the terrace of the Fez house, Nadia in a clean but torn white shirt is just finishing her prayers. She takes the shawl off her head and goes to the mattress on the floor. She sits on it and picks up the open Quran. It is an Arabic-French edition. She turns on the cassette player next to the bed. One hears Kirana recite a verse that she follows in the Quran. She doesn't hear steps on the stairs. She jumps when someone knocks at the door.

NADIA: Who's there?

Kirana opens the door. Nadia gets up and welcomes her warmly. Khaddouj follows, much relieved, almost joyful.
NADIA: I'm so happy you've come. It's been a long time.
KIRANA: (*smiles and kisses her*) I thought about you all the time. I was at Moulai Abdessalam.
NADIA: But you didn't tell us!
KIRANA: Even I had not planned it. But, He called . . .
KHADDOUJ: How lucky! May we benefit from God's *baraka*.
NADIA: (*enthusiastically*) Khaddouj, get the table ready at once. The meal's cooked and you must be hungry.

Khaddouj obeys happily and leaves humming a Hussein Slaoui song: 'Who is the Shaikh of the jbelas? Moulay Abdessalam Allah's wali . . .'

NADIA: I went to see a friend who is a lawyer in town. We thought that the best way to keep the house was to open up a *zawiyya*.
KIRANA: (*interrupting*) What's this story about a black man who comes in the night?
NADIA: (*amused*) Ah, Khaddouj's stories. She doesn't like the Ba Sassi painting. It scares her.
KIRANA: And you? Have you never seen anything?
NADIA: (*smiles sceptically*) Do you believe in that stuff? I don't know. I do know that I have nightmares. Sometimes I am awakened by a feeling of fear . . . Very strange . . . But I remember nothing.

Kirana does not want to make too much of it. She indicates that she wants to change the subject.

KIRANA: Tell me. You talked about opening a *zawiyya*. What a great idea. But it's not so easy . . .

Suddenly, Kirana who is facing the window overlooking the terrace, sees the head of a little girl horribly disfigured. She sits bolt upright in horror.

KIRANA: Did you see? Did you see? In the name of God, the Compassionate.

Nadia, surprised, wonders what's going on. She has not seen anything. Kirana rushes out of the door and Nadia follows.

KIRANA: May God protect us! In the name of God, the Compassionate, the Merciful.

She opens the door and they go out. Kirana runs to the corner of the terrace where the little girl is crouched. She seems to be trying to dig a hole in the wall. Nadia walks ahead because Kirana seems suspicious. She recites verses from the Quran. Nadia kneels next to the little girl, cornered like an animal. Nadia smells the girl's fear as she hides her face. She speaks quietly.

NADIA: Don't be afraid of me . . .

She comes closer to the little girl who is not to be reassured. Nadia strokes her tangled hair as though she were caressing an abandoned cat.

NADIA: Look at me. I'm not going to hurt you. Don't be afraid.

The girl raises her swollen face, covered in blood and tears. Nadia is upset. Kirana cries out and Nadia cannot hold back her tears. She resumes the stroking that horror had interrupted.

KIRANA: My God! My God!
NADIA: Who could have done that to you?

The little one rolls her eyes.

KIRANA: Get up, daughter. Can you get up? God has guided you here. You've nothing to fear any more. No one will ever hurt you again?

A gleam of hope sparkles in the still crazy eyes of the wounded child.

[In the next two scenes, Malika, the little girl, is taken in and tidied up. Her guardians have agreed to leave her with Kirana, Khaddouj and Nadia because they claim she is a trouble maker. Kirana has fetched her personal belongings from her daughter's house. Nadia announces that the zawiyya has just opened.]

In the garden of the Fez house, Nadia is watering the plants close to the door. She hears someone knocking. She puts down the hose and goes to the door. Crossing the courtyard, she hears Kirana reciting the Quran.

KIRANA: Read, in the name of your Lord who created.
He created from a blood clot.
Read!

> For your Lord is the most generous who instructed man
> through the Word and taught him what he did not know.

Before reaching the door, Nadia sees a young woman approaching.

FATIMA: Hello, you're Nadia, aren't you?

*Without allowing Nadia to respond, she runs into the garden and then stops
in the middle of the courtyard.*

FATIMA: It's wonderful! *(Nadia approaches, amused by such open
behaviour.)* You know, they say I'm crazy. But I know that I'm
not. It was a psychiatrist of Berechid who sent me to you. He
knows I'm not crazy. It's just that I see things differently.
(looking around) OK, we have to agree. I like this place.

She sits on the grass and looks up at Nadia with joy in her eyes.

FATIMA: Come, come close to me. It's really comfortable. Sit down.
(Nadia sits down obediently.) This is a foretaste of Paradise.
Really! D'you know what we're going to do? I'll give you my
whole salary. I'm a physics professor at the university. But at
the moment I'm not working. I have to rest. So what I need is
a small room with a key. I sometimes need to lock myself in.
Do you understand . . .? But I think I'll be here a lot. J'aime le
contacte de notre mere la terre. *(stretching on the ground)* So, is
that OK?

NADIA: It seems fine. Only, you shouldn't give all your salary . . .

FATIMA: *(emphatically)* Yes, yes. I want to. I'll never buy anything.
Here!

*She takes out a large wad of banknotes from a soft leather wallet that she
had in a pocket of her sirwal. Nadia is uncomfortable.*

NADIA: But . . .

FATIMA: Why make things complicated? It's so simple.

She throws the coins on the grass and gets up.

FATIMA: It's the *zawiyya's* money.

*As though relieved, she whirls around, dancing and singing. She goes to the
courtyard opposite the large hall. A song of Fairouz is heard.*

[*During the next twenty scenes Nadia's brother is still trying to sell the
house. Nadia has another vision of Ba Sassi. He tells her to hold a Jillali
hadra in the house. During the hadra, Nadia and some other women fall
into a trance. Ba Sassi tells her to dig under the lemon tree. She digs and
finds treasure.*]

Khaddouj hears knocking at the front door and hurries to it. The woman behind the door is shaking. One hears blows and a man's shouts.

HUSBAND: That's it. Daughter of shame. You think you can run away from me! I won't leave before catching you.

Khaddouj arrives at this moment and speaks to the woman.

KHADDOUJ: What's up? Who is it?
BATOUL: It's my husband. He's going to kill me. Don't open for him. Don't open.
KHADDOUJ: (*calming her*) Come, come. Come on in. We're not going to let him in.

She takes her inside while the husband continues to bang and shout.

KHADDOUJ: What did you do to him?
BATOUL: Nothing, I swear.

Kirana arrives.

KIRANA: What's up?
BATOUL: (*while Khaddouj explains*) I put myself into your protection. Above all, you mustn't open. When he's like this, he could do anything.
KHADDOUJ: It's her husband.
KIRANA: (*needs no further explanation*) Bring her in. I'll take care of him. What do you want?
HUSBAND: (*shouts even louder and kicks the door*) I want my wife! Let me in!!
KIRANA: (*behind the door waits for a moment of silence to speak and be heard.*) Listen well. Your wife is here under our protection. She'll come back to you when you've calmed down.

These words make him even angrier. He bangs harder and harder, howling.

HUSBAND: Give me back my wife. You have no right to her.

Kirana does not lose her temper. She grimaces and waits. A man in the street tells him to calm down because his wife is in a zawiyya.
[Batoul explains that her husband did not want her to see her sister and that he had been enraged by her mere visit. Like Malika, B. stays for years.]

Translated from the French
by Miriam Cooke

Nuha Samara

(1944–)

Nuha Samara was born in Tulkarem, Palestine. In 1948 her family fled to Beirut. In 1962, she began to write for a few Beiruti newspapers; many of her newspaper publications have been short stories. In 1973, she published *Fi Madinat al-Mustanqa* (In the Swamp City). During the Lebanese Civil War she published *Al-Tawilat Ashat Akthar min Amin* (The Tables Lived Longer than Amin, 1981). She is one of the Beirut Decentrists. At the end of 1975, she left Beirut for Doha, Qatar and a year later, she moved to London where she stayed for two years. Exile then took her to Paris; in 1982, she returned to the Middle East. She is now based in Limassol, Cyprus, and is the editor of the women's section of the *Al-Shahid* magazine. She has just finished writing a novel about Lebanese and Arabs in exile. In a letter she wrote to Miriam Cooke, she said: 'My primary concern is the Arab woman and her means of expression.'

'Two Faces, One Woman' is selected from *The Tables Lived Longer than Amin* and describes what happens to a woman when her husband, through whom she had experienced the world, leaves the Lebanese Civil War for Paris. The tolerance towards escapees that marked the first stage of the war was beginning to erode. The story traces her transformation in consciousness as she learns to act for and by herself. It is representative of the works of many of the Beirut Decentrists who realised that it was the men who were leaving, the women who were staying behind.

Two Faces, One Woman

1980

❧

Calmly she went to bathe. She had learnt how to hold on to time, how to touch things calmly. She undressed slowly. As she washed her long, blond hair she remembered him and how he had loved and admired her hair: 'The hair of a palomino'; 'It fills me with desire for you'; 'The day it's cut short I'll leave you for another woman.'

Ever since the beginning of the war, she had accustomed herself to bathing quickly, fearing that a shell might hit and kill her when she was naked. Her death would become a funny story for the neighbours to repeat! She felt afraid . . . and decided to finish quickly. Why shouldn't she admit that he had chosen to abandon her with her helpless father!

She dried her hair thoroughly. And then, sitting in front of the mirror, she set up another one behind her and began to cut her hair. She saw the locks fall, but felt no sadness. It's a lie that women make themselves beautiful for men . . . Now that the man had gone she could stop lying. In the mirror her features hardened. Then she had an idea. She took some hair bleach and, mixing it into a paste, she brushed it on to her hair. Then she washed her hair and contemplated it in the mirror. Her features had become more sharply defined; this bleached hair made her look like a Nazi officer. She wanted him to see her now, to rid him of those sweet images. What did he mean by abandoning her in this filthy war, where survival depended on chance alone! He knew perfectly well how the daily chores of wartime existence exhausted her. And her father . . . what an enormous responsibility! How could she take him down to the shelter in his wheel-chair when the shelling got heavy? And what of the neighbours' questioning, infuriating glances: 'He left her the responsibility of this helpless old man!'

Earlier her father had lived with her sister and her four children. It was he who had suggested that they should bring him here to lighten her sister's accumulated responsibilities. He had driven there under the bombs and had quickly brought him back, like a conqueror. Exactly a month later his director had given him the choice between staying or transferring to Paris . . . and he had chosen the latter.

He stuttered a lot as he announced his decision. She remained silent, neither encouraging, nor dissuading him. He knew her well, she didn't interfere in anyone's decision. She muttered under her breath: 'It's your right to choose to stay alive.'

She wondered if he would have chosen to travel had she not aborted the baby a few months ago. Would she have retained her passivity?

Two days after this decision, he told her that he was leaving the next day. Throughout those three days he noticed that she couldn't look him in the eye. She had even lost interest in following the news of the war . . . And when the dining room window shattered after a shell exploded nearby, he had held her tight and said: 'Be strong in my absence!'

And that's how she was now . . . Her features were those of a man, her demeanor that of a Nazi in Hitler's army. She went to the wardrobe, and put on a pair of jeans and a khaki shirt. She looked ready to go into battle, all she lacked were weapons. And then she remembered. She opened an old cupboard and took out his pistol. Why hadn't she agreed at his friend Manah's suggestion to train near the house? She could do that in the early hours of dawn while her father was asleep, when the sounds of shells and death had receded.

She contacts Manah immediately. He responds quickly and tells her that she's made an excellent decision. She tells him of Abdall-ah's departure. He's surprised, and then he understands, and is quiet. Then she hears him reassure her: 'You've made a great decision. Tomorrow morning at six, we'll see you over there.'

In the morning . . . Manah was not there. But he had given her name to the drill master. All those present were men. Not one of them looked at her curiously, nor admiringly nor even lustfully as he had . . . Was it the war? Or was it her new face that made her look like a Nazi officer?

The training exercises were not difficult. The sound of the first bullets exploding out of her pistol didn't frighten or disturb her . . . She was amazed by her lust to kill. When the bullets exploded in quick succession, she wished that the dummies that were falling had been people. When it was over, the drill master congratulated her on her courage, and she answered: 'I want to complete the training. I want to know all fighting techniques.'

At night the shelling increased, but she was no longer afraid as she had been before. She heard the neighbours scream as they rushed down to the shelter. She decided to take her father in his wheel-chair down to the shelter, not forgetting to take some bread and cheese. Probably the toughest thing that day were the neighbours' looks. Ohh! . . . How she hated to be pitied. The only pity she had been able to stand had been his when he returned home and saw her cooking and cleaning. After returning from a day's teaching, he would mutter something she could not understand: 'Ah, the beautiful proletariat!'

She never asked him what that meant, but when she dusted his office, she noticed many titles about revolution and change and books stuffed with the word 'proletariat'. She wasn't at all curious to read any of these books. Maybe she didn't have the time. But then, she'd never seen him read any of them. He preferred to chat with friends, to inhale the aroma of her food and to smoke an ivory *narghile*, of which his friends made fun. At one point Manah had said to him:

'Words! This revolution about which you keep talking doesn't go with this *narghile* of yours!'

Down in the shelter she felt ravenously hungry. She gave her father some bread and cheese. In time with the pounding shells he started to gnaw. She loathed the sound of chewing. All that was left of the people in the war was greedy mouths that did nothing but chew. The shelter was like the Day of Resurrection with all those kids screaming. She touched her stomach where the embryo had been on that day that she had rejoiced to have aborted it. Had she known at the time that her relationship could not stand this?

A neighbour asked her presumptuously: 'Where's Abdallah?'

'He's gone.'

'Where?'

'Paris.

'Why?'

'They transferred him.'

She didn't tell her that his company had given him the choice between staying and leaving, lest the woman pity her even more!

'Has he seen what you've done to your hair?'

'Yes.'

She had to lie. Why should everyone know what she'd gone through. The neighbour went on:

'I'm not surprised that Abdallah's gone. I overheard him talking to my husband a while back here in the shelter, and he said that he couldn't stand it. Don't forget, it's been a year and a half! But why didn't he take you with him?'

'How could I leave my father? My sister's already left with her husband and children.'

The neighbour shook her head, not quite convinced. Then she said pointing to her father: 'May God help you with this responsibility.'

She turned to her responsibility. He was gnawing at the bread and cheese as anxiously as someone eating his last meal. All his appetites in life had turned to eating. Every day he'd ask her what there was to eat, and whether they had enough money for it.

He had given her his whole salary before he left, and as usual had left the money on the table. He knew that she hated to take the money from his hand. He noticed that she hadn't hidden the money and he chided her: 'Be careful! Everyone's become a thief!'

And when it was time for him to go, he stood there in embarrassment wanting to kiss her, and he said: 'Take good care of yourself. If you need anything, go to my brother or uncle. I'll get in touch through my uncle.'

Words . . . words!!

Most of the people in the shelter were sleeping, completely exhausted. They had spread out their bedding and had fallen asleep. Even her father was asleep in his wheel-chair. She covered him with a blanket, and then went up to the apartment calmly. The shells persisted outside, lighting up the skies and then going out, shining and then disappearing. Like red and green traffic lights. She remembered peace time, when the traffic lights used to work.

She felt very calm when she found herself alone. From birth, she had never been quite alone. Her family and siblings had always been there. After marriage, either he or his absence had been there. But now she was completely alone with the night. She sat in front of the hall mirror in her apartment hallway, where there were the safest corners. Suddenly she felt like taking off her clothes. She contemplated her body in the mirror, it was still radiant. She started to touch it as though bewitched, as though noticing it for the first time. She felt a desire to possess it, and she touched herself until she climaxed. Then she thought: I have to have a lover!

She thought about the men she knew, most of whom she knew through Abdallah. She had not once thought of any of them as men. They had different voices. She could remember their voices clearly, but she could not remember their features, their heights or sizes. She saw them through him. Whoever he had liked, she had liked. And he had really liked Manah and praised her in front of him! Manah . . . Maybe he was the one to pursue? He had been his best friend, and his was the only face she could clearly recollect. This was the man. He was almost primitive with his bulging muscles, the hair emerging from the open shirt and his black, piercing, captivating eyes . . .

Manah. Why not? She decided to talk to him the next morning.

She was a bit embarrassed when she saw him at the training

ground. He approached and shyly asked her how she was. Did she
need anything in Abdallah's absence. She didn't hesitate to ask him
if he could find a hospital for her father where she could be sure
that he would be well cared for. He promised to arrange something
as soon as possible.

She went on to tell him about her anxiety for her father during
bombardments. Sometimes she couldn't find him a doctor when he
had a relapse. He praised her for her rational decision. Then he
said before leaving: 'I'll be in touch as soon as I've found something
suitable.'

Manah wasn't long in contacting her. One morning he told her
of a suitable, safe place and he promised to get an ambulance to
transport him. And then he asked: 'How is he?'

She noticed that he avoided mentioning her husband's name.
She answered briefly that he had asked his uncle about her and had
tentatively asked if there was anything she needed.

When Manah left, she hurried to her father to tell him of her
plan. She assured him somewhat harshly and peremptorily that
this was ideal during the war, and that his safety and food would be
surer there than with her. He looked distracted and sad, and shook
his head a lot because he had difficulty in speaking. In the end she
assured him that this was just for the duration of the war, and that
when it was over he would return to her.

She rushed out so as not to burst into tears. In her room she
began to undress. Manah's face leapt out in front of her. Why was
her body beginning to awaken to desires of which she had been
unaware when she had been with him? Was it Abdallah's absence?
Or the repeated reports of death? He had accused her of frigidity,
and she had never responded because she hadn't had the right keys
to her body.

And when he had insistently made love to her during the war,
she had questioned him and he had answered confidently:

'When you keep hearing of death your desires increase. This is
particularly true during wars. Europe went through its moral
decline after its two wars.' And he went on: 'In the face of death all
values go by the board. All that remains alive are the limits of the
body and the pulse of feeling and instinct.'

Another time he had said something that was hard to forget:
'The most important consequence of this war is that our pursuit of
work, social relationships and petty misguided ambitions has
slowed down. It has reduced us to life size . . . But if it goes on we
may lose ourselves once again, but in another way . . .'

How often had she looked back on her life with him before the
war. Her marriage had been a rush between her work as a teacher

and a wife. He had been very concerned about his clothes, his food and the cleanliness of the house. He had often exploded in anger, swearing and slamming the door when he hadn't found things exactly right. She was used to this, because her father had been like this. And her response to these explosions had been the same as her mother's . . . silence! She had only felt a refusal grow in her after he had left. The only difference between her and her mother was that she worked outside the home. The only difference between him and her father was that he didn't object to her sitting with his friends when they came over, and he wasn't ashamed to express his feelings for her openly. Whereas she had never heard her father praise her mother in front of others. Her father was a man: not once had he left his family, and he had shouldered his responsibilities until he was paralysed two years after her mother's death.

How embarrassed she had been by his openness in front of his friends. He had exaggerated, as though wanting them to feel dissatisfied with their wives. But when they had left, he would pick up any old newspaper as though he had not said all those passionate things a few seconds ago. At first, she couldn't under-stand the change, couldn't explain it. She had attributed it to moodiness, because he had often said that he was moody, his temper mercurial.

Manah had been on her mind when she opened the door to him after a wild night of shelling spent in the shelter with her father. He looked a little disturbed:

'Have you prepared all your father's things? The war might last.'

'Will it?'

'Probably. Your drill master has given you an "A". He says that you shoot with an amazing ability that he doesn't find in men. I wonder if you can hit all your targets?'

'Yes. And particularly now that he's gone!'

He interrupted her: 'Where's your father?'

'In the bedroom . . . Here.'

Her father's face was tense, as though he were on his way to the gallows. She loved the way that Manah stroked his tired face and held her father's hand, saying:

'Listen, uncle. We're doing all this for your good. These inhu-man conditions have compelled us to put you in hospital where everyone will take care of you. In the hospital they will protect you against this damned war. You'll get food, drink, shelter, electricity and medicine. I'll always make sure you're O.K. . . . and so will your daughter. If ever you need anything, just let me know . . .'

'And now?'

He carried her father from the bed to the wheel-chair. He indicated that she should bring the case and follow him. Fortunately, the lift was working that day. She rushed after them, and they got into the ambulance.

When they arrived at the hospital after a silent trip, her father's face reflected all the harshness of the war. She followed them into the hospital. She tried not to look through the partially open doors of rooms housing the injured and the maimed of the war. Manah murmured reassuringly:

'He'll be in the geriatrics ward, not here . . .'

She relaxed when she saw how clean the place was and when she realised that he was going to be put into a sunny, private room. She kissed him. Not a single tear. This war was tough. Manah took her hand. She trembled and he must have felt it.

She heard him say: 'I left my car at the hospital entrance so we can return together.' She followed him as though bewitched.

When she sat next to him she was as calm and relaxed as though she were his wife. He said:

'You had no other choice. Imagine what would have happened if your house had been hit, or if you had needed a doctor during a bombardment. What would you have done?'

Silence. Then she heard him say: 'He's in the proper place now.'

When they arrived at the house she asked him if he wanted some morning coffee, and he answered, his black eyes laughing: 'I'd love to have some of your famous coffee!'

In the elevator, he stared silently at the lights that indicated the first floor, the second . . . the fifth then the seventh . . .

She was very embarrassed when they were alone together without his shadow or the shadow of her father. She rushed to the kitchen to prepare the coffee. All this silence excited her. On purpose she started to make lots of noise with the dishes. When she went into the sitting room, he had closed his eyes and he looked washed out. He felt her moving around, and said quickly:

'Imagine! I almost fell asleep. The last three nights I've hardly slept.'

He sat up and asked her gently: 'Are you depressed to be alone now?'

'No. I need to be alone.'

'You're strange . . . Most women living alone complain a great deal.'

'Not me.'

'That's why he was happy with you.'

'Who said he was happy?'

'That's what he had us understand.'

She handed him the coffee and he began to talk about the war, and analysed the reasons for the resumption and intensification of the fighting. Then he got up and said: 'I'll drop around often. I need to talk to you.'

'So do I.'

When he had closed the door behind him, the air was filled with his smell and her father's sad face, and she decided to call and find out how he was.

After taking her father to hospital she hadn't even considered going down into the shelter. Most of the people kept insisting that she go down. But she didn't.

There, on her own, she could dream a lot about Manah, and a little about the future.

What would she do if the war were to end and life returned to its regular pace and he came back. And the school, and his friends' and family's stupid faces and eternal visits, and his anger and whims for what he wanted and didn't want. She felt incapable of touching him after today. In the past she had been content with him and submitted to his moods. But today the balance had been upset. He'd just escaped to Paris. What did he feel when he saw those beautiful, elegant Parisian women who were enjoying themselves while she was a prisoner of her responsibility, her loneliness and her death? Wouldn't he be confused by the comparison? At night whom would he hold? She well knew that he couldn't live without a woman, without touching, especially after the second drink? When his revolutionary friends had left he would sniff and lick her. Once she had fallen asleep with him kissing her body, content as a child, and she had heard him say frantically: 'You're mine . . . mine . . . a thousand times mine.'

It was that day that she realised that however much she submitted to him, he was never fully satisfied that she was his. He had said to her once that she wouldn't let him feel that she belonged to him, that she was like happiness: only felt after it was gone.

The sounds of the shells and the explosions returned, the daily blanket of the city which enfolded the inhabitants like a peasant woman's clothes enfolded her. She began to feel the warm pulse of her new life. The white space of time ahead was hers to contemplate. Again she took off her clothes in front of the mirror in the hallway. She saw Manah's face, and she felt embarrassed as she touched herself, as though he were actually watching. She felt a terrible longing for him. She knew his phone number. Why shouldn't she contact him, and use all her feminine tricks and wiles. Tell him that she was afraid and he would come over and hold her through the night. And she would drown in love in his body. But if that were to happen, how difficult it would be to return to the distant traveller. She knew that she couldn't maintain relationships with two men at the same time. She remembered that his uncle had brought her a letter from him two days ago and she hadn't yet looked at it. His writing was like his body: sensitive, supple and full of curves . . . reading handwriting is like making love to the writer.

'My darling, here, far away it's hard to forget, and it's hard to remember . . . I'm living like someone who is postponing his life. Beirut has not given us the space for expectation and hope. And yet. I am living it. My time and my space are defined by it, even though I'm far away in Paris . . .

'Peace-time Beirut is not as beautiful and passionate as war-torn Beirut. Because of her we become vicious in love with vice, and mystics in love with mysticism. I am filled with loneliness, longing and waiting. I recollect the city's face and yours, and feel that I am still intimately connected to it and to you. I feel that my amputation has been a kind of treachery. My darling, I am suspended between life and death. Every morning I am amazed that I can keep going. As I awake out of the confusion of my dreams I forget where I am, but am filled with the old joy, probably part of my childhood. This joy drives me to get up and wash my face, shave and dress. And as I go through the streets to work I discover the delusion of this joy, and I wonder why and I find it in Beirut and in your face. Both possess me to the point of suffocation. I walk through the streets like a lost child not knowing where the path is leading.

'The women of Paris are beautiful and they remind me of a phrase from Byron: "If all the women of the world had but one mouth I would have kissed it and been happy." How I miss your mouth, your long hair, my corner in front of the TV, my records, my bed, the smell of your cooking when I come home from work. How I long for the warmth of old! I'll be back when the war's over, that's what my director promised when he knew how I was suffering. Today he said to me laughing: "You Beirutis, you're like fish out of water. I don't want you to die like a fish!"

'Pray for peace, so that I can return to you . . . Love always, Abdallah'

His last words revived all her anger at his departure. Was he only with her during times of peace, love, cooking, and warm beds? She hurried to the telephone and dialled Manah's number. He wasn't there. She'd try tomorrow and the day after and even when the war was over . . . And even if he returned from Paris . . .

Translated from the Arabic
by Miriam Cooke

Huda Naamani

(1930–)

Huda Naamani was born in Damascus, Syria. After her father's death in 1938, she was raised in her maternal grandfather's Damascus mansion. She is descended from the Ghazzis, who were landowners and politicians and the Nabulsis, scholars and grand mystics who trace their lineage to the Prophet Muhammad. As a child she mixed with poets, political notables and heads of state.

She attended the Lycée-Français and the Franciscan School and in 1946 received her baccalaureate. In 1947, following family tradition, Huda joined the Law School at the Syrian University. Upon graduation she joined, as a court attorney, the firm of her uncle, Said al-Ghazzi, Prime Minister during the regime of Shukri al-Quwatli. In 1952, she was awarded a graduate scholarship in political science to Stanford University. But her mother objected, and Huda declined the grant and married her cousin A. K. Naamani, twenty-three years her senior. She flew with him to Cairo where he became dean at the American University. During a two-year stay in England, Naamani studied history, sufism, philosophy, classical literature and the Islamic arts at the School of African and Oriental Studies. They went to Beirut in 1968.

Her publications include *To You* (1970), *My Fingers . . . No* (1971), *I Remember I Was a Point I Was a Circle* (1973), her major cluster poem of nationalistic songs calling for universal peace. A member of the Arab Writers Union, she contributes regularly to *Al-Nahar*, the Beirut daily newspaper. Her two plays on the Lebanese civil war are to be published shortly.

The three poems chosen for inclusion are taken from *Tadahujala al-Thalaj* (Tumbling on the Snow), 1978. They express a woman's defiance. She can 'seize' a man's voice and 'scatter it'. By 1980 a woman who has lived through the Lebanese Civil War has gained the self-assurance that allows her to challenge male control so as to shape it and feed it. She even mocks men's words, which have become 'duck's noses'.

From *Tumbling on the Snow*

1982

❦

Pulled by a long thread
Wave after wave you rain down from the Messiah's braids
Should I enter the wall with you, O Snail
    And wait
   Green would embrace green

   . . . . .
     would embrace green

The Hawk was Thrown Down from its Lofty Heights

A bird emerged from the pit and entered the waist
Yesterday you were laughing
I seized your voice and scattered it
I discarded it so that horses might pull it apart
I climbed to the top of the minaret and I sang
The pansy wandered between the calf and the knee
Then she slept
Yesterday you were weeping
I seized your voice and pursed it like a baby's mouth
Suckled it poetry before it slept

I Take You an Orange

I take you an orange and I squeeze you holding you to my face
Spring you blossom in my eyes
A peacock's tail you gaze at me in the dark
I wear you gipsy garb I fold you a nomad's cloak
A flute grass and warmth of sheep flow with you
In the arms of mountains you paint the wreaths of heaven
           And the pains of a goddess

A frame for me I carve you I gild you and
           I fill you with roses
A fish I slaughter you, or a sun
           I bake you
     A star
Lightning flashes from your ring
Your eyes hang on my face coffee grounds honeycombs
Nigerian songs brush my neck, flocks of geese
Your word is suspended on the back of a door a duck's nose

Translated from the Arabic
by Huda Naamani and Miriam Cooke

Fatima Mernissi

(1940–)

Fatima Mernissi was born in Fez, Morocco. She was brought up in a traditional household. She studied Political Science at Muhammad V University in Rabat and at the Sorbonne, and earned her Ph.D. in Sociology from Brandeis University. Between 1974 and 1980 she taught at Muhammad V University. Currently, she is at the Institut Universitaire de la Recherche Scientifique in Rabat. An outspoken feminist, she lectures widely in the Arab world and abroad. She has written numerous articles and several books, including: *Beyond The Veil. Male–Female Dynamics in a Modern Muslim Society* (1975), *Women in Public Space in a Muslim Society: Morocco* (1983), *Le Maroc Raconté par ses Femmes* (1984), published in English as *Doing Daily Battle* (1988), and *Le Harem Politique* (1987), currently being translated into English.

'Who's Cleverer, Man or Woman?' is a very popular Marrakesh folktale that Mernissi transcribed and published in Moroccan Arabic and French in 1983. It has numerous different titles including 'Men's Treachery, Women's Treachery', 'Aisha the Carpenter's Daughter', 'Aisha the Abandoned Living in The Grainroom'.

This tale is told by women to women. Mernissi published a version of this story in Robin Morgan's *Sisterhood is Global* (1984) under the title 'The Merchant's Daughter and the Son of the Sultan.'

Who's Cleverer: Man or Woman?

❧

> There was and there was
> There was basil and there were lilies
> which grew everywhere.

Once upon a time there was a carpenter who had a daughter named Aisha. She gave great care to the basil she was growing on her terrace and she watered it incessantly. The son of the king noticed the young woman and got into the habit of spying on her. He wanted to know her name and found out she was called Aisha. He, therefore, decided to speak to her.
He said to her:

> Lalla Aisha, daughter of the carpenter,
> you who tend and water the basil,
> Do you know how many leaves does the stem hold?

She said to him:

> Sidi Muhammad, son of the king
> you who have studied the book of God
> tell me how many stars are in the sky
> how many fish in the water
> And dots in the Quran!

The prince was suprised and upset by her rejoinder. 'She's mocking me,' he said to himself. He shut the window from which he watched the terrace and he went away. She did the same. The next day she watered the basil again. The prince watched as he had before. On this day Aisha's household was preparing *anhamca*. Someone called her but she wanted to eat the soup on the terrace. It was brought to her in a bowl. She was eating it when a dumpling fell on her breast. She caught it and ate it. The prince was elated. 'I will remind her of this incident.' The next day as she was going up to water the basil, he said:

> Lalla Aisha, daughter of the carpenter
> you who tend and water the basil
> do you know how many leaves does the stem hold?

She replied:

> Sidi Muhammad, son of the king
> you who have studied the book of God
> tell me how many stars are in the sky
> how many fish in the ocean
> and dots in the Quran!

He said to her:

> Remember, you ill-bred glutton
> you didn't hesitate to gobble up a poor lost dumpling
> that fell on your breast
> and you ate it up.

'This young man is always watching me,' she thought. And so for two days she stayed out of sight. She passed much of her time spying on the prince. Finally, she surprised him at a merchant's where he was eating pomegranates. She watched him carefully. He ate happily. Suddenly a seed fell and rolled on the ground to the door of the store. He stooped, retrieved the seed and ate it. Lalla Aisha hurried home. The next morning she rushed up to the terrace to water her basil. The prince was there and said:

> Lalla Aisha, daughter of the carpenter
> you who tend and water the basil
> do you know how many leaves does the stem hold?

She replied:

> Sidi Muhammad, son of the king
> you who have studied the book of God
> tell me how many stars are in the sky
> how many fish in the ocean
> and dots in the Quran!

He said to her:

> Remember, you ill-bred glutton
> You didn't hesitate to gobble up a poor lost dumpling
> that fell on your breast
> and you ate it up!

She responded to him:

> Remember, you ill-bred glutton!
> You didn't hesitate to gobble up a poor pomegranate seed
> that had rolled to the store door
> And you devoured it!

'My God! This young woman is spying on me . . .' He spied on her more discreetly. One day when he was in front of his home, a Jew showed up with a donkey loaded with fish to sell. The prince offered to buy everything – the donkey, the fish and even his clothes. The merchant gladly accepted the deal. The prince, disguised as a Jewish merchant, went to sell his fish in front of Lalla Aisha's home. 'Fish! Fish! Who wants to buy fish!' He praised his goods loudly until Aisha appeared on the doorstep:

> Hey, Jew! Are you selling fish!
> Yes, Lalla! That's what I'm selling.
> How much?
> A kiss on the cheek will be enough.

She was tempted: 'No one's looking. Why not?' She offered her cheek and in return he offered her the donkey and all of the fish. Then he left. She returned to her home with the fish, distributed it to everyone, and let the donkey go free in the street. After this adventure, she didn't do anything for two days. The third day she went up to the terrace and the prince said to her:

> Lalla Aisha, daughter of the carpenter
> you who tend and water the basil
> do you know how many leaves does the stem hold?

She replied:

> Sidi Muhammad, son of the king
> you who have studied the book of God
> tell me how many stars are in the sky
> how many fish in the ocean
> and dots in the Quran!

He said to her:

> Remember, you ill-bred glutton
> You didn't hesitate to gobble up a poor lost dumpling
> that fell on your breast
> and you ate it up.

She responded to him:

> Remember, you ill-bred glutton!
> You did not hesitate to gobble up a poor pomegranate seed
> That had rolled to the store door.
> And you devoured it!

He said to her:

> There was a fish-vendor
> and he kissed the cheek of the carpenter's daughter.

'Lord have mercy!' She cried in amazement. The next day she asked her father to buy her black dye. For seven days she applied it and her skin became black like that of an African woman, a real African slave. She asked her father to take her to the market to sell her. Her father was afraid and absolutely refused. But she insisted, 'Please take me to the market and sell me. Don't worry about me.' So the next day he took her to market and sold her. And guess who bought her? The prince! He took her home, gave her to one of his slaves to be washed and prepared and be brought up to his rooms.

But Lalla Aisha refused to be washed. She assured everyone that she was perfectly clean. She prepared herself for the prince and in the evening she was taken up to his rooms. She spent pleasant moments with him. They played and amused each other very much. The prince never suspected that she had brought with her a razor, a mirror, rouge, a long radish and a sleep inducing herb called *sikran*. When she prepared his tea she put several drops of *sikran* in the brew. As soon as he tasted it he fell fast asleep. She took out her razor and removed the prince's fine beard. She then put rouge on his cheeks, put kohl in his eyes and put the radish in his bottom. Finally she put the mirror in front of his face and left quickly.

It was a long time before the prince opened his eyes. He had been asleep for three long days. When he finally awoke, he looked in horror at his image in the mirror: his shaven beard, his painted eyes and cheeks. He also felt the harsh presence of the radish. He searched for the woman who had been his companion. Nowhere was she to be found! 'God knows who could have pulled this on me!' And the prince locked himself in for seven days, while he waited for his beard to grow back. He carefully got rid of every trace of the make-up and paid special attention to his attire.

During this time Aisha had returned to her home. Each day, she went up to the terrace to inspect her neighbour's windows. When would they open again? Finally, sure enough! He showed up.

He said to her:

Lalla Aisha, daughter of the carpenter
you who tend and water the basil
Do you know how many leaves does the stem hold?

She replied:

Sidi Muhammad, son of the king
you who have studied the book of God
tell me how many stars are in the sky
how many fish in the ocean
and dots in the Quran!

He said to her:

> Remember, you ill-bred glutton
> You didn't hesitate to gobble up a poor lost dumpling
> that fell on your breast
> and you ate it up.

She responded to him:

> Remember, you ill-bred glutton!
> You didn't hesitate to gobble up a poor pomegranate seed
> That had rolled to the store door.
> And you devoured it!

He said to her:

> There was a fish-vendor
> and he kissed the cheek of the carpenter's daughter.

She replies:

> There was a slave
> sold in the market
> who messed with the prince's face and bottom . . .

The prince was stupefied. 'So she's the one who mocked me like this.' On the next day, he went to ask his father, the sultan, to ask for the hand of the carpenter's daughter. The sultan was surprised:
'You ignore the daughters of vizirs, you neglect your own cousins and you choose the daughter of a carpenter!'
'I will marry no one but her,' his son replied firmly. 'I want her, no matter the price. No matter what the conditions!'
Therefore, the king asked for the hand of the carpenter's daughter for his son. The carpenter told his daughter the news immediately. 'Father, give him my hand,' she told him. He tried to dissuade her. She insisted, 'Give him my hand.' He agreed but demanded a fairly high dowry. The king gave it to him immediately. When the marriage was confirmed, Aisha gave her father instructions:
'You know the king's palace. Well, you must dig a tunnel between our house and the palace.'
And so it was done. The carpenter hired some masons who dug a tunnel that connected the two homes. A little while afterwards the prince set the wedding date. He brought his fiancée and moved her into the palace.
When they were alone he said to her: 'You have mocked and ridiculed me!'

'Yes! I'm the one who did it.'

'And now tell me,' he said to her, 'Who is cleverer, man or woman?'

'Woman, my Lord,' she replied.

He was angry and decided to lock her up in the grain room underground. Each day he went to see her in her prison. He brought her a loaf of barley bread, some olives, a jar of water and asked her: 'Aisha, the Defeated, living in the grain room, who is cleverer man or woman?'

'Woman, my Lord.'

As soon as he heard this, he left her. Days and days passed this way. The carpenter, alarmed at his daughter's silence, searched for some news. He found that the prince had locked up Lalla Aisha in a cellar. He met with the masons and told them to unblock the entrance to the tunnel that connected the house to the palace. He demanded that they dig it to the cellar where his daughter was imprisoned. So it was. Lalla Aisha could now come home to sleep comfortably in her father's home. She re-entered the cellar at dawn and the prince never knew. He continued to visit her regularly and each time asked the ritual question.

'Who is cleverer, man or woman?'

'Woman, my Lord.'

One day he came to see her and told her that he was going on a *nzaha* in Sour. She wished him good luck and asked when he was leaving. He told her Friday after next. She went by way of the tunnel to her father and said, 'You must find me a woman to henna my hands for a wedding. I also want a very pretty tent and people to guard it.'

Her father granted her wishes. That Thursday evening, when the prince told his wife he was leaving, she solicitously wished him good luck again and never let on about her plan. When he left, she returned to her father's home.

'My tent must be up in Sour before the prince's is.'

So it was. When the prince arrived at Sour, he saw a beautiful tent set in the middle of the fields and guarded by slaves. 'But who beat me to it here?' he asked, very intrigued. His tent was pitched nearby. The prince called one of his slaves and sent him to find out who was the owner of this mysterious tent. The slave was stopped by Lalla Aisha's guards. He asked them who was there. 'Our mistress,' they replied. The messenger told the prince that the tent owner was a woman. The prince summoned Lalla Aisha. She told the messenger that the prince should know a woman never goes to a man. It is the man who must always go to the woman.

So the prince prepared himself and went to join her in her tent.

They talked for a long time, they drank . . . They denied themselves nothing. They stayed together for three days . . . or perhaps
seven. When the prince finally decided to leave, he offered one of
his rings to Lalla Aisha. When he left, the young woman ordered
camp to be struck before the prince had time to leave the area.
Before leaving, he glanced over and the famous tent had simply
disappeared into thin air. 'Where's this woman now?' he asked his
servants. 'She has disappeared,' was all they could answer.

As soon as he had returned to the palace, he visited Lalla Aisha
in her cellar and said: 'Aisha the defeated, living in the grain room,
you missed a beautiful *nzaha*.'

'I'm glad, my Lord, you had a good time', she replied.

'You should have seen the marvel I met. What a woman!'

'I am thrilled that my Lord had such a charming *nzaha*.'

He left. As for her, she realised she was pregnant and some
months later she gave birth to a son, whom she named Sour. At
night she kept herself busy with the baby, during the day she left it
in her father's home and stayed in her cellar. The prince visited
regularly. He never forgot to bring barley bread, olives and water
and he always asked the ritual question, 'Who is cleverer, man or
woman?'

Invariably she answered 'Woman, my Lord'.

One morning he came to announce that he was leaving right
away for a *nzaha* in Dour. Aisha again asked her father for the
services of a woman to dye her hands with henna, a tent and some
people. The tent was to be different from the first one. She
decorated her hands, and put on her most beautiful garments. She
ordered the tent to be set up before the prince's arrival and settled
in. The prince was as surprised as he had been at Sour that
someone had preceded him. He sent a messenger to find out who
was in the tent. He was told it was a woman. The prince invited her
to join him. But she sent a message to him: 'I do not go to another's
home. Whoever wants to see me must come to me.' So he went and
stayed with her for seven days. On the day he left he gave her his
dagger.

No sooner had he left than Lalla Aisha ordered everything to be
taken down, and she left before the prince. When the prince's
slaves awoke, they could find no trace of the mysterious woman. 'A
woman who acts like that must be, without a doubt, a *jinn*! She can't
be human!' they said.

The prince left Dour and returned to his palace where he visited
Lalla Aisha in her cellar. He brought her the usual black bread,
olives and water and asked her the eternal question: 'Aisha, the
Defeated, living in a grain room, who is cleverer, man or woman?'

'Woman, my Lord.'

He said to her: 'The *nzaha* was terrific. Even better than last time. I met a wonderful woman. I've never seen such beauty.'

'My Lord is worthy of it.'

He left her, quite pleased with himself. A few days later she knew she was pregnant again. When she was reaching the end of her term, she went to her father's home and she gave birth to a second boy whom she named Dour. A little later, the prince came to see her and as always asked the same question. 'Aisha, the Defeated, living in a grain room, who is cleverer, man or woman?'

'Woman, my Lord,' she answered.

'I am going on a *nzaha* to Lalla Hammamat Laqur,' he told her.

'Have fun,' she said.

She asked when he was leaving. He told her the next week. So Lalla Aisha prepared and set up a tent as before. His response was the same. As before, the prince sent a messenger to her. He returned to his master and announced that it was the same woman. The prince told his messenger to have her come to him this time. Lalla Aisha said, 'I will go to no one. If the prince wants to see me, he will come here.'

They spent a very pleasant week together. When he announced his plans to leave, Lalla Aisha wished him a good trip. He gave her his *dalil* before leaving.

Lalla Aisha returned home. She was pregnant a third time. She gave birth to a little girl and named her Lalla Hammamat Laqur.

Months passed. One day, the sultan decided his son should marry. The prince protested, 'I don't really feel like getting married, father.' But the sultan insisted. 'It's absolutely necessary that you marry. I've asked for your cousin's hand.' When the marriage date was set, the prince went to visit his wife.

'Aisha, the Defeated, who lives in a grain room, do you know that my father is marrying me off?'

'To whom?' she asked.

'My cousin!'

'Good luck, my Lord,' she answered.

She inquired about the date of the marriage and found out it was to be the very next day. She gathered her children and carefully fixed their hair and dressed them in their nicest clothes. She gave the ring to the first child, the dagger to the second and the *dalil* to the third. She ordered them to go to the palace where preparations for the wedding were going on, and to turn things upside down, to take the covers off the cushions and to do as much damage as possible. And if anyone tried to stop them they were to repeat the following words:

'This is our father's home and some sons of bitches are driving us out of it.'

And if someone demand that they leave? Lalla Aisha taught them a phrase by which they were to address each other:

'Come, Sour, come, Dour, come, Lalla Hammamat Laqur. Let's go to our mother, Aisha the Defeated, who lives in a grain room.'

When all was ready, Lalla Aisha asked her father to take her children to the palace and leave them at the front entrance. And so it was. When the three children entered the palace, people remarked on their elegance and finery. 'Are they children of vizirs? Children of a friend of the king?' The children set about their task according to their mother's instructions. They attacked and tore up the cushions in the salon prepared for the prince's fiancée. The palace servants tried to stop the children, but in vain. They didn't dare slap the children but tried to persuade them to stop. All they would say to those who tried to reason with them was:

'This is our father's home, and some sons of bitches are driving us out of it.'

Tired of the battle, the palace servants called the prince. He heard the children say to each other:

'Come, Sour, come, Dour, come, Lalla Hammamat Laqur. Let's go to our mother, Aisha the Defeated, who lives in the grain room.'

Intrigued, he asked who they were and they said:

'We are the children of Aisha the Defeated who lives in the grain room.'

More and more intrigued, he asked their names:

'Sour,' responded the first.

'Dour,' said the second, 'and this is my sister Lalla Hammamat Laqur.'

The prince was dumbfounded. He recognised his ring on the first, his dagger on the second, and his *dalil* on the little girl. Then he understood and ran to the grain room. He leant toward Lalla Aisha:

'Aisha the Defeated, who lives in a grain room, who is cleverer, man or woman?'

'Woman, my Lord,' she replied.

'Then give me your hand and come with me.'

She gave her hand to the prince. He freed her from her prison. Lalla Aisha took a long bath, scrubbed herself and put on her finest clothes. It was only minutes before the prince's cousin was to take the place prepared for her! It was then that Lalla Aisha appeared. The prince pushed his cousin aside to make room for Lalla Aisha. And on that day there was an extraordinary feast that woke the dead and they said: 'Get up to celebrate the feast of Lalla Aisha the

Defeated, daughter of the carpenter, who had been held prisoner in the cellar.'

Khalinahum kaiaklu ihdid
w-hna jina naklu trid.
They were left there to eat iron
And we came here to eat pancakes.

Translated from the Arabic and French
by Miriam Cooke and Elise Goldwasser

Chaibia

(1929–)

Chaibia was born in Marrakesh, Morocco. She was married at the age of thirteen. Her first exhibition was held in 1969 in the Casablanca Goethe Institut. She was forty years old at the time. In the same year she also showed in Paris. Subsequently, she has had at least one show a year in France, usually in Paris. Other exhibitions have been organised in Denmark (1969, 1980), Germany (1969), Spain (1974, 1985), USA (1987). She has participated twice in the cultural festival held every summer at Asila. Her powerful murals in Asila have aroused interest as well as some controversy.

This text is based on an interview with Fatima Mernissi in Casablanca, January 1985. Chaibia calls for a sisterhood in which privileged women help others who have not been as fortunate.

My Life

1985

❦

At fifteen I was widowed . . . I was illiterate.

They changed my birthdate so that the wedding could take place. I was thirteen. Then I had a son. My husband died in an accident. I was his seventh wife. I had to survive. I put my son in school. It cost me sixty rials. You see, I was illiterate. My son had to escape from that. I began working with wool, I bought it, washed it, spun it and gave it to a friend who sold it for me. I could have married, of course, I had a lot of offers. But I was afraid it would be somebody who would ill-treat the child and I wanted to live in freedom.

You will find all this in my painting
Listen! don't forget that I am a peasant . . . but that is not all. You must know the rest, otherwise you would not understand my success. You have to know that when I was little I used to do unusual things. I used to make flower crowns and wear them . . . no other girl did that . . . nobody ever did that in the *choutka*. They treated me as crazy. I was crazy for red poppies and daisies. They found me strange, they said: you are queer, like a *Nasranya* (means Christian, different, the enemy).

You must understand, it's important, not being afraid to be different. Don't forget that at that time people were afraid of *Nsara* (Christians, i.e. the French, who were the occupants). They ran away as soon as the *Nsara* approached. I did not. I watched them when they came fishing at the seaside. At the seaside I liked to build houses with stones and shells. I gave them windows and doors. We lived in a tent. But me, I drew them, before I even saw them. I drew houses on the sand. My father took me one day to the city, I was six years old, I was fascinated by the beauty of the decorations on the walls . . . the clocks . . . everything you can hang on a wall . . . I collected pieces of paper and I used to make birds and animals with this paper. I was always fascinated by animals. Do you know how many turtles I have in this garden, right in the centre of Casablanca? Five or six, who knows, nobody counts them anymore. I also love birds, very much. But it was not this love that disturbed people. It's the fact that I covered myself with flowers. My family tried to stop that. They hit me. I ran away. I vanished into haystacks. You do not know what it is to hide in a haystack when fresh rain falls down. You find all that in my painting. How did I became an artist? You know, each of us has his way traced for him.

Before I painted, different events decided my future: a meeting in a *zawiyya*, a feeling and a dream. One day I visited the Moulay Bouchaib *zawiyya*. A holy man saw me and said 'You, you are *mbouhla* (from another planet) you will bring us *baraka* (luck). Pray for us.

Then in the sanctuary, I enjoyed the beauty of the decorated columns and walls. Then a woman came to me . . . she was dressed in her *haik* [a white wrap that Moroccan women used to wear before they changed into the *djellaba*, which is a man's dress. The change from the *haik* to the *djellaba* represents the same change as European women's dresses to trousers]. That woman was deaf and mute. She communicated through gestures, she drew on the wall. I understood what she said. She said I had a talent, that I would accomplish things, create . . .

I dreamt of a blue sky full of colours . . .
I dreamt, just there in the small room near the garden. I was home, the sky was blue, full of colours flashing in the wind, like a storm. From the bedroom to the door, through all the garden, there were lighted candles. The door was open. Men in white came in. They brought me paintbrushes and canvas. There were many young men and two old men with long beards. They said to me: this is your bread-winner. What could an illiterate woman do for a living, what do you think? I was a maid, a house maid. I cleaned houses, and floors . . . I felt I had to do something. I told my sister about the dream, it had to happen. Two days later, I went to the medina and bought paint, the kind you use to paint doors, but that was not important.

My son Talal had a studio, I watched him painting. I always complained when he came home covered with paint. One day, he found *me* all covered with paint. He asked me what was I doing. I said I was painting. He told me to continue. One day Pierre Gaudibert, the director of a modern art museum in Paris, came home with Cherkaoui, a Moroccan artist. They liked my painting. They asked me to show them the rest.

On 8 March 1984, we were invited to celebrate the Year of the Woman at the Ministry of Culture. I went but nobody paid any attention to me. The same year I was invited to France. One hundred and seven women from all over the world were invited as artists. They chose one of my paintings to make a poster. (That was for the exhibition organised in March 1984 by the municipal gallery of Vitry-sur-Seine about women's rights, with the subject: 'A Woman's Role in Contemporary Art'.)

It touched me very much. An artist like me needs that.

Educated women have to take care of us who did not have an education
There must be a joint responsibility between women who were lucky to go to school and those who were not. An educated woman has to help the others, otherwise how can we change society. Morocco will not advance if those who have privileges forget the others. Every time I sell a picture I give to the poor people a part of my earnings. God sees everything, but I see that between women there is no joint responsibility. The educated don't pay attention to the illiterate. What are they doing for them? We have to share in order to progress. I loved it when an educated woman tried to teach me, tried to share something with me. I like to learn and when you have not been to school it is an obsession. When I was a little girl I leaned close to the radio. I wanted people to shut up when a teacher, a minister, a king was talking. At home nobody could be silent when somebody else was talking, I used to say, 'Are you crazy? Don't you want to go beyond ignorance?'

The Muslim sisters are wrong
I have always been a mystic. Even when very young, I used to pray. But I also wanted to be modern. I moved around, was curious about everything. I wanted to learn French to understand what life was about. I didn't stay in a corner like the Muslim sisters of today. Religion helps to organise life but must not be interpreted incorrectly. The other day, at the market, I met a Muslim sister; she couldn't breathe because her face was covered with so many scarves. I told her: 'Do you want to create a new religion? Do you want to change the Prophet's message? He wanted education for Arab women. With the veil we are like donkeys. The French people occupied the country and the women didn't realise what happened. The veil and walls made them *hmarat* (donkeys). Our mothers were maids for the French.

'Muhammad V (the father of the present King Hassan II) changed that. He gave us education and dignity and you Muslim sisters, you want to take us back to the dark age. Now that the Moroccan women are doctors, lawyers and we have begun to be proud of ourselves, you want to give us the *hijab*. It's not Muhammad who wanted that. He was angry when somebody humiliated a woman.'

Translated from the Arabic
by Fatima Mernissi

Sufi Abdallah

(1925–)

Sufi Abdallah was born in al-Faium, Egypt. She had a private Arabic tutor from the age of seven, and later attended British, French and Italian girls' schools. She began to write short stories in 1942, and won the first prize for literature from the Cultural Administration of the Ministry of Education in 1947. From 1948 until 1975 she worked as editor and contributed short stories to a number of Dar al-Hilal's magazines and journals. At the same time, she published synopses of foreign novels and plays in the monthly magazine, *Al-Hilal*. Between 1955 and 1975 she wrote short stories and edited a column called 'Your Problem' for the women's magazine *Hawa*. In 1951, her play *Kasabna al-Brimu* (We Got the First Prize) was performed in the Opera by the New Theatre Company. She has published twelve short story collections which include *Kulluhuna Aisha* (All of Them are Aisha) Cairo, 1956, *Baqaya Rajul* (The Remains of a Man) Beirut, 1958, *Madrasat al-Banat* (The Girls' School) Cairo, 1959, *Nisf Imraa* (Half a woman) Cairo, 1962, *Layalin laha Thaman* (Nights with a Price), 1964, *Arbaat Rijal Wafata* (Four Men and a Girl), 1973, *Shay Aqwa Minha* (Something Stronger Than Her), 1975. Her five novels include *Nefertiti* Cairo, 1952, *Lanat al-Jased* (The Curse of the Body), 1957, *Asifa fi al-Qalb* (A Storm in the Heart), 1961. She has also published two collections of biographies of women: *Nisa Muharibat* (Fighting Women), 1951 and *Nawabigh al-Nisa* (Exemplary Women) 1964.

'Eight Eyes' is taken from her collection *Something Stronger than Her*. The story is a feminist response to blood feud. A mother teaches her son values that do not allow him to follow the paths trodden by his forebears. His inability to do his family tribal duty, that is, to avenge his father's murder, is proof of the success of her teaching which is subversive of patriarchal norms.

Eight Eyes

1975

✿

Night approached. In its captivating silence, Ismail gave in to slumber. Minutes. Who knows? Maybe seconds. A few seconds. Then he opened his eyes, panting as though he had been chased. Yet he was a peaceful man. He had lived his life far from the village in a huge city where he had studied at school and in university . . . And now he was awaiting the nomination speech.

He tossed and turned in bed, the sweat moist on his brow . . . his limbs chilled and the atmosphere suffocating. His thoughts were feverish as he lay there wide awake. The room was pitch black without the slightest glimmer to break the harshness of this frightening ghoul that was spreading its shadow over everything around him.

Everything became solid in front of him. The night was dark, merciless. The emptiness of the room turned into eyes. Stupid eyes that stared at him curiously, questioningly, accusingly.

What was he waiting for? Twenty years had passed . . . twenty years of prolonged waiting. What was he waiting for? It would have been best had he dealt with the matter as soon as he had become a man and was able to carry arms.

Behind him he felt the eyes bearing down on his humble back like daggers, as though to say: The young man is spineless. A city education. Hasanain did not have a son. He had two daughters: Haniya and Ismail. Your youth has been wasted, Hasanain.

That's what the contemptuous, hateful eyes were saying as they looked at him in silence. That's how the man had looked at him when he had seen him sitting with his mother when he had returned. They had had the strangest exchange after his mother had introduced the man as Mahrus the Kurd. His eyes were flashing as he said: 'The village is waiting for you, Ismail . . .'

He spoke quietly, yet the weight behind these words did not escape Ismail.

His feet were rooted to the spot as he turned heavily from the man to his mother and from her to him. She sat like a poor little mouse in front of a wild cat. Her hands were clasped in her lap in complete submission. Her eyes fixed on a spot in the rug with the ornate edge.

Mahrus the Kurd. His father's cousin. He had seen him only once in his life. That was before he had left the village with his mother to go to the city and after his father had been killed in a blood feud. He carried him on his shoulder and gave him a glance that pursued him throughout the following years. Words like fire came out of his lips: 'Ismail, some day you'll return to the village to avenge your father!'

Thereafter his mother never once explained why his father had been killed. Whenever he mentioned the matter she quickly changed the subject. After her husband's murder she had returned to the regional capital with her son Ismail and her daughter Haniya to live with her family.

But a blood feud is a blood feud, and the Upper Egyptians do not forgive cowardice. A son cannot let his father's blood go unavenged. The man's speech was burning as he ate lunch with them. In the afternoon, other men joined him. Three. Three of the strong ones. What they said sounded extremely strange to the young man from the capital who had not set foot on Upper Egyptian soil since his childhood. They agreed with him on the exact date on which he would go to the village. They would prepare everything for him: the weapons and the cloak and all that he needed. But first of all they would introduce him to the victim, the individual who had been chosen. This would take place during a dinner party that they would hold for him. They would take care of the whole affair, they would keep him until his companion had left. Then, as he was returning, he would be there waiting for him in the cornfield. He would shoot him with a rifle and return immediately and the red *jinn* would not find out.

'In other words, there's no anger between you and the individual for whom you are holding the feast and on whom the choice has fallen. Like me, he's victim to an ancient feud about which no one knows anything.'

The eight eyes turned on him, eyes flashing fire as though they were whipping his face. Mahrus shouted:

'Are we to understand from your words that you are flinching from your father's revenge?'

He responded haltingly: 'Hasn't justice run its course?'

Suddenly the ground shook as the four men jumped to their feet as one. The ground shook under their firm feet. They wrapped themselves in their blankets with which they partially covered their faces. Then they followed each other out without looking at or addressing the mother and her son. Rather they looked through them in a silence that was filled with challenge. They stomped out of the large room and down the stone steps.

What a dark night, and the eight eyes almost scorched him with their burning glances.

He tossed and turned, trying to chase away the devil and to sleep. He tried. But finally he leapt out of bed, dressed quickly and opening the door on to the street stole out so as not to disturb his mother.

In the village they were awaiting him. They introduced him to the victim. He was a gentle young man. He felt a shudder that soon dissolved in the atmosphere and which gave him a courage that he had never felt. At a signal from Mahrus he disappeared without anyone noticing. He hid among the corn awaiting his rival. He had wound a scarf around the turban and had the rifle in his hand.

At the first light of dawn he heard the sound of footsteps. He prepared himself, opened his eyes wide, gathered his courage and then his rival appeared. He pulled the trigger and felled him.

The victim uttered a scream at which the blood in Ismail's veins froze. He gathered all his forces and flew off as though chased by the devil. He bumped into something; it hurt and he could not hold back a cry of pain.

He bent over his leg to take a look. Shivering with fear, his terrified eyes swept the darkness around him. The iron leg of the bed – that was what he had bumped into. He sat up and rubbed his eyes. Pouring with sweat, he stared around again.

From deep within him emerged a sigh of relief. In fury, he spat out the bitterness that had collected in his mouth, as though trying to put out the fire in the eight eyes.

The door opened on his mother with her hair dishevelled. She turned on the light and held out her arms in anxiety and grief.

'Ismail, what's wrong? I heard you scream.'

He curled up to make room for her on the edge of the bed.

'Nothing, mother. I had a dreadful dream, really dreadful!'

She looked at him questioningly and her frown increased.

'His eyes were innocent, modest like two doves. Yet the eight eyes continued to chase me and burn my breast with their looks: Be a man, Ismail. Be a man!'

'So I pulled the trigger. Mother, I don't know which one of us screamed the loudest, I or he. . . .'

He shut his eyes. Silently, she stretched out her veined hand to caress his knee.

'Mother, why did God make me a man?'

Her look changed from affection to reproach mixed with pain.

'I've wasted your education, Ismail. I've wasted my life trying to make you into a leader.'

He looked at her in anxiety and confusion.

'A leader, mother? Look, how I'm sweating at a dream in which I tried to do what men do!'

She looked at him with greater reproach as though she had been dealt a treacherous wound.

'I kept silent, Ismail, to give you the freedom of choice and action. I was hoping that you would recognise the truth yourself. And that I would not have educated you in vain. But it seems that you are still not perceptive.'

Her grasp on his knee tightened as though she wanted to plant her fingers with her words into his flesh.

'Man is one thing and animals another. The difference between them is a difference of conscience and barbarism. The difference between them is attested to by the sweat of fear at the barbarism of animals that they wanted to force on you in the name of virility. But I – the mother – I knew more about virility than they. I made you turn your back on the law of the jungle.'

He cast her a long, relieved look, and then slowly smiled.

Translated from the Arabic
by Miriam Cooke

Huda Shaarawi

(1879–1947)

In Cairo in 1944, the Arab Feminist Conference inaugurated
organised collective articulation of pan-Arab feminist ideology and
demands. Delegates came from Egypt, Iraq, Lebanon, Palestine,
Syria, and Trans-Jordan. They included women teachers, journalists and government employees. The Conference produced fifty-
one resolutions addressing political, social and economic goals with
a stress on gender equality within pan-Arab unity. A resolution
aiming at eliminating gender distinctions in language calling for
the omission of feminine endings from Arabic words (which caused
some derision at the time) foreshadowed more recent attempts in
other languages, such as English, to eradicate sexism in language.
In 1945 the Arab Feminist Union was created, as the women
pointed out, before the establishment of the Arab League. The
Union started *The Magazine of the Arab Woman* with Amina Said, the
secretary of the organisation, as editor.

The following selections which we entitle 'Pan-Arab Feminism',
are taken from the opening and closing speeches of Huda Shaarawi, president of The Egyptian Feminist Union which hosted the
Arab Feminist Conference.

Pan-Arab Feminism

1944
❧

Huda Shaarawi

The Opening Speech
Ladies and Gentlemen, The Arab woman who is equal to the man
in duties and obligations will not accept, in the twentieth century,
the distinctions between the sexes that the advanced countries have
done away with. The Arab woman will not agree to be chained in
slavery and to pay for the consequences of men's mistakes with
respect to her country's rights and the future of her children. The
woman also demands with her loudest voice to be restored her
political rights, rights granted to her by the *Sharia* and dictated to
her by the demands of the present. The advanced nations have
recognised that the man and the woman are to each other like the
brain and heart are to the body; if the balance between these two
organs is upset the system of the whole body will be upset.
Likewise, if the balance between the two sexes in the nation is upset
it will disintegrate and collapse. The advanced nations, after
careful examination into the matter, have come to believe in the
equality of sexes in all rights even though their religious and
secular laws have not reached the level Islam has reached in terms
of justice towards the woman. Islam has given her the right to vote
for the ruler and has allowed her to give opinions on questions of
jurisprudence and religion. The woman, given by the Creator the
right to vote for the successor of the Prophet, is deprived of the
right to vote for a deputy in a circuit or district election by a (male)
being created by God. At the same time, this right is enjoyed by a
man who might have less education and experience than the
woman. And she is the mother who has given birth to the man and
has raised him and guided him. The *Sharia* gave her the right to
education, to take part in the *hijra* (referring to the time of the
Prophet Muhammad and his flight from Mecca to Medina), and to
fight in the ranks of warriors and has made her equal to the man in
all rights and responsibilities, even in the crimes that either sex can
commit. However, the man who alone distributes rights, has kept
for himself the right to legislate and rule, generously turning over
to his partner his own share of responsibilities and sanctions
without seeking her opinion about the division. The woman today
demands to regain her share of rights that have been taken from

her and gives back to the man the responsibilities and sanctions he has given to her. Gentlemen, this is justice and I do not believe that the Arab man who demands that the others give him back his usurped rights would be avaricious and not give the woman back her own lawful rights, all the more so since he himself has tasted the bitterness of deprivation and usurped rights.

Whenever the woman has demanded her rights in legislation and ruling to participate with the man in all things that bring good and benefit to her nation and her children, he claims he wants to spare the woman the perils of election battles, forgetting that she is more zealous about the election of deputies than men and that she already participates in election battles, quite often influencing the results. It is strange that in these cases she becomes the subject of his respect and kindness but when the election battle subsides he denies her what she has brought about.

If the man is sincere in what he says let him prove this by first giving the woman her political rights without her having to go through cruel political battles. In our parliamentary life there is wide opportunity for that in the elections of the governorates and municipality councils, and family affairs councils and in being appointed a member of the senate. Gentlemen, I leave room for the conferees to defend the rights of the woman in all areas.

The closing speech
In this final session of the conference please allow me, on behalf of myself and the conference organisers, to thank you for honouring us with your sustained presence during the four days of this conference despite the length of the sessions dealing with issues men are often ill at ease with. I thank you for the concern you have expressed on these matters and for the attention you have given to our objectives, a successful step on the road towards realising our demands. We are proud of this step which signals, thanks be to God, that we have gained the confidence of male intellectuals and reformers in the demonstrated abilities of women in effectively carrying out different kinds of work in the service of country and nation. There are some who still hesitate to give us this confidence and do not understand the benefits that accrue to the nation when women enjoy their political rights. Others fear that the women will compete with them in work. Let me assure you all that if depriving women of the political and civil rights they demand, and that men oppose, would benefit the country, or would increase men's rights, we would relinquish them with pleasure, but, unfortunately, they would be lost rights that men could not use for themselves or for the country. These rights, buried alive, are of no benefit to society.

Every woman who does not stand up for her legitimate rights would be considered as not standing up for the rights of her country and the future of her children and society. Every man who is pushed by his selfishness to trespass on the legitimate rights of women is robbing the rights of others and bringing harm to his country. He is an obstacle preventing the country from benefiting from the abilities and efforts of half the nation or more. He is impeding the advancement of his country and preventing it from being placed in the position it deserves – among the advanced nations whose civilisation was built on the shoulders of women and men together, just as Arab civilisation at the beginning of Islam was built on the co-operation and equality of the two sexes. Now after this feminist conference and the presentation of the cause of women to the public and the placing of its documents in a historical archive, it is incumbent upon man to record on his own page in the historical record that which will honour him and justify his stand before God, the nation, and future generations.

Translated from the Arabic
by Ali Badran and Margot Badran

Zahiya Dughan

This is a speech to the Arab Feminist Conference on 13 December 1944 by Zahiyya Dughan, an educator and a delegate from Lebanon. Dughan calls for the establishment of chairs for women's studies departments in Arab universities. She also advocates the founding of a pan-Arab feminist journal, as well as the institution of women students and women faculty exchanges within the Arab world.

Arab Women's Intellectual Heritage

1944

༄

Our Arab countries have found the path of cultural co-operation easier and clearer than any other field. A glance at our past shows us that they have had long periods under the umbrella of a single culture and language. Each country in its own way has participated in creating this Arab culture and perfecting the Arabic language. Our present is an extension of our past. In every Arab country, irrespective of prevailing conditions and social and cultural variations, we have two streams of intellectual life: the inherited Arab stream and the intruding western stream. Among our main duties at this critical stage in our history is to collobarate in defining our stand on these two cultural streams. We in Lebanon, Syria, Iraq, and Egypt and other Arab countries should agree to a common plan for reviving our Arab heritage and adapting aspects of western culture, strengthening what is good in our heritage and borrowing what is good from western culture.

In this broad cultural effort we must call upon Arab governments, learned societies, and institutions. We must adopt a common position on our own women's heritage. I propose that the literary, political, and social history of the Arab woman and the current contributions and activities of the western woman be assembled in an Arab women's encyclopedia produced by our intellectuals. It will be a resource for educated women in the Arab world and for researchers wishing to study about women. This encyclopedia would enable educated Arab women to view the shining past of her sex, as well as the present condition of the western woman. I believe this would be one of the most fruitful moves towards a unified future. I invite all Arab universities, especially colleges of liberal arts to give the intellectual and literary heritage of the Arab woman the attention it deserves. We are loyal to this heritage in calling upon these universities to create special chairs in liberal arts faculties to promote the study of the literary works of Arab women and the numerous Arab women poets whose work is distinguished by its tenderness and range of feelings not found in the works of men.

Edited and translated from the Arabic
by Ali Badran and Margot Badran

Inji Aflatun

(1924–1989)

Inji Aflatun was born into an aristocratic family in Cairo. Educated in Cairo at the French Lycée, she began painting at an early age. Her mother had wanted to send her to Paris to study art but was concerned about her daughter's political interests. Soon after Aflatun's first exhibition in 1942 she joined the Communist group called al-Sharara, also known as Iskra. She went to Paris in 1945, not as an art student, but as a member of the Egyptian delegation to the World Congress of Women sponsored by the Democratic Federation of Women. That same year she helped found the University and Institutes Youth League and became a member of the National Executive of Workers and Students and the National Women's Committee.

In 1948, she wrote *Thananun Maliyun Imraa Maana* (Eighty Million Women With Us), a strong indictment of imperialism for which the Egyptian writer and Egyptian University dean, Taha Husain wrote a preface. In 1949, she published *Nahnu al-Nisa al-Misriyyat* (We Egyptian Women) which was an analysis of women's oppression and national oppression.

She joined the Movement of the Friends of Peace (*Harakat ansar al-salam*) in 1950 where she met Saiza Nabarawi of the Egyptian Feminist Union. Aflatun joined the youth group of the EFU working with poor women in Cairo. When fighting broke out in the Canal Zone in 1951 she joined the Popular Committee of Women's Resistance.

After the revolution of 1952, Aflatun continued her earlier writing for the liberal Wafdist paper, *Al-Misri*, and also wrote for *Al-Masa*. She worked with the Popular Committee of Women's Resistance during the 1956 tripartite invasion of Egypt. In 1959 during a massive round-up of Communists she was arrested and imprisoned. She continued to paint in prison preserving a powerful visual record of women's prison experience at Al-Kanatar, where al-Saadawi was later imprisoned. She was released in 1963. In 1975, at the start of the International Decade of Women, she helped organise, and participated in the large exhibition, 'Women Painters over Half a Century'. The Egyptian Ministry of Culture sponsored her final exhibition in December 1987. A member of

Tagammu, a leftist opposition party, she was writing her memoirs
when she died suddenly in 1989.

This selection is from *We Egyptian Women*, written during the
liberation struggle of the late 1940s and early 1950s, and the
accelerated battle for women's political rights.

We Egyptian Women

1949

❦

To the women of Egypt
To the ten million women who constitute one half of this people
The Egyptian woman peasant, worker, civil servant, young girl, wife and
mother
To our liberal writers: Qasim Amin, Abd al-Rahman al Rafiq, Taha
Husain, Salama Musa, Khalid Muhammad Khalid, Ismail Mazhar, whose
writings reflect their free conscience and not dissent and prejudices
To the young feminist movement
To the true militants of the Egyptian feminist cause, not the amateurs and
sycophants giving themselves airs and looking for personal profit, or those
crawling far behind
To the Egyptian woman, her supporters, men and women
I dedicate this book . . .

In Egypt today there is a fierce debate about women's rights, between those who uphold equality between men and women and those who oppose it. We are surrounded by the clamour of both groups.

Newspapers and reviews are full of articles expressing conflicting ideas. Although their abundance does not dry up, they are far from clearly presenting the true situation of women in modern Egyptian society. They all revolve around issues which are not supported by facts or based on tangible evidence. I do not suggest that it is the duty of the press to undertake this scientific analysis, supported by facts and based on material evidence. This is the duty of writers rather than newsmen. However, let us recognise here the real need of Egyptian literature for a true scientific study of the status of the Egyptian woman, her problems and her demands. It would be helpful to keep this bitter debate about women's rights a true and matter-of-fact discussion. The present book offered today to the reader is only a quick attempt and a modest contribution. It does not ignore the tumult over the woman issue, but rather explains more clearly and realistically the condition and status of the woman in Egyptian society.

There is no doubt that this book will not be viewed with favour by the enemies of woman, whom Qasim Amin rightly said are the enemies of progress and democracy. It is also certain that it will not be appreciated by certain feminists who pretend to defend the rights of the Egyptian woman but who are actually following in the footsteps of the enemies of woman, crawling behind them and looking only for honours and advantages befitting their elegant personages. The avowed enemies of women are those who proclaim 'Woman's liberation!' This originates in the play of words in which our opponents excel. The slogan 'woman at home' actually means the disruption of this home and the displacement of women and children, and husbands along with them. This means that there will be no contact between the woman working within the house and the society in which she lives. She will know nothing about it, she will not participate in any way in its administration and the solution of its problems. This means the subjection of women to the dominion of men which will result in the obliteration of their personality, dignity and humanity. Society will be deprived of the endeavours of half its members. This means depriving the home of an articulate mistress, conscious of her rights and duties towards her family and society, able to make her family the good and happy centre of a good and happy society.

But these arguments will not suffice to silence the enemies of women. The best way to counter their craft is to confront them with some concrete proofs and plain figures. This is what current Egyptian literature needs and this is the purpose of this book. Because it is their custom to hide behind the ramparts of tradition and religious custom and to use vague terms intended to sow doubt and confusion in people's minds, we invite our opponents to participate in an honest and open discussion.

A final word is needed to defend this book. Today the Egyptian people, on the eve of general elections, are about to be betrayed by its deputies and representatives, a betrayal of the democratic system. Indeed, the right of the Egyptian women to vote and to be elected should be requested at the start of a new age. The recognition of their oppressed rights would be an implementation of the principles of democracy of a representative regime.

I hope this book will fulfil its purpose and will help convince the public of the justice of women's demands and help free them from the fetters which have bound them in their private and public life. It would enable Egypt to join the countries which have granted women their rights and equality with men and enable the country to enter modern civilisation.

Woman and Political Rights
The Egyptian woman is deprived of political rights. She is denied

the right to vote or to run for Parliament. This deprivation is the worst of the prejudices which a woman has to endure in Egyptian society. This deprivation conflicts with the most basic principles of democracy. Democracy recognises the political rights of every member of society, without distinction between rich and poor, influential or otherwise, and advocates the participation of the people in the power structure through the mediation of representatives elected by them through universal suffrage. If we deprive half the members of the nation of the right to enjoy political rights, if we deprive half of the Egyptian people of the right to elect its representatives to parliamentary organisation through universal suffrage, we are going against the fundamental principles of a democratic regime, and will thus find ourselves faced with a demi-democracy instead of a total one. It is our duty to oppose this glaring violation of the principles of a representative regime, and to fill in the lacuna by granting the right to enjoy the privileges of democracy to the second half of society as well. Woman's participation in the political life of society constitutes an important element in a healthy democratic regime and a prime factor in the evolution and development of this society. Women in modern societies are not inactive members living on the fringe of life (as their enemies would like them to be) with no right to participate in politics or power. No, rather they constitute half of the people and have the same importance as the first half in the continued existence and development of society. We have proved that they can participate in every field of labour, culture and science on the same footing as man, and are able to be as productive as man while performing the best services.

It is not true that women constitute an isolated part of society, one which cannot feel its sufferings, its needs or formulate and give directives, thus rendering their participation in political life and power unnecessary. Quite the contrary, women are citizens who are particularly aware of economic, social and national problems. They understand the needs of their country and people, in internal and external matters. Every day they are confronted with the main problems of society, clothing, food, children, housing, health care, education, etc.

To deprive woman of her civil rights constitutes not only an injustice towards her, but also a harmful obstacle in the path of the development and evolution of the people, a lacuna in the country's democratic process.

Now let us listen to the wailings of the enemies of woman who deceive the public with their lies. From their ivory tower, these gentlemen claim that woman should not enjoy the same political rights as man, because this would lead to her degeneration, would make her neglect her duty to the home and children. Woman at home, woman always at home; that is their slogan. For the nth time let us tell these gentlemen that woman, whether they like it or not, has participated effectively in political life in most countries of the world. There is no way to prevent her from participating in various fields of activities, whether they like it or not.

Woman has obtained political rights in India, China and other countries with oriental traditions. Even so, no fanatic would have pretended that families over there were broken or ruined, or that the home in China has no proper structure any longer.

It would be absurd to pretend that woman's participation in universal suffrage once every five years would keep her away from her home, her family and her children. This would lead us to suggest that man's participation in this suffrage distracts him from the task entrusted him as well, whether he be a physician, engineer or civil servant. This would imply that universal suffrage constitutes an alienation for the totality of the population.

Let us follow these gentlemen through their wily reasoning. They pretend that what they mean is a female candidate for parliament and other high functions, such as minister, ambassador, etc. But we will always expose such impudent falsehoods. The fact that woman offers her candidacy to parliament or various diplomatic jobs constitutes only a job that woman accomplishes in society similar to the work of a teacher, physician or peasant. We have already shown the importance of woman's work. We have shown that the combination of running a home and a job is not an illusion. Our efforts to help woman in her work, by supplying her means to accomplish her double duty, will effectively render her 'a woman for society'.

On the other hand, it is frankly ridiculous to assert that the participation of women in parliament or other political offices would lead her to neglect her home and allow her children to go astray. After all, such arguments misinterpreted in this fashion force us to the conclusion that man's participation in parliament or ministries, be he a physician, professor, lawyer or worker, goes against the interest of medicine, teaching, law and industry. We would have to consider universal suffrage as a delaying factor in society's productivity. The theories of these gentlemen would thus lead us to disavow democracy, to destroy the principles of a parliamentary and representative government lest they prevent the whole people, male and female, from attending to their chores.

This is the clear proof that the enemies of woman are the fiercest enemies of democracy.

But these gentlemen return to the fray, stating that men who quit their jobs for politics leave their duties to others, and that thus productivity is not impaired. These arguments completely destroy their claims, since women fulfilling political functions can also entrust the tasks which they cannot accomplish at home and in their family to others.

Thus, this sterile discussion is closed. Is there anything more ridiculous than to ask an educated woman to devote herself to washing dishes, sweeping floors and cooking for the family? If she does not do it, people start whining. They claim that the home has been destroyed and that children have been thrown into the street. With no arguments left, the enemies of woman beat a retreat and look for excuses to justify their unrealistic opinions. Thus, it is not surprising to see these gentlemen raise another factor: Egyptian women are ignorant, illiteracy is twice as high among them as among men. It is easy to reject these faulty pretexts. People should not wait to enjoy democracy in order to learn. On the contrary, obscurantism will only be eradicated and education will only spread under a democratic regime. The Egyptian people realised this fact as a result of their painful experiences. British imperialism dominated Egypt for nearly forty years, during which time illiteracy increased among the people. When the victories of the national movement led to the signing of the 1923 constitution, a new era started; education spread and illiteracy decreased in spite of a tremendous population growth. When a parliamentary system was allowed by the 1923 constitution, the illiteracy rate among the Egyptian people exceeded by far the current rate among Egyptian women.

If these gentlemen mean that we have to deprive the people of its democratic rights and of a parliamentary government as well, all this on the pretext that it has a high rate of illiteracy, their theory is tantamount to a disavowal of democracy as well as the ruin of parliamentarism and popular representation.

This is additional proof, even more blatant, that the enemies of woman are also the enemies of democracy.

Today all our intellectual and political leaders are convinced that the political rights of women will inevitably have to be recognised sooner or later. But the enemies of democracy are fighting to invalidate women's rights. They are fighting to have voting rights granted only to the educated members of the Egyptian nation, both men and women. We are sorry to note that one of the leaders of the Egyptian feminist movement shares the dangerous opinion of these gentlemen and their destructive doctrines. In one of her calls, she has declared: 'How can you allow ignorant and illiterate men to take part in Egyptian political life, while depriving educated women of this same participation? Grant the educated woman her political rights; she deserves them more than illiterate men.'

We must draw attention to the dangers hidden in such views. The opinions held by these gentlemen mean the limitation of political rights to an educated minority of the members of the nation, men and women. This would bring about the destruction of our democratic government rather than its fulfilment. The majority of men in Egypt would be deprived of political rights in exchange for the granting of these same rights to a small minority of women.

Have we not said that the enemies of woman – even if they pose as supporters of educated women – are always the enemies of democracy. The struggle of Egyptian women for their political rights is part of the struggle for the strengthening of democracy in Egypt. The use of this struggle against the democratic regime itself cannot be allowed. Those men and women who are in favour of granting political rights to educated women exclusively, the same people who deny these same rights to ignorant women and illiterate men, should devote their efforts to the immediate eradication of illiteracy and the spreading of education, then the people, men as well as women, will be able to use political rights instead of depriving the overwhelming majority of this people of their natural right to free choice of its representatives and governors.

The solution to the problem is therefore not to deprive illiterate people of their political rights, but to educate them so that they can make good use of these rights. Democracy is not the exclusive prerogative of men, nor of educated men or women only; it is the power of the whole people, men and women together.

The problem of the political rights of women has taken on an international magnitude since the end of the Second World War and the birth of the United Nations. In its preamble, the UN charter states the necessity of equality between men and women. Likewise, the Declaration of Human Rights adopted by the UN General Assembly on 10 December 1948, upholds this equality. Furthermore, on 19 November 1946, the UN General Assembly adopted a resolution recommending that its members implement the equality of rights between men and women in cases where this equality has not yet been established. The UN Economic and Social Council has established a special commission to investigate the woman question and asked it to study the rights and conditions of women in various countries. The deprivation of the Egyptian woman of her political rights is a blatant violation of the United Nations Charter, of the Declaration of Human Rights, as well as of the recommendations of the UN General Assembly of which Egypt is a member. This unlawful attitude adopted by Egypt as a civilised nation doubtless contributes to the decline of her prestige and is detrimental to her reputation in the international arena.

We have recently seen the Syrian government hurriedly recognising political rights for the Syrian woman, but this was limited to educated women. Nonetheless, it is certain that the Syrian woman deserves to be congratulated for having won her cause up to a point. She is the first woman in the Arab East to gain recognition – however partial and limited – of her rights. This step will be followed by others.

Translated from the Arabic
by Michelle Raccagni

Duriya Shafiq

(1908–1975)

Duriya Shafiq was born in the Egyptian Delta town of Tanta where she was educated by Roman Catholic nuns. While still a schoolgirl she wrote to Huda Shaarawi asking to speak at the Egyptian Feminist Union's annual commemoration of Qasim Amin. With support from Shaarawi, Shafiq went to the Sorbonne where she wrote a doctoral dissertation on 'La Femme Egyptienne et l'Islam'. After her return to Egypt from France in 1945, Shafiq founded a magazine, *Majalla Bint al-Nil* (The Daughter of the Nile). With time it came to include a section called *Bint al-Nil al-Siyasiya* (Political Daughter of the Nile) which ran until 1957. She also published a magazine for children called *Katkut* (chick), from 1946 to 1948. She took over the magazine of the New Woman Society called *La Femme Nouvelle*, an art magazine, backed by money from princesses of the royal family. In 1948, she founded the Daughter of the Nile Union (Ittihad Bint al-Nil), a broadly based middle class feminist association with branches in a number of provincial cities. Shafiq focused on female literacy and political rights for women. In 1953, she created the Daughter of The Nile political party. Within a year it was closed down. In 1954, she went on a hunger strike for political rights for women. In the 1960s, she was under house arrest following her call for the removal of Nasser. She died in 1975. Shafiq's writings include: *Al-Mara al-Misriyya min al-Faraina ila al-Yaum* (The Egyptian Woman From the Pharoahs Until Today), and with Ibrahim Abduh, *Tatawwur al-Nahda al-Misriyya: 1798–1951* (The Development of the Women's Renaissance in Egypt), and *Al-Kitab al-Abiyad li Huquq al-Hara al Misriyya* (The White Paper), numerous articles, and unpublished memoirs.

The following piece is taken from *The White Paper* – a collection of statements from the debates on suffrage advanced by secular and religious personalities on both sides of the issue. Here we see an example of Shafiq's outspoken candour and confidence.

Islam and the Constitutional Rights of Woman

1952

❦

The article His Eminence, Mr Hasanain Muhammad Makhluf, the present Mufti, published in *Akhir Lahza* last Friday astonished, not to say dismayed, everyone. His Eminence's article appeared without the supporting evidence from the *Sharia* that one would expect from someone in his position. Moreover, volunteering to discuss the subject of the constitutional rights of the Egyptian woman, and eagerness to express his opinion on the subject are contrary to His Eminence's usual practice of avoiding to speak out on such political and social matters; this has provoked people to question his motives. People had hoped that when the day arrived when His Eminence would decide to speak about matters of life and religion that he would address what we all find to be a serious deviation from Islam and its teachings, rather than discussing matters on which many advanced Islamic nations have already taken a stand, and which His Excellency writes Islam has interdicted. Some of the *ulama* in Egypt have given a different opinion from that of His Eminence. After the article was published, many of these distinguished *ulama* contacted me, offering to respond with a statement backed up with evidence. We look forward to the day when this statement will be prepared.

On 7 May 1952, I wrote the following article in *Al-Misri*, under the title of 'Confidence'.

I have never been more confident that the Egyptian woman would achieve her full constitutional rights than yesterday when the movement against the Egyptian woman's demands for these rights took a new turn. His Eminence Shaikh Makhluf, the Mufti of Egypt, was extreme in his statement saying that Islam, the religion of freedom and true equality among all people, forbids the participation of Egyptian women in all aspects of public life. He implied that the affairs of this country could only be put in order by going back decades and by taking women from the light back to darkness ... to veiling and the life of the harem! The strongest opposition, in the name of religion, to every step towards the advancement of women in Egypt has always been a sign that success is closer at hand. Much more criticism was directed at

Qasim Amin when he called for the liberation of women from the veil and the life of the harem than against what was published yesterday, but such criticism did not prevent the success of Qasim Amin's cause. The whole nation and all classes took up the cause, including some of those who were most hostile in the beginning. Similar criticisms were raised when Lutfi al-Sayyid and Taha Husain permitted the entry of women into the Egyptian University, but this did not prevent the success of this sacred step forward, considered one of the greatest steps towards true progress and civilisation in Egypt.

Let the enemies of women muster everything in their arsenal and let them imagine that they can stop the march of time and progress. They will never succeed, except in harming the reputation of their country and their tolerant and generous religion which when understood truly will not hinder the advancement of nations and the development of their people, men and women. I am calling upon people of true knowledge and eminence in this country – and there are many – to rise up and defend the reputation of their country and their religion and declare relentless war so that people of the entire earth will know that if some people in twentieth century Egypt still believe that woman was created merely for *fitna* that this is not in keeping with the generous tenets of Islam regarding women.

On 14 May 1952, *Al-Misri* published my article entitled, 'Whom Shall We Follow ... The Present Mufti or the Previous Mufti?' The following is the text of the article:

I did not think that His Eminence, Shaikh Hasanain Makhluf, would openly (and without warning) attack women. He is a genteel man who associates easily with people. I have often met him at public events where women and men mix and where his fine qualities were evident when he spoke with women and men. I remember last meeting him at the Syndicate of Journalists at a reception attended by women and men journalists to which His Eminence, the Mufti gave his blessings.

I did not think His Eminence, being such a social man, would publicly move to stop women from becoming judges or governing, or doing other things men do, and state without any hesitation that Islam did not give women the right to vote thus robbing her of her humanity and depriving her of her right to be present in the society in which she lives.

His Eminence, the Mufti decided that women working in teaching or medicine or law or other professions restricted to men is an unforgivable sin and a crime of which Islam disapproves and that the entire Egyptian society – government and people – is sinful for allowing three thousand women students to attend lectures side by side with male students and for permitting women teachers, doctors, lawyers, engineers, and journalists to take up men's positions.

The Mufti said all that for one very good reason: the woman should stay at home; she should not go to the ballot box every five years and have women representing her in the Senate or Chamber of Deputies. His Eminence wants Egyptian life to go back a hundred years and eradicate from history and from the march of time what happened in Egypt so that his view that Islam deprives women of the right to vote should triumph.

I am a believer in God, His Prophet, and the Day of Judgement. I practise the words of God, Almighty, 'Obey God and obey the Prophet and those among you who have been given command.' Therefore, I have decided to stay at home, quit journalism, and remain with my daughters in my house and not allow them to be educated. I shall ask the state to expel women students from the universities and fire women employees as well as nurses, doctors, lawyers, and engineers because these professions are suitable only for men. All this, in response to the appeal of His Eminence, the Mufti of Egypt, Shaikh Hasanain Makhluf. But another *shaikh* who was Mufti of Egypt, an *imam* among our *shaikhs*, His Eminence Shaikh Alam Nassar, said something that differed from what the present Mufti said. When he was Mufti of Egypt he said, 'Islam looks at the woman as it looks at the man with respect to humanity, rights, and personality. Islam does not distinguish between the sexes with respect to humanity.' The former Mufti continues to contradict the present Mufti saying, 'Woman and man in the judgement of Islam are equal. A man is condemned to death if he kills a woman and a woman is condemned to death if she kills a man, therefore the two are equal.' The Shaikh supports this, saying, 'Islam also gave the woman the freedom to choose her husband and to contract and consummate marriage as long as she is of age. This is proof that Islam has made guarantees to the woman in the most important aspect of her life.'

I understand that the woman who has the right to select a man to be her life partner, should have the same right as men to select whomever she wants to represent her concerning public matters, because the two are equal.

This is the opinion of His Eminence, Shaikh Alam Nassar Bey whom I respect as much as Shaikh Hasanain Makhluf in accordance with God's command: 'Obey God and obey the Prophet and those who have command among you.'

Should we follow what the present Mufti advocates or what the former Mufti advocates? Should we renounce the principle of exclusion advanced by Shaikh Makhluf or rest assured with the view of Shaikh Alam Nassar that there is no principle of exclusion in Islam among those who believe in the plenitude of religion?

People may disagree concerning the opinion of the two respected shaikhs, but I believe what the former Mufti advocates. He speaks to me in a way my mind understands, and my heart feels comfortable with, and reassures me in my belief that I shall attain the maximum to which the Egyptian woman aspires, and the day for this is near at hand, and that the Mufti will witness that day. I shall meet the Mufti in the Syndicate of Journalists or some other place and shall remind him of what he has said to the people. There is no barrier between us and the Mufti. He is an amiable, generous, and genial man attending public functions where men and women journalists convene and where the woman does the same work as the man.

Translated from the Arabic
by Ali Badran and Margot Badran

Amina Said

(1914–)

Amina Said was born in Asyut, Egypt. During the 1919 revolution, her mother, with the help of women servants in the household, took part in acts of sabotage against the British in Asyut. Later, her father took the family to Cairo to give his daughters a good education. Amina attended the Shubra Secondary School for Girls in Cairo, the first state school of its kind to provide girls with an education equal to that of boys. At school she met Huda Shaarawi who invited her to give a speech at the Egyptian Feminist Union. She later joined the youth group of the Egyptian Feminist Union, Shaqiqat, becoming the Arabic secretary. She entered Cairo University in 1931 (the third year that women were admitted). In 1945, she became the editor of *Al-Mara al-Arabiyya* (The Arab Woman magazine), the short-lived organ of the newly founded Arab Feminist Union. Said became the first woman in Egypt to make a full-time life-long career, in journalism. She worked for *Al-Mussawar* and in 1954 founded *Hawa*, a mass circulation magazine for women, which also sought a male readership. Said was a member of the Board of the Press Syndicate in 1956, vice-president in 1959, and went on to be the first woman to become a member of the Executive Board of the publishing firm Dar al-Hilal. In 1975, she became president of the Administrative Council of Dar al-Hilal, a position she retained until her retirement in 1981. Said has published two novels: *Al-Jamiha* (The Shrew), 1946 and *Akhir al-Tariq* (The End of the Road); and *Wujuh fi al-Zalam* (Profiles in the Dark), a collection of articles taken from the women's column she edited. She also wrote children's stories and translated Kipling's *Jungle Book* and Louisa May Alcott's *Little Women*.

Amina Said's editorials in *Hawa* from 1954 to 1981 reached a broad readership in Egypt and elsewhere in the Arab world. Her provocative essays inspired many and antagonised many. The two editorials that follow were published in the 1970s when conservatism and religious fundamentalism were on the rise in Egypt. In the first piece Said commemorates the fiftieth anniversary of the Egyptian Feminist Union and the removing of the veil by Huda

Shaarawi and Saiza Nabarawi. At a moment when the veil was returning she called it the biggest obstacle to women's advancement and lamented the lack of activism in the current generation. In the second piece published three years later she confronted a prominent religious leader who had attacked her in the press at a time when her writings were increasingly disturbing the new religious conservatives.

Feast of Unveiling, Feast of the Renaissance

1973

❧

At the end of this week, Egypt celebrates the fiftieth anniversary of the Huda Shaarawi Society for the Feminist Renaissance. This is the same society that for forty years or more was called The Egyptian Feminist Union. Circumstances dictated that the name of the immortal leader would be given to the Society in honour of our beloved departed lady who has first and foremost credit for changing the status of the Muslim woman and in laying the foundations of the feminist renaissance whose fruits we reap today.

The fiftieth anniversary of the Huda Shaarawi Society carries with it the most important event in the history of the Arab woman. In this same week in the year 1923, Huda Shaarawi in the company of two of her colleagues, Saiza Nabarawi and the late Nabawiya Musa represented Egypt for the first time in an international feminist conference in Rome, the capital of Italy. Conference members who came from throughout the advanced world were greatly surprised to see the three Egyptian women in the conference at the most elevated level of culture, consciousness, *élan*, and civilisation. The image of the Arab woman in the minds of the western woman was of a backward woman living behind the walls of the harem, ignorant, veiled, and crippled in effort and movement, totally incapable of performing any role in the service of her country. But, Huda Shaarawi, Saiza Nabarawi and Nabawiya Musa by their presence at this important feminist cultural and political meeting were able to break the detestable old image of the Arab woman in the minds of westerners. They were able through their knowledge, education, and intelligence to stand on the same footing with their sisters from England, France, the United States, Austria, Italy, and Switzerland. By their efforts and through their political speeches they commanded admiration which the international press echoed. This news got back to Egypt to awaken Egyptians from their sleep and to turn their attention to the ability of the daughters of their country to bring benefit to their nation if given the chance.

One of the most obvious traits of Huda was her outstanding moral courage in stating her own views as well as her steadfastness in supporting reform. She was not a coward in the face of the anger of reactionaries like some of today's women. She did not leave it to others to wage cultural battles as we see in many Arab feminist circles representing the modern woman in our present time.

The Biggest Obstacle

After her experience at the Rome conference she saw that the veil was the biggest obstacle in the way of progress of the Muslim Arab woman. Thus the veil had to fall so that with it the strongholds of reactionaries preventing women from being educated and participating in public life would fall.

Following this sound view, with her colleagues she decided to be the first to unveil. Upon their arrival by train at the station in the capital, they met those gathered there to receive them with their faces unveiled. When signs of disapproval became apparent in the crowd, women in the crowd immediately supported the unveiled women by also removing the veils from their faces and throwing them on the ground. Hence, the greatest victory in the history of the Arab woman.

The veil started to disappear in our country with great speed. In just a few years unveiling had spread throughout the country and the walls of reactionaries separating men and women and crippling half of the Arab people from making any effort to serve the country had collapsed.

With the crumbling of the walls of reactionaries and with the woman going out of her home, unveiled, there was nothing to prevent her from education. In 1925, the first secondary school for girls preparing them for the general certificate was opened, with girls following exactly the same curriculum as boys. Only a few years passed after this, when the university opened its doors to women. The first group who entered were admitted to the colleges of liberal arts, law, and medicine. Year after year others entered and women graduated with honours and marched into jobs in government and the private sector until they had entered all fields, as we see nowadays, and were present at every level even holding seats in the Chamber of Deputies and in the Cabinet.

It is important to mention that the tide of the unveiling movement that changed the face of life in our country, moved to our sister Arab countries. In Lebanon a courageous leader like Huda Shaarawi appeared; she was the Lebanese Muslim leader, Ibtihaj Kaddura. She lifted the veil like Huda Shaarawi to become the first example for her own people. At the same time in Syria the leader, Adila Abd al-Qadir al-Jazairi appeared and did the same, leading the women of her country from the darkness of the harem to the light of progress.

A Good Example

This story that I tell you on the fiftieth anniversary of the Huda Shaarawi society is the gift that I present to the daughters of the new generation throughout the Arab world as a good example. Not only that but to make clear that veiling is the greatest enemy of civilisation and advancement, and that nationalism cannot be worthy of mention nor respect if it does not exist in the form of courageous, constructive acts based on belief in values and morals. It is important that every good woman citizen should perform these acts if she feels it her duty to serve her country so that the Arabs would regain their former dignity that has unfortunately gone as a result of rigid thinking dominating the minds of the ignorant majority causing us to move backwards, from being at the forefront of the world, to being at the rear. It had made us who have the greatest and most civilised religion in the world be despised by our enemies and pitied by our friends.

I'm addressing my words in particular to the young women of the modern Arab feminist generation. While in Egypt we celebrate the golden anniversary of the liberation of women, I want them and us to ask themselves what they have added to the efforts of the feminist vanguards? Unveiling and education at various levels were achieved through the efforts of those generations who have gone before. Work (for women) at various levels was also realised through the efforts and struggle of the first vanguards. Even the political rights that women in some Arab countries enjoy have come about in later years as the fruit of the early feminist struggle and the great political roles played by Egyptian, Syrian and Lebanese women, in the battles of national liberation against foreign colonisation.

I believe that if the modern Arab woman is honest in examining herself on this magnificent, historical occasion, she will discover that she has not added anything new to the efforts of those who have gone before and that she has not been part of any effort worth mentioning in advancing the feminist liberation movement in spite of the wide horizons before the woman of today, the abundance of opportunities and the advancement of social thinking and the development of life outside our area.

The modern woman of today can make miracles with her own hands. She can make gains and achieve suitable status in the world of civilisation, knowledge, freedom and advancement but she chooses to stand still, content with the little that has been realised for her by others imagining that she has attained everything while, in spite of the early victories, she has not achieved more than the crumbs from the table. In all Arab countries she is veiled, underdeveloped, and unqualified to perform national roles to help reconstruct her society. Even in those countries where the veil has disappeared the great majority of women are still prey to illiteracy. We remain in the era of the midwife while other nations are living in the space age and walk on the surface of the moon.

This is our greatest tribulation. How long will it last?

Translated from the Arabic
by Ali Badran and Margot Badran

Why, Reverend Shaikh?

1976
၆ၣၥ

On Friday morning, 6 January 1976, I read an interview with Faraj
al-Sanhuri in *Al-Ahram*. The least I can say to describe how I felt
afterwards is to say I was deeply sad and sorry. If the speaker had
been an insignificant person we might have saved ourselves the
trouble of discussing what he said and refuting his affronts and
accusations. But, the Reverend Shaikh is not at all insignificant. On
the contrary, he is a well-respected *alim* among Egyptian religious
leaders. *Al-Ahram* referred to him as the 'Shaikh of Shaikhs'
because of his long history as a *shaikh*, sixty out of his eighty-five
years. The words of a man like that can never be taken lightly. His
position, knowledge, and age entail that he be held responsible for
what he says in public. We find it appropriate to have him
penalised for the 'trash' he says in public. We are, therefore,
compelled to discuss his offensive accusations of honourable
people, or at least what concerns us.

The interview was offensive to quite a few people and institutions, for example, the Institute of Islamic Research, which the
'Shaikh of Shaikhs' condemned to a death sentence when he
announced to the public, and in the pages of the most widely
circulated Arabic newspaper, that its members were not properly
qualified for their positions. It was an implication that their
judgements should not be taken seriously. This attack on the
Institute of Islamic Research has been a blow to a major institution
upon which we had pinned hopes for the transformation of Islamic
thought from the darkness of rigidity and stagnation to the light of
flexibility and progress. We are disappointed to see it condemned,
but we do not concern ourselves with its defence. This must be left
to its members whose religious reputation has been seriously
damaged.

The Institute of Islamic Research was not the only victim of the
interview with the 'Shaikh of Shaikhs'. He also talked about a past
official, the Mufti of Egypt, saying that he had written complaints
about his wife to Imam al-Shafai in his shrine. The story obviously
places the religious integrity of the man at stake. The Mufti has
been dead for quite a few years and was always admired not just in
Egypt but in the Muslim communities of all countries. I have also

Opening the Gates

been informed by a trusted *alim* that the Mufti had been a teacher
of the 'Shaikh of Shaikhs' instructing him in legal matters; this man
earned such treatment by his own student after his death. However, we shall also leave this matter to those among the *ulama* who
know the contributions of their master to Islamic thought.

What concerns us is the issue of family law to which the Shaikh
has devoted at least half of his words and was, unfortunately, far
from successful in what he said. I would like to make it clear that I
do not mind the objection of Shaikh Sanhuri, nor anyone else, to
our request to change some of the laws we see as obsolete and
reminiscent of past ages of occupation. We do not deny him nor
anybody else the right to defend the legislative committee which he
himself headed, although we do not see this project as worth much.

Freedom of expression and debate of public issues is a right of all
concerned. It is the most democratic way of deciding what is right
and the more opinions expressed the better the chance to reach the
truth. Shaikh Faraj al-Sanhuri, then, is free to say what he likes
about the family law and so are we free to request changing what
we consider detrimental to the public welfare. However, the
Reverend Shaikh has absolutely no right to offend or abuse
honourable people with his 'trash'. This is not only a violation of
the basic teachings of Islam, a shameful practice from a man of
religion, but it is also a civil offence punishable by law.

Before I get to the central issues I would like to reply to a side
issue that came up in that interview which was a failure from start
to finish. Dr Sanhuri in his attempt to slight feminists mentioned
that they still demand the same things Huda Shaarawi demanded
at the end of the nineteenth century; I think this remark was made
without his thinking what it means. The Shaikh, himself, was born
in the nineteenth century and is still living – may God grant him
long life – as a respectable Muslim *alim* in the Arab world. Why,
then does he hold it against the feminists that they – for as long as
he had been living – continue to say what they had said at the time
of Huda Shaarawi as long as they are not granted their demands
and as long as ills still exist destroying the moral principles of our
society. Our persistence in the same demands since the nineteenth
century is only an indication of the crisis we are living through,
characterised by intellectual rigidity and the inability of intellectuals to innovate. We lack the ability to serve Islam through
modernising its teachings and laws that are inflicted on its people
regardless of their contradiction of the spirit of Islam, a religion
meant to be flexible enough to respond to the changing nature of
styles of life and their demands. This remark, therefore, is against
the Shaikh and not to his credit, but as I have mentioned earlier it is

but a side issue with which we would not have bothered, had it not been for the Shaikh's worse offence later when he spoke of the women who requested change in the family laws.

The Shaikh told the reporter that he gives each of them a different title. One he calls, 'grandma', another he calls 'aunt', and the third he calls something which he says is not fit to print. Imagine how maligning his words are and how they transgress Islamic ethics. We shall overlook his sarcasm in using words like 'grandma' and 'aunt' as trivial and focus on the matter concerning the unprintable word.

We all know that what is not fit to print must be extremely offensive – libel punishable by law. I wonder who among our feminist leaders who have spent the best years of their lives in the service of their nation deserves such defamation?

This is, indeed, a blunder humiliating for any Muslim, even if he were a less than average individual, but especially so for a major Islamic figure. How did he who has read the Quran and knows the Quranic penalty for such a transgression allow himself to do this? If the 'Shaikh of Shaikhs' has forgotten, we remind him that the Quran says: 'Those who defame honourable women shall be cursed in this world and the next.' And: 'Those who defame honourable women and cannot produce four witnesses shall be given eighty lashes. No testimony of theirs shall be admissible, for they are great transgressors.' (Sura of Light). This is the clearly stated punishment which he deserves. However, we shall consider his poor health, old age, and past services and drop the request to inflict any physical punishment on the Shaikh.

We leave him to the sterner punishment of God. We pity him for the outcome of such slips in defaming other people without any evidence or proof of ill conduct. Unfortunately, this seems to be a character trait. He insulted us a few years ago in the pages of *Al-Ahram* and afterwards, when we responded to his accusations he sent a letter of apology which he wished us to keep confidential.

I was generous enough to accept a confidential apology for an insult in public hoping it would be the last slip of the 'Shaikh of Shaikhs'. I seem to have been too optimistic for he has gone back to his old habit and this time has gone too far in his abuse and offences. May God bless our earlier Shaikhs, Muhammad Abduh, Al-Magharghi and Shaltut, and may God help all Muslims.

Translated from the Arabic
by Noha Radwan

Challenges Facing the Arab Woman
at the End of the 20th Century

1987

୧ଊ୨

The Association

The idea of the Arab Women's Solidarity Association (AWSA) arose at the beginning of the 1970s. We were a group of independent Arab women, appalled by the various kinds of subjugation suffered by Arab men and women. We knew that the liberation of the people as a whole could not take place without the liberation of the women, and that this could not take place without the liberation of the land, and liberation from economic, cultural and media domination. The liberation of women and of the country demanded solidarity for power. Rights without power are useless, easily lost.

The idea of the Arab Women's Solidarity Association became a tantalising dream. We held some preliminary meetings in Egypt, Lebanon, Kuwait, Tunisia, Syria, Jordan, Morocco, Sudan, Algeria, Yemen and elsewhere. In 1982, we laid the first foundations of the Association as an international Arab organisation. We submitted an application for consultative status with the Economic and Social Council of the United Nations. This was granted in April 1985. AWSA then had consultative status in the Economic and Social Council of the United Nations as an international, Arab, non-governmental, non-profit-making body. Its aims were to promote the Arab woman and Arab society through various political, economic, social and cultural means; and to strengthen the bonds between women from different Arab countries.

A large number of Arab and Egyptian women, as well as Arab women in exile all over the world, joined the Association. There was enthusiasm from the beginning. In the current period, rights that Arab women gained in the 1950s and 1960s are being attacked. This attack is an integral part of growing setbacks the Arab peoples are experiencing as they lose their independence, their freedom and their struggle.

It has become clear that the traditional stance towards women and their rights undercuts progress in Arab societies. The present situation demands a deeper, more modern look at women's roles in society as well as in the family. These objectives must be clarified in the light of the objectives of the Arab feminist movement which aims to make life in our countries more just, free and responsive to the needs of millions of men and women crushed by economic, intellectual and moral crises.

General Objectives of the Association

AWSA's principles and objectives can be summarised as follows:
1. Women's active participation in the political, economic, social and cultural life of the Arab world is essential for the realisation of true democracy in Arab society.
2. Justice in the family demands the elimination of gender discrimination in both private and public realms.
3. The Arab woman's moral growth depends on her ability to criticise values and ideologies that have subverted women's historic struggle for freedom. This struggle must be informed by an understanding of the modern Arab woman's needs.
4. Application of intellectual endeavours and practical actions to improve conditions of work and the quality of life of as many Arab women as possible, including poor women living in rural as well as urban areas who are overwhelmed by work both in and out of the home.
5. Active participation in projects to raise the political, economic, social and cultural level of Arab women in private as well as public domains.
6. Opening up the workplace to allow for the liberation of women's minds and to encourage their budding talents.
7. Open membership to young and old men who believe that the liberation of Arab society is not possible without the liberation of women.

Difficulties the Association has Faced

It was not easy to found AWSA under the conditions that Arab nations are suffering: fragmentation makes solidarity a distant hope.

This fragmentation has been reflected on Arab women. The woman still belongs to the man in the home, in the state, in the political party, in the trade union and in all kinds of public and private institutions. It is not surprising that these difficulties should affect Arab women's solidarity.

Nevertheless, we were able to bring together a large membership of Arab and Egyptian women. We were surprised by a number of difficulties when we wanted to register the Egyptian branch of AWSA. Egyptian law does not allow any association to be registered without the permission of the Ministry of Social Affairs. This

Ministry rejected our first demand to register the Egyptian branch of AWSA.

They sent us an official letter on 9 August 1983 informing us of the rejection because we did not have permission from the State Security Police and the Criminal Control Department. We took this letter to a number of intellectuals in Egypt and began a campaign for the registration of AWSA in Egypt. During this campaign we relied on a number of well-known Egyptian personalities like Fathi Radwan, Mustafa Amin and Salah Hafiz. The branch was officially registered on 7 January 1985.

No Association Headquarters
Until today AWSA has no headquarters of its own[1]. We hold meetings in the headquarters of the Arab Human Rights Organisation in Egypt. On 3 June 1985 this organisation agreed to accommodate AWSA. AWSA has participated in a number of activities related to Arab women at the regional and international levels. It sent a delegation to the International Women's Conference (Nairobi, 1985) and organised a panel on Arab women and social values. Our delegates participated in meetings and marches and issued a statement that was distributed with the conference documents to all the delegations.

AWSA was part of the campaign against the rescinding of the Personal Status Code in Egypt in 1985. It organised a number of meetings, issued statements and submitted modifications to the draft law to the People's Assembly. AWSA also organised a number of cultural seminars about women between 1982 and 1987. During the first week of April 1985, AWSA invited the black American activist writer Angela Davis. Her visit included meetings with various feminist groups in Egypt.

AWSA played a role in warning against birth control methods used in Egypt, such as the depo provera[2] injection and nuroplant[3]. Members met with the Minister of Health about this matter, they published articles in newspapers and sent a proclamation to the Medical Syndicate.

The Conference
This book contains most of the studies presented at the pan-Arab conference on challenges facing the Arab woman at the end of the twentieth century held between 1 and 3 September 1987.

These studies were discussed in public sessions and meetings of the four committees – political, economic, social and cultural – into which the conference was divided.

This conference is one of the most important of the AWSA's

activities. About 500 women and men attended the opening session. There were 159 registered participants from all over the Arab world. The conference achieved its three basic objectives:

1. To study the political, economic, social and cultural challenges facing the Arab woman at the end of the twentieth century.
2. To bring together many Arab women to co-operate and work together to become an effective force in the liberation of themselves and Arab society.
3. To convene the general assembly of AWSA; to hold elections for its board of directors and its representatives to the United Nations; to amend some statutory articles and to approve projects for the future.

Conference Emblem
It was agreed that the conference emblem would be: 'Women's Power – Solidarity – Lifting the Veil from the Mind'.

This emblem combines AWSA's two basic goals: solidarity without which women's power is not possible; awareness which can only come after the veil has been removed from the mind. This emblem was put on all correspondence and official documents, including invitations to the conference. We wanted this emblem to have a wide appeal so as to include many women from different political, intellectual and party persuasions as well as women from different governments, trade unions and non-governmental organisations. Is there anyone who can object to solidarity or freedom of thought and mind?

AWSA was eager to broaden the scope of its invitation to the Arab women's conference, because it was not an academic conference in the narrow sense, but rather a scientific sociological cultural conference in the broad sense of the term. It was the assembly of Arab women for solidarity, and to strengthen bonds among women from all Arab countries. We also invited men concerned with women's issues.

Success of the Conference
The Arab League witnessed an Arab feminist conference of a new order because it was not sponsored by a government or a party. Young people came, anxious to contribute. The conference and the four committees deliberated for three days during which twenty-four papers were discussed. There was an Arab women's bookfair with books on science, literature and the arts. Egyptian, Arab and international media covered the event.

Attitudes of Political Movements to the Conference
Some political groups tried unsuccessfully to control the conference. The position of the political groups can be summarised as follows:

1. *Fundamentalist Islamic*: Most of these groups boycotted the conference from the beginning. They considered our emblem: 'Lifting the Veil from the Mind' and 'Arab Women's Solidarity' as a kind of corruption or violation of the commands of God and the *Sharia*. Hence they refused to attend and did not allow their women to participate. However, some fundamentalist Muslim women with minds free of such attitudes actively participated. Newspapers belonging to these fundamentalist groups attacked us as infidels and atheists. They also accused us of treason because we received funding from non-Islamic, non-Arab foundations.

2. *Traditional Right*: These groups also boycotted the conference from the start; they considered AWSA to be communist because we associate women's oppression with patriarchy. The word 'class' is one that these groups' dictionary has expurgated. They want us to be a women's welfare association volunteering to help the sick and war victims, to give them candy without getting involved in politics or having a historical or class perspective on women's issues. We were accused of being communists and of working for the Soviet Union.

3. *Traditional Left*: They accused us of being agents of American zionism because we accepted Ford Foundation funding. When these accusations failed they turned to distorting our words so that it appeared that we were separating women's issues from those of the state. Or they would concentrate on the gender issue and ignore the political and economic aspects.

4. *Governmental Constituencies*: The Ministry of Social Affairs ignored the conference and did not respond to our invitation. Some government-sponsored newspapers attacked the conference and pressured the authorities into conducting an investigation. However, the Ministry of Foreign Affairs was supportive and helped us book the Arab League rooms in Cairo.

The Crisis of Democracy and the Press
Some AWSA writers tried to respond to the government and opposition newspapers attacks. However, most of these responses were never published. The few that did get published were greatly edited and the titles changed. This despite the fact that the Egyptian press law provides for the right to respond. But this did not happen in most newspapers, whether they were government or party run.

This is not strange. Journalism, like politics, does not acknowledge rights but only power. Rights are taken, they are not given in the world of the media. That is why the first proposal adopted at the last general assembly on 3 September 1986 was to establish a publishing house for the AWSA and to issue a journal or a newspaper in which we could express our ideas so that we would no longer need others' newspapers.

Edited by Nahid Toubia and translated from the Arabic
by Miriam Cooke

NOTES

1. This has changed. In 1987, AWSA moved into its permanent headquarters in Cairo not far from the site of the first destination of women's organised nationalist demonstration in 1919.
2. Depo-Provera is a long-term estrogen injection; the problem with this form of contraception is that the amounts of estrogen cannot be controlled; breast and uterine tumours can develop.
3. This is probably noimplant. This is an intra-uterine device that is known to cause abdominal cramps and pubic infections.

Nahid Toubia is a Sudanese surgeon. She studied at Cairo University and at the Royal College of Surgeons in London. She writes in Arabic and English on women's social and health issues, especially on female circumcision.

A Group of Egyptian Women

Aziza Husain, Inji Rushdi, Saniyya Salih, Awatif Wali, Mervat Ittalawi, Muha Zulfiqar and Magda al-Mufti, leading Egyptian women in different professions, came together in order to advance the lives of women in the political, economic, and social spheres at a time when women are being pushed back into the home. Their approach is pragmatic. They have recently published a pamphlet setting out in clear, concise, accessible prose women's rights as guaranteed in the Egyptian Constitution, state laws and decrees, and international agreements that Egypt has signed. We include here the 'Open Letter' announcing the purpose of their project. This is testimony of an aspect of the current feminist struggle at a time when, in the words of the authors of the pamphlet, 'currents have appeared trying to take her (the woman) back to the Ottoman era, that is, the harem era . . .'

Legal Rights of the Egyptian Woman: Theory and Practice

1988

❧

We present to you this pamphlet which we consider a vital document supporting every Egyptian woman who seeks the realisation of a better life for herself and her family. We would like to remind you that you are not alone. There are millions of women and men struggling for the defence of the rights of the woman as the development of the woman is part of the development of society. Accordingly, it interests every citizen, man and woman, alike.

This pamphlet includes a comprehensive review of all rights guaranteed by Egyptian law for the woman in society including her work rights, rights relating to *ahwal shakhsiya* (personal status) and political rights. We believe that a knowledge of legal rights enables a person to exercise them more effectively. It has been proven that the citizen who understands well their rights is a strong citizen able to share in life and participate in the building and development of society and to realise happiness and well-being for themselves and their family.

We would like to remind you that woman's equality to man in rights means equality in duties. We hope that efforts to enlighten the woman about her rights will lead to greater attention to her duties.

History has proven that persons who have deprived the woman of her human rights in social, economic and political equality have paid a dear price. It has been proven that adopting a policy of subjugation and injustice against half of the population deprives society of half of its power and productivity.

On the other hand, we find that the enlightened nations are those that have realised that woman is half of the society and that her liberation and the release of her energies leads to the liberation and release of the energies of every individual in society.

These societies have recognised that the family is the foundation of society and that man and woman form its basic unit. They have recognised that society composed of the totality of families becomes strong or weak according to whether families are united or not.

The holy Quran has promoted the unity of the family and love

and compassion among its members and has declared that all
people come from a single origin, 'Ye, people fear your God who
created all of you all from one soul.'

The case of the woman is threatened not only by rigidity, but by
the danger of being pushed backward tens of years, while some
work to create a public climate that would lead to depriving woman
of her rights, by placing obstacles in the way of the exercise of her
rights, and by supporting certain customs and traditions or wrong
interpretations and applications of public laws and religious law, or
by misquoting them.

Therefore, it is necessary to establish a platform to defend
woman's vital causes and to strike at this backward movement. We
must, in an organised way, deal with this public climate and what is
written about woman and refute or support what is published.

Signed,
*A Group of Women Concerned with Affairs Relating to the Egyptian
Woman*
Mrs Aziza Husain, President of Family Organisation Society in
  Cairo
Mrs Inji Rushdi, writer in al-Ahram
Dr Saniyya Salih, Assistant Sociology Professor, Social Research
  Centre, the American University in Cairo
Mrs Awatif Wali, President of Friends of the People Society
Mrs Mervat Ittalawi, Egyptian Ambassador to Austria
Lawyer Muna Zulfiqar, Attorney at Law and Partner in Shalakani
  Firm for Legal Consultation
Mrs Magda al-Mufti, Instructor of Simultaneous Interpretation at
  the American University in Cairo

Translated from the Arabic
by Ali Badran and Margot Badran

Amatalrauf al-Sharki

(1958–)

Amatalrauf al-Sharki was born in Ibb, a town in North Yemen. In 1967, her family moved to Sanaa. Her life has been bound up with the media in Yemen: radio, television, and journalism, and she is widely known in Yemen and abroad as Raufa Hassan, her radio and television name. She started off in a children's programme and by the age of twelve had her own programme. She began television broadcasting when it first came to Yemen in 1975, following her first year at university. She was prominent in reviving the Yemeni Women's Association which had been shut down by Islamic fundamentalists in the mid-1970s. She became its president in 1979. She studied mass communications at the University of Norwich in America where she received a master's degree in 1984. She is now at the University of Paris working towards her Ph.D. in sociocommunications. Her articles, sometimes taken from segments of her radio and television programmes, have appeared in Yemeni newspapers and journals such as *Al-Thaura*, the major daily newspaper where for two years she edited a weekly column for women and *Al-Taawun* (where she was editorial secretary) now called *Al-Majalis al-Mahaliyya*.

Amatalrauf al-Sharki reflected on her life in an oral memoir with Margot Badran in Cairo in 1988 where they had taken part together in the second conference of the Arab Women's Solidarity Association in Cairo on Contemporary Arab Thought and the Woman. The two had previously worked together in Yemen planning a women's community development project for several cities and towns.

The following fragment from al-Sharki's memoir is a stunning portrayal of the unfolding of feminist consciousness and activism as she threaded her way through society's barriers, taking advantage of the rise and spread of new technologies in the media, especially radio and television. She dared to pay the price for her feminist beliefs at a liberal moment in the history of Yemen when men in government and in the state-owned and state-run media were willing to assist a gifted and courageous young woman.

An Unveiled Voice

1988

❧

I have a family that helped me, finally, to be the way I am now. But, not at the beginning. At the beginning I had to prove myself for them to accept me as different from the person they wanted me to be. We are six children – four girls. I am the eldest. I was born into a family of *qadis* on both sides. *Qadis* are professionals but they also constitute a class. The positions are hereditary.

Because Amatalrauf is a hard name to pronounce, people used to know me as Raufa after I started working in the radio. But, it was not really to make my name easy to say that I changed it but to keep my family from knowing I was working in the radio. At school and at work, officially, my name was Amatalrauf al-Sharki. But on radio, I was introduced to the people as Raufa Hassan.

I used to sing in a children's programme on the radio. The names of who was singing or who was telling the stories were not announced. The programme was run by Baba Abdul Rahman Mutahar who still has programmes for children and sometimes for women too. He was the one who introduced me to the radio. I was in the sixth grade. They used to give me pocket money. It was fun. I enjoyed the money and I did things. One day they asked me to be a broadcaster – it was by accident actually. I was doing the children's programme when a regular broadcaster was absent and they needed someone to fill the place immediately. So one of the broadcasters came to me and asked me to do the job. He wasn't sure that I could do it, but I did. I imitated the broadcasters on the BBC (the BBC has extensive Arabic language broadcasting). It worked out beautifully. They thought they had discovered a voice. So everyone talked about having me as a broadcaster. At the time I was twelve going on thirteen. The programme I took over was called 'Jaula fi Alam al-Tarikh' (Journey through the World of History).

When I did the programme well, they discussed having me as an official broadcaster. Without a moment's thought, I told them my father would not agree. I came from a certain kind of family and my father would be angry if he knew I was working in radio. They thought the solution was to change my name and to start another programme. So, I said to them, 'I should at least ask my mother.' I told her. My mother thought if nobody knew there wouldn't be a problem and I would have my own salary. So she thought it was all right and that it would be kept a secret. We never thought it would become a career or an important part of my life.

The name was not decided the day they made the offer. The first job had been going on for a few weeks when the head of the Yemeni Women's Association, Hurriya al-Muayid, took me to the office of the Minister of Information. She was a friend of mine despite our difference in age – she was the first Yemeni woman to graduate from university in 1970. The Minister of Information was Abdallah Humran, a poet. I remember he was very nice to me at the time. It was he who suggested the name. It was part of my name, but different, and no one would recognise it. Instead of Amatalrauf it would be Raufa and instead of Husain, my father's name, my last name would be Hassan (Husain is the diminutive of Hassan). It would be my professional name. Nobody would know who my family was.

Everything went smoothly for the first six months. After school I used to go to the radio station to record the programmes and then return home. One day a broadcaster from another programme announced on the air, 'We have a new voice, Raufa Hassan,' and by mistake he added, 'Al-Sharki'. Then the trouble started. It was a scandal for the family. Everybody came to talk to my father. Some people were quite hostile so I went to my grandfather's house. He loved me very much. I was his favourite. I went to him crying and got his sympathy. He told me I could do whatever I wanted and that no one could push me around. He said if I wanted to be a broadcaster I could be a broadcaster. I was free.

My father, a civilian *qadi*, meantime was planning to remove me from the radio and not allow me to continue that kind of scandal. The whole family was involved. But one day something unexpected happened. One of these relatives went to my father and said, 'If your daughter is working at the radio because she needs the money, I am willing to give her her salary every month so she can stay at home.' That made my father angry. He said, 'It is none of your business. My daughter is not working because of the salary. She doesn't need your money and she will work for as long as you don't want her to work.' So, that helped me. My father believed that no one had the right to decide things like that for me and to insult him. I survived. I continued working for the radio.

But, there was a secret in this. I was working and I was veiled. At the radio I took off the veil to record because a voice through the veil would be muffled. Everyone working at the radio understood that no one must know that I was showing my face while I was recording. The only persons permitted to be present with me were the producer of the programme and the engineer. Someone always kept watch to see if anyone was approaching because there were other studios and someone might pass by and see me and talk and the news would get to my family. This continued for about five years. It is amazing how all those people protected me and not one said a word. I think of that to this day and I am still amazed. I really carry a lot of appreciation in my heart for these people and their solidarity. They did everything unconsciously, not because they felt what was going on was right or wrong, but because they liked working with me and didn't want harm to come to me. To this day, I think my father and mother still believe I was totally veiled when I used to record those programmes but we have never discussed it.

Inside me I didn't like that veil anymore. I felt it was a big lie. I hated and still hate the idea of being a liar. I wanted to be me. Just me, accepted the way I was. But I was doing something and hiding it. I was not convinced that wearing the veil was right. At the same time, I was not completely convinced that I should not wear the veil. That was around 1973 when I still thought that women were supposed to wear the veil and that was the way it was.

There was someone working with us in the radio who was a leftist. He used to say derogatory things about the veil. I didn't really understand what he was saying when he told me that I was hiding myself inside something that was not even Islamic. I didn't understand, but I wanted to. I began to read to understand him, not so much to understand the veil. I was interested in this man because he was different. No one had ever told me these things before. He was interested in me and proposed to me and my family agreed. The engagement was announced because he was going to the Soviet Union for his studies. We were to get married after he finished and returned home. But I changed my mind while he was away.

I started to read. This man introduced me to someone who was connected with the Communist Party which I only discovered some time later. I was introduced to someone who could lead me to things to read. This person gave me books and discussed books and ideas with me. We had a schedule for meeting and this continued for a year, when one day he was taken to a jail, or something, and no one ever contacted me after that. I had always read a lot, it was my hobby, but through reading these different kinds of books, I began to realise that the veil was just something to hold me back in life and not really for my benefit. Since then this started to rage inside me. I wanted to do something different, to prove myself, even though I wore the veil. I had become a different person.

At that time I joined a theatre group. We put on plays at the cinema which had a stage because there were no theatres in Yemen. I acted with the veil. Once I played the part of a mother in her house and had to imitate the voice of an older woman. We did four plays in the cinema theatre. That angered my father. He said radio was all right because nobody could see me, but the theatre was not all right. So when we did a play for Mother's Day, I asked him to come and see it. The play was about obedience of children towards their parents and things like that. He thought it was a good play, and that I was properly dressed. After that he never said anything more.

But some male relatives made threats and the women talked. The pressures started to get to my mother. Sometimes she came home angry, sometimes sad over the things she heard at the women's afternoon gatherings. Sometimes she was angry at me. She realised I was not doing anything wrong. But, she was hurt because they said that a girl working in the radio and performing in plays had a bad reputation. She knew it was not true, that I was not immoral but the gossip hurt her. She would come and discuss it with me. We talked a lot and were close. Between us there are only thirteen years. So we could discuss things and she was able to understand my position, and she soon realised how independent I had become. I never asked her for money. I gave her money. I did not have the problems I was supposed to have. I did my homework. I was good at school. My marks were good. I was doing well at my job and had a radio programme for women. She liked what I was saying to women.

Around that time, there were four of us who began to see that our reputation was being unfairly ruined, not for anything we had done but only because we had become known. One woman worked in the Ministry of Education and was a member of the Yemeni Women's Association. She did whatever she could to publicise the aims and goals of the YWA. The second, Fathiya Jirafi, had done programmes for the radio. She is a relative of mine and now the wife of one of our very famous poets, Abdallah al-Baraduni. Another woman, Fathiya al-Nidari, worked in the Ministry of Education and is now in the United Arab Emirates. She took out citizenship and is working with the women's association there. She couldn't bear it for long in Yemen. There were the three of us and Hurriya al-Muayid, the head of the Yemeni Women's Association, who was, as I have said, the first Yemeni woman to graduate from university. She now has psychological problems, almost mental problems. She is no longer in Sanaa but in a nearby village. She was married but is now divorced. She has a daughter who is twelve now.

She had so many difficulties because she comes from a Hashemite
family (which traces its origins to the Prophet Muhammad). They
refused to have any connection with her because she was the head
of the Yemeni Women's Association and because she married
someone not of their class. Also, because she stood up for things
they opposed on religious grounds – they were a very religious
family. She was not veiled, had new ideas, travelled alone, went to
conferences – things like that. She was another victim.

The four of us started a project for the girls and women who just
sat in their houses talking about us. Towards the end of 1973, we
started a school to give them literacy classes. We volunteered our
time and established that school. Now one of the girls who was my
student was the head of the school. She finished high school and
wanted to study at the university but her brother threatened the
family saying that if she went to the university he would stop
studying. So the family asked her to stay home. She didn't actually
stay home but went to work in the school.

At that time I was acting in the theatre, working in the radio,
studying in high school, and teaching in the literacy school, so I
didn't have any time to meet anyone. I didn't have to prove to my
mother that I didn't have time to meet men. People talk because
they think a girl who is educated and free is a girl who meets men
and does things they don't consider to be good.

I had a family affairs programme at the time. It continued for
three years. It was very successful in the cities, but later I realised
we did not really reach the people in the villages. We didn't know
how to speak to them. But, we had great response from different
kinds of people in the cities. For them the programme was very
effective. I was trying to reach men, women and children. I was
trying to talk to all of them telling them that the family affairs
programme was not just for women. I was saying that both the man
and the woman are responsible for the family. I wonder how I had
that consciousness at the time. I would have an interview with a
minister, say the Minister of Health, and tell him that I had talked
to both men and women and that they and their families were
affected by programmes in the Ministry, and we would go on to
discuss concrete issues. The typical family affairs programme used
to deal with household decor, the woman's responsibility for the
house, how a woman should smile at her husband and make him
comfortable – things like that. That was not the aim of my
programme even though sometimes I talked about the wife's
responsibility toward her husband and spoke of her as someone
dependent on a man, not about her own independent roles. I did
that unconsciously. It was normal. Now when I think back to my

programme, after my own way of thinking changed, certain things are clear to me now that were not then. I was also working in the Yemeni Women's Association without knowing exactly what I was doing. Then came 1975 and the end of high school and my desire to go somewhere to continue my studies.

The seventies in Yemen was the most liberal time in its history. There was the civil war from 1962 to 1967 with Egyptians supporting the republicans and the Saudis backing the royalists. The war was hard for everybody. Every house was divided between republicans and royalists. People from both sides were killed. Then came the compromise or the reconciliation, I don't know what it was called. This was after the withdrawal of the Egyptians from Yemen in 1967. There was the siege of Sanaa, called the siege of seventy days, by the royalists who were about to take the city but the leftists and others defending the capital succeeded in putting down the siege and the republicans won. We were in Sanaa then, my family and I. I had grown up in Ibb, a city in the part of Yemen we call 'The Green Province'.

The government was liberal then – more open and willing to try new things. Around 1971 and 1972 a group of us girls had military training for three weeks to prepare us to march in the Day of the Revolution parade during the celebrations for the revolution. During the military training held inside the headquarters of the Yemeni Women's Association, we learned how to walk, how to move and to carry guns. The training was done by the man who is now the Minister of Health. It was the first and last time in the history of Yemen that women marched. Some of us were veiled and some weren't. Another girl and I who were veiled wore military uniforms under our *sharshafs*. We marched in the military parade holding the banner of the Yemeni Women's Association. Behind us were three girls a year ahead of me in school. They marched unveiled in military uniform holding a gun. They were from families that allowed them to be unveiled. There were very few unveiled women at the time. Behind them were huge lorries full of women. Some were veiled – half-veiled or fully-veiled. One of the latter was my mother. She was veiled, she accepted it. She and some of her friends were holding pens and books in their hands showing that they were in the literacy school of the Yemeni Women's Association. Some carried banners and the flags of the Republic. Hurriya al-Muayid, the head of the Yemeni Women's Association made preparations for the march but was not in it herself.

However, at the end of 1973, the Women's Association was closed by a religious group who shut down the building and sealed it with red wax. They looted and destroyed everything inside. They took all the books. They wrecked the sewing machines. What I discovered later – at the time I was not aware of what was happening – was that the person giving us the training was a leftist and the Association was supported by leftists. The government was leftist and liberal. Around 1973, the Islamic forces start to come back. After the forced closing of the association it did not open again until I restarted it myself in 1977.

Another association that I was not part of was established under another name, Jamiya Nahda al-Mara al-Yamaniya, the Society of the Renaissance of the Yemeni Woman, headed by the wife of the prime minister at that time. However, the government was not directly involved in what was happening with the women's associations – neither with closing the first nor starting the second one. The women of the association were from the élite and not very interested in a women's movement in the true sense. I knew the prime minister's wife and her wish to do something for women, but her education and ideas were limited. All she had was the will. Also, her husband had problems because of her actions. She was not veiled and someone took a picture showing her face and distributed it in the streets to show that the prime minister's wife was unveiled implying she was not a good woman. Her husband was a liberal who had finished his studies in France. His education made him more open-minded, but, nevertheless, it affected him. She is now veiled again.

After finishing high school in Sanaa I wanted to go to university in Cairo. To go to Egypt I had to endure other problems. My family refused to let me go without a *mahram*, a male relative to act as a guardian. That was a time of great struggle with my family. They said no and I kept insisting. So I started studying administration and business at the University of Sanaa. I stayed for almost a month and a half but I couldn't stand it. It was not me. This was not what I was going to study. So I went back to my mother again and cried. I went to my grandfather who melted in front of my tears. He said he would support me. I went to my father and he said, no. So, I threatened my father saying, 'All right, I will get married to this man who is in the Soviet Union and I am going to become a communist like him in the country he is in and I will always ask God to punish you because you made me marry someone I didn't want.' Of course he thought about it. He thought I might do it and even though he liked the man he didn't like the idea of my being communist and living in that country.

The other problem came from inside the Ministry. I went to the Ministry of Education and got a scholarship. However, the person in charge of scholarships was married to a cousin and he proceeded to put every kind of obstacle in my way to make my trip nearly impossible. He tried to prevent me from getting my scholarship money and from going to Egypt in order to protect the reputation of the family. I should stay home not go abroad without a *mahram*. This same person now has three daughters at university, one of whom is about to become a doctor. So I had difficulties, but I went to Egypt after all the tears and threats. It was because of my grandfather's influence, and because they found a solution. There was a neighbour living with his daughters in Egypt. One of his wives had given me milk when I was an infant so she was my 'mother', that is my milk-mother (*umm bi-ritha*). So I could live with them because they were my family. That was the idea. So they said, 'You can go to Egypt, but you must go directly to this family. They will take care of you.' Of course, I didn't see this woman or her family. I had decided that I was not going to be guarded by anyone. They did not know I was coming. The letters and papers were with me and I kept them with me.

At about that time there was going to be a labour conference in Libya and they wanted someone to represent Yemeni women. So the minister suggested that I go and that on the way back I could settle in Egypt. That solved the problem of the ticket which was paid for by the Ministries of Social Affairs and Labour. On the way to Libya we passed through Egypt for three days. During this time I was introduced to a family who were very nice to me. They had a girl of about ten and two boys. So I asked them, 'Can I live with you?' They said, 'Yes, and if you want to pay something, it doesn't matter.' So after returning from Libya I went to stay with them.

There were many difficulties that year. The man in charge of scholarships in Yemen decided to make my life hell in Egypt to force me to go back home, so he cut off my scholarship. I didn't get my money until a year later. At that time, my mother, thinking I might need some extras while I was in Egypt, sent me money not knowing that I needed the money to *live* on. The first year was very hard. Then it happened that the president of Yemen, al-Hamadi, was coming to Egypt. At the time, the Minister of Supplies was in Egypt. He was a friend of mine – I knew him through my family affairs programme and he told me that the president was coming and that he would talk to him about the scholarship. The president ordered that my scholarship come directly from the presidency and so the problem of money was solved.

At the end of the academic year I returned to Yemen. I knew that I didn't want the veil anymore. Not only this, but people who support the veil can do evil things. I thought, look what they do.

They hurt me, they cut off my scholarship. They do all these things in the name of religion, and this is not religion. So it was a sort of reaction to all the hardships I had endured that year. While I was in Egypt, I had sent several pictures home showing me with friends from Yemen and other places and the way I was living in Egypt waiting for a comment. But, no one said anything so I thought that meant acceptance. I didn't inform anyone of the day of my arrival so no one was there to meet me. I walked down the street and no one recognised me. They looked at me as if I were a foreigner. They probably thought that I was an Adeni because at that time the girls from Aden were unveiled. There was a man I knew walking down the street, one of our neighbours, so I said, 'Good morning.' He answered me with surprise in his eyes. Then I said, 'Don't you know me?' He said, 'No.' Then I put my hand over my nose and mouth showing only my eyes. He recognised me immediately and said. 'Raufa this is impossible.' I said, 'Yes, it's me.' He replied, 'Well, how was your trip,' and so on. He told everybody I was back and of course in his heart was telling himself – she has come back without her veil; look what happens to girls when they go abroad.

I got to my house and my mother opened the door. Ah, what a shock. She was happy to see me. She hugged me, but she was shocked to see me without my veil. She tried to prevent my father from noticing but he had seen me enter. Everybody came to the house to see me and welcome me back. My parents postponed talking about the matter until later. That day we were supposed to have lunch at my grandfather's house. My mother gave me a *sharshaf*. When I saw it I said, 'What's that?' she said, 'You will wear it because we are going to your grandfather's house.' I said, 'No, I will not. I am sorry I am not going to wear it.' She said, 'You listen to what I say.' And I said, 'No. I have to make things clear. I have my return ticket with me. I am like this in Egypt and I am going to be like this in Yemen. If you accept me, it's all right. If you don't, I shall go back to Egypt and never return.' It was a drama. My mother cried. My father got angry. I went without my *sharshaf* to my grandfather's house and we had lunch. I stayed on with my grandfather and for the first time in my life my grandfather who loved me more than anyone else in the world was very angry. He said, 'I helped you go to Egypt. It was I who forced everyone to give you the freedom to go. But you were not supposed to take off your veil.' I spoke about the sayings of the Prophet Muhammad and the stories about him and his views. I said that women had participated in the wars, and had done various other things and that they could not have done these things inside a *sharshaf*. I said the *sharshaf* was Turkish. We had a long discussion, but he was not persuaded. I told him, 'All right, you are not convinced. For me the matter is obvious. Either I shall not wear the veil in Yemen, or I shall not come back again to this country. If you are really religious you would not allow me to be unveiled in Egypt because Islam exists in all Muslim countries, not just in some places and not others.' He said, 'You are behaving like the people there behave.' I said, 'All right that means it's not a matter of religion.' It was a long discussion. He remained angry with me but I stayed the night at his place because even though he was angry he was less hostile than everyone else. So we kept talking and he was trying to persuade me because he respected me. He thought I had a good mind and could be persuaded. It was an effort. He brought me books and I discussed them. My father simply said, 'No, I do not accept it,' end of discussion.

It was the summer vacation of 1975, after which things got worse. At that time television had just started in the country. They wanted to use the radio team for television. Going on television was the worst thing I could do to my family. Anybody who didn't know I had already taken off the veil would know when they saw me.

My family saw my first programme and declared it was a scandal. Once again everyone came and talked to my father, my mother, and my grandfather. It even became an affair for the whole city, I believe. Then my father and mother said, 'All right. We agree that you are unveiled and that our neighbours see you, but why should everybody in the whole country?' I told them, 'I am studying information and mass communication and this is my work. I am going to do it. I am not doing anything wrong. I am covering my hair. It is only my face that is showing.' It was really hard on them, but my mother had learned from the first experience that people talk in the beginning and make a lot of noise and then things calm down. People respect you as long as you insist. She had learned that lesson. She kept telling my father and grandfather, 'Everything will calm down. Don't let other people run your lives. Our daughter is doing what she wants. She is not bad. She is good and nobody is speaking badly of her and nobody has seen her do anything bad.' She defended me. But, when we were alone she told me, 'You are wrong, but I have to stand by you.' I told her, 'No, I am not wrong.' I wanted her to believe I was doing right. But she said, 'No, you do everything too aggressively for people and to your family you bring harm.' I told her there was no harm. I left Yemen to return to university in Egypt.

Transcribed in English
by Margot Badran

Assia Djebar

(1936–)

Assia Djebar was born Fatima-Zohra Imalain in Cherchell, Algeria. She grew up in a traditional, middle class Muslim family. She attended a French lycée in Blida, and later studied history at the Sorbonne in Paris. In 1955, she returned to Algeria for a while but soon left for Tunisia and Morocco where she taught and worked as a correspondent for the Algerian paper *Al-Moudjahid* during the Algerian Revolution, 1954-62. It was during the war that she began publishing novels. In 1957, she published *La Soif* which was translated into English as *The Mischief*. Her other novels are *Les Impatients* (1958), *Les Enfants du Nouveau Monde* (1962), *Les Alouettes Naïves* (1967), *Femmes d'Alger dans leur Appartement* (1980), *L'Amour, la Fantasia* (1986) and *Ombre Sultane* (1987). She has also published a collection of poems entitled *Poèmes pour l'Algérie Heureuse*. She has directed two films: *La Nouba des Femmes du Mont Chenoua*, which won the International Critics Prize at the Biennale in Venice in 1979, and *La Zerda et Les Chants de l'Oubli*.

In 1986, she translated and introduced Nawal al-Saadawi's novel *Woman at Point Zero* under the title *Ferdaous: Une Voix à l'Enfer* (Ferdaous: A Voice from Hell). The introduction to the novel follows. *Woman at Point Zero* is a story told to Nawal al-Saadawi, a psychiatrist, by Ferdaous on the eve of her execution for the murder of her pimp. It is a story of a woman's attempt to escape male domination: father, uncle, husband, employer, pimp. The only choice she is given in life is death. Djebar's introduction signals a woman writer's recognition of another's contribution to a growing body of feminist literature.

Introduction to Nawal al-Saadawi's
Ferdaous: A Voice from Hell

1983

☙❧

What is a feminist novel in Arabic? First of all, it is a voice – here, a voice 'in hell' of a woman called Paradise – a night murmur, a lament across the hurdles of twilight that finds birth in a suddenly lit private interior of heaven. An ancient wound finally and gradually opened up to assume its song. The revolt evolves as it searches for new words: the revolt develops here in the circular, repetitive rhythm of its speech.

I imagine that for centuries and in the silence of the seraglios this feminine rhetoric in Arabic was whispered from ear to ear of watched women: sights, internal screams grazing the sisterly ear itself incarcerated. I imagine that it could not take off, not so much because of fear of guardians and a master, but rather because of ignorance of a horizon outside the harem. Open, dancing, moving space free of others' eyes was inconceivable. What Arabic word would it have suggested?

The voice of Ferdaous, a righteous prostitute in Cairo – and behind her, appearing through the detours of this fiction, the voice of Nawal al-Saadawi, a contemporary Arab writer – is a strong voice.

It is no longer a question of explaining, of justifying the challenge. It is enough that there is a challenge in this confession of one woman to another. It is enough that the challenge of the feminine voice rises higher and higher with a throbbing energy.

We, from the Maghrib, who have dreamt the western dream of the re-emergence of the couple, we women who have rolled about in the Arabic language as though in a grotto of heat, of memories and of ancestors' whisperings (so much so that although we walk through the streets veiled there are further veils, the-words-of-the-French-language, a turning away from our history ...) find inspiration at hearing a woman revolt in Arabic.

A new, fresh discursive field is imperceptibly traced for other Arab women. A point for take-off. A combat zone. A restoration of body. Bodies of new women in spite of new barriers, which in the internal, interior language at once retracted and proclaimed, public and no longer secret find roots before rushing forth ... A loud voice that gives body. Body and new forms restoring a darker, deeper texture to other louder voices.

This book is dealing with birth – birth of a word.

Ferdaous in Arabic means 'paradise', and it is a woman called 'Paradise' who, on the eve of her hanging for having killed a man, addresses with a 'voice from hell' all the women in a society where sexual oppression is only just beginning to be recognised.

Successive stages in the life of Ferdaous, turned prostitute by revolt after having undergone unspeakable exploitation: childhood in Upper Egypt where her father, crushed by misery, spares his cow but not his wife and daughter; adolescence in Cairo where her uncle, a professor, refuses to send her to university 'where there are men', and forces her to marry an old man. Battered, Ferdaous chooses the street where her first protector turns against her, where the police of the poor quarters, the wealthy clients of whorehouses, the bad boys, and an ambitious upwardly mobile journalist reflect for Ferdaous a scarcely exaggerated image of other men. After a number of desperate escapes, Ferdaous becomes a murderer out of spite.

Fiction can thus be made into a film scenario for a Salah Abu Saif (an Egyptian film-maker whose thirty-odd films depict the reality of the popular streets of Cairo). A box-office hit. But is this novel written by Nawal al-Saadawi (first known in Egypt as an essayist whose studies of sexuality were based on her experience as a doctor, whose novels are now read by a large number of Arabic-speaking youth, but who is still opposed by official culture), a 'populist novel'? There is realism, there is also a powerful warmth in the novel. The fiction is anchored in the social and sexual dramas of contemporary Arab reality.

The writing itself is marked by points which cut up and interrupt the flow of the narrative. I notice them in this compulsive repetition of somatic notations first in the interior of the phrase, then in the paragraph, then in the chapter, finally in the entire dialogue.

In the beginning, the listening of one woman to another – the psychiatrist to the woman condemned 'in flesh and bone' – is not so much a simple interview, as the physical setting in motion of the searcher for the word:

> I was as though sleep-walking. The ground under me was hard; the ground under me was cold; the cold did not touch me. It was the cold of the sea in a dream. I swam through its waters . . . her voice too was like the voices one hears in a dream . . . Such voices seem to come from the depths of the earth, to fall from the heavens or to drop from the rooftops
> . . .

The place, a cell, doors and windows closed; two women seated on the bare earth. It was as though the primitive seating, the sparse decor – outside the warden was washing the floor – the purifying poverty emphasised the bodies.

As Ferdaous, yesterday a high-class prostitute, searches for her identity in her faraway peasant childhood, the reader has two vivid sensations: two eyes, sometimes stable sometimes threatening, symbol of love or of the fear of the Other: and the swelling emergence of an erotic awakening.

> Two eyes that I watched and that watched me. Two eyes that followed me even when I hid from them. Whenever I tripped when I was learning to walk they would hold me up ... I felt like a pebble thrown into a sea without shores and without a bed; hit by the waves when it starts to sink and by the wind if it starts to float. It sinks and floats in turns between heaven and water. Nothing but these two eyes held me as I oscillated ... I knew that it was my mother.

Birth with the mother which more or less in the same terms prefigures that with the girlfriend from the Iqbal boarding house and later that with the beloved Ibrahim.

Almost simultaneously, a sexual awakening:

> I trembled with a previous pleasure that I could neither locate nor define as though its source were outside me, as though it poured forth from me and drowned my body. A shudder that began as a pain and finished as a pleasure. An unknown that I would have liked to grasp, to touch even if only for a second, but it escaped like air, like a mirage, like a dream ...

Six or seven times during her confession, Ferdaous numbly repeats this double sensation, the climax and frustration of nascent pleasure: children's games with Mohamdine, adolescent problems in the boarding house, love with the journalist Ibrahim between the two periods, passive then freely demanding, of prostitution. This refrain that the voice repeats each time comes up out of an anger that accuses the patriarchal, marital, police, bureaucratic, political system. It is as though Ferdaous were finding again courage and latent strength in the memory of her body.

This body mutilated so young by her mother and her accomplice, a 'woman with a razor', the delegate of male fear. This excised body. This is said as though secretly, as though in an obscure parenthesis, whereas it is here that the real trauma lies:

> At one point I asked my mother about my father: 'How could you conceive me without a father?' Her response was to hit

me. Then she went for a woman armed with a knife or a razor.
She cut out a piece of flesh from between my thighs. I cried
the whole night long. The following morning, my mother did
not send me to the fields as she usually did.

This experience will not be alluded to in the rest of the narrative.
Ferdaous mutilated at her mother's command; almost fetishistic –
the automatic shameful transmission of the damnation, this solidarity toward . . . And the thickening silence leads Ferdaous to
hate the pleasure/pain, pain/pleasure of her body. This body which
constantly bumps up against countless other male bodies. From
excision to prostitution.
    Male bodies. The other site of this discourse. The look of a little
girl with a jar on her head but who guns down the village men at
the mosque exit on the feast day when 'they' pray, parade and
congratulate each other. For their piety is ostentatious, noisy,
gesticulating.

> They nodded their heads, rubbed their hands one against the
> other, pressed their fingers against their foreheads. They
> murmured, invoking God's name and praying . . . I saw
> them: they nodded, coughed, blew their noses loudly, con-
> stantly scratching themselves under their arms and between
> their legs.

The portrait of the father eating alone, and often in front of the
starving children, is more vivid than a caricature: 'I watched while
he ate . . . Mouth as big as a camel's impressive jaws, the one
moving above the other noisily. His teeth ground . . . His tongue
rolled around in his mouth . . . He ate and belched . . . He
coughed . . .' And the little girl concludes: 'I knew that that man
could not be my father.'
    Life for Ferdaous was a stream of such invading, aggressive
bodies obstructing everything, all hope. The uncle, who would,
however, give her the opportunity for education, is at first a
hypocritical hand which moves up the girl's leg from behind an
open book; the husband, old and sick, is a stinking mouth and a
pair of inquisitorial eyes at the dinner table; the clients who appear
in this progressive fall are of two kinds: those with dirty or clean
nails, those who are sweaty or perfumed; but all have the same
weight that Ferdaous supports with eyes closed.
    When the first one leaves anonymity by the expression of a
simple human concern ('Are you alright?'), and another wants to
talk to her and in spite of himself utters the insult, 'women without
dignity', Ferdaous flees. It is as though the 'hero-saviour' is more

dangerous and oppressive than the body of a man who pays: 'Above all, I hated the men who tried to moralise or said that they wanted to save me ... They thought they could save me by assuming the role of saviour, a mission they had not been able to accomplish elsewhere.'

These breaks, experienced as reprieve or as an acceleration in despair, all take the form of escape into the streets.

'A woman in/of the streets', this is a refrain of this narrative. In the colloquial Arabic of my country, this euphemism means prostitute. By regression, this same expression is applied to women who work outside the home. The street, place for the monetary exchange of bodies, is also the place for their transformation through work. Never mind. It seems to come to the same thing. Is it not there precisely that the looks of men seize hold of the female body? Indeed, does prostitution not mean the exhibition of the female body that has escaped the control of father, brother or master, escaping the bonds of blood.

For Ferdaous the street is the place where each of her successive changes happens. She rushes out into it, not to expose herself but to explode.

Trying to avoid a forced marriage, to get away from a husband who beats her with impunity (has he not been told that according to God a wife must submit even to a beating?), to escape from the first protector who imprisons her. Each time she finds herself outdoors where she is oppressed by the crowds, by the threatening eyes of strangers. But during her third flight she claims that 'the street has become my refuge'.

Thereafter she chooses the street, and she herself interprets an experience: she leaves Cherifa and her whorehouse in a second, she undercuts her first financial success as an independent prostitute: 'I started walking along the street my head held high, and I looked people in the eye.' When 'honest' loves turns into a catastrophe, there is one source of liberty: 'I spent my time wandering through the streets.'

In the wanderings of this lonely body (there is never any question of veiling), nature comes into existence ('the night was silent, the darkness magnificent, the Nile flowed seductively') and the plot (a succession of changes of personality) finds its dynamic in the street. 'I understood', 'I realised', 'I uncovered the mystery'. The confused thought that is coming into its own needs the body of a woman freed from other bodies ... Ferdaous advances, no longer for sale, just moving along trying to rid herself of the multiple layers of internalised oppression.

When at the end the police take her away it is because she has become the woman 'with a dangerous and wild truth'. The street becomes the site of her slow asceticism, of her drunkenness. But there lies hell also, because she rarely meets other women. The only place where a woman's words can be transmitted to another woman is in a cell with doors and windows closed and that will only open up on and for death.

Others more competent than I, specialists or critics, will have to situate the Egyptian Nawal al-Saadawi in comparison with the Lebanese Laila Baalbaki (whose novel *I Live* in the 1960s marked the beginning of women's poetic romanticism) and with the Syrian Ghada Samman, whose psychological romance novels have faithful readers all over the Arab world. About ten years ago, Nawal al-Saadawi's first essays denouncing sexual misery and oppression and linking them to social immobility and religious conformity shocked the Arab conscience. This shock came on the heels of about fifty years of reformist liberalism which brought Arab women some new rights.

One could also make a study for a French or western audience of how this novel renews a socio-literary understanding of contemporary Egypt which has until now been mediated through three classics translated into French. In 1941, Gide introduced Taha Husain's *The Days*; in 1974, Taufiq al-Hakim's *Journal of an Administrative Assistant in the Country* appeared in the collection *Human Land*; finally, Najib Mahfuz's trilogy *The Alley of Miracles*, was published by Sindbad. In each of these novels the images of rural and urban women are multiple and undeniably real. But the originality of *Woman at Point Zero* lies in a look that upsets and cuts through the traditional sexual dichotomy of space, a look that impregnates so as to resist at all costs the suffocation. Novelty resides in the tone of a voice that does not sigh, that does not complain, that accuses.

Before travelling through the pages that follow and pursuing Ferdaous' journey through hell, I dream suddenly of the first origin — alas, lost, or perhaps to be found some day — of our women's literary tradition.

'The emancipation of woman, relatively advanced under the Ummayads, enriched the sexual language. Inversely and despite religious prescriptions this helped men and women to communicate,' writes Tahar Labid Djedidi, a scholar of udhri Arabic, the ancestor of courtly love.

From the ninth to the eleventh centuries a whole literature of love developed for a refined public, male as well as female, in the court of Baghdad. Of these works, some anonymous, only a few titles survive: *The Story of the Dancer; The Story of the Woman Free as the Wind*, etc. Were these *Stories of Female Love* between two women, or love stories written by women or were they collective creations? There are only twelve titles that Ibn al-Nadim, a Persian historiographer, has catalogued: *The Story of the Myrtle and the Carnation, The Story of the Pearl and the Diamond, The Story of Salma and Suad* . . . Shimmerings of a lost murmur, of a happiness that – even today – people wanted to kill, because they first of all suppressed its words.

Translated from the French
by Miriam Cooke

Nawal al-Saadawi

(1931–)

Fedwa Malti-Douglas and Allen Douglas both teach at the University of Texas at Austin. They taped the following conversation in Nawal al-Saadawi's Cairo apartment, on Shariah Murad, during the evening of 15 August 1986. The interview was conducted in a mixture of English and Arabic and it covered the following topics: growing up feminist; feminism: from marriage to political activism; publishing and society; religion and the Quran.

The book which she wished to write in 1986 and which she discusses in the interview was published two years later as *The Fall of The Imam*. It was almost immediately translated into English.

Reflections of a Feminist

1986

❧

Fedwa Malti-Douglas: I thought it might be appropriate to start by talking about how you became interested in feminism, how you became a feminist?

Nawal al-Saadawi: I became a feminist when I was a child. Starting to feel the discrimination between myself and my brother, and how he was treated, how he had more privileges than I. I did very well at school. He did not. But over the summer holiday, he was rewarded by being allowed to travel, and I was rewarded with nothing. So for me, it was really a lot of injustice. It started unconsciously when I was a child. I felt the discrimination. My parents and my family were quite liberal, relative to other people, of course. But, anyway, I felt that my brother was privileged. And then when I grew up and I became a physician, and I worked in the rural areas, etc, I started to become aware of the fact that what I had felt years earlier was the truth. And that is how I became a feminist.

Allen Douglas: You make it sound like the first chapter of your *Memoirs of a Female Physician*. Does that express your reactions as a child? Where the heroine says 'My brother had the right to do this but I didn't.'

N.S.: Yes. Exactly. Though my *Memoirs of a Female Physician* is not strictly autobiographical, parts of it are. How I was really furious when I received my certificate, how I was the first in my class and my brother was a failure. And then he goes and plays football in the street, while I have to make his bed and cook his food. What made me more furious was when I asked why this should be so, my parents, the family, would answer: 'Well, that is what God has said.' So, I felt a lot of hostility towards God when I was a child. I felt that He was very unjust.

F.M.-D.: If I remember correctly, you mention the same conflict in *The Hidden Face of Eve*, the sibling rivalry between yourself and your brother.

N.S.: Yes.

A.D.: But, how would you explain that this emerged in your case? When you were a child, there were millions of other Egyptian girls growing up at the same time. Was it anything in your environment that made you react to this injustice, while others simply survived it, or said nothing?

N.S.: It is really quite strange, because, for instance, my cousins, all the girls in the family, were obedient. They were completely the opposite of me – they married very young and never got divorced. They cannot understand why I get so upset, since I was much better off than they are – I was sent to school and then to university. We were nine children and my father believed in education. So I received some privileges and an education. But, I was not satisfied. I had five sisters, none of whom rebelled at all. But they were stronger, relatively more powerful than other girls. What happened in our family was that my father and mother gave us some space to rebel by giving us some freedom and education. They gave us the elements of rebellion. Because in order to rebel, you need some awareness, some knowledge, and also some courage. They gave us this.

F.M.-D.: And this was unusual?

N.S.: This was quite unusual at that time in urban, middle-class families like ours. My father's family, in the village, was different. My father's sister married when she was nine or ten. Most of my cousins in the village married when they were eleven or twelve. A girl, in those days, if she was thirteen or fourteen, and still not married, would be considered an old maid.

A.D.: But, you were given some education. When was this? What decade are we talking about?

N.S.: I was born in 1931, so it was the end of the thirties and the beginning of the forties. I went to primary school, an ordinary Egyptian school. But, at the beginning, I went to an English school in a village called Minuf. Then two years at primary school, and then on to a secondary school in Helwan. It was a boarding school. This was during the forties. Then I went to the university, to the Faculty of Medicine in 1950. I graduated in 1955.

F.M.-D.: Were there many women in the Faculty of Medicine at that time?

N.S.: No not very many. But, there were some. I think in my year, we were around forty or fifty women.

F.M.-D.: Among how many in total?

N.S.: Hundreds.

F.M.-D.: That's interesting. Because I read a statistic somewhere which claimed that half the medical population in Egypt were women.

N.S.: Now, yes, yes. It is true *now*.

F.M.-D.: Why did you choose to go into medicine yourself?

N.S.: Well, I didn't choose to, in fact. But, at that time, and up until the present, the Faculty of Medicine takes the best students, those with the highest grades. I went there because I had the highest grades. And I also loved science more than history. The way they taught us history was very dull: to memorise dates, etc. However, I also loved literature and I wanted to go to the Faculty of Arts. So there I was . . . torn between two things. I loved science, but I also loved the arts. I wanted to write. But I hated the subjects in the Faculty of Arts. So, I chose science. Since I was at the top of my class, I went into medicine.

F.M.-D.: And then you decided to become a writer . . .

N.S.: No. Ever since I was a child, I wanted to be a writer. Since I started to learn the alphabet I loved writing.

F.M.-D.: Isn't this basically also the conflict that takes place in *Two Women in One*? This problem of science versus art?

N.S.: Oh, yes, exactly. That is the dilemma of my life, that my life was oriented towards medicine, science, facts, and my love was always with art.

A.D.: Do you regret the years you spent in medicine?

N.S.: In a way, yes, but I gained a lot. Because I think that writing is like dissection. When you dissect the body, anatomically, it gives you a lot of insight into the secrets of the body. By studying psychiatry and psychology, I began to understand character. So I don't regret it, because it gave me, as a writer, a lot of insight into the nature of human beings. But, still, I lost many years, studying medicine and working as a physician. But I never regret it, because medical practice, especially in the villages, gave me a lot of material.

F.M.-D.: I think your expression that writing is like dissection is very interesting. Can you tell us a little bit more what you mean by that?

N.S.: Well, in fact, I don't distinguish very much between art and science. Both of them are searching for the truth. Why do we write? Because we are searching for the truth. What's the end, the aim of science? To know, to know life, to understand the human being. In medicine we dissect the body to understand the nerves, or the liver, and the relationship of each part to the others. It is the same with the community. The human being is a microcosm of the whole society. So when you understand the body, you understand society. And vice versa. I think every writer should understand both the human body and the psyche.

But this does not mean that one must spend ten years studying medicine. And the profession itself was a strain when I had a clinic and was working in the hospital. It was a strain to work till three or four o'clock in the afternoon and then come back tired and write till three o'clock in the morning. So, I was torn between two professions and I had a lot of problems, you know. I had problems with my first husband. I had to get rid of him. [*laughter*] And then the problems with the second husband. And looking for ways to get rid of him also.

A.D.: Were you a feminist when you married the first husband?

N.S.: I have been a feminist since I was a child. I didn't accept any authority, not even the authority of my father. He did not agree to me marrying my first husband. But I married him anyway. I took my bag and said, well, I am going to get married, and I married him. And then I left him.

F.M.-D.: What was his occupation?

N.S.: He was a doctor like me. He is the father of Muna. I divorced him when she was very young. And when she reached sixteen or seventeen, she visited him, or he visited her, or something like that. And she came and told me, 'You know, Mama, I am so happy that you divorced my father.' [*laughter*]

A.D.: Where in this sequence of events did you decide to become politically active? Your feminism as a child was basically an instinctive rebellion, or even a reasoned rebellion. When did it become a politically mature and conscious development?

N.S.: When I worked as a physician in rural areas. Then I started to be shocked by many things. And also by my life. I started to feel the conflict, as a wife. My first husband, a physician, didn't want me to work as a physician. He was jealous of my colleagues, and he told me: 'You shouldn't meet those men.' Can you imagine such a mentality? This shocked me, and it gave me insight into the problems of women: private life and public life.

My second husband was a lawyer. When I published a short story in a magazine his colleagues in the Council of State told him: 'Oh, it's a very courageous story. How well your wife writes.' He came to me and said to me: 'You shouldn't write. You have to choose between me and your writing.' So I said to him, 'Well, I choose my writing.' [*laughter*]

F.M.-D.: And that was it?

N.S.: Yes. This shook me up, and made me politically active. Because, really, I felt that women had such major problems. I didn't have many problems as a physician, but I did as a writer. I could work in a hospital and have equal pay. I competed with men, and I have bested them. I was very prominent in my work, as a physician and as a writer. I didn't have problems with men outside. But once I opened the door and entered my home I faced problems as a wife. In Egypt, under Nasser, women were encouraged to work. It's not like that now. Now, in the public sector, women like my daughter suffer, women are being discouraged from working, because of unemployment, because of the veil. This is the regression in our society. But during the 1960s we were pushed to work. Every day, I opened the newspaper and found people saying: 'Women should be doctors, lawyers, should participate in the socialist change in the country.' So I didn't find many problems outside. And I received a salary like my colleagues in the public sector.

A.D.: When did you write *The Hidden Face of Eve*?

N.S.: I started writing fiction first, when I was a student. I wrote stories. I published them in the magazines of the Faculty of Medicine. I wrote short stories, during the 1950s. During the 1960s I wrote novels and more short stories. In the 1970s, I started writing about women. I wrote *Woman and Sex, Female is the Origin* and *The Hidden Face of Eve* in Arabic. I wrote five books one after the other.

A.D.: Had you read many western feminists at the time when you started writing?

N.S.: Only very few, very very few.

A.D.: It strikes me that you were ahead of them.

N.S.: Sometimes, when I read the literature of some of the very progressive feminists – you know, in the States – I remember that I had felt that way when I was in high school. I think the problems are common.

F.M.-D.: I think that the radical way in which you look at the social roles of men and women is rare even in America, in western writings on women.

N.S.: I wrote *Memoirs of a Female Physician* in 1959.

A.D.: That's extraordinary for something like that. It still shocks people.

N.S.: Yes. No one can believe it. Everyone thinks that we write such things in imitation of the West.

F.M.-D.: How were the books on sexuality received here?

N.S.: They were best-sellers, but they were censored. As soon as the first book *Woman and Sex* was published here, it was removed very quickly when the authorities began to become aware of its impact on people – it was very progressive. They gave orders to the publisher to remove all the copies from the market and put them in storage. Since then, I have published in Beirut.

F.M.-D.: When did you start publishing again in Egypt?

N.S.: After I came out of prison, I published the *Memoirs From the Women's Prison*, but it was censored in Egypt first. Then I published it serially in *Al-Tadamun* [an international Arabic magazine published in London]. Later, in 1983 I published it as a book in Dar al-Mustaqbal in Cairo. I also published two volumes of *My Travels in the World* in Cairo, with Dar al-Hilal. And I am publishing *Isis*, the play with Faiq at Dar al-Mustaqbal. So there is some progress now.

F.M.-D.: Do you think that there is an opening up?

N.S.: Not in television. I am black-listed on television. I cannot appear on television or on the radio. I am also censored in the newspapers – they cut three quarters of an article, and then they publish it.

F.M.-D.: How do you see your role as a writer in the Arab world?

N.S.: Well, I judge from what happens at public lectures. For example, when I am invited to Arab countries to give lectures, in Yemen, Tunisia, Morocco, Algeria, Lebanon or Syria, thousands of young people come. I remember once in Tunis I cancelled the lecture because I couldn't breathe. The lecture was at 6 pm, in Qaat Ibn Khaldun, in Tunis. And at 4 pm, not only was the hall full, but the streets leading to the hall were full of people, to the point that I couldn't enter the hall. Finally, they squeezed me in. I found myself sitting on a platform surrounded by bodies. So I said: 'Really. I cannot speak.' And then I apologised. We had to shift the lecture to al-Qairawan, which is far away from the capital. The train journey is two or three hours. And we had to cancel that too. Can you imagine? The people took trains and came to al-Qairawan. [*laughs*]

F.M.-D.: And most of these were young people?

N.S.: Yes. But there is another group who are fundamentalist now, veiled, and so on. It's part of a universal phenomenon. But it's very visible here. And these fundamentalists reject me totally. Both the men and the women.

F.M.-D.: Do you think they have read you?

N.S.: Some of them have read me. And, of course, they are affected. But they are antagonistic to what I have written and there is a lot of conflict. They see that I'm touching on the problems they feel, especially the young women. But, still, they have to wear the veil, etc. Some of them come to me here with a lot of psychological problems.

F.M.-D.: Veiled women?

N.S.: Yes. They come to me as a psychiatrist. Or they read my books, and they are so puzzled, and they want to discuss these things with me. And they are torn up. Some of them come to attack me, you know. It's rejection and attraction.

A.D.: Do you have any unfulfilled literary ambitions?

N.S.: Yes. I am writing a novel which is a breakthrough in terms of both language and content. My love is fiction. My love is novels. When I am writing a novel, I am happy. When someone criticises a short story or a novel to me, and he or she states the pros and cons, I am interested, I listen. But when someone criticises a book on women, I listen, but not as attentively. You know, it's something related to my constitution. My constitution is not political, it is not social. My constitution is artistic.

F.M.-D.: I see you both as a writer and as a feminist.

N.S.: Yes. Because I am a woman. And you know when you are a writer, you reflect your agony. It's part of you.

A.D.: Do you think that as a feminist writer, as a woman writer, as a writer in the Arab world, that your writing makes a difference in the evolution of society, in the evolution of people's attitudes? Your fiction, I mean.

N.S.: Well, the effect of fiction is very remote. People read a novel and they think about it. But they don't change their lives so quickly. But when they read a book, a straight-forward book, like *The Hidden Face of Eve* ... Oh, I remember women coming to me and saying that after they read *The Hidden Face of Eve*, they divorced their husbands or asked for a divorce. [*laughter*] I remember some men coming to me and quarrelling with me. But not a single person ever comes to me after a novel and says: 'This happened to me.' Because the effect of fiction is deep, but remote. It takes a longer time. It touches life. It eliminates gradually. It moves in a different way. But facts shock you very much. When you bring contradictions to light, people start to say: 'Yes, that's true, that's true.'

F.M.-D.: To me, a novel like *Woman at Point Zero* is really just as radical in its own way as the theoretical writing.

N.S.: Yes. Because *Woman at Point Zero* is half way between fiction and fact. I was so affected by this real woman, that I wrote it as it was. Imagination is only twenty per cent, maybe ten per cent. So, it's fiction. Sometimes a novel can be more effective. It depends.

A.D.: You said that you're experimenting with language in a novel you're working on now?

N.S.: Yes. As you know the Arabic language, like the English language, is very male-oriented. And the language of the Quran is very male. You remember that I wrote in *The Hidden Face of Eve* how the women went to the Prophet Muhammad and told him: 'The Quran is very male-oriented. We fought alongside men like you. Why are we not mentioned in the Quran as women?' And then the verses, the language of the Quran, started to be both feminine and masculine. And, after this event, you will find verses in the Quran that are masculine and feminine. Now, many women in the West are changing language. But, in the Arabic language, I feel that there is a barrier. When Marilyn Booth translated my *Memoirs from the Women's Prison*, she told me she had a problem with the translation because most of the language was male-oriented. For example, we say, '*al-insan wa-ka-annahu* ...' [man, as though he] and she doesn't know if she should say 'he' or 'she'. Because I use '*al-insan*' [man]. So I told her: 'Yes. You know, in my new novel, I am changing this.' I am really trying to change the language. Because when you change the content, you have to change the form. But it's difficult.

A.D.: Do you think you're going to end up with something which is a woman's literary language?

N.S.: Not exactly. But it will be more reflective of what I feel. Because we are still using a language that is alienating us. I remember Mubarak said in his last speech, as reported in the newspaper: '*Misr al-rijal — aqwa min khazain al-mal*' [The Egypt of men is stronger than treasure houses of wealth]. As if it were men only, and no women. So I thought that I should answer him and say: 'Why didn't you say *Misr al-rijal waal-nisa?*' [Egypt of Men and of Women]. Like those women who went to the Prophet Muhammad and asked him why the Quran only mentioned men?

F.M.-D.: So you're changing the language. Are you also changing the syntactic structure of your style?

N.S.: Yes. Because, in fact, I want to . . . I want to put more of myself on paper.

A.D.: Do you mean that you want your writing to be more subjective?

N.S.: Not more subjective, but more uncensored. Because, you know, in spite of the fact that I am freer, relatively speaking, than other women in my writing, there is still an internal censorship, from different repressions and oppressions. So all my books, all my writings, do not really reflect me. Of course, I can't write with all the courage I want. For many reasons: because I live in the Arab world, because I am limited by the publishers.

A.D.: What would you like to write that you don't write because of internal censorship?

N.S.: Oh, many things. Many things. I want to write freely about . . . religion, sex, God, authority, the State. But the publishers also censor me. Even in Beirut. I'll give you an example: my book *God Dies by the Nile* – they rejected the title, totally. We settled on *Maut al-Rajul al-Wahid ala al-Ard*, [Death of the Only Man on Earth], which is very bad.

F.M.-D.: Yes, it's true, the other one is much better.

N.S.: And there are concepts that cannot be accepted at all in the Arab countries. Therefore no one would read my books. So, while my books are read because of this compromise, and I want to be read rather than be totally isolated, I pay a price for this.

F.M.-D.: So in this novel, you will try to break out of these constraints.

N.S.: That's right. Even if it's not published in the Arab world. Because now I feel that I have reached a certain stage. I have twenty-four books in Arabic. They are in almost every home. I have made an impact. Now I have to experiment. Before, I didn't have the pleasure or the freedom to experiment. But, now I want to go beyond that, to experiment with the language, to experiment with ideas, to have more freedom. Even if the book is not published in the Arab world. At first, I wrote for the Arab people, men and women. And I had to consider my audience. I was not writing for angels in the sky. My audience was the Arab people. So, if I spoke about something they would totally reject, I would not be there at all. But now I don't care.

A.D.: Do you think that Arabic letters are heading towards more revolutionary or experimental positions nowadays? Or are they becoming more conservative as society is becoming more conservative?

N.S.: It's becoming more conservative. Especially male writers. You know, even some of the Marxists have become Islamic writers – from pragmatic political considerations, of course. And there are many progressive writers who now start their works with the *bismallah* and end them with *al-hamdulillah ar-rahman ar-rahim* [Praise be to God, the Compassionate, the Merciful].

A.D.: So, you're not optimistic about male Arabic literature at this point?

N.S.: Well, I am optimistic by nature. When I was in jail, I was very optimistic. Even when I'm dying, I will be optimistic. You have Islamisation and retrogression. But you also have conflict and progress. Both happen together. In spite of the fundamentalist revival, you also have a revival of the progressive forces. And the fight goes on. We must go forward.

Transcribed
by Allen Douglas and Fedwa Malti-Douglas

Glossary

abaya   cloak-like wrap
abu   father (when followed by a name means father of X)
afrit   devil, imp
alim   religious teacher or scholar; plural, ulama
Allah yi barek fi omrek   God bless you (North African)
arusa   bride
asalam alaikum   greeting meaning 'Peace be with you'
aya   verse
baraka   blessing
bismallah   literally 'In the Name of Allah'. First line of all but one of the
    chapters of the Quran
bulgar   cracked wheat
burnous   long woollen cape worn by men in the Maghrib
dalil   a sacred text that protects the wearer
daya   midwife, wet nurse
djellaba   man's garb
Fatiha   opening chapter of Quran
feddan   a measure of land, a little over an acre
fellah/in   Egyptian peasant/s
fitna   temptation and civil strife
gallabiya   long, loose, shirt-like garment
gnawi   member of Islamic mystical group in Morocco
habara   wrap
hadra   exorcism ritual
haik   North African women's woollen wrap
Hajj   annual Pilgrimage to Mecca
hajja/hajji   honorific bestowed on women and men who have made the
    Hajj
hammam   bath, particularly public baths
harem   women's quarters; a man's wife or wives
henna   reddish-orange dye for hair and hands gained from leaves and
    stalks of the henna plant
hijab   veil: covering the head and neck and in some cases the face as well
Hijra   Muhammed's emigration from Mecca to Medina. This event
    marks the beginning of the Muslim calendar.
hmarat   donkeys
imam   religious functionary

imma   a shaikh's turban
izar   wrap, covering
jabal   mountain
jbelas   cloak
jinn   a spirit
kishk   Upper Egyptian dish made with yoghurt and cracked wheat
kohl   antimony
kuttab   quranic school
Lalla   Mrs/Lady (Moroccan)
mabruk   literally 'blessed', congratulations
mahram   a man who acts as a woman's guardian, usually a male relative
majlis   session, sitting room
maktub   literally 'written', used in the fatalistic connotation
maazun   official authorized by qadi to perform civil marriage and
    divorce
medina   old city, often walled
msettia   mad (Moroccan)
milaya   black wrap worn by Egyptian women
minbar   mosque pulpit
muezzin   one who calls faithful to prayer from a minaret
mulukhiya   Jew's mallow. Also, thick soup made of this herb in Egypt
    and Syria
nabi   prophet
nahda   cultural renaissance of the Arab world in the nineteenth and
    twentieth centuries
narghile   waterpipe
nasranya   Christian, accidental, other, the enemy
niqab   veil (face covering)
nushuz   Islamic Law: violation of marital duties
nzaha   picnic
oke   unit of weight in Egypt
qadi   Islamic judge, magistrate
qasida   poem of praise consisting of twenty-five to a hundred verses
raka   bending of the torso from an upright position, followed by two
    prostrations in Muslim prayer ritual
Ramadan   Muslim month of fasting
Rasul Allah   God's messenger, i.e., Muhammed
sayyid   Mr; see 'sharif'
sharif   descendant of the Prophet Muhammad
shaikh/a   village/clan/tribal leader (male & female); term of respect
Sharia   canonical law of Islam
Sunna   The Prophet's sayings and doings, later established as legally
    binding precedents
sharshaf   enveloping garment worn by Yemeni women
shishah   waterpipe
sikran   sleep-inducing drug

shur   cloth envelopes (Turkish), made out of silk and embroidered in silver and gold, typical gifts for female guests at marriage ceremonies among the upper class.

sirwal   loose trousers

sitt   Mrs, woman

suffragi   waiter, steward

sufi   Muslim mystic

suq   market

sura   a chapter in The Quran

taimat   law court (Algerian)

tajmâat   meeting hall (Algerian)

taleb   village witch doctor (Algerian)

tarbush   gentleman's headgear, also called a fez

tarha   head veil

umda   village headman, mayor

umm   mother (when followed by a name means mother of X)

umm bi-ritha   milk mother

ulama   religious leaders/scholars

waqf   religious endowment

zaghruda   ululation or trills of joy or grief

zar   ritual exorcism meant to rid a person (usually a woman) of an evil spirit by means of a frenzied dance accompanied by incantations and quranic verses

zawiyya   North African Muslim sanctuary

INDEX

❧

OTHER BOOKS OF INTEREST FROM VIRAGO

Letter to Christendom

Rana Kabbani

What is it like to grow up a Muslim?
What is it like to live as a Muslim in the West?

In this impassioned book, Rana Kabbani leads the reader through the labyrinthine world of Islam. Setting the historical record of western prejudice against Muslims alongside her own experience of life in the West, she demonstrates that deep misunderstanding and fear continue to inform the way Islam is perceived today.

With particular reference to the Salman Rushdie affair, she illustrates how quickly the old forms of hatred and bigotry surface in order to wage contemporary political battles, and makes a plea for a new dialogue, free from historical bias or personal animosity, between these two civilisations.

Harem Years
Memoirs of an Egyptian Feminist

Huda Shaarawi

These memoirs – candid, poignant, unconventional – offer a unique portrait of a private world, rarely observed and seldom documented from within. For Huda Shaarawi came from the last generation of upper-class Egyptian women to spend their childhood and married life in the closed confines of a harem. At twelve she was told she was soon to be married: 'I stood sobbing for hours . . . my spirit was broken.' At fourteen, after a year of marriage, and to the consternation of many, Huda began a seven-year separation from her husband, experiencing for the first time the exhilaration of independence and a growing awareness of the price women paid for their confinement. Delighted by her friendships, seaside holidays, her first visit to Alexandria's department store, she began, in the harem, to assert her new-found activism: she was the youngest woman to attend Cairo's first women's salon, and she organised lectures for women on wearing the veil. Increasingly, too, she became involved in Egypt's nationalist struggle, culminating in independence in 1922. Then, in 1923, in Cairo's railway station, she removed her veil: an act of daring which signalled the end of the harem years for herself, and the beginning of the end for others.

Khul-Khaal
Five Egyptian Women Tell Their Stories

Nayra Atiya

These marvellous life stories of five Egyptian women were recorded by Nayra Atiya over a period of three years. The women tell us about every aspect of their experience: what it's like to grow up in a country where 'boys are more precious than girls,' where childhood is seen only as a preparation and training for marriage, and where a girl's main purpose is to have children.

Vividly they describe the details of their everyday lives: involvement with extended families, paid work, attitudes to men, particularly husbands, bringing up their children, coping with illness, the pressures of living cheek by jowl with neighbours in Cairo, and how each women manages her family's meagre resources. Individual events, too, are dramatically recounted: Om Gad tells of the death of a beloved brother struck down by the 'evil eye', Dunya her hilarious rejection of an unwanted suitor, Om Naeema the rituals surrounding her circumcision and wedding night. From the narratives there emerges a rare philosophical breadth and candour as the women reflect upon their destinies. *Khul-Khaal* brings to life five very distinct personalities and offers fascinating insights into aspects of contemporary Egyptian culture.